METHODS OF TEACHING CHEMISTRY

By

Kolasani Sunil Kumar
M.Sc., (Chemistry) M.Ed.
Lecture in Physical Science
St. Peter & G. Krishna College of Education
Burripalem, Tenali, Guntur, (A.P)

K. Rama Krishna
M.Sc., M.Ed.
R.V.R. College of Education
Guntur–522 006

General Editor

Dr. Digumarti Bhaskara Rao
M.Sc., M.A., M.A., M.Ed., Ph.D.
Reader
R.V.R. College of Education
Srinivasa Nagar Colony
Guntur–522 006
Andhra Pradesh
India

DISCOVERY PUBLISHING HOUSE
NEW DELHI-110002

Published by:

Namit Wasan

DISCOVERY PUBLISHING HOUSE PVT. LTD.

4383/4B, Ansari Road, Darya Ganj

New Delhi-110 002 (India)

Phone : +91-11-23279245; 23253475; 43596065

E-mail : discoverybooksindia@gmail.com
discoverypublishinghouse@gmail.com
namitwasan9@gmail.com

web : www.discoverypublishinggroup.com

***Edition:* 2020**

ISBN: 978-81-7141-913-5

Methods of Teaching Chemistry

Printed at:
Infinity Imaging Systems
Delhi

Foreword

Teacher education is quantitatively marching ahead towards quality education. The central and state governments through the NCTE and the Directorates of School/Higher Education are rendering their legitimate service in improving the quality of teacher education by formulating and implementing various academic policies and educational programmes. Along with these policies and programmes, the teacher educators and the prospective teachers teaching and studying in teacher education institutions need good curriculum and quality books.

The methods of teaching each subject play a pivotal role in enhancing the efficiency of their practitioners. Identifying the very importance of the methods of teaching and the quality of books, a series of books on the methods of teaching different subjects have been developed by experienced teacher educators for the benefit of teachers in making in teacher education institutions. Thanks to the authors.

Valuable suggestions for the improvement of these books are welcome from fellow teacher educators, prospective teachers and other academicians involved in the arena of teacher education.

The authors and the editor dedicate this series of books on the methodology of teaching to Mr. Tilak Raj Wasan Proprietor, Discovery Publishing House, New Delhi, for taking up this commendable task of publication to meet the felt needs of teacher education faculty and clientele.

Dr. Digumarti Bhaskara Rao
Research Director in Education
Nagarjuna University
br_digumarti@rediffmail.com

PREFACE

The movement of modern education in India is almost two century old. It has come of age now. Over the decades, great educationists have contributed towards the development and evolution of education, as a discipline. Thus, education in India has been enriched a lot.

As a result, the Indian education system can be placed at par with any advanced education system in the modern world. In fact, education is a vast sea and Teachers' Training is a stream in it. So, it makes it essential that the responsibilities of the faculty members are focused on the task of providing better training to the future teachers, for their better learning and proper development. And this responsible exercise can only be undertaken, if the trainers are equipped with all the needed skill and knowledge of the subject, they are supposed to teach. Hence, it becomes essential for making adequate provisions, for each course to the teacher-trainees. Methods of Teaching are very important for the successful training of teachers and for their career in future.

In order to provide all related material in one cover, here is this book, on this important subject. Of course there are several books on the subject in the market, but, every book has its own style and way of presentation. Similarly, the present one, too has its own merits and advantages.

During the course of the preparation of this book, the undersigned has done his best for the accomplishment of the job. He would be pleased and feel contented, if this book is acknowledged, as a textbook and a reference tool for the teachers and students, alike.

Author

CONTENTS

Chemistry and Mathematics ▪ Correlation between Chemistry and Social Sciences ▪ Correlation between Chemistry and Physics ▪ Correlation between Chemistry and Biology ▪ Correlation between Chemistry and Work Experience ▪ Creativity and Chemistry Teaching

1

INTRODUCTION

"Teacher! I saw a satellite!" "Look! One baby mouse is white!" "Can we attempt the experiment this way?" "I have collected all the data – use of log tables and even slide rule is too time consuming and out of date for calculations. May I use a calculator? Please! Now we have computers."

Everyday, they are different – but everyday greetings like these begin the day for science teachers. One day it is satellite, one day the moon, one day how the seesaw operates, one day the why of earthquakes – or another question everyone is asking. Science teachers as well as students; government as well as commentators – everyone needs the answers to questions in science.

It is a wonderful world when you look at it this way – and science is like a key that opens doors everywhere – on the bottom of the ocean – with the astronauts in space – with the plants, animals, and man here on earth – with thousands of conveniences of our daily lives. Learning about science – as you already know – stretches your mind, but gives you a lot in return. You always have something new to bring to your classes. And you as a science teacher have many satisfactions that come from working with young students.

You have been a practising science teacher and now you are ready to be regular science teacher, teaching a class of physics or chemistry, biology or integrated science, you will surely like to be a good science teacher. This is the right time to ask yourself some questions like these:

- What does it take to be a good science teacher?
- How can I use my teacher's training to be a good science teacher?
- Where can I get some more information about good science teaching?
- What things should I do to begin with to be a good science teacher?
- What should I do to be happy as a science teacher?

TEACHERS' ROLE

Everyone needs an education in science in order to understand the world and to be a good citizen and good worker. Scientists, leaders in government, industrialists, and the public in general need to be able to understand scientific problems and to make good judgements about them. We need scientific literate and informed people to make decisions about such things as major government projects in space exploration and medical science; health problems, environmental and population problems, such as air and water pollution; diseases such as cancer or tuberculosis and epidemics; or the possible effects of chemical pesticides upon us and our environment.

More and more people will need science in their work, and they must depend on teachers to help them get the knowledge they will need. Each new "breakthrough" or the expanding frontier of science and technology, and the public's need to be informed, require a never-ending supply of well-trained people to fill the ranks. This is also true in engineering, medicine and other fields related to science. The next generation of youngsters, as it passes through school, must be as well-educated in and about science as its talent will permit if we are to continue to prosper in our democratic society. Moreover, the ever-increasing scientific and technological progress challenges man's ingenuity to improve his methods of processing, storing, retrieving and reporting all sorts of scientific information. In a sense, we need "new breeds" of people who can combine science with other talents, as for example, the scientist, librarian and the science reporter.

Good science teaching is one of the most valuable ways to meet this urgent need for science-educated citizens and workers. Enthusiastic, intelligent, and well-educated science teachers inspire and prepare students to investigate the great questions of science and the questions raised by the scientific discoveries which affect us and our society.

Mainly through the inspiration of devoted science teachers, great number of students develop lifelong scientific interests and learn to appreciate and understand the nature of science and its usefulness to mankind.

The science teacher derives great satisfaction from this special importance of his work. And added to it is the great satisfaction that comes from mastering a field of scientific study and from affording a special kind of service to others.

So, when you ask yourself: "What do science teachers do?" You may answer:

"Everyone today needs to understand what science is about. We need it because discoveries in science affect many aspects of society. To be responsible and useful citizens, we must be able to judge how the discoveries of science may be best used for ourselves and society. Many among us will make a career of science, engineering, or technology. We need a good foundation in science to become competent in our chosen work. Therefore, we can say in general that a science teacher, at whatever level he is teaching, is laying the foundations for an understanding of science."

A science teacher is a teacher first and then a science teacher. As a teacher he should be understanding, sympathetic. Teachable and free of prejudices. Science teaching requires a sound knowledge of the subject and a real interest and ability in sharing this knowledge with others. It also requires keeping up-to-date. The work is not easy, but it is creative, and it can be extremely exciting and satisfying. It takes thought, energy, and enthusiasm. Here is an example of what one good school expects of its science teachers:

1. He plans his work for the whole year before school starts its session.
2. He plans his lessons well in advance before he enters the classroom for teaching science.
3. He knows the various practical skills needed in his particular field.
4. He guides and assists his students in their laboratory experiments, field trips and projects. He is also responsible for the safety of the students and the condition of the laboratory and its equipment. He decides in what way each aspect of his subject can best be taught. Some of the ideas and problems can be most effectively presented by demonstration, others through student investigation, field trips, or by films or lectures. He also masters the finer art of asking the questions that will stimulate his students to think for themselves and to search for answers.
5. He organises class procedures, plans the use of the laboratory, discusses with the class, and helps his students learn how to find information outside the classroom in school and city libraries, local industries, or by consulting experts in the community.
6. He encourages his students to develop a lasting interest in science, its changes, and its methods. He guides both individual and group projects and help the students

participate in various programmes of awards and recognition. He may sponsor a school science club and with the help of other science teachers and students, organises a science fair or plan field trips.

7. He keeps both himself and his students informed on the most recent developments in his field. He draws his students attention to the social, economic, political, and other aspects of the relationship between society, people and modern science. Thus he and his students always see that science study is not limited to the classroom.
8. He attends orientation courses in his field (seminars, workshops, summer institutes), as well as science conventions and science conferences for his academic growth.
9. He participates in science curriculum development programme conducted by various agencies like DIETs, SCERTs, LASEs and NCERT etc.
10. He conducts action research in science education and actively participates in innovative science programmes for better science teaching.
11. He always efforts for quality science education to his students. Now you can figure out yourself what should be the competencies for a good science teacher (Physics/Chemistry/Biology).

A GOOD TEACHER

After completing your teacher training programme, this is the right time to ask yourself whether you possess the basic intellectual and personal qualities necessary to be a good science teacher. Do you have the attributes, such as integrity, drive, and a high sense of responsibility, which are valued in teaching specially science teaching. Besides these, there are special characteristics of successful and happy science teacher.

Checking the following questions may help you decide, how good a science teacher you are going to be.

		Yes	No
1.	Do you enjoy reading and studying in science as well as in other academic areas?	.....	.....
2.	Have you been a good science teacher?	.....	.....
3.	Do you like working with students and other science teachers?	.....	.....
4.	Do you like to help your students?	.....	... .
5.	Do your students and other science teachers like to work with you?	.....	.....
6.	Could you enjoy and adopt to a career in which the subject is constantly and rapidly changing because of new discoveries?	.....	.....
7.	Do you/ on your own, sometimes do more work than is required by teachers?	.....	
8.	Have you developed science projects and participated in science fairs?	.....	
9.	Do you like to find answers to problems on your own?	.....	
10.	Do you have a sense of humour?	.....	.....
11.	Can you accept criticism and profit from it?	.....	.....
12.	Do you consider that preparing students for living in the World of the future is a challenging job?	.....	.....
13.	Are you developing the ability to read quickly and with comprehension and to express yourself clearly and interestingly in speaking and writing?	.....	.....
14.	Are you in good health, both physically and mentally?	.....	...

If you have checked thoughtfully YES for most of the above questions, you very likely would enjoy teaching science at any level, and you should read on to learn how you prepare for this type of exciting career.

2

SCOPE AND INFLUENCE

A reasonable short definition of the scope of chemistry has been given as, "chemistry is the integrated study of the preparation, properties, structure and reactions of the chemical elements and their compounds and of the systems which they form."

Interpreted in the broader sense, this definition would include most of natural science, a consequence of the considerable areas of overlap which chemistry has with physical, biological, earth and material sciences.

Chemists tend to work on molecular rather than atomic systems, and on molecular structures and transformations rather than on phenomenon associated with simple substances only.

Chemical science is dynamic in scope and many chemists find themselves working in areas currently described as interfaces (*e.g.* molecular biology, solid state physics).

THE SUBSTRUCTURE

The traditional substructure of physical, organic, inorganic, and some times analytical chemistry has origin in the past activities of chemists and still continues to determine how chemistry is taught. Another possible sub-division would be the following: The structure and physical properties of pure substances, chemical transformations and applications of chemistry to complex systems. Application of chemistry would include such fields of current activity as molecular biology, material science and geochemical phenomenon.

RISE AND GROWTHS

The scientific method emerged in the 16th century with the realisation that investigation must supplement logic and intution in probing nature. This view point which owes its initiation to scientists like Bacon, Boyle, Galileo, Hooke, Newton and others, recorded its early successes in astronomy and mechanics. The method came to be gradually applied to chemical behaviour of matter, thanks to the pioneering efforts of Antoine Lavoisier in the late 18th century and this marked the birth of chemical science as we know it today.

SIGNIFICANCE OF THE SUBJECT

Chemistry as considered an important subject in school curriculum as many professional and applied courses, directly or indirectly use the knowledge of chemistry. Moreover, the present age is the era of science and more number of people are being employed in scientific pursuits which require knowledge of chemistry.

Chemistry education is also necessary because of its immense value in the students' individual life as well as in society.

Chemistry is essentially a secondary school subject. At this level, it may be taught as a subject in its own right or as part of a broader science course identified by a variety of titles, *e.g.* integrated science, general science and modular science. The discipline may also feature as a component of courses in physical or biological sciences.

The most significant aspect of modern science is the impact it has had in solving a variety of problems of practical and technological importance as well as those related to the pressing problems of mankind. A large number of these problems require a proper understanding and application of chemical principles and processes.

The major threats to the present day civilisation are population explosion, hunger and disease, environmental pollution, depletion of sources of energy as well as natural resources. The growth of population is probably the greatest problem facing us.

In solving most of these pressing problems, chemists have a lot to do. Paracelus (1493-1541) said, 'the true use of chemistry is not to make gold, but to prepare medicines'. The problem of atmospheric pollution, if and when it is solved will only be done through an understanding of chemical dynamics.

Chemistry has made a significant contribution in the fields of drugs, fuels, agriculture, animal farming, fibres etc. In addition to these there are many other inter-disciplinary areas where the contribution of chemists is significant. In the area of *environmental pollution,* chemists arc finding better methods of analysis and solutions to get rid of pollution. There is the entire area of *marine chemistry* to investigate new sources for food and chemicals.

PRACTICAL APPLICATION

The involvement of chemists in real life problems has been pointed out in the previous section. In this section we take up a few specific areas in some details.

Drugs : Many a substances from natural sources have been used since times immemorial for treatment of diseases. For example, an extract from the bark of poplar, olive or willow trees was recommended more than two thousand years ago by Hippocrates—the father of medicine—for treating fever. At present we can isolate and purify the drug from natural sources and establish their chemical structure Sparsely occurring substances can be synthesized in the laboratory and in this way made available in abundance. More over even such drugs which do not occur in nature have also been obtained by synthesising them in the laboratory. *Aspirin* (Acetyl salicylic acid) is one of the earliest synthetic drug. *Salvarsan* was synthesized for treatment of syphilis. Some other prominent synthetic drugs are *Sulpha drugs, antibiotics, anaesthetics, antimalarials* and wonder drug *cortisone.*

Food : Chemist have done a lot to increase food grain production and helped to bring about green revolution. *Synthetic fertilizers* were developed which provided the essential elements for growth of plants. The use of these fertilizer led to higher yield of plants. *Insecticides, weed killers, fungicides* developed by chemists have contributed a lot to increase the availability of food grains for the mankind. In many countries farmers use laboratory made chemicals as *defoliants*. For example, magnesium chlorate when applied to ripened cotton crop causes the leaves to fall of thus making harvesting much cheaper and faster. Chemicals are also used in animal farming. For example, 'marlate'-a new insecticide-used as a dip or as a spray-kills' blood-sucking hornflies which attack cows. This step alone leads to 10% increase in milk supply.

Fuels : Till the middle of this century only naturally occurring substances such as wood, coal, coke etc. were used as fuels but now the situation has been completely changed by *processsing of petroleum Petrochemical industry* also provides many a useful chemicals like benzene, toluene, xylene, naphthalene etc. *Petrochemicals* provide the base of synthetic fibres, rubber, resins, detergents, refrigerants and explosives.

Fibres : Now a days we are producing *synthetic fibres* like *nylon, rayon* and *terylene*. These fibres in some respects excel the natural fibres. They are longer lasting, crease resistant and quick drying.

In addition to these there are many inter-disciplinary areas where contribution of chemicals is significant. For example production of glasses and ceramics, electronic, magnetic and optical materials; fibre-based composites; etc. In the area of *environmental pollution* chemists are finding better methods of analysis and solution to get rid of pollution. *Marine chemistry* is concerned with investigating new sources of food and chemicals.

HUMAN RESOURCES

A nations most valuable resource is its people. The intelligence, creativity and talent that resides in the human mind awaits only its release and full development through education.

Chemistry in particular, is close to a nations' health and strength and to the well being of its people. Since chemistry touches the lives of every individual (through agriculture, industry, nutrition, industry, medicine, home environment etc.). We can easily say that an individuals' *every moment* is directly influenced by the understanding and therefore the utilization he or she can make of chemistry. Scientific discoveries, technological advances, the efficiency of work force, the exercising of citizens rights and quality of life are directly tied to the teaching of chemistry.

As a teacher of chemistry our goals should he

(i) to provide appropriate education in chemistry to everyone.

(ii) to fully develop human resources.

Having set our goal we should establish strategies to achieve the goals and should periodically evaluate our progress. We should always have an open mind to set even higher goals for some thing better,

For chemistry teaching in future the goals have to be set in a different light than in the past. This is due to the fact that in the past we aimed to educate a few scientists and engineers for our country. Now we aim at educating every one in basis of chemistry. With this in view students have to be classified on the basis of diversity in student interest and goals. The following five grasp can be easily identified.

(i) Those interested to become future chemists.

(ii) Those interested in other science-based professions (*e.g.* the biological and earth scientists, engineers, physicians, nutritionist etc.).

(iii) Those who are interested to become technical personnel. They will comprise the support system for science and technology.

(iv) Those who are likely to join industries, in health sciences and in agriculture.

(v) Ordinary citizens.

Every body needs sufficient knowledge of chemistry to function effectively in present day society. At present our society is being influenced by new drugs, synthetic materials, green revolutions in agriculture, micro-computers, micro-electronics etc.

In developing human resources we should aim at providing high quality education in chemistry. Such an education should provide opportunity for working in laboratory and for solving mathematical and intellectual problems. Students be encouraged to investigate, to explore, to use the library, to use the natural environment and to discuss chemical concepts and issues in order to provide them sufficient opportunity and experience to cope with benefits from products and processes of chemistry through out their lives.

Thus in future we shall have to give a much different chemistry curriculum which may either be in the form of a course suitable for every one at secondary level or of several streams for providing chemical education for every one. The syllabus for science students and non-science students has been discussed in chapter on curriculum.

a staff salary of Rs. 600.00 p.m. in addition to his registered pay and allowances." Calcutta Medical College established in 1835 under a number of capable teachers, became an important institution, for the study of anatomy, physiology and medicine (along with surgery), as well as of chemistry, botany and natural philosophy.

First Research Institutions : Indians asked for Western Education in Science from the Government. The Colonial power agreed to create facilities but with miserly financial provision just sufficient to train a few clerks able to operate in English in Government offices and European Commercial houses, and not to enable the native people to pick up treasures from European science. So the hard way of working for science began. Mahendra Lal Sircar *(born* in 1833), an M.D. of the Calcutta Medical College, clearly saw that science would never develop and strike deep roots in this country under foreign tutelage and that Indians themselves must come forward to raise funds and found institutions for the training of scientists and organisation of research. In 1876 Dr. Sircar himself founded India's first research institution, "The Indian Association for the Cultivation of Science," completely under Indian Management and control with finances derived from private subscriptions. In the first half of the twentieth century the association developed into an important centre for research in the physical sciences - in optics, acoustics, scattering of light, X-rays and magnetism; and C.V. Raman performed his Nobel Prize Winning Experiments in its unassuming laboratories, *i.e.* western India. Jamshedji Tata a businessman, prepared plans for a similar institution for technical and scientific education and research which finally took the shape of "The Institute of Science" at Bangalore in the beginning of the twentieth century.

First College of Science : The Educational Despatch of 1854 paved the way for University education. In 1857 the three Universities of Calcutta, Bombay and Madras came into existence, but they came out just as examining bodies with powers to grant degrees. The actual teaching and academic work were left to the colleges. Fortified by the University Act of 1904, which empowered Universities to appoint professors and lecturers, to hold and manage educational endowments, and to erect, equip and maintain libraries, laboratories and museums, Asutosh Mookerji, Vice Chancellor of Calcutta University took the initiative in establishing the, first University College of Science. Undaunted by the Government's refusal to provide funds for the creation of professorships and other facilities, Asutosh obtained princely endowments from Sir Tarak Nath Palit and Sir Rash Behary Ghosh, who had amassed enormous amounts of money and property in the legal profession, and established a number of chairs in Chemistry, Physics, Applied Mathematics and Botany. According to the terms of the endowment, professorships could be filled only by Indians, a clause which further irritated the Government firmly entrenched in the view that only Europeans were suited for such high positions. This University College of Science, although starved financially all through, produced a group of physicists and chemists who received international recognition for their scientific developments and institutions staffed by high salaried Europeans and maintained and patronised by Government funds cut a sorry figure.

NATIONAL SCIENCE POLICY

The development of science in India was greatly accelerated after independence (August 1947). In 1950 the Government of India appointed a Planning Commission for preparing a blueprint of all-round economic development. In 1954 the Indian Parliament accepted socialism as a political goal. Declaring these objectives, fullest emphasis was laid on the development of science and technology on all fronts. In 1957, the Government took one step further in adopting a National Science Policy Resolution that envisaged the cultivation of science and scientific research in all its aspects, assured an adequate supply, within the country, of research scientists of highest quality through an intensive programme of training, promised the availability of conditions and an atmosphere of academic freedom in which the creative talent of men and women would find full scope in scientific activity. The resolution thus reaffirmed the Government decision to encourage science and develop a healthy scientific community as a sound basis after a balanced economic development.

SCIENCE EDUCATION IN SCHOOLS

- In the beginning of twentieth century science was not a school subject in our country. The Report of the Secondary School Commission 1953, recommended the teaching of General Science as a compulsory subject in the high and higher secondary schools.
- The All India Seminar on the Teaching of Science in Secondary Schools (1956) dealt with almost all the problems facing the inclusion of General Science as a Core Subject for the Higher Secondary Classes - syllabus, apparatus, teaching aids, textbooks, science clubs, science museums, examination techniques etc. It suggested a uniform system of science teaching for the entire country, suited to its needs and resources.
- Indian Parliamentary and Scientific Committee (1962) studied the allied problems of science education in schools like
  - growth of school population,
  - shortage of qualified science teachers,
  - accelerated achievement in science,
  - demand for increase in technically trained manpower,
  - growing importance of science in the affairs of mankind, and
  - changes in the processes and goals of science.
- UNESCO Planning Commission (1963-64) worked on the problems of science education in India and suggested ways to improve it. As a follow up programme, Department of Science and Mathematics Education of the NCERT took up the pilot project of preparing new disciplinary science curricula at middle (VI-VIII) level text books (Physics, Chemistry, Biology), teachers' guides, science kits, kit guides, teacher training films and evaluation material. This Disciplined Science Programme was changed to Integrated Science Programme in mid-eighties.

- In 1970 under UNICEF Assisted Science Education Programme (SEP) Primary "Science is Doing" Programme was developed by NCERT, which was used in primary schools throughout the country. This Programme was a package of classes I and II Science Syllabus, Class III-V Science Texts, Teachers Guides, Primary Science Kit, Kit Guide, and Teacher Training Films. This Programme was changed to EVS Programme in mid-eighties.
- Kothari Commission (1964-66) recommendations were implemented in 1975 when Science for All (SFA) was introduced as a part of general education during the first ten years of schooling. With this 10+2+3 education scheme started with an additional year of schooling, in the country. First Disciplined Science Course (Physics, Chemistry, Biology) was introduced at secondary level (IX-X). This was changed to Disciplined Science A-Course (Physics, Chemistry, Biology) and Integrated Science B-Course. Students had an option either to take Science A-Course or to take Science B-Course. This again changed to just one Integrated Science Course for all. At +2, Senior Secondary level (XI-XII) Disciplined Science Course (3 different science subjects - Physics, Chemistry, Biology) started from the very beginning of 10+2+3 education scheme.
- Then in 1986 the National Education Policy Document (NPE-1986) came out (Chapter 23). If some one asks, "What is new in this new education policy (NPE-1986), "Implementation" perhaps will be the right answer. Much emphasis has been given to quality pre-service and in-service teacher education in the policy document. For this District Institutes of Education (DIETs) and Institutes of Advance Studies in Education (LASEs) were established throughout the country for Elementary and Secondary Education respectively.

LATEST DEVELOPMENTS

India is now engaged in a broad spectrum of scientific research, both fundamental and applied, in Government, Universities and Private Research Establishments. In recent years there has been extraordinary success in developing new polymers, ceramics, composites, superconductors, nanomaterials, smart materials and biomaterials. Biotechnology, Genetic Engineering and Biomedical Research are some other fields in which India has started entering.

AIDS (Acquired Immuno Deficiency Syndrome) poses a threat to India as a large number of people are infected with HIV (Human Immunodeficiency Virus). There are no drugs today for AIDS. The problem which has dogged anti HIV drugs is that resistant mutant forms of virus are formed within mere weeks. Lot of research work is to be done in search of a vaccine against HIV.

Per capita consumption of energy in India is very low compared to developed countries, and even that we are unable to afford. In the years to come when we have already entered twenty-first century, we will need much more energy. The major effort in next decade would have to be through an increase in the production of coal and a search of new reserves of oil. We should also give due emphasis to new technologies for solar energy and hydrogen energy. India is also to expand its nuclear power programmes. Nuclear energy could play an important role in meeting our bulk energy requirement. Our expertise in the field of nuclear power technology as well as related research areas, is an asset for us.

For all this we need huge amounts of funds, as scientific research has become costly. If we compare the funds available for scientific research in India compared to some other developing countries, India has a very gloomy picture. South Korea had planned to increase its R&D spending to over 5 per cent of its GDP by year 2000. China had planned to increase its R&D investment from 0.5 per cent to 1.5 per cent of GDP by the year 2000. Unfortunately India's R&D expenditure has come down to 0.89 per cent of GDP from 1.1 per cent earlier. We need to realise that in order to be able to do competitive scientific research and development we have to bring our R&D expenditure to at least about 1.5 per cent of GDP and focus our efforts on a few selected programmes and projects.

Our scientists want people to support them and understand their needs, and they are to inform people about science, why science is needed, what they are doing and why. They (our scientists) are to build up partnership with public, industries, politicians and bureaucrats. They need informed friends of science at all places.

When changes which affect our future, are happening and will happen at such a rapid rate, and are based on science and technology, it is necessary that our scientists be more close to decision making.

In the existing state of scientific advancement and development of resources for research, the rate of scientific growth of developed countries is likely to continue to be faster than that of the developing countries like India. Science has become deeply involved with defence and big industry, with the result that big sciences like atomic energy, space, etc., has been and probably will remain concentrated in super powers, In nuclear, space, computer and few other sciences, developing nations like India are already at the mercy of super powers. To be self-sufficient we are to change our science curriculum right from the school stage. We are not just to teach science but also scientific method. We are not just to teach science content but also science processes, the ways in which scientists advance their knowledge and solve problems. Science should be presented to students as a way in which they can conduct an inquiry into the nature of things as well as a body of information built up by other people. The science processes are being neglected and the school science has been concerned almost exclusively with the content—the body of information. Science is not just content. Science is content plus science processes. If we want to advance in science like other developed countries, science processes should be given due importance like science content in school science curriculum, and students should be encouraged to become personally involved in solving problems and in discovering some science for themselves.

Questions

1. What was the position of science education in ancient India?
2. "During the British Empire introduction of modern science in India was extremely slow." Discuss.
3. Discuss very briefly how the development of science was greatly accelerated after independence.
4. Discuss the role of the curriculum developers when science is developing so fast in our country.
5. "Knowledge of science becomes double every decade." What should be the role of our science teachers in this context?

4

OBJECTIVES AND AIMS

In order to accomplish the task of teaching chemistry, it is essential for us to be very clear about the purpose of teaching chemistry. If we have a clear idea of what is to be achieved them it would be easier to implement any prescribed course in chemistry. This clarity of purpose would also be quite helpful in measuring the effectiveness of teaching chemistry. The purpose of teaching chemistry is based on certain aims and objectives to be achieved. Teacher may use different methods of teaching to achieve the purpose. Many educational reform committees have emphasised spelling out aims and objectives of teaching a particular course of study.

The aim of teaching chemistry refers to the advantages that can be drawn or purposes that can be served by the study of chemistry. The important aims of teaching chemistry are as follows:

Knowledge Aim : The teaching of chemistry should increase the knowledge of the individual and such an increase in knowledge should help him in understanding himself and his environment. Thus this knowledge should help him in his daily life.

Practical Aim : The knowledge gained should be of practical use to an individual. The individual should not only know the principles, and facts but should be able to use these principles in understanding his environment. For this the knowledge should be related to the materials, with which the pupil is familiar and should not be based on obsolete devices and ideas.

Development of Scientific Attitude : Chemistry being a physical science it aims at the development of scientific attitude among the learners. It should be helpful in removing the superstitions, false beliefs, wrong notions spread in the society and cultivate the habits of proper reasoning, observation and experiment action. One of the major aims of chemistry like any other science subject is to develop scientific attitude and science related values amongst students. It should train the student in the method of science and should help develop in scientific temper.

Cultural Aim : Present day civilisation owes much to the development of chemistry and for any further development we have to strive for progressive improvement in the study of chemistry. For this the chemistry be taught in schools in such a way as (i) to grasp the progress in the field of chemistry (ii) apply it for enhancement of our cultural heritage and development of civilisation and (iii) appreciate the study of chemistry in the progress and development of culture and civilisation.

Social Aim : The study of chemistry should help inculcate social virtues among the students for leading a well adjusted social life and contributing significantly towards welfare and progress of society. It should imbibe in him essential social qualities and virtues for becoming a responsible useful citizen.

Vocational Aim : The knowledge of chemistry in the present day world is essential for almost all the professions, and vocations. To achieve the vocational aim we must prepare our students for the different occupations and vocational courses. This knowledge should also provide them proper opportunity for adoption of some chemistry hobby and engage themselves in small scale industries and self employment projects.

Utilisation of Leisure Time : The knowledge of chemistry should be useful to an individual to learn ways and means of utilizing his leisure hours more fruitfully.

Psychological Aim : Teaching of chemistry provides to an individual various opportunities for satisfying his varying psychological needs and this help him grow and develop as a well balanced individual.

Skill Aim : Like any other science subject, the teaching of chemistry should aim to develop useful skills pertaining to scientific observation, experimentation and practical use of scientific facts and principles.

CRITERIA FOR SELECTION OF AIMS

Thurber and Collette have proposed the following criteria for selection of aims.

(i) *Usefulness.* The knowledge gained should be useful to the students in their lives.

(ii) *Timliness.* The knowledge given should be concerned with materials/objects with which student is familiar.

(iii) *Fitness.* The knowledge should fit into sequence that leads him to broad objectives.

(iv) *Appropriateness.* The learning should be appropriate for maturity and background of the students.

(v) *Practicability.* It means that experience required for development of learning should be possible.

The chemistry team of the institute for the Promotion of Teaching Science and Technology (IPST) in Thailand formulated the following broad aims which they felt valid for any science course.

1. To develop an understanding of the basic principles and theories of science.
2. To develop an understanding of the nature, scope and limitations of science.
3. To develop a scientific attitude.

4. To develop skills important for scientific investigation.
5. To develop an understanding of the consequences of science on man and his physical and biological environment.

Aims of chemistry curriculum should be as follows:

(i) To make students interested in chemistry.

(ii) To familiarise the students with the important role played by chemistry in their life.

(iii) To develop in students a scientific culture.

(iv) To provide a training to students in methods of science.

(v) To emphasise upon students the role of chemistry on social behaviour.

(vi) To prepare students for those vocations which require a sound knowledge of chemistry.

(vii) To increase students understanding to such a level that he can understand various concepts and theories which unify various branches of chemistry.

THE DIFFERENCE

Though the two terms 'aims' and 'objectives' are considered as synonyms and used interchangeably yet in a deep sense there is a lot of difference between 'aim' and 'objective'.

Values and aims are quite inter related and interdependent. We aim at a thing because we value it. The values or advantages that we can draw by achieving a thing become our purposes or aims. These may be taken as the broader purposes or goals or targets that can be anticipated through the teaching of chemistry.

To achieve these aims we have to proceed systematically. For achieving these aims, these are usually divided into some definite, functional and workable units named as objectives. Objectives are, therefore, the ways and means of achieving the aims in a more practical and definite way.

Objectives are the specific and precise behavioural outcome of teaching a particular topic in chemistry. The objective of a topic in chemistry help in realising some general aim of teaching chemistry. The characteristics of a good objective are as under:

(i) It should be specific and precise.

(ii) It should be attainable.

Probably the most common educational objective in the *acquisition of knowledge.* By knowledge, we mean that the student can give evidence that he remembers either by recalling or by recognising, some idea or phenomenon which he has had experience in the educational process. Knowledge may involve more complex processes of relating and judging.

Another important objective is development of *intellectual abilities and skills.* This has been labelled as 'critical thinking' by some, 'problem solving' by others.

Arts or skills + knowledge = ability 'Arts and skills' refer to modes of operation and generalised technique for dealing with problem. The arts and skill emphasise the mental processes of organising and recognising material to achieve a particular purpose. *Intellectual abilities* refer to situations in which the individual in expected to bring specific technical information to bear on a new problem

Objectives are the specific and precise behavioural outcomes of teaching a particular topic or lesson of chemistry. Objectives actually control other factors of chemistry teaching to a great extent, therefore more emphasis be laid on writing objectives in behavioural terms for each unit of class room instructions in chemistry.

TAXONOMY

"Classification especially of animals and plants according to their natural relationships".

Taxonomy of educational objectives is intended to provide for classification of the goals of our educational system. It is expected to help in the discussion of curricular and evaluation problems with greater precision. It is expected to facilitate the exchange of information about curricular developments and evaluation devices.

Bloom's taxonomy is a classification of instructional objectives in a hierarchy. It is found quite useful in communicating the objectives of a chemistry lesson as also a criterion for evaluation of chemistry teaching. Under this scheme the specific objectives are classified as falling into the following three domains.

1. Cognitive domain objectives.
2. Affective domain objectives.
3. Psychomotor domain objectives.

COGNITIVE DOMAIN

Probably the most common educational objective is acquisition of knowledge. Knowledge, as defined here, involves the recall of specifics and universals, the recall of methods and processes or the recall of a pattern, structure or setting.

The cognitive domain can be summarised as under:

Classes	*Instructional Coverage*
Knowledge	Recall and recognition of facts information, principles, laws and theories of chemistry.
(i) Knowledge of specifics	The recall of specific and isolable bits of information.
(ii) Knowledge of terminology	Knowledge of refrents for specific symbols (verbal and non-verbal) *e.g.* to define technical terms.
(iii) Knowledge of specific facts	Knowledge of dates, events persons, places, etc.
(iv) Knowledge of ways and means of dealing and with specifics	Knowledge of the ways of organising, studying, judging, critisising.
(v) Knowledge of conventions	Familiarity with the forms and conventions of scientific papers.
(vi) Knowledge of trends and sequences	Knowledge of the process directions and movements of phenomenon with respect to time.

Contd.

Classes	*Instructional Coverage*
(vii) Knowledge of Classification and categories	To recognise the are encompassed by various kinds of problems and arguments.
(viii) Knowledge of criteria	Knowledge of a criteria by which facts, principles opinions and conduct are tested or judged.
(ix) Knowledge of methodology of evaluation.	Knowledge of scientific methods
(x) Knowledge of principles and generalisations	Knowledge of important principles.
Comprehension	It represents the lowest level of understanding.
(i) Translation	The ability to understand non-literal statements.
(ii) Interpretation	The ability to grasp the thought of the work as a whole at any desired level of generality.
(iii) Extrapolation	The ability to deal with the conclusions of a work in terms of the immediate inference made from the explicit statements.
Application	Application to phenomenon discussed in one paper of the scientific terms or concepts used in other papers.
Analysis	The breakdown of a communication into its constituent elements or parts such that the relative hierarchy of ideas in made clear and/or the relation between the ideas expressed are made explicit.

Contd.

Classes	*Instructional Coverage*
(i) Analysis of elements	The ability to recognise unstated assumptions, skills in distinguishing facts from hypothesis.
(ii) Analysis of relationships	Ability to check the consistency of hypothesis with given information and assumptions.
(iii) Analysis of organisational principles	The organisation, systematic arrangement and structure which hold the communication together.
Synthesis	The putting together of elements and parts so as to form a whole.
(i) Production of a unique communication	Skill in writing, using an excellent organisation of ideas and statements. Ability to tell a personal experience effectively.
(ii) Production of a Plan	Ability to propose ways of testing hypothesis.
(iii) Derivation of set of abstract relations	Ability to formulate appropriate hypothesis based upon an analy-sis of factors involved and to modify such hypothesis on the basis of new factors and considerations.
Evaluation	Judgement about the value of material and methods for given purposes.
(i) Judgement in terms of internal evidence	The ability to indicate logical fallacies in arguments.
(ii) Judgements in terms of external evidence	Judging by external standards, criteria ability to compare a work with the highest known standard in its field.

Contd.

Classes	*Instructional Coverage*
(iii) Psychomotor	Development of skills such as of handling pieces of apparatus, their assemblies, drawing diagrams and circuits, repair of apparatus and appliances.

A brief discussion of these objectives is given below:

The Knowledge

To impart knowledge in the basic aim of education and so it naturally is the basic aim of teaching of any subject including science. By imparting knowledge of science to the student it is expected that he acquires the knowledge of:

(i) Natural phenomenon.

(ii) Scientific terminology.

(iii) Scientific concepts and formula.

(iv) Modern inventions of science.

(v) Importance of animal life and plant life to man.

(vi) Manipulation of nature by man.

(vii) Correlation and inter-dependence of various branches of science.

(viii) Environment.

Knowledge objective is considered to have been achieved if the student is able to recall and recognise terms, facts, symbols, concepts etc.

The Understanding

This objective considered to have been achieved if the student is able to:

(i) Interpret charts, graphs, data, concept etc., correctly.

(ii) Illustrate scientific terms, concepts, facts, phenomenon's.

(iii) Explain facts, concepts, principles etc.

(iv) Discriminate between different facts, concepts etc. that are closely related to each other.

(v) Identify relationships between various facts, concepts, phenomenon etc.

(vi) Change tables, symbols, terms etc. from any given form to some other desired form.

(vii) Find faults, if any, in statements concepts etc.

The Applications

This objective seems to be the most neglected one in our educational system. The common observation that supports it is that a science graduate fails to insert even a fuse wire in the electric circuit of his house. This objective is considered to have been achieved to a great extent if the pupil can:

(i) Analyse a given data.

(ii) Explain giving reasons various scientific phenomenon.

(iii) Formulate hypothesis from his observations.

(iv) Confirm or reject a hypothesis.

(v) Correctly infer the observed facts.

(vi) Find cause and effect relationship.

(vii) Give new illustrations

(viii) Predict new happenings.

(ix) Find relationships that exist between various facts, concepts, phenomenon learnt by him.

The Skills

This objective can be considered to have been achieved if a pupil learns (i) handling piece of apparatus, (ii) assembling pieces of apparatus for experiment (iii) drawing diagrams and illustrations, (iv) constructing things, and (v) carrying our repairs of apparatus and appliances.

Thus here we aim to develop three types of skill in the pupil. These are (a) drawing skill (b) manipulative skill and (c) observational and recording skill.

The drawing skill is considered to have been achieved if pupil is able to draw labelled sketches and diagrams quickly.

The manipulative skill is considered to have been achieved if pupil is able to

(i) Keep and handle the apparatus properly,

(ii) Improvise models and experiments,

(iii) Observe various precautions while handling apparatus and doing experiments.

The observational and recording skill is considered to have been achieved if the pupil can

(i) Read correctly the instrument or apparatus,

(ii) Record observations faithfully,

(iii) Make calculations correctly and

(iv) Draw inferences correctly.

The Interests

To achieve this objective the pupil is provided with scientific hobbies and other leisure time activities. By providing such activities our aim is to inculcate, among pupils, a living and substaining interest in environment in which he lives.

The aim is considered to have been achieved if the pupil becomes curious and develops such an interest in science that he is always eager and is on look out to:

(i) Take to some interesting scientific hobby.

(ii) Visit places of scientific interest.

(iii) Undertake some chemistry projects.

(iv) Meet and interact some reputed person in the field of chemistry.

(v) Read scientific literature.

(vi) Collect scientific photographs, scientific biographies etc.

(vii) Participate in science fair, science exhibition, science club etc.

(viii) Actively participate in scientific debates, declamation contents, quiz etc.

The Attitudes

Development of scientific attitude is one of the major objectives of teaching chemistry. The development of scientific attitude makes pupil open minded, helps him to make critical observations, develops in time intellectual honesty, curiosity, unbiased and impartial thinking etc.

This objective is considered to have been achieved if a pupil

(i) becomes free of superstitions and prejudices.

(ii) depends for his judgement only on verified facts and not on opinion.

(iii) is readily willing to reconsider his own judgement when some more facts are brought to his notice.

(iv) has an objective approach.

(v) is honest in recording and collecting scientific data.

The Abilities

By the teaching of chemistry we expect to develop the following abilities in the pupil.

(i) Ability to use scientific method.

(ii) Ability to use problem solving method.

(iii) Ability to process information.

(iv) Ability to report things in a technical language.

(v) Ability to collect scientific data from suitable source and to interpret it correctly.

(vi) Ability to organise science fair, science exhibition, science club etc.

The Appreciation

To achieve this objective the teaching of chemistry has to be done in an evolutionary way. For this the curriculum should include such topics where it is possible to reveal stirring biographical anecdotes, some scientific stories having some incidents of adventure, charm and romance. It is possible to achieve this objective by teaching history of chemistry including life stories of some chemists. This objectives can also be achieved by telling the impact of modern chemistry on life.

This objective of teaching chemistry may be considered to have been achieved if the pupil:

(i) Appreciates the contribution of various chemists to human progress.

(ii) Appreciates the history of development of chemistry.

(iii) Realises the importance of chemistry in modern civilisation.

(iv) Takes pleasure in understanding the progress made by science.

Providing Vocational Career

In the modern world majority of Career Courses depend to a large extent on the basic knowledge of chemistry. Some Vocational Courses can be taken up only by students of science. *e.g.* Engineering, medicines, Agriculture etc. For various courses offered by I.T.I's the knowledge of chemistry is the basic requirement. Thus chemistry opens a vast field of opportunities for taking up any vocational course and choose a career. Not only this the knowledge of chemistry develops in a pupil the manipulative skills and he can easily improvise apparatus and experiments and can use his knowledge and skill to make many a common things like ink, soap, candle, chalk, cosmetics, boot polish, nail polish etc. All these provide the pupil with a profitable leisure time work.

SCIENTIFIC ATTITUDE

One of the major aims of teaching chemistry is the development of *scientific attitude* in the pupil. Following are some of the various aspects included in the scientific attitude:

(i) Making pupils open minded.

(ii) Helping pupils open minded.

(iii) Developing intellectual honesty among pupils.

(iv) Developing curiosity among pupils.

(v) Developing unbiased and impartial thinking.

(vi) Developing reflective thinking.

NSSE (National Society of the Study of Education) has defined scientific attitudes "open mindedness, a desire for accurate knowledge, confidence in procedures for seeking knowledge and the expectation that the solution of the problem will come through the use of verified knowledge".

The views regarding scientific attitude expressed at a work shop conducted by the National Council of Educational Research and Training (NCERT) at Chandigarh in 1971 can be summarised as follows. A pupil who has developed scientific attitude:

(i) is clear and precise in his activities and makes clear and precise statements.

(ii) always bases his judgement on verified facts and not on opinion.

(iii) prefers to suspend his judgement if sufficient data is not available.

(iv) is objective in his approach and behaviour.

(v) is free from superstitions.

(vi) is honest and truthful in recording and collecting scientific data.

(vii) after finishing his work takes care to arrange the apparatus, equipments etc. at their proper places.

(viii) shows a favourable reactions towards efforts of using science for human welfare.

DEVELOPING AN ATTITUDE

In the previous pages an effort was made to define the term *'scientific attitude's* By developing scientific attitude in a person certain mind-sets are created in a particular direction. Such mind-sets may be developed either by direct teaching in schools or by out of school experiences gained by the pupil. Though out of school experiences contribute to a large extent yet according to *Curtis* direct teaching does modify the attitude of young pupil.

Tyler also made some suggestions for planning learning experiences in order to inculcate scientific attitude in the pupil. These are summarised below:

(i) The increase in the degree of consistency of the environment helps in developing and inculcating scientific attitude in the pupil.

(ii) The scientific attitude can be inculcated in a pupil by providing him more opportunities for making satisfying adjustments to attitude situations.

(iii) The scientific attitude can also be developed in the pupil by providing him opportunity for the analysis of problem or situation so that a pupil may understand and then rest intellectually in desirable attitude.

ROLE OF TEACHER

The major role can be played by the chemistry teacher in developing scientific attitudes among his students and this he can do by manipulating various situations that infuse among the pupils certain characteristics of scientific attitudes. He can also help in developing a scientific attitude among his students if he possesses and practices various elements of these attitudes. The practical examples given by the teacher leaves an indelible mark on the personality of his students.

Teacher can use one or more of the ways for developing scientific attitude among his pupils.

Making use of Planned Exercises: A large number of exercises for development of certain scientific attitudes are reported by various journals and magazines. Teacher can frequently use such exercises for developing certain scientific attitudes among the pupils. He can also make use of cuttings from newspapers and science magazines and can display such materials on bulletin board so that it is used again and again for direct teaching.

Exercises which are always included in good text books can also be used by the teacher for developing scientific attitude among his pupils.

Wide Reading: On the basis of a study conducted by him, *Curtis* reported, that those pupil who engage themselves in wide reading in science, develop scientific attitudes more than those who study only one textbook. Thus a teacher should encourage his students to read library books and supplementary books on chemistry. For this it is essential that each school at least has a science corner in its library. The teacher himself must be in habit of making proper use of science library so that his students get encouragement for use of science library. The teacher himself be familiar with the latest new titles in his subject and be willing to share his joys of new readings with his pupils. He should refer some suitable books to his students.

Writing about teachers, Rabinder Nath Tagore has observed, "A teacher can never truly teach unless he is still learning himself. A lamp can never light another unless it continues to burn its own flame. The teacher who has come to the end of his subject, who has no living traffic with his knowledge, but merely repeats his lessons to his students, can only load their minds. He cannot quicken them".

Proper use of Practicals Period: A student of chemistry gets many an opportunities for learning scientific attitudes during his practical periods. It is for the teacher to properly use such opportunities for developing scientific attitudes amongst his pupils. Teacher should take extra care to state the problem of the experiment and should present hypotheses on solution. He should practice the proper method of testing the hypotheses. He should actively participate in discussion and interpretation of results after the experiment. He must inculcate in his students the habit to postpone judgements in the absence of sufficient evidence to support a hypotheses.

Personal Example of the Teacher: Personal example of the teacher is perhaps the single greatest force that is helpful in inculcating the scientific attitudes amongst his pupils. Psychologist have found a great tendency amongst the students to copy their teachers. In this regard some have stated, "As is the teacher, so is the student". It is therefore essential that chemistry teacher is free from bias and prejudices while dealing with his pupils. He should have an open mind and be critical in thought and action in his everyday dealings. He should be totally free from superstitions and unfounded beliefs and should be objective and impartial in his approach to his everyday problems. He should be truthful and should have faith in cause and effect relationship.

Study of Superstitions: There are different types of superstitions that still prevail in Indian society. Simply taking of these superstitions and calling them bad and out of date, will not leave a lasting impression on the minds of the pupils. It will be more useful if the teacher can encourage at least a few of his students to carry out practicals on some popular superstitions such as that the presence of a broken mirror in any home leads to disharmony in that home or that if a cat crosses your way when you are going out for some work, then your work will not be done on that day etc. etc.

Such beliefs can easily be discarded by a student if he keeps a broken mirror at his home and finds to his satisfaction that it has not created any type of disharmony in his home. Similarly, other superstitions and misbeliefs can be tested and easily discarded by a student of chemistry. Various researches carried out in the field have drawn the same conclusion *i.e,* by practical survey and study of such common beliefs, students have developed permanent mind-sets or attitudes towards such superstitions.

Co-curriculum Activities in Chemistry: Various co-curricular activities such as organising science club, hobbies club, chemistry society, organising scientific tours and excursions etc. can be taken up by chemistry teacher. Such activities should be properly organised by chemistry teacher under his direct supervision but students be given enough freedom to plan their activities. It will help inculcate in students some desirable scientific attitudes. Co-curricular activities may include making of chemistry charts and models, making of improvised chemistry apparatus etc.

Atmosphere of the Class: A proper atmosphere in the class room provided a desirable atmosphere for inculcating of certain scientific attitudes in the pupils. By a proper class atmosphere we mean that the room is properly arranged and suitably decorated in such a manner that it provides for incentive to the pupil to inculcate the habit of cleanliness and orderliness. In addition to such a congenial physical atmosphere of the class room, the teacher's behaviour also contributes to the development of proper class room atmosphere. For inculcating the scientific attitudes amongst his pupils teacher should encourage them in their various activities. He should also take care to see that his lessons content are such as to encourage the students to ask a large number of intelligent question. He should feel pleasure in answering and explaining such questions and must not snub his pupils for asking so many questions.

SCIENTIFIC METHOD

It has already been pointed out that two basic aims of teaching chemistry are (i) development of scientific attitude and (ii) training in scientific methods.

In previous section we have discussed some ways for developing scientific attitude and in this section our aim is to concentrate mainly on training in scientific methods.

A 'scientific method' is 'a method which is used for solving a problem scientifically. It is also referred as 'the method of science' on or 'the method of a scientist. Sometimes it is called as 'problem solving method'. So far it has not been possible to arrive at any commonly agreed definition of scientific method.

The scientific method of teaching chemistry is based upon the process of finding out results by attacking a problem in definite steps, therefore there cannot be any one 'particular method' but such methods have certain common characteristics.

According to Fitzpatrick, "Science is a cumulative and endless series of empirical observations which result in the formation of concepts and theories, with both concepts and theories being subject to modification in the light for their empirical observation. Science is both the study of knowledge and the process of acquiring and refining knowledge". From this it becomes quite clear that students of chemistry be exposed to the scientific method of finding out. Scientific method helps to develop in a student the power of reasoning, critical thinking and application of scientific knowledge. It also helps in developing positive attitudes amongst the pupils. A list of such traits as given by Woodburn and Oburn is as under:

(i) A scientist must have an unsatiable curiosity, inquisitiveness and a spirit of adventure.

(ii) He should be capable of independent thinking and be ready to abandon the disproved.

(iii) He should be knowledgeable, enlightened and informed.

(iv) He should possess a power of sound judgement and prudent foresight.

(v) He should possess a high degree of perseverance.

Steps of Scientific Method : Since we don't have any single well defined scientific method so we cannot have any well defined fixed steps for a scientific method. However in general the scientific method of teaching chemistry proceeds in the following steps;

(i) Problem in an area of chemistry learning is identified and well stated.

(ii) Relevant data is collected.

(iii) Certain hypothesis are proposed for testing.

(iv) Experiments are set and done to test the proposed hypothesis.

(v) Prediction of other observable phenomenon are deduced from the hypothesis.

(vi) Occurence or non-occurence of predicted phenomenon is observed.

(vii) From observations, the conclusion are drawn to accept, reject or modify the proposed hypothesis.

Thus the scientific method is a sequenced and structured way of finding out the results through experiments. Various steps of scientific method are discussed here.

Statement of the Problem: A student comes across so many things which arouse his curiosity and he has a large number of questions to ask. A good chemistry teacher always encourages his students to ask questions and tries to answer them in a simple and understandable manner. However in answering a particular question the teacher brings to the fore many new problems and it has rightly been said that, "when we double the known, we quadruple the unknown".

Most of the question asked are about 'what?', 'why?' or 'how?' type and these can be conveniently classified as under:

(i) 'what' type of questions are *predictive*

(ii) 'why' type of questions are *explanatory*

(iii) 'how' type of questions are *inventory*

The most important thing in a scientific method is a simple and well defined statement of the problem. The statement of the problem be such that it clearly defines the scope of the problem as also its limitations.

Data Collection: When the problem has been stated in clear terms an effort be made to collect the data from as many different source as is possible. Such data may be available in books in chemistry, library which are an important source for data collection. Data may be collected by use of certain instruments etc. and observations. In data collection an effort be made to minimise the errors that are likely to be caused due to apparatus and instruments used *(mechanical errors)* and those which are likely to be caused due to personal bias *(personal errors)*.

Proposing a Hypothesis: On the basis of collected data a tentative hypothesis is proposed for testing. A hypothesis is in fact a certain tentative solution to the problem. The hypothesis should be proposed only after an objective analysis of the available data because any number of hypothesis can be proposed for a problem. For an objective analysis the student be given a training so that he is free from all his bias towards the problem.

Conducting Experiments: After a hypothesis has been proposed suitable experiments are designed to test the validity of the hypothesis. From the observations of such experiments the validity of the hypothesis is tested. The experiments will show the occurrence or non-occurence of the expected phenomenon and from this we will be able to accept or reject or modify the hypothesis.

The Advantages

Some of the advantages of scientific methods are:

(i) Students learn chemistry by their own experiences and the teacher is just a guide who provides them an opportunity and proper environment for learning chemistry.

(ii) It trains the students to identify and formulate scientific problems.

(iii) It gives enough training to students in techniques of information processing.

(iv) It develops in students the power of logical thinking as he is required to interpret data in a logical way.

(v) It helps to develop an intellectual honesty in the student because he is required to accept or reject the hypothesis on the basis of evidences available.

(vi) It helps the students to learn to see relationships and patterns amongst things and variables.

(vii) It provides the students a training in the methods and skills of discovering new knowledge.

The Disadvantages

Some important disadvantages of scientific methods are as under:

(i) It is a long drawn out and time consuming process.

(ii) It can never be a full fledged method of learning chemistry.

(iii) Majority of chemistry teachers cannot implement it successfully because of their back of exposure to such a method.

(iv) It is not suitable for all students as it suits only bright and creative students.

Summary **:** We summarise the aims and objectives of teaching chemistry at various stages in India. These are taken from the reports submitted by various commissions, committees etc. which form the basis of chemistry curricula to be taught at various stages of school education.

In 1950 a report was published by Ministry of Education, Govt. of India which listed the aims of teaching of chemistry (science) in schools as follows:

Upto Middle School Level

(a) To develop interest in nature and environment.

(b) To develop creativeness and inventiveness of students.

(c) To inculcate scientific methods.

(d) To develop ability to generalise facts.

(e) To make them understand various social implications of chemistry.

(f) Development of some chemistry-based hobbies and leisure time activities.

At Secondary Level

(a) To enable students to adjust to their environment after understanding it.

(b) To help them to get a feel of scientific methods.

(c) To develop scientific attitude and scientific temper in them.

The major objectives of the syllabus developed, for secondary-schools in India by, National Council of Educational Research and Training (NCERT) are as under:

(i) To strengthen the concept developed at a secondary level and further develop near concepts to provide a sound back ground for higher studies.

(ii) To develop a competence in students to offer professional courses like engineering, medicines etc. as their future career.

(iii) To acquaint the students with different aspects of chemistry used in daily life and enable them to recognise that chemistry plays an important role in the service of man.

(iv) To expose the students to different processes used in industries and their technological applications.

(v) To provide relevant content materials useful for vocational courses.

(vi) To develop an interest in students to study chemistry as a discipline.

5

TEACHING UNDER SCHEME

Percentage of our science teachers (Physics, Chemistry and Biology) have good background in their respective subjects, and they take interest in teaching and trying out new science programmes. Even in the schools which have enough science equipment and the science labs are well equipped, the lecture-demonstration method is the one most commonly used, as our science teachers are heavily loaded and they get a very little or sometime even no time for planning their lessons during school hours. Our schools have usually 8 periods of 30-40 minutes duration. Regular teachers also work as substitute teachers (where in America if a teacher is on leave, a substitute teacher is invited from outside to teach his classes) during their planning periods besides their teaching 6-7 (out of 8) periods daily, six days a week (where in Western countries schools work five days a week), and Sunday is the only holiday.

Our textbooks are written in a traditional way. If our science teachers could have well sequenced programmed materials, it would be a great help to them, as mentioned above, they are heavily loaded. Also if the programmed materials provided activities of 20-25 minutes duration, students would have more opportunity to do the experiments themselves even in smaller periods. So well sequenced programmed materials would be more useful for teachers to teach and for students to learn than the materials now available.

THE DEFINITION

Let us look at some of the definitions of programmed instruction.

(1) Cronbach describes a programme of instruction as follows: "A programme is a pre-arranged sequence of explanations and questions. A programme whether for a brief unit or for an entire course, is a carefully planned progression of ideas, beginning with elementary notions and working upto relatively complex theories or applications.

(2) According to B.F. Skinner a programmed instruction is simply a matter of breaking the material to be learned into easy steps, arranging steps in logical order with no gaps, making sure the student understands one step before moving to another and then incidently, making sure that he is successful.

(3) According to Espich and Williams a programmed instruction may be defined as a planned sequence of experiences, leading to the proficiency, in terms of stimulus response relationships. By this definition a programme is an educational device that causes a student to progress through a series of experiences, which lead to the students proficiency. The experience here is student's own experience in the learning process, not just the teacher telling. Planned sequence determines what experiences and in what order should occur. What is the student supposed to be able to do after completing

the programme? How well? How quickly? All such questions implied in leading to proficiency in terms of stimulus-response relationships refer to the basic behavioural science concepts on which programmed instruction is based, and which are taken into consideration when a programme is written.

PSYCHOLOGY IN APPLICATION

No one knows for certain how or why programmed instruction works, but it is generally agreed that basic behavioural psychology is somehow involved. At least the originators of programmed instruction attributed its success to some basic tenets of behavioural psychology.

The results of the change in behaviour called learning are observable or measurable. All behavioural changes of students as a result of learning may be of three types: (1) Psychomotor; (2) Cognitive; and (3) Affective (Chapter 3). (1) and (2) are comparatively easier to measure than (3).

In any teaching situation for effective learning the best method is:

1. Present the stimulus to the student.
2. Help the student to make the desired response to the stimulus by giving him clues, by leading him towards it, or by telling him the response itself.
3. When die student makes the desired response to the stimulus, immediately reinforces that response.

Programmed instruction takes advantage of the basic human drive for success. The programmer guides the student toward making the correct response. He then shows or tells the student that he has given the desired response – that he has been successful. Each time he makes the correct response, he is positively reinforced by being told that he is correct, his drive for success is satisfied. Each time his drive for success is satisfied, the probability increases that he will make the correct response to the given stimulus in future situations.

The Advantages

The programmed instruction does have a number of advantages over conventional methods. It allows for individual rates of learning and it gives immediate reinforcement of correct responses. According to Burner the technically most interesting features of automatic devices are that they can take some of the load of teaching of the teacher's shoulders. For this time the teacher can be used by his students who need him and whenever they need him. According to James this type of teaching is very frustrating and tiring but extremely rewarding. When science teachers have worked as long at individualized instruction as they have to make grouped instruction workable, the rewards may be proportionally increased.

PRACTICAL INTEGRATION

In teaching science, a continuing area of concern to educators has been the problem of integrating laboratory experimentation with instruction in scientific theory. The need to individualize course content for students is also recognized. Programmed instruction may offer one solution to both of these difficulties. If the science curriculum can be programmed so that individual rates could be dealt with more effectively, and if laboratory material can be developed which enable students to conduct experiments effectively on an independent basis, laboratory experi mentation may be integrated more satisfactorily into the typical science course.

A summary of the subject area in which programmed instruction has been used reveals that these areas which require laboratory activities are rare. Cowan indicated that there were no auto-instructional materials available in physics that provided students with laboratory experiences Cowan and Siddiqi developed and used such materials in their research studies.

Hundreds of good science textbooks are available in the market They are not designed to teach but to convey information to the student. In a programme a programmer determines for a student, what he should and what he should not assimilate. In a programme, the student is guided along a path and given those experiences that will cause him to learn those things. No such guidance is given with a textbook Adjunct programming can be a link between programmed instruction and a good textbook. It combines some of the progressive features of programmed instruction with the comprehensiveness of textbooks. The goal of adjunct programming is to enable the student to learn as effectively as possible from a good textbook.

An Adjunct Programme may be one of two types (1) The text itself is kept intact and the programme is supplied as a separate unit, or (2) sections of the textbook are extracted vibration and used in the programme as the basic information. The most popular procedure as used by Cowan and Siddiqi is to leave the textbook intact. Their programmed materials which they developed for the PSSC Physics Text, provide a very good example of adjunct programming. They used these materials in their research studies. Students using the auto instructional materials studied from the same text, worked the same problems, viewed the same films, and performed the same experiments as regular physics students. Cowan did not use a qualified physics teacher in the classroom to direct their studies. The use of auto instructional materials prepared for this study evidently provided a good physics programme, as students using these materials were able to demonstrate as well in achievement as those not using these materials but taught by a qualified PSSC physics teacher. In Siddiqis study students of experimental group used the auto-instructional materials under the guidance of their physics teacher, while, the students of the control group did not use such materials, they were taught by their teacher in a conventional way. The experimental group demonstrated statistically higher mean level of achievement in PSSC physics.

STUDENTS' OPINION

Siddiqi developed an Adjunct Programme for PSSC physics. It was student self-directed study guide m PSSC physics. Here are the comments (unedited) of some of the students who used it.

Strengths

1. "Students can do whenever they want to do. If we do not understand anything now, we can do it some other time."
2. "When you learn on your own, you are more apt to remember it."
3. "Student learns more if he goes on his own rate. In conventional classes superior students get frustrated. They want to go ahead. Slow students don't understand. Teacher stops the whole class. With these materials superior students also have an opportunity to go ahead. Every student is able to go on his own rate, not waiting for anybody, not trying to catch up with anybody."
4. "Teacher gets more time, when he can go and help other students. He goes to the student who has problems, and not to the student who does not have any problem; so he does not waste his time. Teacher's time can be put to better use. We do not need the teacher all the time. We only use him when we need him. Teacher can enrich the student more when he talks individually."
5. "PSSC text was easy to understand with these materials. Text was too complicated, and the guide made it simplified."
6. "Guide has more hints to do labs than does the lab manual."
7. "Self-tests were good. When I missed something, I went over it and it helped me very much to learn physics."

Weaknesses

1. "These materials were unable to motivate those who were not self-motivated to use these materials."
2. "This approach did not work for lazy students. Some students need a push and without a teacher always available to keep them working they have a tendency not to study. It's hard for some people to pace. It requires more discipline to work on your own."
3. "This approach is good for those who want to learn by this approach. If the student is the type who cannot go on his own, this approach is not good; he should (probably) be taught by the conventional method."
4. "Sometimes a student is isolated by this approach—text guide, problems, lab, text, guide; that's all he has to work with."
5. "Physics is such a hard subject that you have to have more teacher help."
6. "I did not like it too much, because I am lazy by nature."

TEACHERS' OPINION

Teachers who taught the students using programmed instruction materials also pointed out some strengths and some weaknesses of mis approach of teaching.

Strengths

1. "These materials are excellent for {hose who have difficulty with PSSC physics."
2. "These materials enabled some students to achieve what they were unable to achieve without them."
3. "These materials developed in students an attitude of doing independent work, which they will need when they will go to College and University."

Weaknesses

1. "Only those students who feel responsibility learn more by this approach."
2. "These materials are not good for slow learners."
3. "Some students go behind and behind not because they were not capable to move but because they were lazy. Some students can read but they don't want to read. There is a problem of keeping the student motivated."
4. "This approach is more time consuming. Some students took more time to finish the same material."
5. "When working on their own only half of the students use their time effectively while others use their time doing something else."

The conclusion of a group of students regarding the auto-instructional material was: "With autoinstructional materials, the text, and a teacher to explain, the self-study would be most practical and best for students."

In general most of the students and teachers liked the programmed instructional materials and this approach of instruction. They pointed out individualisation, independence, self-pacing, self-evaluation, and better use of teacher's time as some of the major strengths of this type of instruction. More than half of the students and teachers liked individualised instruction. They reported that using this approach for instruction, the teacher got more time to interact with individual students. They pointed out that the PSSC Physics Students Guide made PSSC Physics easier for the students. They also pointed out that this approach of instruction was best suited for superior students. More than half of the students liked the idea of moving according to their own pace, but the teachers did not like this idea very much, as it was hard for them to cope with their students, when different students were doing different things in the same period. Most of the students and all the teachers pointed out that lack of self-motivation was the main weakness of this type of instruction.

UNIT DEVELOPMENT

Some of you as a science teacher will like to use programmed instruction materials in your science classes. Usually programmes are not available in the market. Though developing programmed instruction materials is a time consuming job, yet some of you will like to develop some programmed instruction units. It will be a good project for your instruction.

Before developing programmed instruction units, it will be nice if you learn how to develop them. One such programmed unit "Structure of an Atom" is given here as a Sample. You go through it, and after that we will discuss, how it is developed.

PROGRAMMED UNIT

Structure of an Atom
(A Programme Unit)

Instructions to Students

This is not a test. This is a Programme designed for you to learn the Structure of Atom.

In this Programme you will find numbered paragraphs.

These paragraphs are called Frames. Read each Frame carefully and answer the questions given after each Frame.

Check your answers from the Answer key given at the end of the programme.

Frame 1. Matter is made up of very small particles called atoms. The smallest particle of matter is........

If answer is correct go to Frame 2, otherwise Repeat Frame 1.

Frame 2. Atom is made of various particles called electrons, protons and neutrons. Electrons are negatively charged particles. Protons are positively charged particles. Neutrons have no charge, that is, they are neutral.

Complete the following sentences:

(a) The positively charged particle of an atom is.....

(b) An electron has ...... charge.

(c) A neutral atomic particle is called.......

If answers are correct go to Frame 3 otherwise Repeat Frame 2.

Frame 3. Check the statement below that is true. A proton is:

(a) positively charged.

(b) negatively charged.

(c) neutral.

(d) sometimes positive, sometimes negative.

If answer is correct go to Frame 4, otherwise Repeat Frames 2 and 3.

Frame 4. Check the statement below that is true. A neutron is:

(a) positively charged.

(b) negatively charged.

(c) neutral.

(d) sometimes positive, sometimes negative.

If answer is correct go to Frame 5, otherwise Repeat Frames 2 and 4.

Frame 5. Check the statement below that is true. An electron is:

(a) positively charged.

(b) negatively charged.

(c) neutral.

(d) sometimes positive, sometimes negative.

If answer is correct go to Frame 6, otherwise Repeat Frames 2 and 5.

Frame 6. The weight of a proton is approximately equal to the weight of a neutron, and the weight of an electron is so small compared to the weight of a proton or a neutron that it can be neglected.

Check the statement below that is true.

The weight of a proton is approximately equal to the weight of:

(a) electron.

(b) neutron.

(c) each of them.

(d) none of them.

If answer is correct go to Frame 7, otherwise Repeat Frame 6.

Frame 7. The charge of an electron is equal and opposite to the charge of a proton. If the charge of an electron is -4 units, then the charge of a proton should be:

(a) –4 units

(b) +4 units

(c) more than 4 units

(d) less than 4 units

If answer is correct go to Frame 8, otherwise Repeat Frame 7.

Frame 8. If the charge of a proton is +x units, the charge of an electron should be.......

If answer is correct go to Frame 9, otherwise repeat Frames 7 and 8.

Frame 9. An atom can be assumed to be spherical in shape. At its centre there is a very small space (compared to the atom as a whole) containing protons and neutrons. This space is called nucleus.

Check the statement below that is true. The nucleus of an atom contains:

(a) protons only.

(b) neutrons only.

(c) protons and neutrons both.

(d) none of them.

If answer is correct go to Frame 10, otherwise Repeat Frame 9.

Frame 10. Around the nucleus some hollow spheres of different sizes can be assumed. The space between any two of such hollow spheres is called a shell (Fig.).

∇ – boundary of first hollow sphere.

Δ – boundary of second hollow sphere.

Fig.

Check the statement that is true.

(a) A is a shell.

(b) A is a shell.

(c) Both A and Â are shells.

(d) None of them are shells.

If answer is correct go to Frame 11, otherwise Repeat Frame 10.

Frame 11. As the number of electrons is equal to the number of protons and the charge of an electron is equal and opposite to the charge of a proton the atom as a whole is neutral.

Example—Sodium atom has 11 electrons and 11 protons. If charge of an electron is $-x$ units, the charge of a proton will be $+x$ units.

Charge of 11 electrons = $-11x$ units.

Charge of 11 protons = +11x units.

Therefore total charge of sodium atom is equal to –11x plus +11x = 0.

Complete the following statements:

(a) A neutral atom has 40 electrons, then it should have .... protons.

(b) If an atom has 10 electrons but only 9 protons, then the atom .... neutral (will be, will not be).

If answers are correct go to Frame 12, otherwise Repeat Frame 11.

Frame 12. Nucleus has protons and neutrons. Around the nucleus there exist electrons in various spherical shells.

Complete the following statements:

(a) Electrons exist in the.........

(b) Protons exist in the..........

(c) Neutrons exist in the..........

If answer is correct go to Frame 13, otherwise Repeat Frame 12.

Frame 13. In a particular shell the electrons are assumed to be moving in various circular orbits. The total number of electrons in all the shells of an atom is equal to the number of protons in its nucleus. This number *i.e.* the number of protons or electrons in an atom, is called atomic number.

(a) Sodium has 11 protons in the nucleus. The total number of electrons in all the shells of sodium will be........

(b) The atomic number of sodium is.......

If answers are correct go to Frame 14, otherwise Repeat Frame 13.

Frame 14. The atomic number of oxygen is 8. What will be the number of protons in the nucleus, and the number of electrons in the shells?

(a) Number of protons is......

(b) Number of electrons is.......

If answers are correct go to Frame 15, otherwise Repeat Frames 13 and 14.

Frame 15. The sum of the number of neutrons and protons is equal to the atomic weight of an atom.

Example. Oxygen has 8 protons and 8 neutrons. Thus the atomic weight of oxygen is 8 + 8 = 16.

Sodium atom has 11 protons and 12 neutrons. Check the statement below that is true. Atomic weight of sodium is:

(a) 11

(b) 12

(c) 23

(d) 1

If answer is correct go to Frame 16, otherwise Repeat Frame 15.

Frame 16. Nitrogen atom has 7 protons and 7 neutrons. The atomic weight of nitrogen is..... .

Frame 17. The atomic weight of hydrogen is 1. It has 1 proton, then the number of neutrons in hydrogen atom is......

If answer is correct go to Frame 18, otherwise Repeat Frames 15,16 and 17.

Frame 18. The number of shells in an atom may vary from 1 to 7, that is the number of shells in an atom cannot exceed 7, though it can be less than 7 i.e. (6, 5,4,3, 2,1) depending upon the total number of electrons in a particular atom.

The number of electrons present in each shell is governed by 2 rules. *Rule 1* – The nth (n is the number of shell) shell cannot have more than $2n^2$ n electrons.

Example

For the first shell $n = 1$

therefore $2n^2 = 2.$ f $= 2$

It means 1st shell cannot have more than 2 electrons (if the atom has more electrons they will be in the other shells), though it can have less than 2 (if there are not enough electrons in a particular atom).

For the 2nd shell $n = 2$

Therefore $2n^2 = 2 .2^2 = 2 .4 = 8$

It means 2nd shell cannot have more than 8 electrons though it can have less than 8 (as explained above).

According to this rule, there should not be more than:

(a)..... electrons in 3rd shell.

(b)...... electrons in 4th shell.

(c)..... electrons in 5th shell.

(d)..... electrons in 6th shell.

(e)..... electrons in 7th shell.

If answers are correct go to Frame *19,* otherwise Repeat Frame 18.

Frame 19. Oxygen has 8 electrons. According to the above mentioned rule write down the number of electrons in different shells.

Shell 1.......

Shell 2.......

Shell 3.......

If answers are correct go to Frame 20, otherwise Repeat Frames 18 and 19.

Frame 20. The atomic number of chlorine is 17. Write down the number of electrons in different shells.

Shell 1.......

Shell 2.......

Shell 3.......

Shell 4.......

If answers are correct go to Frame 21, otherwise Repeat Frames 18, 19 and 20.

Frame 21. *Rule 2* – Last shell cannot have more than 8 electrons in an atom, and the last but one shell cannot have more than 18 electrons. Complete the following statements:

(a) An atom has 5 shells. The number of electrons in its 5th shell should not exceed......

(b) The number of electrons in its 4th shell should not exceed ....

If answers are correct go to Frame 22, otherwise Repeat Frame 21.

Frame 22. The atomic number of sodium atom is 11 and its atomic weight is 23. Write down the number of the following items of a sodium atom.

(a) Electrons...........

(b) Protons.........

(c) Protons and neutrons........

(d) Neutrons..........

(e) Electrons in 1st shell........

(f) Electrons in 2nd shell..........

(g) Electrons in 3rd shell...........

(h) Electrons in 4th shell...........

If answers are correct go to Frame 23, otherwise Repeat Frames 13-22.

Frame 23. The atomic number of carbon is 6 and its atomic weight is 12. Complete the carbon atom by putting at proper places the number of electrons, protons and neutrons.

If answer is correct congratulations, you learned what we wanted to teach you through this programme. If not please repeat Frames 13-23.

ANSWERS

Frame 1

Atom

Frame 2

(a) proton

(b) negative

(c) neutron

Frame 3

(a) positively charged

Frame 4

(c) neutral

Frame 5

(b) negatively charged

Frame 6

(b) neutron

Frame 7

(b) +4 units

Frame 8

X units

Frame 9

(c) protons and neutrons both

Frame 10

(b) B is a shell

Frame 11

(a) 40 protons

(b) will not be

Frame 12

(a) shells

(b) nucleus

(c) nucleus

Frame 13

(a) 11

(b) 11

Frame 14

(a) 8 protons

(b) 8 electrons

Frame 15

(c) 23

Frame 16

14

Frame 17

0

Frame 18

(a) 18

(b) 32

(c) 50

(d) 72

(e) 98

Frame 19

shell 1=2, shell 2=6, shell 3=0

Frame 20

shell 1=2, shell 2=8,

shell 3=7, shell 4=0

Frame 21

(a) 8

(b) 18

Frame 22

(a) 11

(b) 11

(c) 23

(d) 12

(e) 2

(f) 8

(g) 1

(h) 0

In developing this unit the System Approach was used. The System Approach (Fig.) has the following steps:

1. Identify problems and state terminal objectives.
2. Conduct task analysis.
3. Describe entry behaviours of students.
4. State sub-objectives in behavioural terms.
5. Develop evaluation instruments.
6. Determine instructional sequence.
7. Select appropriate media and instructional procedures.
8. Develop instructional materials.
9. Conduct formative and summative evaluation.

Given the atomic weight and atomic number of an element the students will find out the number of protons and neutrons in the nucleus and the number of electrons in the various shells of the atom.

Hierarchical methodology (Fig.) was chosen for the programme Structure of an Atom. There is an ordered relationship between sub-skills which ultimately help to learn the terminal objective. The simple things are given first that makes the basis for more complex concepts.

DIFFERENT BEHAVIOURS

The assumed entry behaviours for this programme were the following:

1. Knowledge of some common elements such as oxygen, hydrogen, nitrogen, carbon, sulphur, sodium, chlorine etc.

2. Simple addition, subtraction, multiplication and division.
3. Knowledge of positive and negative charges.
4. Basic skills of reading, writing, generalizing, and following directions.

Behavioural objectives were prepared in such a way that they were consistent with each task in the task analysis.

All the behavioural objectives contain an observable response, important condition under which the behaviour will be evaluated, and the criterion for satisfactory performance.

INSTRUMENTS FOR TESTS

The test was made to test all the eleven behavioural objectives. It contained 16 test items. There were one or two test items to test each behavioural objective. All the test items are multiple choice tests and seems to be appropriate to test the task required in the behavioural objectives. The language used in writing test items was kept easy enough to be understood by the students.

This test was used as a Pre-Test, in which the items are sequenced m the same manner as they would appear in the programme (in the Sequence of Tasks and Behavioural Objectives). The same test can also be used as Post-Test (though a separate Post-Test is preferred), whose items should be scrambled, so that they are not in the same order as in the programme. In the multiple choice questions the order of correct responses was random.

The frames were constructed in the same sequence as shown in the task analysis. The frames were sequenced in such a way that by completing all the frames the terminal objective might be achieved by the students.

SIGNIFICANCE OF MEDIUM

The strategy of linear programming was chosen. The self-learning unit was an instructional programme, having enough practice frames

PROGRAMME EVALUATION

Formative Evaluation. After writing the programme and the tests (pre-test and post-test) one IX class student was selected for one-on-one evaluation. This student was of an average ability. Two copies of the programme were prepared, one for the student and other for the programmer. When the student was using the programme, the programmer noted down his reactions and suggestions, which seemed to be important in revising the programme. The following feedback was received from one-to-one evaluation.

1. There was smooth flow or material in the programme, that is, the arrangement of the frames was logical.
2. At some places difficult language was used.
3. The programme needed more practice frames.
4. Frame No. 18 was not well explained, cue and prompt were also needed in this frame.

The programme was revised according to the feedback received from one-on-one evaluation. Then the programme was tried out on a small group consisting of five IX class students. Each student was given pre-test, the programme and the post-test. Before starting the programme the group was told about the programme and the importance of the criticism. They were also asked to write any suggestions if they have. They all took 40-55 minutes to complete the programme. Finally they were interviewed by the programmer and were asked to give their suggestions. The programme was further revised according to the feedback received from small group evaluation.

Simmative Evaluation. The revised programme was given to the target population, (150 IX class students) after giving the pre-test. There were few students who asked questions when going through the programme, but when they were asked to read the matter again they seemed to understand it. All of them were able to complete the programme in time (about 2 periods of 30 minutes duration). Post-test was given the next day.

The pre-test and post-test gain shows that 72 per cent of the students achieved 80 per cent or more objectives. The majority of the students used in the summative evaluation programme showed enthusiasm in working with the programme. Many of them said that they liked the new system of instruction and wanted to have more programmes like this. The vast pre-test to post-test gains exhibited by most of the students generated a great deal of excitement and confidence. This fact alone made the whole project a worthwhile experience for the students.

Constructed Response Frame. As the word Constructed implies, no choice are presented to the student in a Constructed Response Frame. He does not select one response from many, as in the Discrimination Frame. Instead, the student constructs his own response each time. That is, he supplies the answer from his own knowledge.

The response the student constructs can take many frames. He may be asked to write or supply a word or statement, draw a diagram, or perform any other type of over action requiring a response from within his own repertory.

Examples. Frames No. 1, 2, 8,11,12,13,14,16,17,18,19,20, 21,22 and 23. The Constructed Response frame is basically a two-part structure, the set frame and at least one *practice frame.* It may be desirable to have several practice frames with each set frame.

Set Frame. Whenever the response asked for is found in the data portion of the frame, it is known as a set frame. The student may never have seen the desired response prior to reaching this frame, but he is able to supply this response simply by deducing it from the data within the frame itself.

Examples. Frames No. 1, 2,11,12,13,14,16,18 and 21.

Practice Frame. The set frame is followed by a practice frame. The practice frame gives the student a chance to practise what he has learned in the set frame.

Examples. Frames No. 8,19, 20, 22 and 23.

Discrimination Frame. As the name implies, this construction technique is used to teach student to make discrimination. A student who has been taught to make fine discriminations through the use of Discrimination Frame sequence will find that he can go beyond the programme material and approach the subject matter from any direction. For example, if taught a definition by Discrimination Frame Sequence, he will be able to define it when given the term; if given the definition, he will be able to name the item; if physically possible, he will be able to illustrate it.

Examples. Frames No. 3,4,5,6, 7,9 and 15.

Baboon Frame. In this frame the student is asked to make a choice from among four answers: Choice A, Choice B, both A and B, or neither A nor B.

Examples. Frame No. 10.

Basically, the Baboon Frame Sequence consists of three frames similar in purpose to those of the Constructed Response Frame Sequence. The first frame is a set frame; it contains enough information to enable the student to come up with the correct response when asked to respond. This frame is followed by a practice frame; here the student is asked to demonstrate, with a little prompting. In the final frame, the minimum amount of stimulus is presented to the student and a maximum response is called for.

Examples

1. A Trapezium is a figure with four sides, two of which are parallel. Place a check mark (^) before the correct statement below check only one Answer.

.... A. Figure A is a trapezium.

.... B. Figure Â is a trapezium.

.... C. Both Figure A and Figure Â are trapeziums.

.... D. Neither Figure A nor Figure Â is a trapezium.

B. Figure A is a trapezium.

2. Place a check mark (^) before the correct statement below. Check only one answer.

Fig. A *Fig. B*

(a) Figure A is a trapezium.

(b) Figure B is a trapezium.

(c) Figure A and Figure B are trapeziums.

(d) Neither Figure A nor Figure B is a trapezium. D. Neither Figure A nor Figure B is a trapezium. 3. Define "Trapezium" and draw two figures. A trapezium is a figure with four sides, two of which are parallel (or words to this effect). The example figures that you have drawn should match this definition.

VARIOUS PROGRAMMES

Linear Programme. In linear programmes, all of the students are normally required to take all of the frame.

Example. The self-learning unit, "Structure of an atom" is a linear programme.

Linear Programme strategy was used in writing this Programme due to the following reasons:

1. The topic was new for most of the students for whom it was developed, and they were needed to be provided with a lot of practice.
2. The topic of the programme was of such nature that the subject matter involved ascending order of complex skills to be learned/ therefore it was felt that all the students should be required to take all frames.
3. The type of learning task necessitated mostly constructed response answers.

Branching Programme. The word branching suggests any deviation from the straight line, A Branching Programme allows for greater differences in student abilities.

The Branching Frame Sequence Technique. "Systematics" is given in Appendix I-1. This technique presents the student with remedial information/ if necessary and permits him to take steps that are as large as his capabilities allow. A particularly adept student may go through a programme in a minimum number of steps, whereas his less able cohort may require twice that number to learn, the same amount of material. The Branching Programme offers the student alternate paths from which to choose, and the path he takes depends upon the response he makes in each frame.

Hence now you know how to develop a programmed instructional unit. Identify some topics in your field, on which you feel good programmes may be developed. Develop, evaluate and revise programmed instructional units on these topics, and share these self-learning units with your fellow teachers.

Questions

1. What is the need of programmed instructional units in effective science teaching?
2. What is programmed instruction?
3. What are the bases of Behavioural Psychology for learning through programmed instructional materials?
4. What are the advantages of programmed instruction?
5. What is the scope of integrating science practicals with theory in programmed instructional materials?
6. What is adjunct programming? What are its two types? Discuss how adjunct programming can help in better science teaching.
7. Write some strengths and weaknesses of teaching or learning science through programmed instructional materials.
8. Write down the steps for developing a programmed unit using system approach.

9. What do you mean by:

   (a) task analysis, and (b) entry behaviours? Illustrate your answer with examples.

10. Distinguish between:

    (a) formative, and (b) summative evaluations.

11. What are:

    (a) Constructed Response Frames, (b) Discrimination Frames, and (c) Baboon Frames. Illustrate your answer with some examples..

12. Differentiate between:

    (a) linear, and (b) branching programmes. Illustrate your answer with examples.

6

METHODS OF TEACHING

By teaching chemistry we aim at bringing about a desirable behavioural changes among pupils. Teaching is thus a most difficult task and every body is not fit to be a teacher. Some persons may have a 'flair' for teaching and such persons have the ability to awaken interest and arrest the attention of the students. Some others who are not so fortunate can improve their teaching through practice if they are fully acquainted with various methods of teaching. In order to make children learn effectively the teacher has to adopt the right method of teaching. For choosing right method for a given situation the teacher must be familiar with different methods of teaching. In this chapter an effort will be made to discuss common methods used for teaching of science.

LECTURE METHOD

Lecture method is the most commonly used method of teaching chemistry. This method is most commonly followed in colleges and in schools in big classes. This method is not quite suitable to realise the real aim of teaching chemistry. In lecture method only the teacher talks and students are passive listeners. Since the students do not actively participate in this method of teaching so this method is a teacher controlled and information centred and in this method teacher works as a sole resource in class room instructions. Due to lack of participation students get bored and some of them some times may go to sleep. In this method students is provided with readymade knowledge by the teacher and due to this spoon feeding the students loses interest and his powers of reasoning and observation get no stimulus.

In this method the teacher goes ahead with the subject matter at his own speed. The teacher may make use of black board at times and may also dictate notes. This teacher oriented method in its extreme from does not expect any question or response from the students.

Advantages : It has the following advantages:

(i) It is quite economical method. It is possible to handle a large number of students at a time and no laboratory, equipment, aids, materials are required.

(ii) Using this method the knowledge can be imparted to the students quickly and the prescribed syllabus can be covered in a short time.

(iii) It is quite attractive and easy to follow. Using this method teacher feels secure and satisfied.

(iv) It simplifies the task of the teacher as he dominates the lesson for 70-85% of the lesson time and students just listen to him.

(v) Using this method it is quite easy to impart factual information and historical anecdotes.

(vi) By following this method teacher can develop his own style of teaching and exposition.

(vii) In this method teacher can easily maintain the logical sequence of the subject by planning his lectures in advance. It minimises the chances of any gaps or over-lappings.

(viii) Some good lectures delivered by the teacher may motivate, investigate, inspire a student for some creative thinking.

Disadvantages : The disadvantages of lecture method can be as under;

(i) In this method the students participation is negligible and students become passive recipients of information.

(ii) In this method we are never sure if the students are concentrating and understanding the subject matter being taught to them by the teacher.

(iii) In this method knowledge is imparted so rapidly that weak students develop a hatred for learning.

(iv) It does not allow all the faculties of the student to develop.

(v) In this method there is no place of 'learning by doing' and thus teaching by this method strikes at the very root of chemistry.

(vi) It does not take into account the previous knowledge of the student.

(vii) It does not provide for corrective feed back and remedial help to slow learners.

(viii) It does not cater to the individual needs and differences of students.

(ix) It does not help to inculcate scientific attitudes and training in scientific method among the pupils.

(x) It is an undemocratic and authoritarian method in which students depend only as the authority of the teacher. They cannot challenge or question the verdict of the teacher. This checks the development of power of critical thinking and proper reasoning in the student.

Summary : After considering various merits and demerits of method it may be concluded that this method may be suitable for teaching in higher classes (XI, XII) where we aim to cover the prescribed syllabus quickly. In these classes this method can be used successfully for imparting factual knowledge, introducing some new and difficult topics, make generalisation from the facts already known to the students, revision of lessons already learnt etc.

Teaching by this method these students of classes XI and XII will also help those students who intend to join college so that they can prepare themselves for college where lecture method of teaching is a dominant method of imparting instruction.

This method of teaching can be made more beneficial if the teacher encourages his students to take notes during the lesson. After the lesson teacher can give his students some time for asking questions and answer their queries without any hesitation. While delivering his lesson the teacher may see that the lesson is delivered in good tone, loudly and clearly. He should use only simple and understandable words for delivering his lesson. If a teacher can introduce some humour in his lesson it would keep students interested in his lesson.

LECTURE DEMONSTRATION METHOD

This method of teaching is sometimes also referred to as *Lecture-cum Demonstration Method.* This is considered to be a superior method of teaching in comparison to lecture method. In lecture method the teacher speaks and students listen so it is a one way traffic of flow of ideas and students are only passive listeners. This one sidedness is the major drawback of lecture method. A teaching method is considered better if both teacher and taught are active participants in the process of teaching. This particular aspect is taken care of in demonstration method.

This lecture-demonstration method is used by good chemistry teachers for imparting chemistry education in class room. By using this method it is possible to easily impart concrete experiences to students during the course of a lesson when the teacher wants to explain some abstract points. This method combines the instructional strategy of 'information imparting' and 'showing how'. This method combines the advantages of both the lecture method and the demonstration method.

In this method of teaching the teacher performs experiment before the class and simultaneously explains what he is doing. He also asks relevant questions from the class and students are compelled to observe carefully because they have to describe each and every step of the experiment accurately and draw inferences. After thorough questioning and cross-questioning the inferences drawn by the students are discussed in the class. In this way the students remain active participants in the process of teaching. The teacher also relates the outcomes of his experiment to the content of the on-going lesson. Thus while in lecture method teacher merely talks in demonstration method he really teaches.

Principle : This method is based on the principle: *Truth is that which works.*

Requirements for a Good Demonstration : For success of any demonstration following points be always kept in mind:

(i) It should be planned and rehearsed by the teacher before hand.

(ii) The apparatus used for demonstration should be big enough to be seen by the whole class. It would be much better if a large mirror is placed at a suitable angle above the teacher's table which will enable the pupils to have a view of everything that the teacher is doing while performing the experiment.

Alternately, if the class is well disciplined the teacher may allow the students to sit on the stools placed on the benches to enable them to have a better view.

(iii) Adequate lighting arrangements be made on demonstration table and a proper back ground be provided.

(iv) All the pieces of apparatus be placed in order before starting the demonstration. The apparatus likely to be used should be placed on the left hand side of the table and it should be arranged in the same order in which it is likely to be used. After an apparatus is used it should be transferred to right hand side. Only things relevant to the lesson be placed on demonstration table.

(v) Before actually starting the demonstration, a clear statement about the purpose of demonstration be made to the students.

(vi) The teacher must make sure that the demonstration-cumlecture method leads to active participation of the students in the process of learning. This he can achieve by putting well structured questions.

(vii) The demonstration should be quick and slick and should not appear to linger on unnecessarily.

(viii) The demonstration should be interesting so that it captures the attention of the students.

(ix) The teacher must be sure of success of the experiment to be demonstrated and for this he should rehearse the experiment under the conditions prevailing in the class room. However even after all the necessary precaution the experiment fails in the class room due to one reason or the other, the teacher should not get nervous instead he should make an effort to find the reasons for the failure of the experiment. Sometimes in this process a good teacher may draw very useful conclusions.

(x) No complaints about inadequate and faulty apparatus he made by the teacher. In such a situation a good teacher finds an opportunity to show his skill.

(xi) It would be much better if the teacher demonstrates those experiments which are connected with common things which are seen and handled by students in their every day life.

(xii) There should be a correlation between the demonstrations and the sequence of experiments performed by the students in their practical classes.

(xiii) For active participation of students, the teacher may call individual student, in turn, to help him in demonstration work.

(xiv) During lecture-cum-demonstration session, teacher must act like a 'showman' and a 'performer'. He should know different ways of arresting the attention of the students.

(xv) He should write, a summary of the principles arrived at because of demonstration, on the black board. The black board can also be used for drawing necessary diagrams.

Conducting Demonstration Lesson : We commonly find chemistry teachers making use of demonstration method for teaching of chemistry. The conduct of a demonstration lesson is very difficult and here we will try to discuss some of the essential steps that should be followed in a demonstration lesson.

Planning and Preparation : A great care be taken by the teacher while planning and preparing his demonstration lesson. He should keep the following points in mind while preparing his lesson:

(a) subject matter,

(b) questions to be asked;

(c) apparatus required for the experiment.

To achieve the above stated objective the teacher should thoroughly go through the pages of the text book, relevant to the lesson. After this he should prepare his lesson plan in which he should essentially include the principles to be explained, a list of experiments to be demonstrated and the type of questions to be asked from the students. These questions be arranged in a systematic order that has to be followed in the class. Before actually demonstrating the experiment be rehearsed under the conditions prevailing in the class room. Inspite of this, some thing may go wrong at the actual lesson, so reserve apparatus is often useful. The apparatus should be arranged in a systematic order on the demonstration table. Thus for the success of demonstration method a teacher has to prepare himself as thoroughly as a bride prepares herself for the marriage.

Introduction of the Lesson : As in every other subject so also in case of chemistry the lesson should start with proper motivation of the students. It is always considered more useful to introduce the lesson in a problematic way which would make students realise the importance of the topic. The usual ways in which a teachers could easily introduce his lesson is by telling some personal experience or incident, a simple and interesting experiment, a familiar anecdote or by telling a story.

A good experiment when carefully demonstrated is likely to leave an everlasting impression on the young mind of the pupil and it would set his pupils talking in school and out of it, about the interesting experiment that had been demonstrated to them in the chemistry class. This should be kept in mind not only to start the lesson but be used, on every suitable occasion, during the lesson.

It is not possible to give an exhaustive list of such interesting experiments but as an illustration we can consider the opening of soda water bottle in the class room, by the teacher, following by a direct question to his pupil, have they seen any gas coming out of the bottle? At this stage the teacher can introduce the topic of carbon dioxide.

Presentation : The method of presenting the subject matter is very important. A good teacher should present his lesson in an interesting manner and not in a boring way. To make the lesson interesting the teacher may not be very rigid to remain within the prescribed course rather he should make the lesson as much broad based as is possible. For widening of his lesson the teacher may think of various useful applications of the principle taught by him. He is also at liberty to take examples and illustrations from other allied branches of science to make his lesson interesting. The life history and some interesting facts from the life of the great chemist whose name is associated with the topic under discussion can also be cited to make the lesson interesting. Thus every effort be made to present the matter in a lively and interesting manner and a lesson should never be presented as 'dry bones' of an academic course.

Constant questions and answers should from part of every demonstration lesson. Questions and cross questions are essential for properly illuminating the principle being discussed. Questions be arranged in such a way that their answers form a complete teaching unit. Though an effort be made to encourage the students to answer a large number of questions but if students fail to answer some questions teacher should provide the answers to such questions. It is unwise to expect all the answers from the pupil and a teacher should feel satisfied if he has been able to create a desire in a student to know what he does not know.

The lesson be presented in a clear voice and the teacher should speak slowly and with correct pronunciation. He should avoid the use of any bombastic and ambiguous terms. The continuous talk is likely to monotony and to avoid it experiments be well spaced throughout the lesson.

Performance of Experiments : A good observer has been described as a person who has learned to use his senses of touch, sight, smell and hearing in an intelligent and alert manner. We want children to observe what happens in experiments and to have ample opportunities to state their observations carefully. We also want them to try to explain what happens in reference to their problem, but we want to make certain.

There is separation between observations and generalization and conclusions. We will be violating the true spirit of chemistry if we allow children to generalise from one experiment or observation.

The following steps are generally accepted as valuable in developing and concluding chemistry experiments with the children;

1. Write the problems to be solved in simple words so that every one understands.
2. Make a list of activities that will be used to solve problems.

3. Gather material for conducting experiments.
4. Work out a format of the steps in the order of procedure so that every one knows what is to be done.
5. The teacher should always try the experiment himself to become acquainted with the equipment and procedure.
6. Record the findings in ways commensurate with the maturity level and purposes of the student.
7. Assist students in making generalisations from conclusions only after sufficient evidence and experiences.

The demonstration experiment be presented by the teacher in a model way. He should work in a tidy, clean and orderly manner while demonstrating an experiment. Some of the important points to be kept in mind while demonstrating an experiment are as under:

(i) Experiments should be simple and speedy.
(ii) The experiments must work and their results should be clear and their results should be clear and striking.
(iii) Experiments be properly spaced throughout the lesson.
(iv) Keep some reserve apparatus on the demonstration table.
(v) Keep the demonstration apparatus intact till it has to be used again.

Black Board Summary: A summary of important results and principles be written on the black board. Use of black board should also be frequently made for drawing necessary sketches and diagrams. The black board summary should be written in neat, clean and legible way. Since black board summary is an index to a teacher's ability he should keep the following points in mind while writing on black board.

(i) Proper space be left between different letters and words.
(ii) Always start writing from left hand corner of the black board.

(iii) Start a new live only when the first one has extended across the black board.

(iv) Take care not to divide the words at the end of a line.

(v) Make all efforts to keep all the paragraphs and similar signs in calculations under one another.

(vi) While drawing sketches and diagrams preferably use 'single lined' diagrams.

(vii) All the diagrams drawn on the board be properly labelled.

Supervision : Students be asked to take the complete notes of the black board summary including the sketches and diagrams drawn. Such record will be quite helpful to the student for learning his lesson. Such a summary will prove beneficial only if it has been copied correctly from the black board and to make sure that students are copying the black board summary properly the teacher should check it by frequently going to the seats of the students.

Common Errors : A summary of common errors committed while delivering a demonstration lesson are given below:

(i) The apparatus may not be ready for use.

(ii) There may not be an apparent relation between the demonstration experiment and the topic under discussion.

(iii) Black board summary is not upto the mark.

(iv) Teacher may be in a hurry to arrive at generalisation without allowing sufficient time to arrive at these generalization from facts.

(v) Teacher may some times fail to ask right type of questions.

(vi) Teacher some times may use a difficult language.

(vii) Teacher some times takes to talking more which may mar the enthusiasm of the students.

(viii) Teacher may not have allowed sufficient time for recording data etc.

(ix) Teacher has not given proper attention to supervision.

Merits : Following are the merits of this method:

(i) It is an economical method as compared to purely student centred approaches.

(ii) It is a psychological method and students take active interest in teaching learning process.

(iii) It leads students from concrete to abstract situations and thus is more psychological.

(iv) It is a suitable method if the apparatus to be handled is costly and sensitive. Such an apparatus is likely to be damaged if handled by students.

(v) This method can be more safe if the experiments to be demonstrated are dangerous.

(vi) In comparison to Heuristic method, project etc., it is time saving but lecture method is too speedy.

(vii) It can be used successfully for all types of students.

(viii) In this method such experiments which are difficult for students can be included.

(ix) This method can be used to impart manual and manipulative skills to students.

Disadvantages : Some of the disadvantages of this method are as under:

(i) It provides no scope for 'learning by doing' for students as students just observe what the teacher is performing. Thus students fail to relish the joys of direct personal experience.

(ii) Since the teacher performs the experiment in his own pace, many students cannot comprehend the concept being clarified.

(iii) Since the method is not child centred so it makes no provision for individual differences. All types of students including slow learners and genius have to proceed with the same speed.

(iv) It fails to develop laboratory skills in the students. It cannot work as a substitute for laboratory work by students in which they are required to handle the apparatus themselves,

(v) It fails to impart training in scientific attitude.

(vi) In this method students many a times fail to observe many finer details of the apparatus used because they observe it from a distance.

Summary : It is thoroughly accepted that success is greater with experiments in elementary schools if they start with a real purpose, are simply done with uncomplicated apparatus, are done by children under careful direction of the teacher, and help the children think and draw valid, tentative conclusion.

This is considered as one of the best methods of teaching chemistry to secondary classes. An effort be made to involve a larger number of students by calling them in batches to the demonstration table.

Chemistry teachers should encourage more direct experimentation by children in order to help children broaden their range of fact finding skills beyond three T's-teacher, textbook, television.

HEURISTIC METHOD

Heuristic method is a pure discovery method of learning chemistry independent of teacher. The writings and teachings of H.E. Armstrong, Professor of Chemistry at the City and Guilds Institute, London, have had much influence in promoting chemistry teaching in schools. He was a strong advocate of a special type of laboratory training—heuristic training ('heuristic' is derived from the Greek word meaning 'to discover'). In Heuristic method, the student be put in the place of an independent discoverer. Thus no help or guidance is provided by the teacher in this method. In this method the teacher sets a problem for the students and then stands aside while they discover the answer.

In words of Professor Armstrong, "Heuristic methods of teaching are methods which involve our placing students as far as possible in the attitude of the discoverer—methods which involve their finding out instead of being merely told about things".

The method requires the student to solve a number of problems experimentally. To almost every one - especially children- experiments and chemistry are synonymous. Once an idea occurs to a chemist he immediately thinks in terms of ways of trying out his ideas to see if he is correct. Trying to confirm or disprove something, or simply to test an idea, is the backbone of the experiment. Experiments start with questions in order to find answers, solve problems, clarify ideas or just to see what happens. Experimenting should be part of the elementary school chemistry programme as an aid to helping children find solutions to chemistry problems as well as for helping them to develop appreciation for one of the basic tools of chemistry.

Procedure of the Method : The method requires the students to solve a number of problems experimentally. Each student is required to discover everything for himself and is to be told nothing. The students are led to discover facts with the help of experiments, apparatus and books. In this method the child behaves like a research scholar.

In the stage managed heuristic method, a problem sheet with minimum instructions is given to the student and he is required to perform the experiments concerning the problem in hand. He must follow the instructions, and enter in his note-book an account of what he has done and results arrived at. He must also put down his conclusion as to the bearing which the result has on the problem in hand. In this way he is led to reason from observation.

Essentially therefore, the heuristic method is intended to provide a training in method. Knowledge is a secondary considera-tion altogether. The method is formative rather than informational.

The procedures and skills in chemistry problem solving can only be developed in class rooms where searching is encouraged, creative thinking is respected, and where it is safe to investigate, try out ideas, and even make mistakes.

Teachers Attitudes : One of the most important aspects of the problem solving approach to children's development is scientific thinking in the teachers attitude. His approach should be teaching science with a question mark instead of with an exclamation point. The acceptance of and the quest for unique solutions for the problem that the class is investigating should be a guiding principle in the teacher's approach to his programme of chemistry. Teachers must develop sensitiveness to children and to their behaviour. Teachers should be ready to accept any suggestion for the solution of problem regardless of how irrelevant it may seem to him, for this is really the true spirit of scientific problem solving. By testing various ideas it can be shown to the child that perhaps his suggestion was not in accord with the information available. It can then be shown that this failure gets us much closer to the correct solution by eliminating one possibility from many offered by the problem.

In this method teacher should avoid the temptation to tell the right answer to save time. The teacher should be convinced that road to scientific thinking takes time. Children should never be exposed to ridicule for their suggestions of possible answers otherwise they will show a strong tendency to stop suggestions.

For success of this method a teacher should act like a guide and should provide only that much guidance as is rightly needed by the student. He should be sympathetic and courteous and should be capable enough to plan and devise problems for investigation by pupils. He should be capable of good supervision and be able to train the pupils in a way that he himself becomes dispensable.

Merits : This method of teaching chemistry has the following merits:

(i) It develops the habit of enquiry and investigation among students.

(ii) It develops habit of self learning and self direction.

(iii) It develops scientific attitudes among students by making them truthful and honest for they learn how to arrive at decisions by actual experimentations.

(iv) It is psychologically sound system of learning as it is based on the maxim, "learning by doing".

(v) It develops in the student a habit of diligency.

(vi) In this method most of the work is done in school and so the teacher has no worry to assign or check home task.

(vii) It provides scope for individual attention to be paid by the teacher and for closer contacts. These contacts help in establishing cordial relations between the teacher and the taught.

Limitations : Main limitations of this method are as under:

(i) It is a long and time consuming method and so it becomes difficult to cover the prescribed syllabus in time.

(ii) It pre-supposes a very small class and a gifted teacher and the method is too technical and scientific to be handled by an average teacher. The method expects of the teacher a great efficiency and hard work, experience and training.

(iii) There is a tendency on the part of the teacher to emphasize those branches and parts of the subject which lend themselves to heuristic treatment and to ignore important branches of the subject which do not involve measurement and quantitative work and are therefore not so suitable.

(iv) It is not suitable for beginners. In the early stages, the students needs enough guidance which if not given, may greatly disappoint them and it is possible that the child may develop a distaste for studies.

(v) In this method too much stress is placed on practical work which may lead a student to form a wrong idea of the nature of chemistry as a whole. They grow up in the belief that chemistry is some thing to be done in the laboratory, forgetting that laboratories were made for chemistry and not chemistry for laboratories.

(vi) The gradation of problems is a difficult task which requires sufficient skill and training. The succession of exercises is rarely planned to fit into a general scheme for building up the subject completely.

(vii) Some times experiments are performed merely for sake of doing them.

(viii) Learning by this method, pupils leave school with little or no scientific appreciation of their physical environment. The romance of modern scientific discovery and invention remains out of picture for them and the humanizing influence of the subject has been kept away from them.

(ix) Evaluation of learning through heuristic method can be quite tedious.

(x) Presently enough teachers are not available for implementing learning by heuristic method.

Summary : This method cannot be successfully applied in primary classes but this method can be given a trial in secondary classes particularly in higher secondary classes. However, in the absence of gifted teachers, well equipped laboratories and libraries and other limitations this method has not been given a trial in our schools. Even if these limitations are removed this method may not prove much useful under the existing circumstances and prevailing rules and regulations. Though not recommending the use of heuristic method for teaching of chemistry it may be suggested that at least a heuristic approach prevails for teaching of chemistry in our schools. By heuristic approach we mean that students be not spoon fed or be given a dictation rather they be given opportunities to investigate, to think and work independently alongwith traditional way of teaching.

ASSIGNMENT METHOD

The heuristic method is based exclusively on laboratory work where as the lecture method and demonstration method do not give any opportunity for laboratory work. For teaching of chemistry, assignment method is best suited because it involves a harmonious combination of training at the demonstration table and individual laboratory work. In this method of teaching chemistry, the given syllabus is split into well planned assignments with a set of instructions about solving the assignments. It is also possible to plan assignments based on the individual needs of the students.

Procedure : The whole of the prescribed course is divided into so many connected weekly portion or assignments. One topic is taken and a set of instructions regarding the study is drawn up. The printed page containing instructions or the assignment is handed to the pupil a week in advance of their practical work. They are then required to read the pages of the text book referred to in the assignment and write answers to a few (generally not more than three or four) questions in a note-book. The students then hand over these answers to the teacher a day before the practicals. The teacher corrects the answers. If there are a lot of mistakes in the assignments then the teacher sets the remedial and corrective assignments.

The second part of every assignment consists of laboratory work. Full instructions about laboratory work *i.e.* fitting up of apparatus, recording of results, precautions to be taken etc. On the day of the practical work the students are returned their note-books and those students whose preparatory work is found satisfactory by the teacher are allowed to proceed with the practical work.

Teaching by this method demands a lot of careful planning by the teacher and generally two out of six periods allotted to chemistry in time-table are reserved for demonstration work and remaining four for practical work. During periods reserved for demonstration work teacher gives a demonstration on a topic that is considered to be a difficult one by the pupils. These period can also be utilized by the teacher to clarify some facts which are not very clear to the pupils. For the success of assignment method the teacher should prepare a list of experiments to be demonstrated by him and another list of experiments which are to be done by the students. The success of this method mainly depends on properly drawn assignments. If the teacher keeps a progress chart he can easily distinguish between a good and an average or dull student. He can then prepare special assignments according to the needs of the student. An assignment chart may be of the following type:

The Aims : Aims of assignment method are as follows:

(i) To provide a synthesis of various methods of learning.

(ii) To provide students a training in information processing.

(iii) To develop a habit of self study among the students.

(iv) To develop scientific attitude and a habit of critical thinking among students.

(v) To expose students to various resources of leaning.

To achieve these aims the following points be kept in mind while drawing up an assignment.

(i) The assignment must be based on one textbook.

(ii) The assignment should clearly state what portion of textbook are to be read.

(iii) It should draw attention to particular points and give explanation of difficult points.

(iv) It should also indicate those portions of matter which can be omitted by the students.

(v) Questions are an essential part of the assignment and the questions be so designed that

(a) they test whether the student has read and understood the portion assigned.

(b) their answers are short.

(c) their answers require diagrams to be drawn

(d) they ask for a list of apparatus for coming laboratory work.

(vi) In each assignment the teacher should indicate portion of book dealing with the same or allied topics.

(vii) The assignment should include detailed instructions about the experiment. This portion of instructions should include.

(a) the procedure of the experiment.

(b) the method of recording results.

(c) the precautions to be observed.

(d) a diagram illustrating the set up of the apparatus.

Features of a Good Assignment

(i) It should be related to subject matter under study.

(ii) It should be concise and balanced which can be finished by student easily and quickly.

(iii) Its purpose should be clear and its objective be made known to the students.

(iv) It should be so worded that it fosters thinking and independent learning.

(v) It should be such so as to suit to the age, aptitudes and interest of the student.

(vi) It should be able to combine various methods of teaching.

Teachers Role : The teacher has to do the following for the success of assignment method of teaching.

(i) He should split up the prescribed course in chemistry into successive and progressive assignments.

(ii) He should list down the objectives for each assignment which students must achieve.

(iii) He should prepare a progress chart for each student.

(iv) He must prepare and provide a list of reference material required for each assignment.

(v) To cover up the learning gaps he should prepare remedial assignments.

(vi) He should also prepare activity sheets for laboratory work and experiments.

Merits : This method of teaching has the following advantages

(i) It provides the students an opportunity for self study.

(ii) It synthesizes various methods of teaching of chemistry and makes the learning process very effective.

(iii) It provides an opportunity to the student to learn at his own pace and thus the progress of the brighter students is not hindered by weaker students.

(iv) In this system teacher gets the central role of contingency manager and facilitator of learning. The teacher acts as a guide and interferes least in the student's work.

(v) It places more emphasis on practical work and provides students a training in skill of information processing.

(vi) It provides a feel for the scientific methods to students.

(vii) In this process the learning process can be individualized to a great extent by having differential assignment.

(viii) It provides for corrective feed back and remediation.

(ix) The progress chart with the teacher shows the progress of each student at a glance which gives the teacher an idea of a gifted and weaker students.

(x) In this process the student learns to work himself because in laboratory he is not provided with any laboratory attendant.

(xi) Habit of extra study is developed because a number of books for extra study are recommended by the teacher. Such a study helps in widening the outlook of the pupil.

(xii) Since the burden of work lies on pupil so he learns to take responsibility.

(xiii) Since the students perform experiments at their own speed so owing to their different speeds they do not perform the same experiment at the same time. Thus a large quantity of same kind of apparatus is not required.

Disadvantages : Some of the disadvantages of assignment methods are as follows:

(i) It burdens the teacher with a lot of planning and thus increases his work load to a large extent. It requires the teacher to prepare a well thought out scheme for the year before starting the method.

(ii) No source material is available in the market for assignments and preparation of assignments for different students becomes an uphill task for the teacher.

(iii) The success of method depends on the availability of rich library and laboratory facilities. It makes the method very expensive.

(iv) Before starting with this method teacher must satisfy himself that the apparatus and chemicals required for practical work are available in the laboratory. He should also satisfy himself about the availability of text books, laboratory manual, note book etc. and see that each student possesses them.

(v) Teacher should also be vigilant to see that weak students do not get a chance to copy the answers from the note books of brighter students.

(vi) Weaker students need a lot of help and guidance at individual level and it becomes an unnecessary drain on the teacher's energies.

(vii) This method is suitable only for a small group of students.

Summary : Though the method has some limitations but can be used successfully if following points are given due consideration:

(i) The teacher should prepare a well thought out plan for the year.

(ii) He should find some good resource book and use the same after necessary changes.

(iii) He should be very particular to check copying by weaker students. As remedial measures the teacher should clearly explain difficult topics and principles to the students during demonstration class and set only a limited number of questions in his assignment.

(iv) The availability of apparatus and chemicals needed for experiment be confirmed before hand.

(v) Only those students who have text book, laboratory manual and note book whose preparatory work has been found to be satisfactory be allowed to do the practical work.

(vi) A new experiment be allowed to a student when he has completed his previous experiment and has shown it to the teacher.

(vii) Students be asked to record all their observations directly in the fair note book. They should be asked to complete their practical note book in the class itself.

(viii) Teacher can provide necessary help to needy students and for this he should move from one table to another when the students are performing the experiment.

PROJECT METHOD

This method was given by Dewey - the American philosopher, psychologist and practical teacher. The project method is a direct outcome of his philosophy. According to Dr. Kilpatrick "A project is a unit of whole hearted purposeful activity carried on preferably, in its natural setting". According to Stevenson "A project is a problematic act carried to its completion in its natural setting". According to Ballard, "A project is a bit of real life that has been incorporated into the school".

The project method is not totally new. Project equivalents are advocated for the adolescent period by Rousseau in Emile (BK-

III). A project plan is a modified form of an old method called "concentration-of-studies". The main features of "concentration of studies plan" is that some subject is taken as the core or centre and all other school subjects as they arise are studied in connection with it.

Project method is based on the following principles:

(i) Learning by doing.

(ii) Learning by living.

(iii) Children learn better through association, cooperation and activity.

What is an Educational Project? Various definition of project has already been considered. A modified definition of project is given by Tomas and Long. They define it as "a voluntary undertaking which involves constructive effort or thought and eventuates into objective results".

Considering various definitions of project we may consider it as a kind of life experience which is an outcome of a craving or desire of the pupils. This is a method of spontaneous and incidental teaching. "Learning by living" may be a better meaning of project method, because life is full of projects and individuals carry out these projects in their every day life.

The projects may broadly be classified as:

(i) Individual projects, and

(ii) Social projects.

Individual projects are to be carried out by individuals where as social projects are carried out by a group of individuals.

Steps in a Project: For completing a project we have five stages in actual practice. These are:

(i) Providing a situation.

(ii) Choosing and proposing.

(iii) Planning of the project.

(iv) Executing the project.

(v) Judging the project.

Recording the project is also essential.

Providing a Situation : A project should arise out of a need felt by pupils and it should never be forced on them. It should be purposeful and significant. It should look important and must be interesting. For this the teacher should always be on the look out to find situation that arise and discuss them with students to discover their interests. Situations may be provided by different methods. Some such methods may include talking to students on the topics of common interest *e.g.* how did they spend their holidays, what did they see in Delhi etc.

Choosing and Proposing : From various definition of an educational project we get the same underlying ideas (a) school tasks are to be as real and as purposeful as the tasks of wider life beyond the school walks (b) they are of such a nature that the pupil is genuinely eager to carry them out in order to achieve a desirable and clearly realised aim.

According to Kilpatrick, "the part of the pupil and the part of the teacher, in most of the school work, depends largely on who does the proposing". The teacher should refrain from proposing any project otherwise the whole purpose of the method would be defeated. Teacher should only tempt the students for a particular project by providing a situation but the proposal for the project should finally come from students. The teacher must exercise guidance in selection of the project and if the students make an unwise choice, the teacher should tactfully guide them for a better project. The essentials of a good project are:

(i) It should have evident worth for the individual or the group that undertakes them.

(ii) The project must have a bearing on a great number of subjects and the knowledge acquired through it may be applicable in a variety of ways

(iii) The project should be timely

(iv) The project should be challenging.

(v) The project should be feasible.

It is for the teacher to see that the purpose of the project is clearly defined and understood.

Planning **:** The students be encouraged by the teacher to plan out the details of the project. In the process of planning teacher has to act only as a guide and he should give suggestions at times but actual planning be left to the students.

Execution **:** Once the project has been chosen and the details of the project have been planned, the teacher should help the students in executing the project according to the plan. Since execution of a project is the longest step in the project method so it need a lot of patience on the part of the students and the teacher. During this step the teacher should carefully supervise the pupils in manipulative skills to prevent waste of materials and to guard accidents. The teacher should assign work to different students in accordance with their tastes, interests, aptitudes and capabilities. Teacher should see that every member of the group gets a chance to do some thing. Teacher should constantly check up the relation between the chalked out plans and the developing project and as far as possible 'at the spot' changes and modification be avoided. However if such changes become unavoidable these should be noted and reasons explained for future guidance.

Evaluation **:** The evaluation of the project should be done both by the pupils and the teacher. The pupils should estimate the qualities of what they have done before the teacher gives his evaluation. The evaluation of the project has to be done in the light of plans, difficulties in the execution and achieved results. Let the students have self criticism and look through their own failings and findings. This step is very useful because as a result of the project, the pupils can know the values of the information, interest, skills and attitudes that have been modified by the project.

Record **:** A complete record of the project be kept by the students. The record should include every thing about the project. It should include the proposal, plan and its discussion, duties allotted to different students and how far were they carried out by them. It should also include the details of places visited and surveyed, maps etc. drawn, guidance for future and all other possible details.

Role of Teacher

(i) In project method of teaching the role of a teacher is that of a guide, friend and philosopher.

(ii) He helps the students in solving their problems just like an elder brother.

(iii) He encourages his students to work collectively, amicably in the group.

(iv) He also helps his students to avoid mistakes.

(v) He makes it a point that each member of the group contributes some thing to the completion of the project and in this process helps the shy and Weaker students to work along with their classmates.

(vi) If the students face failure during execution of some steps of the project the teacher should not execute any portion of the project but should only explain to his students the reasons of their failure and should suggest them some better methods or techniques that may be used by them next time for the success of the project.

(vii) During the execution step teacher also learns something.

(viii) Teacher should always remain alert and active during execution, step and see that the project goes to completion successfully.

(ix) During execution of the project teacher should maintain a democratic atmosphere.

(x) Teacher must be well read and well informed so that he can help the students to the successful completion of the project.

The Merits

(i) It is a method of teaching based on psychological laws of learning. The education is related to child's life and he acquires it through meaningful activity.

(ii) It imbibes the spirit of cooperation as it is a cooperative venture. Teacher and students join in the project.

(iii) It stimulates interest in natural as also man made situations. Moreover the interest is spontaneous and not under any compulsions.

(iv) The method provides opportunities for pupils of different tastes and aptitudes within the frame work of the same scheme.

(v) It upholds the dignity of labour.

(vi) It introduces democracy in education.

(vii) It brings about a close correlation between a particular activity and various subjects.

(viii) It is a problem solving method and places very less emphasis on cramming or memorising.

(ix) It helps to inculcate social discipline through joint activities of the teacher.and the taught.

(x) A project can be used to arouse interest in a particular topic as it blends school life with outside world. It provides situations in which the students come in direct contact with their environment.

(xi) It develops self confidence and self discipline.

(xii) A project tends to illustrate the real nature of the subject.

(xiii) A project affords opportunity to develop keenness and accuracy of observation and produces a spirit of enquiry.

(xiv) It puts a challenge to the student and thus stimulates constructive and creative thinking.

(xv) It provides the students an opportunity for mutual exchange of ideas.

(xvi) This method helps the children to organise their knowledge.

The Drawbacks

(i) Projects require a lot of time and this method can be used as a part of science work only.

(ii) Though the method provides the student superficial knowledge of so many things it provides insufficient knowledge of some fundamental principles.

(iii) In the project planning and execution of the project the teacher is required to put in much more work in comparison to other methods of teaching.

(iv) The teacher has been assumed as master of all subjects which is practically not possible.

(v) Good text books on these lines have not yet been produced.

(vi) It is an expensive method is it involves tours, excursions, purchase of apparatus and equipment etc.

(vii) The method of organising instructions is unsystematised and thus the regular time table of work will be upset.

(viii) The method may fit those who cannot listen but it is very questionable if it has the same value for those who can listen.

(ix) The method leaves a gap in pupils knowledge.

(x) It under estimates man's power of imagination which enables him to savour the full experience of another without the necessity of undergoing the experience himself.

(xi) Some times the projects may be too ambitious and beyond pupils capacity to accomplish.

(xii) Larger projects in hands of an unexperienced teacher lead to boredom.

(xiii) The education given by projects is likely to emphasise relationships in breadth than in depth.

Summary : The project method provides a practical approach to learning of both theoretical and practical problems. If it is difficult to follow this method of teaching it would be better at least not to ignore the spirit of this method.

This method has been found to be more suitable for primary and middle classes and is of restricted use for high and higher secondary classes. This method may be tried alongwith formal class room teaching without disturbing the school time-table. With this in view some projects may be undertaken by the students to be completed on certain fixed days of a week. Alternately first half of the day may be devoted to class room teaching and the project work be carried out in the remaining half day. To help solve the problem of fund's shortage such projects be choose which are self-supporting or the projects selected be such that their final products can be sold to partially support the funds. Some such projects are improvising chemistry apparatus, etc. Costly projects should be avoided. As it is not suitable for drill and continuous and systematic teaching, it is not very desirable to use it freely.

CONCENTRIC METHOD

This is a system of organising a course rather than a method of teaching. It is therefore better to call it *concentric system* or *approach.* It implies widening of knowledge just as concentric circles go on extending and widening. It is a system of arrangement of subject matter. In this method the study of the topic is spread over a number of years. It is based on the principle that subject cannot be given an exhaustive treatment at the first stage. To begin with, a simple presentation of the subject is given and further knowledge is imparted in following years. Thus beginning from a nucleus the circles of knowledge go on widening year after year and hence the name concentric method.

The Procedure : A topic is divided into a number of portions which are then allotted to different classes. The criterion for allotment of a particular portion of the course to a particular class are the difficulty of portion and power of comprehension of students in that age group. Thus it is mainly concerned with year to year teaching but its influence can also be exercised in day-to-day teaching. Knowledge be given today should follow from knowledge given yesterday and should lead to teaching on following day.

The Merits

(i) This method of organisation of subject matter is decidely superior to that in which one topic is taken up in particular class and an effort is made to deal with all aspects of the topic in that particular class.

(ii) In provides a frame work from science course which is of real value to students.

(iii) The system is most successful when the teaching is in hands of one teacher because then he can preserve continuity in the teaching and keeps his expanding circle concentric.

(iv) It provides opportunity for revision of work already covered in a previous class and carrying out new work.

(v) It enables the teacher to cover a portion according to receptivity of learner.

(vi) Since the same topic is learnt over many years so its impressions are more lasting.

(vii) It does not allow teaching to become dull because every year a new interest can be given to the topic. Every year there are new problem to solve and new difficulties to overcome.

The Drawbacks : For the success of this approach we require really capable teacher. If a teacher becomes over ambitious and exhausts all the possible interesting illustrations in the introductory year then the subject loses its power of freshness and appeal and nothing is left to create interest in the topic in subsequent years.

In case the topic is too short or too long then also the method is not found to be useful. A too long portion makes the topic dull and a two short portion fails to leave any permanent and lasting impression on the mind of the pupil.

Summary : It is a good method for being adopted for arranging the subject matter. It should be kept in mind, by the organisers, while organising the subject matter that no portion is too long or too short. It would also be much useful if the same teacher teaches the same class year after year so that he can reserve some illustrative examples for each year and thus can maintain the interest of the students in the topic.

UNIT METHOD

It is one of the latest methods in the field of education. It involves pupils more actively in learning process.

Different authors define unit in a different way. Hanna, Hageman, Potter define it as, "a unit is a purposeful learning experience that is focussed on some socially significant understanding which will modify the behaviour of learner and adjust him to adjust to a life situation more effectively".

However all the definitions of unit imply that it possesses the following characteristics:

(i) It is an organisation of activities around a purpose.

(ii) It has significant content.

(iii) It involves students in learning process.

(iv) It modifies the students behaviour to such an extent that he can cope with new problem and situations more competently.

Types of Units : Mainly the units may be classified as:

(i) Subject matter units.

(ii) Experience units.

(iii) Resource units.

The teaching of chemistry can be carried out in a better way and it is better understood and appreciated by the students if it is taught as units of immediate interest to the pupils. Such units may be (i) life centred (ii) environment centred (iii) life and environment centred.

For this The Tara Devi Seminar (1956) recommended the following:

Life Centred Units

1. The air we breathe.
2. The water we use.
3. The food we eat.
4. The clothes we wear.
5. Our mineral resources.
6. The universe we live in.

Environment-centred Units

1. The atmosphere.
2. Water, a vital need of life.
3. The earth surface.
4. Civilization and the use of metals.

Environment of Life-centred Units

1. Using mineral resources for better living.
2. The weather and what we can do about it.
3. Chemistry for our homes.

Interesting lessons can be developed on 'Air', 'Water' etc. These can be used for teaching of hydrogen, nitrogen, water, carbon dioxide etc.

Essentials of a Good Unit

(i) It should deal with a sizeable topic.

(ii) It should emerge out of students past experiences and should lead to broader interests.

(iii) It should be of appropriate difficulty in terms of child's understanding, interest.

(iv) It should provide scope for using a variety of materials and activities like community resources, audiovisual materials etc.

(v) It should allow use of sufficient amount of books and other learning materials.

(vi) Units should be such as to draw materials from several fields so that children may develop richer insight into human relationships and processes.

(vii) It should be functional and should be in accordance with the maturity level of the learner.

The Merits

This method of teaching has the following advantages:

(i) It brings about a closer integration between various branches of science.

(ii) It makes subject matter more interesting and realistic.

(iii) It provides a better understanding of the environment and life.

(iv) It focuses attention on significant facts and avoids confusion.

(v) The unit because of its flexibility provides facility in adopting instructions to individual's differences.

The Limitations

(i) This method cannot be used if the teacher is required to complete some prescribed course in a specified time.

(ii) There are only a few teachers who are so widely read that they can introduce material and illustration from various branches of science while keeping before their students one central topic.

Unit method or *topic method* is a varied slightly in America. In American schools the teacher announces one topic and the students are asked to say what they already know about it. Then the topic is discussed in a question and answer session and those questions which no member of the class could answer are noted down for investigation. From this list of questions, such questions as are considered as too difficult for a particular class are eliminated by the teacher and the remaining questions are arranged in a planned manner for answers. These questions are then dealt within the class according to the plan. The great thing about such a course is that boys feel that it is their course and not some thing thrust upon them by authority.

HISTORICAL METHOD

Some teachers prefer to develop a subject by following the stages through which the subject has passed during its course of development from its early beginnings. This type of teaching has a fascination which appeals to pupils. Various science subjects such as Chemistry, Bacteriology etc. Which have an interesting historical background can be taught successfully by such a technique. It is possible to develop a topic starting from its early history and the various stages through which it developed before attaining the modern shape.

Chemistry, has a very interesting history and the works of Priestley, Lavoisier, Davy, Black and Dalton etc. can be given this type of treatment. The gradual development of atomic theory can be unfolded gradually by this method which will be quite interesting.

Through such a treatment may not be possible for all the topics but an occasional resort to such a treatment has its own uses.

DISCUSSION METHOD

This method is found quite suitable for those topics in chemistry which cannot be easily explained by demonstration or other such techniques. The discussion may be about a certain specimen or model or chart.

In this method the topics for discussion is announced to the students well in advance. The teacher gives a brief introduction about the contents of the topic and them suggests to his students various reference books, text books and other books. Students are then required to go through the relevant pages of these books and come prepared for a discussion of the topic on a specified day. During actual discussion period teachers poses a lew problems and thus provides the necessary motivation. The students are then asked to answer the question one by one and when ever thinks fit advises some students not to go out of the scope of a particular question or topic under consideration. This check is essential otherwise immature students may go out of the scope of the topics.

Following points if kept in view will help make the discussion successful:

(i) The topics for discussion should be of common interest of students.

(ii) Teacher should establish a favourable atmosphere in the class before starting the discussion.

(iii) Teacher should see that every one participates in the discussion. The whole essence of discussion is "Thinking together".

(iv) The teacher should talk to the bare minimum and also should not allow any one student to dominate the whole discussion.

(v) It is for teacher to see that the discussion remains a discussion and it does not change into a debate.

(vi) Teacher should keep a check on answers of the students and should not allow a student to go beyond the scope of a topic under discussion.

(vii) Teacher has to maintain discipline and he should see that only one student speaks at a time.

It is a combination of two methods. To be able to understand this combination it is necessary to understand them separately.

INDUCTIVE METHOD

In this method one is led from concrete to abstract, particular to general and from complex to general rule. In this method we prove a universal law by showing that if it is true in a particular case it is also true in other similar cases.

This method has been found to be quite suitable for teaching of chemistry because most of the principles of chemistry or the conclusions are results of induction. This process of arriving at generalisation can be illustrated as under:

Illustration. Take a piece of blue litmus paper and dip it in a test tube containing hydrochloric acid, observe the change in colour. (It turns red.)

Take another piece of blue litmus paper and dip it in a test-tube containing nitric acid. Observe the change in colour. (It turns red.)

Repeat the experiments with other acids in different test tubes (*e.g.* oxalic acid, acetic acid etc.). (In each case blue litmus turns red.)

From the above experiments we can make a generalisation that *acids turn blue litmus red.*

The Merits

(i) It helps understanding.

(ii) It is a scientific method.

(iii) It develops scientific attitude.

(iv) It is a logical method and develops critical thinking and habit of keen observations.

(v) It is a psychological method and provides ample scope for students activities.

(vi) It is based on actual observations, thinking and experimentation.

(vii) It keeps alive the students interest because they move from known to unknown.

(viii) It curbs the tendency to learn by rote and also reduces home work.

(ix) It develops self-confidence.

(x) It develops the habit of intelligent hard work.

The Drawbacks

This method suffers from the following limitations:

(i) It is limited in range and cannot be used in solving and understanding all the topics in chemistry.

(ii) The generalization obtained from a few observations are not the complete study of the topics. To fix the topic in the mind of the learner a lot of supplementary work and practice is needed.

(iii) Inductive reasoning is not absolutely conclusive. The generalization has been done from the study of a few (three or four) cases. The process thus establishes certain degree of probability which can be increased by increasing the number of valid cases.

(iv) This method needs a lot of time and energy and thus it is time consuming and laborious method.

(v) This method is not found to be suitable in higher classes because some of the unnecessary details and explanations may make teaching dull and boring.

(vi) The use of this method should be restricted and confined to understanding the rules in the early stages.

(vii) This method may be considered complete and perfect only if the generalization arrived at by induction can be verified through deductive method.

DEDUCTIVE METHOD

Deductive method is opposite of inductive method. In this method the learner proceeds from general to particular, from abstract to concrete. Thus in this method facts are deduced or analysed by the application of established formula or experimentation. In this case the formula is accepted by the learner as a duly established fact.

In this method teacher announces the topics of the day and he also gives the relevant formula/rule/law/principle etc. The law/formula is also explained to the students with the help of certain examples which are solved on the black board. From these students get the idea of use or application of the concerned law/principle/formula. Then the problems are given to the students who solve the problems following the same method as explained to them earlier by the teacher. Students also memorise the results for future application.

Following example illustrates the procedure:

Principle: Cooling is caused by evaporation.

Confirmation by Application: It can be confirmed by numerous application, such as, by wearing wet clothes, observing feeling after taking bath, by applying alcohol on your hand etc.

The Merits

(i) It is short and time saving and so this method is liked by authors and teachers.

(ii) It is quite a suitable method for lower classes.

(iii) It glorifies memory because students are required to memorise a large number of laws, formulae etc.

(iv) For practice and revision of topic it is an adequate and advantageous method.

(v) It supplements inductive method and thus completes the process of inductive-deductive method.

(vi) It enhances speed and efficiency in solving problems.

The Limitations

(i) It is not a scientific method because the approach of this method is confirmatory and not explanatory.

(ii) It encou: ages rote memory because pure deductive work requires some law; principle formula for every type of problem and it demands blind memorisation of large number of such laws/formulae etc.

(iii) Being an unscientific method it does not impart any training in scientific method.

(iv) It causes unnecessary and heavy burden on the brain which may some times result in brain fag.

(v) In this method memory becomes more important than understanding and intelligence which is educationally not sound.

(vi) It is an unpsychological method because the facts and principles are not found by the students themselves.

(vii) In this method students cannot become active learners.

(viii) It is not suitable for development of thinking, reasoning and discovery.

Summary : A careful consideration of merits and limitations of these two methods leads us to conclude that Inductive Method is the fore-runner of Deductive Method. For effective teaching of chemistry, both inductive and deductive approaches should be used because no one is complete without the other. Induction leaves the learner at a point where he cannot stop and the after work has to be done and completed by deduction. Deduction is a process that is particularly suitable for final statement and induction is most suitable for exploration fields. Induction gives the lead and deduction follows. In chemistry if we want to teach about *composition of water* then its composition is determined by a endiometer tube (inductive process) and confirmed by the process of electrolysis of water (deductive process).

SCIENTIFIC METHOD

This method of teaching of chemistry is based upon the process of finding out the results by attacking a problem in a number of definite steps. It is possible to train the students in scientific method.

In this method student is involved in finding out the answer to a given scientific problem and thus actually it is a type of discovery method.

Fitzpatrick defines science as, "science is a cumulative and endless series of empirical observations which result in the formation of concepts and theories, with both concepts and theories being subject to modification in the light of further empirical observation. Science is both a body of knowledge and the process of acquiring and refining knowledge".

Considering this definition of science it becomes imperative that the students be exposed to the scientific way of finding out. Scientific method of teaching helps to develop the power of reasoning, application of scientific knowledge, critical thinking and positive attitude, in the learner.

This method proceeds in the following steps:

(i) Problem in identified.

(ii) Some hypothesis are framed and these are proposed for testing.

(iii) Experiments are then devised to test the proposed hypothesis.

(iv) Data is collected than observations and the collected data is then interpreted.

(v) Finally conclusions are drawn to accept, reject or modify the proposed hypothesis.

Scientific method is therefore a well sequenced and structured method for finding the results through experiments.

Role of Teacher : For the success of scientific method the role of teacher is very important. He should act as a co-investigator along with students and must also find sufficient time and have patience to attend to students' problems. Under the proper guidance of the teacher the science laboratory should become the hub for implementations of this method.

The Merits : Scientific method has following advantages:

(i) Students learn chemistry of their own and teacher works only as a guide.

(ii) It helps students to become real scientists as they learn to identify and formulate scientific problems.

(iii) It provides to students a training in techniques of information processing

(iv) It develops a habit of logical thinking in the students as they are required to interpret data and observations.

(v) It helps to develop intellectual honesty in students.

(vi) It helps the students to learn to see relationships and pattern among things and variables.

(vii) It provides the students a training in the methods and skills of discovering new knowledge in chemistry.

The Limitation : Some important limitations of the method are as under:

(i) It is a long, drawn out and time consuming method.

(ii) It can never become a full fledged method of learning chemistry.

(iii) Due to lack of exposure to this method most of the chemistry teachers fail to implement it successfully.

(iv) This method is suitable only for very bright and creative students.

PROBLEM SOLVING METHOD

In this method of teaching chemistry the student is required to solve a problem by an experimental design making use of his previous knowledge.

In chemistry problem solving has been presented by Ashmore, Frazer and Casey. They define problem solving as a result of the application of knowledge and procedure to a problem situation and propose four stages:

(i) definition of the problem,

(ii) selection of the appropriate information,

(iii) putting together the separate pieces of information, and

(iv) evaluation of the solution.

Many other authors in the field have taken up different approaches and some have given even 20 to 30 steps in the problem solving approach for teaching of chemistry.

Inspite of the enthusiasm for designing stages in problem solving, there is hardly any impact an chemical education.

Difficulties in Problem Solving in Chemistry : There were a many fold difficulties, some of these are:

(i) To formulate problem which will be real but still have only one solution.

(ii) To select such problems which include relatively simple chemistry.

(iii) To get teachers interested in research, which is considered as the best method of developing problem–solving skills.

(iv) To construct problems for chemistry teaching and learning which will be of help not only at tertiary, but also at secondary level.

To construct problems for teaching problem solving skills the following procedure has been developed.

(i) Select a paper from research journal. (This paper should not be easily available to students).

(ii) Take out the research data from the selected paper and handed over to the students as a list of experimental results.

(iii) Students are then asked to attempt to solve the problem as well as to design their problem–solving network.

(iv) Students network are compared and analysed, to identify the reasons for success or failure.

(v) This forms the basis of discussion on problem solving, problem solving network and problem solving skills in which teacher and students participate.

(vi) In some cases the problem is given to different groups and results are compared for evaluation.

In well structured examples, in which students use more or less the same network independently, efforts are made to develop the similar problems for lower level. This is known as 'funnel approach' (Fig.)

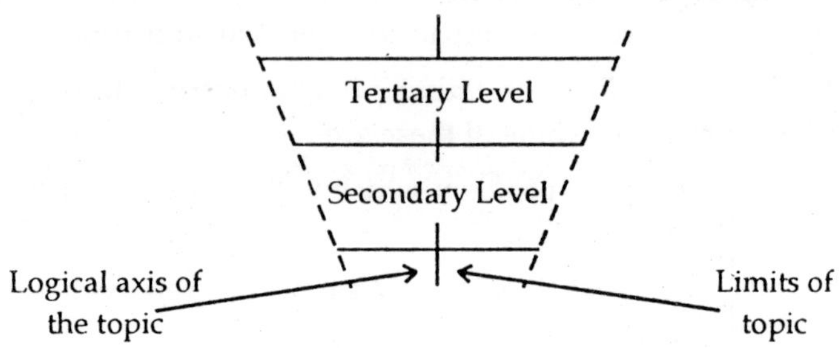

Fig. The Funnel Approach

To illustrate it the problem selected is from chemistry of natural products.

Selection of Research Paper. The paper on "The structure of viscumamide, a New Cyclic Peptide Isolated from *Viscum album* Linn. Var. *Coloratum* Ohwi" was selected.

This paper was selected because

(a) of its high quality

(b) of its relevance to undergraduate course

(c) of its demanding relatively simple knowledge of chemistry

(d) of its having a sufficient amount of experimental data.

Useful Data that was Available in the Paper was

(a) The unknown compound was isolated from the neutral fraction of the methanol extract of *Viscum album* Linn.

Var. *Coloratum* Ohwi by column chromatography on activated alumina.

(b) m.p. of crystalline substance is 622.7 – 624.2 K.

(c) The optical activity of the compound is given by $[\alpha]_D^{25}$ = –49.1°C = 0.199, ethanol)

(d) Elemental analysis etc. gives the formula as $C_{30}H_{55}N_5O_5$.

(e) Molecular weight in 565.8.

(f) I.R. Spectra gives bands (absorption) at 3315, 3050, 1658, 1530 cm^{-1}. No absorption bands are obtained which may indicate the presence of free amino group or a carboxyl group.

(g) Potentiometric titration of 0.01 m HC1 with 0.1 m NaOH gives the same curve as that of a blank titration.

(h) It gives no reaction with ninhydrin.

(i) It is sparingly soluble in most of the common solvents.

(j) Hydrolysis in 6 m HC1 at 383.2 K for 120 hours gave two products, 60.6% of substance A and 39.4% of substance B.

(k) Both A and B have the molecular formula $C_6H_{13}O_2N$ and both are optically active.

$[\alpha]_D^{27}$ = +12.1° (for A) (C in 20% HC1 = 0.40) = + 34.8° (for B) (C in 20% HC1 = 0.39)

(l) Products of A and B form esters with butan-1-ol saturated with HC1.

(m) Products A and B from amides with trifluoroacetic anhydride in dichloromethane.

Problem : Try to hypothetize what the isolated substance would be.

Design of Networks : Students were free to design their network and it was observed that the networks of successful students were almost similar.

Analysis of Students' Results : Various groups were involved in solving the problem. Following generalisation were made.

(i) Since most of the groups were able to give good results, this should be included in every curriculum to develop problem-solving skills.

(ii) Some students were careless and they 'lose' pieces of information.

(iii) A large number of students had no patience to build up the network and got lost in speculation.

(iv) Most of the students forgot to check their solution by comparing it with the given experimental data.

Development of a Similar Example for Secondary Level : The following example was developed and tried out in secondary schools:

Problem : Hydrolysis of proteins gives a solid compound A which dissolves in water. In electrolysis it migrates towards the cathode or anode—depending on pH. It is not optically active. On heating it yield another solid B having a molecular mass 114. What is A?

Students Results : In most cases students could reach only second level. Coming to linear conclusions. 50% of students could reach the hypothesis that A may be glycine but most of the students failed to check if substance B could be cyclic peptide.

Conclusion

(i) Research papers are good source for construction of problems for teaching chemistry through problem-solving method.

(ii) Students be asked to solve the problem as also to design the problem-solving network.

(iii) Instead of individuals, individualised groups be encouraged for problem-solving. It gives more confidence to the students.

(iv) Original network that leads to problem-solving should be encouraged.

(v) Positive and negative results should be carefully analysed and discussed with students.

(vi) A speculative approach should be discouraged.

(vii) Similar types of problems for different school levels be designed.

Learning Chemistry by Pattern Recognition : This method of chemistry learning is based on the following hypothesis. In chemistry we find the existence of periodic system. It is a recognised pattern of a number of facts about elements and their relationships.

Similar pattern of compounds exists in matter. However to reach a bigger pattern of compounds we should first aim at subsystems.

The main idea of learning chemistry *by pattern recognition* is to encourage the students to select a specific field of compounds or reactions or properties to search for their characteristics and and to try to construct patterns and check them.

This is illustrated by taking example from the course of secondary level.

***Example 1.* Organic Compounds of Oxygen**

Students learn organic compounds only in fragments however they may be presented as a chain of knowledge.

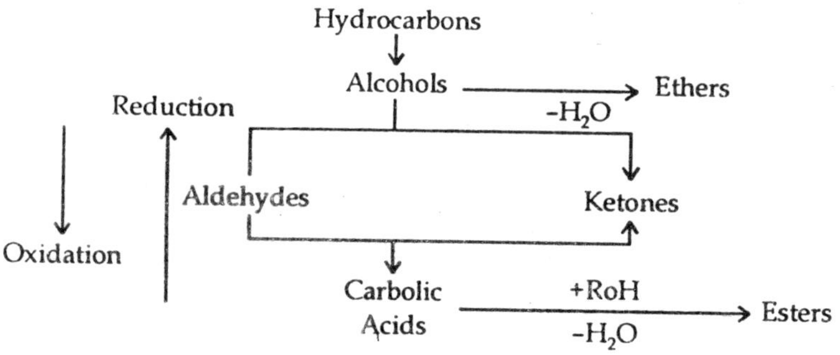

This chain of knowledge is a pattern. It is repeated at a higher level in chemistry of carbohydrates.

Considering only a fragment of carbohydrate molecule (*i.e.* dioxycarbohydrates) we can find some analogy with hydrocarbons. It helps the students in learning more about the carbohydrates and their inter-relationship with oxygen compounds.

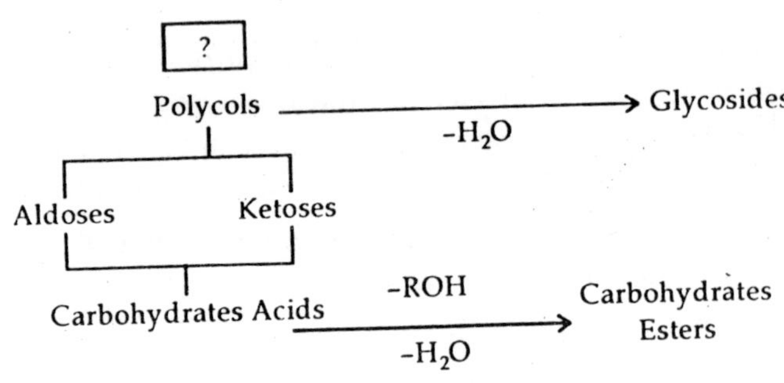

Example 2. **The Chemistry of –OH group**

The compounds containing -OH group can be classified as acidic, neutral or basic.

Acidic	*Neutral*	*Basic*
Phenol	Methanol	Sodium hydroxide
C_6H_5-OH	CH_3-OH	NaOH

A large number of compounds can be added to each group and from this students can generalise that the nature of –OH group is decided by the other part present in the molecule.

The Advantages

1. It makes use of different sources of data, their comparison and critical analysis.
2. It motivates students for research and data organisation.
3. It helps organise learning towards higher cognitive levels.

4. It develops the ability to organise the data, to find an classify parameters, to search for regularities, systems and patterns.
5. It provides support for prediction, design for checking hypotheses.
6. It helps orientation towards curriculum design.
7. It provides design of research.
8. It provides a support for industrial decisions.

The Drawbacks

1. It is too vague.
2. In the absence of sufficient data students might end in speculation.
3. It involves danger of over simplification and also of 'model thinking'.

Summary : Pattern recognition can combine teaching and learning situations with research design and is also helpful in taking industrial decisions. It is one of the most efficient methods in teaching of chemistry.

To avoid the drawbacks of the method the process of pattern recognition should be considered more important than the pattern produced. Critical evaluation of a pattern be taken up carefully. Every pattern design has to be faced not only with facts and their relationships, but in a dialectic approach, in which the recognition of their changing nature is also essential.

CHOICE OF THE METHOD

In the previous pages a number of methods for teaching of science have been discussed. Some of them have been recommended for use, some have been disapproved and some have been recommended for use with caution. Out of the methods available a choice is not entirely left to the whims of the teacher but has to be made by the teacher in the light of facilities available and nature of work to be done. This does not mean that a teacher may select any one method and then cling to it lavishly throughout his service or even an entire academic session. This is a great mistake because each method has its own merits. Our preference for any one of the methods deprives us of the merits of other method. A good teacher should therefore try to imbibe the good qualities of all methods instead of depending on any one method. The teacher should keep himself on the right side of every method. The best method of a teacher is his own individualised and personalised method which is the result of his varied and long experience in teaching. Some of the points which a teacher should keep in mind are as under:

(i) Heuristic approach be used to start a lesson. Thus the lesson be introduced in a problematic way so that the students feel that they are going to learn some thing really useful and worth learning.

(ii) He should choose a pupil—dominated method in preference to a teacher dominated method.

(iii) He should have a bright manner of presentation and should illustrate his lesson with experiments, pictures, charts, diagrams etc. specimens and models are preferred for illustration.

(iv) Teaching should be made a cooperative enterprise. Teacher should give maximum opportunity of participation to the students so that they feel that their active participation in quite important for the solution of problem and successful growth of the subject.

(v) Teacher should made all possible efforts to properly correlate the topic in hand with other subjects.

(vi) Teacher should avoid the use of difficult phrases, scientific expressions and lengthy definitions.

(vii) Through Heuristic approach dominates that the historical method of teaching be utilized at places and the lives and achievements of famous scientists be told to the students. These are a source of inspiration to the students.

(viii) Instructional method and plans must be flexible. In a lesson if, in addition to planned illustrations and experiments students want some more experimental evidence then the teacher should make all possible efforts to satisfy the students.

(ix) After a constant use of some method teacher can break the monotony by using project method and laboratory method.

Thus we conclude that no single method could be the best method and a good teacher will have to evolve his own individual method consisting of good points of all the methods. He will never become a slave to any method and will remain a true master of all of them.

7

ROLE OF TEACHER

According to F. Diesterweg, "A bad teacher teaches the truth; a good teacher teaches how to find it".

A good teacher is a congenial and conscientious person who leads an ordinary normal life. He is respected and intelligent person. He possesses a sense of humour and also an aptitude for teaching.

Another requirement for a good teacher is that he should have a high sense of principle and an aptitude for creative work and scientific curiosity.

In this chapter we will try to make a distinction between a good teacher and a good chemistry teacher we will also discuss the kind of training required to produce a good chemistry teacher.

The training of a good chemistry teacher, to a large extent, depends on the following factors:

(i) The careful selection of the candidates.

(ii) The educational process.

(iii) The efficacy of retraining programmes.

SELECTION OF CANDIDATES

The search for potential teachers should begin while future candidates are at school. For such a selection very useful role can be played by university and college teachers in taking part, with school teachers and pupils, in chemistry competitions, evening get-togethers, science clubs etc. It is essential because only personal contacts and close acquaintance with potential teacher-training candidates can ensure success in the search of boys and girls who are sufficiently talented and gifted to became good teachers.

This process of selection should continue through out the academic career of the prospective candidate and should not end even at the end of university education.

For any one who opts to become a teacher the basic requirement is that he must be dedicated and sincerely interested in communicating knowledge. He must also be willing to undertake the ardous task of educating younger generation.

While looking for potential teachers we must ensure that only such boys and girls are selected, for being trained as chemistry teachers, who are sufficiently talented and motivated to become 'good' teachers the search for such 'good' teachers should be carried out by teachers at all levels, among secondary pupils, undergraduates and graduates. The number of teachers depend directly on the number of young people choosing this difficult career.

EDUCATION AND TRAINING

The preparation of a secondary school chemistry teacher involves three elements *i.e.*

(i) The academic study of chemistry,

(ii) Educational and professional studies and

(iii) School experience.

In most of the countries those who obtain their M.Sc. degree in chemistry or subjects in which chemistry plays a major role and who opt for teaching profession are trained for a year or so in special institutions (*e.g.* College of education) and awarded a degree in teaching (*i.e.* B.T., B.Ed. etc). It is a general belief that a thorough knowledge of chemistry is first and foremost for becoming a good chemistry teacher. It is also desirable for a chemistry teacher to become acquainted with those aspects of physics, biology and other natural sciences which chemists need and use.

Secondary school chemistry teachers are in short supply in most countries and even developed countries also face difficulties in recruiting specialised teachers. A serious shortage of teachers inevitably entails additional concern about quality. Not surprisingly, therefore, both these concerns, together with the need to respond to innovation in school curricula, have been important in promoting a reconsideration of the structure and content of teacher training programme in many countries.

Teachers for primary classes are usually trained in colleges of education, which may or may not be attached to the university. Teachers for senior secondary classes have followed a science course in a university.

These days there is an increasing number of university courses devoted to chemistry and education and students have to choose before going to university whether or not they wish to teach. In Malaysia B.Sc. Ed. course was introduced in four universities. Such a system with slight variations can be seen in a wide range of developed and developing countries.

In some universities an inter-linked study scheme has been introduced. *e.g.* In Yugoslavia. This type of structure is also seen in U.K. At one university in U.K., a chemistry-with-education course allows students to spend about 65% of their time working alongside chemistry undergraduates, taking the same classes and examinations. The remaining 35% of the curriculum time is used for educational studies but students still have to take a fourth-year, postgraduate course of training for the teaching profession.

In Sri Lanka some elements of chemical education have been introduced into university chemistry courses. Chemical education is also available as an optional study for a small proportion of the chemistry undergraduates in united kingdom.

In the United States, 4-year courses of concurrent study of chemistry and other sciences and of education is the common pattern. This leads to courses of approximately **60%** science, 20% education and 20% general education.

In 1980's yet another approach of teacher education has emerged. It is based on Schon's notion of reflective practitioner'. This approach is committed to analysing how 'professionals think in action' and it seems to hold much promise for teacher education in general.

Recently some initiatives have been taken in United Kingdom to increase the role of schools in the teacher training process. This is quite evident in the 'articled teacher' scheme, which requires student teachers to spend most of a 2-year training period working under supervision in a school that shares responsibility for students' professional development with a training institution.

Thus we can see that the three elements of training described earlier must be inter-related: the acquisition of knowledge in the sciences; the foundation in education; and teaching methods and practice. The relative importance attached to the three parts and degree of integration between them varies from country to country.

One aspect of moving the balance in favour of methodology is the need to arrange as much teaching practice as possible. Methodology courses include not only methods of teaching but also a study and evaluation of curricula being studied at schools. The content of the methodology part of the course must also include an appreciation of assessment techniques because these will be crucial part of their pupils work and thorough training in setting questions and marking answers is needed.

WORKING CONDITIONS

Appropriate working conditions for a good chemistry teacher should include the following:

(i) Provision of graduates with certainty of employment.

(ii) Encouragement of society by giving them the esteem they deserve.

(iii) Providing them the material conditions necessary for their work, *e.g.* chemistry laboratory, library etc.

(iv) Providing them opportunities for strengthening the education and training received by them in their pre-service training.

Various ways in which school teachers can receive further training are:

By Self Improvement : It requires reading books, pamphlets and journals, consulting specialists etc. In this self improvement process T.V. programmes can contribute a lot. For success of self-improvement programme the teacher must have the time and money to buy books and pay for subscription of journals. However, secondary school teachers have seldom been found interested to utilise this opportunity of self improvement.

Organisation of Refresher Courses : Refresher courses are organised by universities for the improvement in the quality of their teachers. Such refresher courses provide an opportunity to secondary school teachers to establish working links with scientific groups, obtain first hand knowledge and become immersed in main stream of modern scientific thought.

Participation in Revision and Improvement : By such a participation teachers get an opportunity to come in close contact with each other and discuss their problems and elicit their concrete suggestions for further training.

CURRICULUM DEVELOPMENT

The type and extend of educations that training institutions can offer to their students depends on various factors. A need is felt to identify the skill areas which the trainee teacher ought to develop.

A survey was conducted in 'United Kingdom and it revealed that the seven most important skills out of a list of twenty-seven in which trainee science teachers should gain competence are:

(i) Lesson planning and preparation.

(ii) Lesson presentation.

(iii) Practical work organisation.

(iv) Teacher demonstrations.

(v) Safety in the laboratory.

(vi) Discipline and class room.

(vii) Class-questioning skills.

These areas are concerned with the short-term aim of pre-service training. Thus they aim to prepare and equip the student for first few years of class room teaching. They ignore the long-term aspects of the teacher's job. They also assume that the teacher has a mastery in his subject.

For a long-term aim such prospective teachers must be acquainted with the history, philosophy, sociology and economics of educational system.

Various curriculum development projects in teacher education have been started in different parts of the world. The aims of such projects are:

(i) Indentification of those aspects of science teaching methods which must be covered in pre-service training.

(ii) Pooling up the experience and expertise of leading teacher trainer and to share them with others.

At the university of Monash in Australia, the Australian Science Teachers Project (1976) was coordinated with science teacher educators across Australia participating. ASTEP introduced forty-seven units of activities and experiences in six sections.

1. Understanding Science (7 units)
2. Undestanding pupils (6 units)
3. Models of teaching (12 units)
4. Considering the curriculum (8 units)
5. The laboratory as a teaching resource (9 units)
6. The Australian context (5 units)

The Thai Science Teaching Project (Thai-STEP) is another such projects which aims at improving the pre-service training in all higher education institutions with teacher training responsibility across Thailand.

In United kingdom, the Nuffield Foundation provided funds for the Science Teacher Education Project (STEP). STEP pooled the ideas of over fifty science tutors in training institutions and developed and tested materials.

Such projects have been found useful even beyond their countries of origin as they provide range of activities and materials that be used selectively or modified and also provide guide lines for curriculum development in teacher education.

STEP has devised many an activities in different areas such as: aims and objectives; the nature of science and scientific enquiry; the pupil's thinking; language in science lessons; teacher-pupil-interaction; methods and techniques; resources for learning; adapting to the pupil; feedback to teacher and pupil; curriculum design; safety; laboratory design and management and the social context of science teaching.

We find that emphasis is laid on devising such activities which not only cover the identified skill areas but also give due consideration to what is likely to motivate the student teacher.

IN-SERVICE EDUCATION AND TRAINING

It is now universally accepted that in-service education is a career-long necessity, although the means of carrying it out arc not readily available. The in-service training is quite expensive and be provided most economically.

In many countries, in-service training is a semi-voluntary activity, often taking place during school holidays. Some times such training is compulsory. In Malaysia such a training was made compulsory when the new integrated science curriculum was introduced. Similar was the situation in Thailand when IPST chemistry was introduced.

In the USSR, all teachers are required to attend refresher courses every five years.

In Yugoslavia, in-service-training, of at least 3 days annually is compulsory since 1972.

In United States, chemistry teachers are expected to earn a Master's degree or its equivalent with in their first 5 years of teaching.

In India, NCERT (New Delhi) has conducted courses for over 500 teachers to help them with new senior secondary school curriculum.

In Japan there is a provision which allows groups of teachers to study abroad for upto a month.

Similar arrangements can be found in many other countries.

Science teacher's associations are also actively participating in such in-service-training programmes. National chemical societies also make some distinctive contribution to make to the professional development of chemistry teachers. Institutions of higher education and universities are also participating in such programmes.

The following advantages accrue to the teacher by in-service-training:

(i) He can reorient himself with the latest knowlege and developments in chemistry.

(ii) He gets acquainted and acquires the latest strategies, techniques and methodology of teaching chemistry.

(iii) He can develop proper scientific attitude, temper and interests and learn scientific method for solving the problems and discovering scientific facts.

(iv) He can acquire necessary competency in motivating the students for learning chemistry and applying it to their day to day life.

(v) He can acquire necessary skills to guide his students in the form of educational, personal and vocational guidance.

(vi) He can be in a position to take active part in reconstruction and revision of curriculum, in preparation and revision of text-books, instructional material, teaching aids, evaluation scheme etc.

MAKING TEACHING INTERESTING

Chemistry is a compulsory subject in curriculum of secondary schools in many a countries. It is a must for further education required by many a socially attractive occupations (medicines, engineering etc.). In view of this we should expect no problem in motivation for chemistry learning but it has been found by majority of chemistry teachers that their students consider chemistry as hard, dull and boring. To change this attitude teacher and curriculum developers made an attempt by concentrating on the materials to be learnt. Changes in curriculum occur slowly and to avaoid any frustration due to these slow changes teachers should find other ways to tackle the problem.

To make chemistry learning more interesting there should be a clear linkage between the affective and cognitive aspects of learning on the concerned culture.

Johnstone proposed the model for the situation of a learner confronted with the heavily conceptual content of chemistry. If information content does not over-load the concept understanding, perceived difficulty will be low and feeling will be positive.

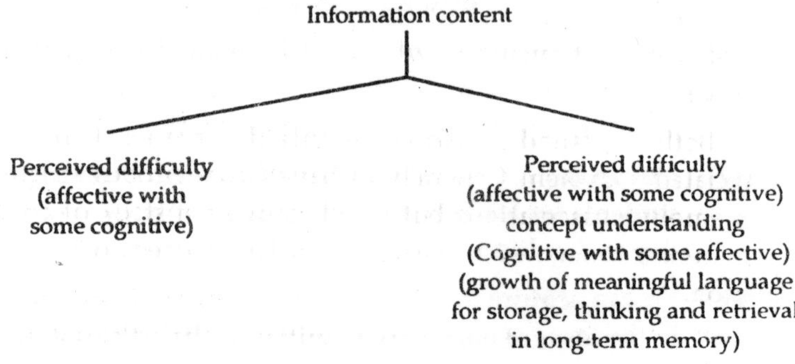

Fig. A model for learning situation confronting pupil in chemistry

For its success the teacher should explicitly explain 'Chunking' strategies. Teacher should use a consistent language and should avoid providing any unessential information. The effective use of chemistry laboratory and chemistry practicals be made by the teacher to make chemistry learning more interesting.

EFFECTIVE USE OF LABORATORY

There are various types of activities that could be taken up in the chemistry laboratory. However in some countries we lack laboratory fecilities and in some others where such fecilities are available they have not been put to proper use.

Researches have proved beyond any doubts that the pupil's time in laboratories does contribute positively to their enjoyment of the subject, thus any increase in the component of a course should make it more interesting.

Karplus *et al.* developed a series of laboratory exercises for teacher in-service education that are based on Piagetian research and theory.

Gagne and White have developed a model of ways in which memory can aid or inhibit learning. Two of these postulates are more relevant for making effective use of laboratories. The first are called *images*. They are figural representation in memory of diagrames, pictures or scenes. This type of memory can be built up by chemistry teacher in the class room or laboratory.

The second are called *episodes*. There are representation in memory of part events in which the individual was personally involved.

Both *images* and *episodes* are useful aids for recall of knowledge associated with them. Generally we have those episodes which have less emotive associations but which provide a stock of concrete experiences from which meaning can be attached to new information.

Teacher should use opportunities to link the laboratory experience of the students to the learning process. He should choose images and episodes carefully and associate them with key topics in the course of study. By such an association teacher can give meaning to the abstractions of chemical knowledge.

DUTIES AND RESPONSIBILITIES

The duties and responsibilities of a chemistry teacher can be summarised as under:

1. He should be fully acquainted with and should have a full knowledge of school time table, the ideals of school and the social environment of the school.
2. He should be very consentious in performing his duties of teaching chemistry to various classes assigned to him.
3. He should take special interest in arranging and performing demonstration relevant to chemistry teaching in his classes.
4. He should help the students of his class to carry out practical work in the laboratory.
5. He is responsible tor organisation of chemistry laboratory, chemistry library etc.
6. He is also expected to organise various Co-curricular activities such as science fair, science exhibition, hobbies etc.
7. He is expected to help and organise the evaluation of students' progress and their achievements specifically in terms of realisation of aims and objectives of chemistry education.
8. He is also required to help in preparation and production of quality books in chemistry.
9. He is expected to select and recommend good text-books to his students.
10. He should provide active assistance in unproving chemistry curriculum.

11. He should assign appropriate and relevant home-work and assignments to his students and to check such assignments regularly.
12. He should keep a proper record of the progress of his students. Such record would be quite useful for better results.
13. He is expected to make proper use of various audio-visual aids in teaching of chemistry.
14. He is expected to help in setting up of audio-visual room in the school.
15. He is expected to help in preparation and collection of audio-visual materials and improvised apparatus.
16. He must strive hard for his own personal growth and keep himself acquainted with (i) the latest knowledge and development in the subject and methodology of teaching chemistry (ii) chemistry journals and instructional material (iii) new trends and experiments in teaching chemistry (iv) attending work-shops, summer institutes etc. (v) joining chemistry teachers association (vi) keeping himself in touch with schemes and provisions for progress of students like science scholarship, NTSE etc.
17. He should maintain a diary and make proper records in it.
18. He is expected to help in school administration and in carrying out the inspection of school specifically concerned with chemistry department.

8

MEASUREMENT AND EVALUATION

It has long been recognised that for curriculum development to be successful, the assessment of students must be sensitive to the aims and objectives of curriculum. It judiciously employed assessment results can be used to evaluate curricula, particularly to determine difficulties. ·*Evaluation* is a new term in the field of education that has been introduced to replace the terms like testing or examination etc.

Evaluation has a wider meaning as compared to testing or examination. Concept of testing is very much limited in terms of objectives, scope, methodology etc. where as evaluation has a very wide meaning as it includes to assess all educational outcomes and outputs which have been brought about by teaching-learning process. Recent trends in learning and evaluation link them to behavioural objectives specified for a course of study in chemistry. Actually a total change in behaviour of the learner related with all the three domains (conative, cognitive and affective)is expected by learning experiences provided to him.

In this chapter an attempt will be made to study the specific procedures for evaluating the effectiveness of chemistry teaching-learning.

MOVEMENT FOR REFORM

The sense of discontentment with the prevailing system of examination, in India, can be easily traced back to British days. A report submitted by Zakir Hussain Committee in 1938 recommended for longer duration test so as to cover the whole of the curriculum. The examination be given in such a form that would make marking objective and independent of individual judgement.

The examination committee of the Central Advisory Board of Education gave its report on, "Post War Examination Developments in India" in 1944 and recommended as under, ".....every attempt should be made to devise and standardise objective-type tests for use in this country so that they may supplement and ultimately replace the old type of examinations".

These recommendations were never implemented and they remained on paper only.

After attaining independence in 1947, proper attention was given to examination reforms. Radhakrishanan Commission (The first Education Commission) on university education (1949) reported as under to bring to the fore the weaknesses essay-type examination prevailing in our universities.

"An unsound examination system Continuous to dominate instructions to the detriment of a quickly expandinag system of education. In our visits to universities we heard from teachers and students alike, the tale of how examinations have become the aim and end of education, how all instructions is subordinated to them, how they kill initiative in the teacher and the student, how capricious, invalid, unreliable and inadequate they are and how they tend to corrupt the moral standards of university life".

".....we are convinced that if we are to suggest one single reform in university education, it should be that of examination".

The Secondary Education Commission (1953) also recommended a reform in system of examinations. In this report we find, "In order to reduce the element of subjectivity of essay-type tests, objective tests of attainment should be widely introduced side by side. Moreover the nature of the tests and type of questions should be thoroughly changed. They should be such as to discourage cramming and encourage intelligent understanding".

Another commission commonly known as Kothari Commission (1966) made the following remarks in its report, about reforms in examination system.

".....But the task is a stupendous one, and it will take considerable time for new measures to make their impact on objectives, learning experiences and evaluation procedures in schools education".

The commission made many recommendations for lower primary, middle and other examinations.

Examination reforms have also been advocated with National Policy on Education (1968). It states, "A major goal of examination reform should be to improve the reliability and validity of examinations and to make evaluation a continuous process aimed at helping the student to improve his level of achievement rather than at 'certifying' the quality of his performance at a given moment of time".

THE EVALUATION

In words of Kothari Commission (1966) "Evaluation is a continuous process, it forms an integral part of the total system of education, and is intimately related to educational objectives. It exercises a great influence on the pupil's study habits and teachers' methods of instruction and thus helps not only to measure educational achievement but also to improve it the techniques of evaluation are means of collecting evidences about the students development in desirable directions".

Evaluation, thus may work as a connecting bridge between the objectives of teaching science and the ways and means of attaining these objectives in the form of learning experiences, learning methods and learning environment.

A students' learning is evaluated in terms of the extent of achievement and then behavioural objectives specified for a course of study in chemistry. Behavioural objectives are specific, observable and measurable aim and serve as a guide for learning and are desired for the eventual achievement of a general objective.

Relationship among Objectives, Learning Experiences and Evaluation : The close relationship that exists between objectives, learning experiences and evaluation is depicted in Fig.

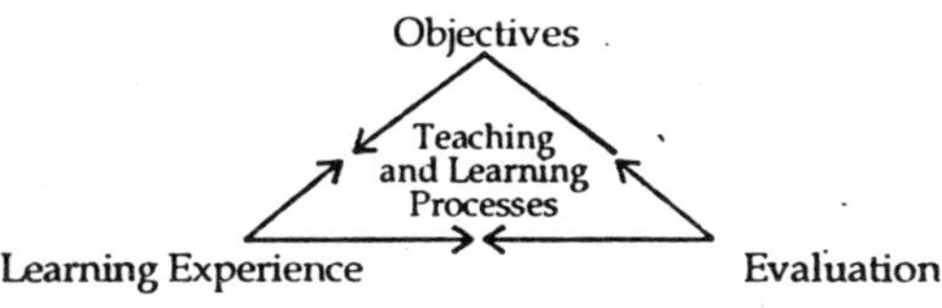

Fig.

The learning experiences for any topic in a subject are designed keeping in view the study of that topic. These learning experiences are likely to bring about behavioural changes in the learner as specified through different objectives. Evaluation of students' performance is generally done in terms of marks or grades competitively. Sometimes students may be compared with some absolute performance standard instead of making comparison with other students of a given group. Thus there are two kinds of evaluation (i) criterion refernced evaluation and (ii) Nonrefernced evaluation.

Criterion-Referenced Evaluation : It assesses the students performance in term of a specified performance standard or criterion without any mention of the performance levels of the other students of the group. This evaluation method is related to mastery and developmental tests.

Norm-Referenced Evaluation : It assessed the students performance relative to other students of the group. Students are awarded marks and relative ranks in this method of evaluation.

PURPOSE OF EVALUATION

Evaluation fulfills the following purposes:

(i) It assesses the extent of learning by students and gives them the feed-back about their performance.

(ii) It gives feed-back to the teacher about the learning gaps of the students. It also provides the teacher a feed-back about the quality of his class room instructions.

(iii) It provides the student an opportunity to show his worth.

(iv) It serves as a screening tool for selecting students for special purposes.

Our evaluation has another goal besides assisting the teacher in assessing and modifying her teaching procedures. This goal *self-evaluation* is not solely for the students. As teacher and students actively engage in all levels of a study such as initial planning, organizing and carrying out activities they can be guided in developing ability to evaluate themselves. Knowing the general and specific goals can aid the pupil in checking himself all along the way. This makes the learner an active participant in class room activities. It also places same of the responsibility on him for learning and assessing what and how much he has learned. Self guided evaluation stimulates healthy and realistic achievement goals. A logical first step self evaluations is setting up of realistic goals. These goals for chemistry teaching in elementary schools are:

(i) *Functional understandings* such as concepts, principles, generalizations, and the facts needed.

(ii) *Problem Solving Skills* such as defining problems, proposing hypothesis and techniques necessary for the solution of the problems, observational techniques, discussion and interpretations skills.

(iii) *Scientific attitudes, interests and appreciation* such as open mindedness and humanity.

The easiest area to evaluate is functional understanding because a rich variety of tests are well known and are widely used in elementary schools. Before we proceed to actual discussion of these tests let us consider the criterion of a good examination and pre-requisites of a physical test.

CRITERIA OF A GOOD EXAMINATION

Though a variety of tests are available to test the functional understanding of the child but for true assessment of such aspects of growth as the elements of reflective thinking, scientific attitudes, resourcefulness, creativeness or such other objectives or interests we require more precise and accurate instruments of evaluation. According to most of the psychologists and educationalists the following are essential criteria of satisfactory evaluation.

Validity. Any good test should measure what it claims to measure.

Reliability. A good test is one that is reliable *i.e.* it gives same rating to a candidate even if he is examined by different examines and even at different times.

Objectivity. *A* test can be considered objective if the scoring of the test is not affected in any way by the examiner's personal judgment. Thus the opinion, bias or judgment of the examiner can have no influence on the results of an objective test.

Comprehensiveness. By comprehensiveness of a test we mean that it covers the whole or nearly the whole course content and the questions are uniformly distributed to cover the course content.

Practicability. A test is called practicable if it can be easily administered and is acceptable to average examines. While preparing such a test, the time and cost of administration must be taken into consideration. The test should be usable and should serve à definite need in the situation in which it is used.

Interpretibility. A lest can be considered as interpretable if its scores can be used and interpreted in terms of a common base having natural or accepted meaning.

Easy to Administer. A good test should be easy to administer so definite provision be made for collection and preparation of test material. It should give simple, clear and precise instructions.

Pre-requisites of a Good Test

There are certain pre-requisites for preparing a good test. These are as under:

Aspects		*Description*
Aims	–	Acquisition of knowledge of various concepts and skills.
	–	Development of scientific attitude and interest.
	–	Development of laboratory skills.
	–	Highlighting the application of chemistry in every day life and technology.
	–	Development of skills of information processing, observation, enquiry and design.
	–	Acquisition of problem-solving abilities.
Knowledge :		Recall and recognition of factual information such as:
	(i)	definitions of various terms.
	(ii)	statement of laws, principles, rules, conventions etc.
	(iii)	Description of construction and working of devices and instruments.
	(iv)	Description of events, processes and phenomenon.
	(v)	Recognising the parts of devices, instruments, appliances and apparatus.
	(vi)	Identifying known physical phenomenon, events and occurrences.
Comprehension :		Understanding facts, laws etc.
	(i)	Comparing and contrasting various phenomenon.
	(ii)	Locating errors, limitations and defects.
	(iii)	Illustrating scientific phenomenon.
	(iv)	Reasoning events on the basis of scientific principles and laws.
Applications :		Using knowledge in various situations.
	(i)	Solving numerical problems.
	(ii)	Making use of various scientific laws in various situations and events.
	(iii)	Relating various scientific variables.

Contd.

Aspects		*Description*
Skills :		Using psycho-motor skills.
	(i)	Laying out an experimental set-up.
	(ii)	Drawing diagrams, graphs, histograms, flow charts etc.
	(iii)	Reading various measuring instruments.
Analysis :		Breaking up information into parts to reach conclusions:
	(i)	Interpretation of observations.
	(ii)	Drawing inferences from observations.
	(iii)	Generalising conclusions.
Synthesis :		Combining parts of information to grasp a concept.
	(i)	Designing an experiment.
	(ii)	Improvising and experiment, apparatus or device.
	(iii)	Improving the accuracy of an instrument.

DESIGNING A TEST

A good test should be constructed in accordance with a definite design or plan. The steps in designing a test are as under:

(i) Allocation of marks for the different cognitive levels to be tested.

(ii) Allocation of marks for different chapters or units.

(iii) Blue print for the question paper.

(iv) Allocation of marks to various types of questions.

Table : Allocation of Marks for Abilities to be Tested

Ability	*Symbol*	*Marks*
Knowledge	K	45
Comprehension	C	26
Application	A	17
Skills	S	6
Analysis and Synthesis	An/Sn	6
Total		**100**

After the blue-print is ready the actual question paper is set. Some of the commonly used tests in chemistry are fill-ins, true-false, multiple-choice, short-answer or essay-type etc.

Now we shall take up the discussion of some of these tests.

EVALUATION OF FUNCTIONAL SKILLS

Concepts, Generalization and Principles : The need of written tests becomes increasingly important as children progresses through the elementary school grades. This is so because of the following reasons:

(i) In upper grades pressures for more "objective evaluation" in chemistry are greater as children are exposed to greater emphasis upon "subject matter grades".

(ii) As children's use of language increases, there can reasonably be greater emphasis upon meaningful written and verbal concept development.

(iii) As the child builds a background of chemistry concepts, facts, understandings and inter-relationships, a greater need is presented for accurately assessing the child's knowledge.

(iv) With larger classes, as is generally the rule for the intermediate and upper grades, teachers require evaluation techniques that are fast, accurate, and easy to apply, score and interpret.

One of the types of written testing devices is the *short-answer tests*. One major disadvantage is the superficiality and isolation of factual materials asked for rather than a breath and depth of understanding. They do however offer the teacher:

(i) opportunities for including wide ranges of items to be tested.

(ii) an ease of writing questions because of the shortness of each.

(iii) a minimum of time and effort is needed for scoring because of the shortness of answers expected, and

(iv) opportunities for involvement of pupils in the self-evaluation because of the ease of scoring and following up incorporate responses.

Basically there are two types of short answer testing devices recall and recognition examinations.

Recall Tests

As the term implies, recall questions ask the student to bring back to mind information that the student was exposed to in the past. Psychologists have indicated that the people usually associate items to be recalled with other items and information and rarely, if ever, completely isolate them. The way in which individuals associate isolated items is still much of a mystery. Even tests of isolation such as the inkblot design used in *Rorschach test,* evoke widely divergent responses because of unique back grounds and associations of individuals. Recall with children thus becomes a problem of framing questions in such a way as to stimulate the remembrance of the situation in which the intended information occurred. One of the ways in which this can be accomplished on recall tests is formulation of a question so that only one word or a few words is needed to answer the query. This simple question and answer procedure might look like this.

What is the approximate %age of oxygen in air at sea level?

Another way of accomplishing recall of information in a chemistry content study is by supplying statements with blanks to be filled in.

For Example

Two by-products of the process of photosynthesis are ________ and __________.

Recognition Tests

True and False tests are probably the most commonly used recognition tests in use today. The basic idea involved is illustrated as follows.

True	False

Carbon dioxide is a product of photosynthesis.

Such tests encourage guessing and it greatly reduces the validity and reliability of the Tests. Because it is very difficult to frame questions that are neither too obvious nor too ambiguous, this type of examination should be used very sparingly. Whenever possible other types of recognition tests such as multiple choice test should be given.

Multiple Choice Test

In this type of test, several alternatives are presented to the pupil from which he must select the one that makes the statement most correct. Such test items can reduce the subjectivity in marking and inter-examiner variability in marking. These tests are the most popular these days and are most useful because in this way guessing is minimised and intelligent thinking is encouraged. Some examples of this type of tests are:

A scientist who studies rocks is called (a) a chemist *(b)* a geologist (c) a geometer *(d)* a geopolitist.

Reasoning power can play a big part in answering this type of questions and so called educated guesses should be encouraged. Actually these educated guesses usually are formulated from vague relationships that are seen or sensed. Very often the person cannot explain his reason for selection of correct choices in this type of questions, he just knows. Because there are so many aspects of learning and teaching that are still mysteries to us, teacher should not stand in the way of children learning. Intuition plays an important part in learning as well as in the scientific way of working.

Guidelines for Constructing Multiple-Choice Test Items : While constructing multiple choice test items following guidelines be followed:

1. A test-item should have a single concept to be tested.
2. A test-item should be such that it can be used to discriminate a group of students as low, medium and high achievers.
3. The statement of test-item should be very clear and unambiguous.
4. Be sure that of the plausible answers only one answer is correct.

Parts of Multiple Choice Item : There are generally two parts of a multiple choice test-item, *viz.*, stem and plausible answers. The stem of the test-item contains the statement of the question or problem. There are some important styles of writing the stem of a multiple choice questions. These are:

1. Stating the stem in the form of a question.
2. Writing the stem as an incomplete statement.
3. Writing the stem as a problem to be solved.

The plausible answers are the options available to the student from which he has to choose the correct answer. These are generally written according to following guide lines:

1. Write the answers in such a way that to a student who has not read the topic thoroughly each answer seems to be plausible.
2. Include common misconceptions which an average student holds about a particular learning segment.
3. Options which are true on their own but defy the statement of the problem given in the stem of the test item.
4. Do not provide clues for the right answers.

Cognitive Levels and Multiple Choice Items : Generally at the school level, the multiple choice questions in chemistry are related to three cognitive levels, *viz.,* knowledge, comprehension and application.

The Limitation : Some of the limitations of objective type tests are:

(i) They fail to test the ability to organise material.

(ii) They cannot test how well a thought is expressed.

(iii) They encourage guess work.

(iv) They are difficult to design.

MATCHING TESTS

Besides the true and false and the multiple choice tests, there is a third type of recognition test, *the matching lest.*

In this type of test items two mismatched columns are given, one working as problem statement and the other working as options. The questions and answers given in two columns are required to be matched or compared by the students. By giving the pupil two columns of items and asking him to match the related items, the teacher can quickly and easily see if his student recognises the relationships that exist between the items. There is less of a stress upon sheer memory or recall of fragmentary information because the materials are presented to the student for his correlation.

Because matching tests are focused mainly to measuring subject matter, it is not always indicative of the pupils ability to perceive the deeper meaning or real understanding of the relationship between the items used on the tests. Stress upon mere verbalization and memory of isolated bits of information should be avoided. Teachers will find it necessary to use all types of testing instruments so as to get a broad picture of the formulation of his children's chemistry concepts.

SHORT ANSWER TESTS

With all the drawbacks of the short answer tests, there is a wide use for these tests in chemical education in schools. They are becoming quite popular these days. As the name suggests such questions expect brief, to the point, limited short answers. Generally the length of answers is specified. They offer the teacher an ease of construction and scoring not possible with other types of tests. The tests offer a greater degree of objectivity than other evaluating techniques and the results of tests can be helpful to the teacher for evaluating and reporting children's progress in chemistry education to their parents. With the teacher's guidance, the simplicity of tests can be useful for self-evaluative examinations for the children. Children can also be involved in writing examinations of this type as well as in scoring them. Teachers can be assured that the objective tests being discussed warrant the expenditure of time and effort required to construct them in correct way. Correctly made, administered and interpreted, the short answer test offers many advantages to the teacher; however, they should never be used as sole testing device. They should only be used in conjunction with other types of oral and written tests as well as teacher observation.

Advantages of Short Answer Questions : Some of the important advantages of this type of questions are:

(i) They are easy to design.

(ii) Scoring is less subjective and easy.

(iii) The question paper becomes comprehensive i.e. it covers the entire syllabus. The students lose the chance of spotting questions or topics.

Short Answer and Structured Questions : Perhaps the most interesting development over the past twenty years or so is that of the structured questions of the following type:

5.0 cm of 2.0 m aqueous solution of Y chloride (where Y is a metal) was placed in each of eight similar test tubes. Different volumes of 2.0 m aqueous solution of silver nitrate were then added to the solution in each of the test tubes. The resulting mixtures were shaken and allowed to settle. The heights of the precipitates obtained in each test-tube were plotted against volumes of the silver nitrate solution added. The graph obtained is shown in Fig.

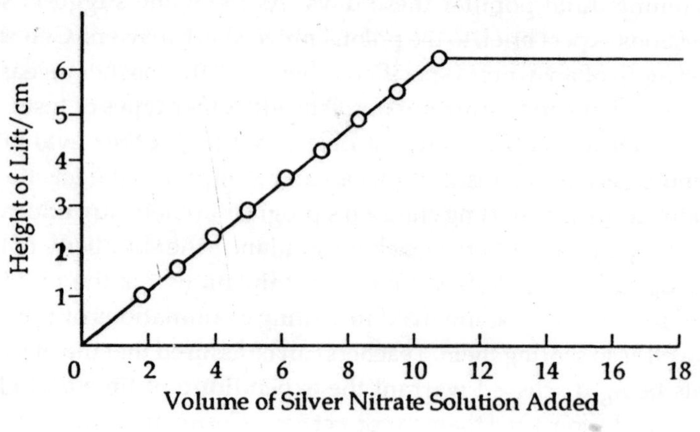

Fig.

(a) (i) Name the precipitate formed.

(ii) What is the initial colour of the precipitate?

(b) How many moles of Y chloride is present in 5 cm^3 of 2.0 m solution of Y chloride?

(c) What is the volume of silver nitrate solution that will be just sufficient to react completely with 5.0 cm3 of Y chloride solution?

(d) Calculate the number of moles of silver nitrate that will react with one mole of Y chloride.

(e) If the volume of aqueous solution of Y chloride used in slightly more than 5.0 cm^3, the maximum height of the precipitate obtained will be different. Sketch the graph you would expect to obtain on Fig.

(f) 14.0 cm^3 of silver nitrate solution is mixed with 5.0 cm^3 of Y chloride solution. The precipitate formed in filtered.

(i) What will be observed if the precipitate obtained is exposed to sun light for a few hours?

(ii) Metal Y is above copper in the electro-chemical series, describe what will be observed when a piece of copper foil is placed in the filtrate.

(Malaysian Certificate of Education)

This involves the art of *questioning,* questioning so structured and phrased as to stimulate a response from most of the students and thus lead them to the understanding of the whole.

A *structured question* is essentially one in which the student is asked to study information given in the stem, usually complex and generally unfamiliar, and is then asked to respond to it through a series of questions, each requiring a short answer.

Though the use of such structured questions is on increase but training in their construction is not so readily available. Teacher can use the following guidelines for constructing such questions guidelines given below also summarise the form of this type of assessment.

Guidelines for Framing Structured Questions

1. The *stem* should provide information and act as a focus for the set of questions which follow it.
2. The questions following the stem should relate to the stem. These questions should be in a sequence according to one or more of the following principles:
   (a) a teaching sequence through which the information normally would be studied.
   (b) a logical sequence of operations such as steps of a calculation.
   (c) increasing difficulty a hierarchy of skills.
3. In formulation of *questions* due thought be given to expected *responses.* For a precise answer the question too should be *precise.*

4. Marks allotted to each question be indicated against each.
5. Enough space be provided, between questions, for expected answers.
6. Normally five or six question are framed from a stem.
7. Discretion be allowed to examiners for marking answers to such questions.
8. Generally choice is not allowed.
9. A set of question may have either a linear structure or a branched structure. The branched type is more common in chemistry. In this type the questions do not depend on one another although they all relate to common stem.
10. Like objective tests, structured questions can be used for formative evaluation and diagnosis.

ESSAY TESTS

The essay-type examinations are in use in India since long and these have been greatly appreciated due to the freedom of response allowed. Essay tests aid in evaluating chemistry understanding in the intermediate and upper grade of elementary school. Like all testing devices, essays present many serious disadvantages. At the same time they present many possibilities for gathering informations. This type of test directs attentions to and places emphasis on a larger segment of the subject or on an integrated total unit. It provides the student a chance to create a new approach to a problem as it requires the student to express his views in writing. He is required to produce some thing and not merely to guess or recognise the answer. These tests can measure verbal fluency, skill of expression, organisation of thoughts and the attitude of examinees towards problems and subjects considered in the class, however it lacks most of the qualities of a good measuring instrument.

Obvious advantages and disadvantages of essay test.

1. Shows how well the student is able to organise and present ideas

   but

   scoring is very subjective due to a lack of set answers.

2. Varying degrees of correctness since there is not just a right or wrong answer,

   but

   scoring requires excessive time.

3. Tests ability to analayze problems using pertinent information and to arrive at generalization or conclusions,

   but

   Scoring in influenced by spelling, handwriting, sentence structure and other extraneous items.

4. Gets to deeper meanings and inter-relationships rather than isolated bits of factual materials,

   but

   Questions usually are ambiguous or too obvious.

The Limitation : These tests have low validity, low reliability and are less comprehensive. Discussing about the weaknesses of this type of tests Ross remarks, "The essay overrates the importance of knowing how to say a thing and under-rates the importance of having some thing to say".

This type of tests are not reliable because there is no agreement between teachers about the marks to be assigned and studies have shown that even the same teachers do not agree with themselves. Sandifoard, in his book on educational psychology refers to a study, "In one department of the University of Toronto, the same subject was set for an essay in different years. The essay which had secured 80 marks in one year, was exactly copied by the students in another year and scored 39 marks".

Ashburn who carried out a study at University of West Virginia concluded that, "the passing or failing of about 40% depends not on what they know or do not know, but on who reads the papers and that the passing or failing of about 10% depends on when the papers are read".

Another general complaint of students about essay type tests is that the questions 'did not suit them'. Certainly nine or ten questions generally set in this type of question paper cannot cover the whole syllabus. Hence this types of test is less comprehensive.

If an effort to offset the disadvantages the teacher must carefully consider the construction of each essay question. The teacher should word the question in such a fashion that the pupil will be limited to a certain degree to the concepts being tested.

To minimise the shortcomings of excessive subjectivity teacher should prepare a scoring guide before hand. Each question be scored separately and a list of important ideas that are expected should be made.

ASSESSMENT OF PRACTICAL WORK

Assessment of practical work is the most difficult operational problem in assessment. The reason for it may that curriculum designers and teachers are not clear in their mind about the objectives to be achieved. In part the major aim of practicals was the mastery of manipulative skill, presently there are many other aims. In one study twenty one aims have been given out.

For assessment of practical work there are three alternatives before us:

(i) The assessment be done by external examiners.

(ii) Internal assessment system may be followed.

(iii) Practical work may not be assessed at all.

Presently most of the practical assessment work is done by external examiners. However this form of assessment of practical work has the following disadvantages:

(i) A large number of students have to be examined simultaneously.

(ii) A large number of similar sets of apparatus, equipment etc. are required for this type of assessment.

(iii) Reliability of single practical examination is suspect.

However inspite of its various shortcomings this system of practical examination is in use because it is thought that any practical examination is better than none.

On a limited scale internal assessment of practicals has been undertaken. This type of assessment is based on the belief that assessment of practical work of students by their own teacher on several occassions during the course of study shall be more reliable than one single examination by external examiners. Source of the advantages of internal assessment of practical work are:

(i) The reliability increases because of increase in frequency of examinations.

(ii) In this system the range of attributes of students is extended and it includes those which are displayed during work as well as at the end of it.

(iii) In this type of assessment range of experiments and types of work can be extended.

However the dual role of teacher in such type of assessment may sometimes result in adversely affecting the relationship between the teacher and the taught.

As a safeguard to such a system of assessment are may take recourse to moderating the scores by source external moderator. But this is a lengthy and cumbersome process. Some other statistical methods such as moderation on the basis of some written examination can also be undertaken.

However it can be easily seen that internal assessment of practical work involves both teachers and administrators in a good deal of work and it demands a high level of competence and professional integrity.

ASSESSMENT OF PROJECT WORK

"In project work, pupils are expected to assume some level of personal responsibility for their work and to organize their time for constructive study".

TYPES OF PROJECTS

There important types of project are:

Report Type. In this type of project students collect information from books, journals and other sources and then prepare a report in the form of a project report.

Discovery Type. In this type of project the students use the results of their own experimentation, observation etc. to answer a specific question of a specific hypothesis. These findings are then summarised as a project report.

Combination Type. In this type the theoretical and experimental aspects of a topic are combined and thus is actually a combination of report type and discovery type of project.

The objective of project work is to develop the skills of planning design, investigation and interpretation.

The assessment of project work becomes difficult because of such tall claims for projects as an educational activity, more over most of the chemistry projects are of co-operative nature and so in such cases it would be difficult to differentiate between the performances and attributes of members of a group is self evident.

This clearly brings about the problems in assessment of projects. However to have same type of project work and same type of its assessment is considered better to the rejection of all project work in chemical education just because it can not be properly assessed.

Summary : If we compare the present with the past (20-30 years ago) we find that these days much more thought and resources go into assessment of attainment of chemistry. The use of micro-processors is on the increase which is likely to lighten the burden of a cumbersome test processing and administration system. It is also likely to facilitate international test banking and application.

An inexpensive electronic information source of large capacity is now available which can be readily used by students during a chemistry examination. It opens up the possibility of a revolutionary open book type of assessment very shortly.

9

Curriculum Development

Dissatisfaction with the existing curriculum is natural in a keen and up-to-date teacher of any subject, particularly if, like chemistry, that subject is itself undergoing change. Such dissatisfaction provides the impulse for reform of science curriculum within schools and leads, usually gradually, to changes in both content and teaching strategy. During 1950's considerable amounts of money were made available in several countries for large scale reforms. Large scale curriculum development started in the united states in 1950's and were taken up in Britain in the 1960's. During 1960's curriculum reforms were initiated in many countries all over the world. It would not be an exaggeration to say that the changes in school chemistry that have occurred on a world-wide scale during the 1960's and 1970's have greatly exceeded those of the previous fifty years.

THE DEFINITION

Curriculum is a gist of lessons and topics which are expected to the covered in a specified period of time in any class. However this traditional concept of curriculum has undergone a change in modern times. Now curriculum refers to the totality of experiences that a child receives through various class room activities as also from activities in library, laboratory, work shop, assembly hall, play fields etc. Thus according to modern concept curriculum includes the whole life of the school. Thus those activities which were previously referred to as co-curricular or extra-curricular activities have now become curricular activities.

According to this concept the curriculum can be considered to include the subject matter, various co-curricular activities etc.

Curriculum is derived from Latin word "currere" meaning "to run". Thus curriculum in the medium to realise the goals and objectives of teaching a particular course of study.

PRINCIPLES OF CURRICULUM FORMATION

There are certain basic principles of curriculum planning which should form the basis for the formation of a good curriculum. These are:

1. *The principle of child centredness:* The curriculum should be based on the present needs and circumstances of the child.
2. Curriculum should provide a fulness of experience for children.
3. The curriculum should be dynamic and not static.
4. It should be related to every day life.
5. It must take into account the economic aspect of life of the people to whom an educational institution belongs.
6. The curriculum should be realistic and rationalistic.
7. While forming the curriculum a balance be struck between the education of nature and education of man.
8. It should lay emphasis on learning to live rather than on living to learn.

9. In curriculum such activities must be included, which help in preserving and transmitting the traditions knowledge and standards of conduct on which our civilisation depends.
10. It should be elastic and flexible.
11. It should be well integrated.
12. It should provide both for uniformity and variety.
13. It should be able to serve the needs of community.

As far as chemistry curriculum is concerned it should be elastic and variable, child-centred, community centred, activity centred. It should be such as to be use for adjustment in life and helps to integrate the activities of the child with his environment. It should be helpful to conserve and transmit the traditions, culture and civilisation. It must help in arousing the creative faculties of the children.

APPROACHES TO CURRICULUM PLANNING

There are a number of approaches to curriculum planning in chemistry. The extremes of such approaches are given in Table

Table : The Extreme of Curriculum Formation

One extreme	*Other extreme*
Integrated	Disciplinary
Child-centred	Teacher-centred
Flexible	Structured
Process-based	Content-based
Conceptual	Factual

Actually no single way of curriculum planning exclusively based on one approach can fulfil the curricular needs of pupils. It is always better to combine different approaches to plan an effective curriculum in science.

CURRICULUM STYLES

Curriculum can be classified as:

(i) Instrumental curriculum.

(ii) Interactive curriculum.

(iii) Individualistic curriculum.

Instrumental Curriculum : In this type of curriculum more emphasis is placed on the utility value or vocational value of chemistry. It makes learning an intense competition among students.

The basic approach in such a curriculum is disciplinary and emphasises the acquisition of knowledge or information. The role of teacher is that of a dominant teacher in such a curriculum.

Interactive Curriculum : This type of curriculum is society oriented and lays more emphasis on the social development of child. In this type of curriculum class room instructions becomes an interactive or a cooperative process. The approach is interdisciplinary and the curriculum is 'loosely structured and consists of learning packages.

Individualistic Curriculum : In this type of curriculum more emphasis is placed on the personal development of the individual and it is based on interdisciplinary approach. It helps to develop creativity in the individual. This type of curriculum is based on self-calculation by the student.

VARIOUS PROJECTS

In this section an attempt will be made to describe some of the chemistry curricula that have been developed over last thirty years or so. An attempt will also be made to give reasons for their introduction as also the way in which they were introduced.

The three early projects in chemistry were the following:

1. Chemical Bond Approach (C.B.A.) in United States.
2. Chemical Education Material Study (CHEM study) in United States.
3. Nuffield O-level chemistry in United Kingdom.

These projects influenced the mechanism for science curriculum reform in many countries through out 1960's and beyond.

Though there are a number of significant differences between the three projects cited above but they all arose at a time when a shortage of qualified scientific personnel was felt world-wide. Keeping in view the short comings of the existing curricula all these projects emphasised the following:

(i) Updating chemistry in the light of modern knowledge of the subject.

(ii) Giving the students a good understanding of the subject.

To achieve these ends the new curricula placed particular emphasis on such concepts as *periodicity* and *the mole.* They also incorporated some major chemical ideas underlying the *structure of materials, chemical bonding kinetics* and *energetics.* These are some tunes referred to as 'concept-based' which indicates the attention given to the principles of chemistry in their development. To make aware the students about the importance of chemistry topics like plastics, synthetic fibres, elastomers, detergents, drugs and insecticides were also included.

These curricula also emphasised the role of practicals (laboratory work) in chemistry which was seen as having a dual role. Firstly to illustrate and 'make real' the chemistry being taught and secondly to encourage scientific mode of thinking.

These projects were adopted by schools because of the participation of leading scientists like Glenn Seaborg (nobel prize winner) in united states and Sir Ronald Nyholm in United Kingdom.

REGIONAL PROJECTS

In 1960's, in addition to national projects for curriculum development a number of projects were started to serve a large regional area consisting of several countries. One such project was the *UNESCO Pilot Project for Chemistry Teaching in Asia.* This project was aimed at bringing together chemical educators from various Asian countries in touch with one another and with their counterparts at other places in the world for the purpose of providing the necessary training in curriculum development. The well equipped laboratory at Bangkok in Thailand served as a regional meeting and working centre. The 'study groups' located in each Asian country provided information and consultancy services on innovations in chemistry teaching. The project lasted from 1964 to 1970.

Another regional project was the one which came to be known as the *school science project* in *East African Countries* of Kenya, Uganda and the United Republic of Tanzania. On the initiative of science teachers of these countries a British organisation then known as the Centre for Curriculum Renewal and Educational Development Overseas (CREDO) helped and G. Van Praagh ran courses for chemistry teachers. At a conference held in Nairobi in 1968, representatives from Uganda, Kenya and United Republic of Tanzania agreed to work together to produce new, 4- year courses in biology, chemistry and physics. These courses were intended to be up-to-date and relevant to the needs of the countries concerned. They were to be so designed as to stress understanding and for this purpose a substantial laboratory based component is to be incorporated in them. For curriculum preparation the ideas found in Nuffield Chemistry Project were extensively used. Drafts were prepared and tried in some schools and on the basis of feed-back they were revised. United Republic of Tanzania withdrew from the scheme in 1970. In Kenya and Uganda now a decision has been taken to fuse the traditional and newer courses into a single programme of study.

The project helped to raise the standard of awareness of and interest in, modern chemistry curricula in East Africa. It also helped to the publication of easily read background readers such as *salt in East Africa, Fermentation and Distillation*. CREDO played the role of coordinator.

The decision to choose between 'traditional' and 'new' curricula was left to schools. They may be considered as a good decision keeping in view the difficulties involved in preparing all teachers adequately and in a short-time, for large-scale science curriculum reform.

NATIONAL PROJECTS

Modern Chemistry Project in Malaysia is one such project. It not only concerns with development of modern curriculum but also concerns to help teachers to use it effectively, to improve the provision of laboratories and equipment and to produce a more appropriate form of examination for students who complete the course.

Another example is the nationally based chemistry project of Cuba. The new curriculum for schools in Cuba was developed with the assistance of specialists from USSR and the GDR. The new curricula is based upon two cycles, the first in grades 8 and 9 (two lessons per week) and the second in grades 10 to 12 (three lessons per week). In the first type, students study the principal types of inorganic compounds, their properties and general behaviour. They are also introduced to some fundamental chemical concepts and phenomenon. It includes teaching of the periodic law, electronic structure of atom and introduction to organic chemistry. The second cycle contains theory of electrolytic dissociation, energetics, chemical kinetics and chemical equilibria and organic compounds. The selection of content clearly illustrates the importance of Cuba's developing chemical industry.

ADVANCED PROJECTS

Important advanced courses include those developed in Thailand and in India.

Thailand Project. New advanced chemistry course which is now in use in all secondary schools hi Thailand is built around the chemical themes illustrated in figure.

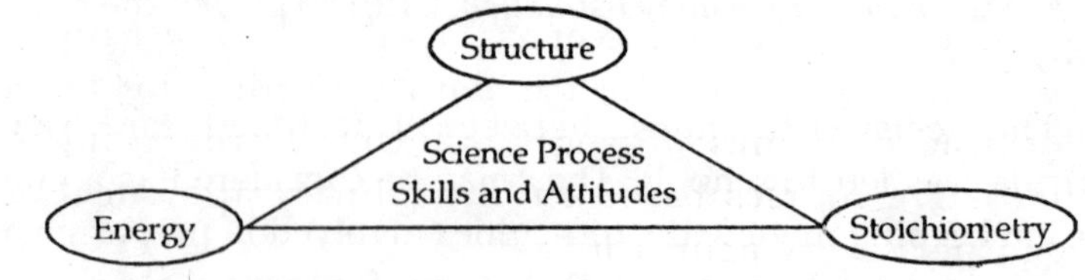

Fig. Theme for chemistry curricula, grades 11 and 12 (Thailand)

A frame work was built around these themes and then ideas and topics were shifted from one chapter to another during the process of development of curriculum.

There were many a difficulties in implementation of the new curriculum. However inspite various difficulties including those of finances the programme has been implemented across the whole of the Thailand. It has been well received and no need has been felt to make much revision in the course.

Indian Project. National Council of Educational Research and Training (NCERT) has developed a model senior-secondary level curriculum which has been adopted either as such or with slight modifications by a large number of states in India.

In a major change from traditional chemistry courses in India, in the new curriculum chemistry is presented as a unified subject. There is no traditional classification as physical, inorganic or organic chemistry. Some basic chemical concepts are developed in the beginning and these are later on applied during the study of elements and their compounds. An effort has also been made to relate macroscopic behaviour to microscopic behaviour. Two separate text books have been developed for classes XI and XII. Though some traditional open-ended and environmental investigations have been retained in the laboratory part of the course but the course is basically designed to develop skills, scientific attitudes and future training for research. Keeping in mind the interests of students who are likely to join vocational and professional courses an effort has been made to blend facts and theory by putting emphasis on the applications of the principles rather than their derivation. Equal emphasis has been given to chemical principles and descriptive chemistry.

Chemistry course at secondary level has also been revised. A review committee set up by the Ministry of Education to reduce work load, made drastic changes in the course recommending two alternative courses based on 'disciplinary approach' and a 'combined science approach'.

In some countries physics is more dominant in curriculum than chemistry.

In many countries, curriculum innovation in 1970's became increasingly involved with chemistry, not so much as a single subject, but as a part of a larger whole, chemistry now forms a part of courses in (i) physical science (ii) general science and (iii) integrated science.

Physical Science course adopted in some countries combines physics and chemistry courses together with omission of some subject matter.

General Science course combines the courses of physics, chemistry and biology. This type of course was based on the idea that general science should form an essential part of general education of all young people but unfortunately general science to meet the ideals.

Chemistry as a Component of Integrated Science

Some difficulty arises in the terminology in using 'General Science', 'science' and 'combined science' as all these have similar meaning. It may be clearly understood the 'integrated science' is in no way possesses a higher degree of integration than that possessed by science' or 'general science'.

Integrated science is generally more closely integrated usually with an element of social and environmental sciences. Most of the applications and social implications of science (*e.g.* Fertilisers; motor cars etc.) involve more than one science. Integrated science is widely associated with the movement to teach science for the majority. Making use of integrating theme 'Investigating the Earth' was an ambitions effort which exerted a considerable influence on the junior secondary curriculum in the United States. It includes structure, properties of matter and chemistry of the oceans, soils, minerals and atmosphere. This curriculum inspired many texts. Many countries are now adopting some form of integrated science, particularly in the early years of secondary school.

We can conclude the discussion by observing that despite disappointment with outcomes of some earlier projects, the 1980's brought a renewed commitment to science curriculum reform. In comparison to the earlier reforms the recent science curriculum initiatives identify the teacher or the teacher and learner as the focus of the reform so that curriculum improvement becomes essentially a matter of teacher development. Some curriculum initiatives have tried to accommodate 'metacognition' by fostering students' knowledge and awareness of, and thereby control over, their own learning.

The changed social and political context of 1980's has also had a marked effect upon school science education. Now we have courses which are concerned with science *e.g.* technology and society (STS) and the Chemical Education for the Public Understanding of Science Project (CEPUP).

However one trend has been remarkably constant, that towards laboratory work. Actually speaking, the school chemistry curriculum, in many countries, is now essentially laboratory based.

CHEMISTRY IN FOREIGN COUNTRIES

In China : In junior middle schools chemistry starts with a study of common things such as air and water. Then carbon, a very common element is introduced and also an important and common system of dispersal solution. The course concludes with the concepts of acids, bases and salts, the nature of an oxide and the rules of reactions.

In senior middle schools, the structure of matter and periodic table are introduced. These are based on the study of sulphur and alkali metals. From here they proceed to nitrogen and phosphorus. Other concepts included are rate of reaction, chemical equilibrium, electrolysis etc. The elements magnesium and silicon are also dealt with organic materials appear when oil industry and macromolecular compounds are simply explained.

In Germany : Students from class 7 to 10 are acquainted with fundamentals of structure of matter, the process of chemical change, important aspects of chemical production and applications of chemistry in other fields.

After their first few lessons on *structure of matter* students can differentiate between metal, molecular substances, ionic substances etc. from here they pass on to polymers.

At the end of the chemistry course the students are familiar with the fundamentals of chemical bonding, can differentiate between atomic bonds including polarised atomic bonds, ionic bonds and metallic bonds. They can relate the kind of bond to the property of the substance and are familiar with the structure.and phenomenon of substances. They can also workout relationship between the structure and the reaction of organic substances. Chemistry imparts basic knowledge about major industries. Students also acquire knowledge about application of chemical science in other branches of production and spheres of life as well as about the inter-relationship between chemical industry and other industries. In the process they also realise the need of applying chemistry to well being of mankind.

FUTURE CURRICULUM

In future we are likely to move to more student-centred programme. For knowing the needs of various types of students (science and non-science) evaluation and research are essential. However the following general observations can be made for science and non-science students.

Science Students : Science students will be required to learn the qualitative and quantitative aspects of chemistry and so they should be given a rigorous course with mathematics through introductory calculus in secondary schools. This class of students is also expected to accept a more theoretical, more abstract approach in understanding chemistry. They require practical experiences in the laboratory and experiences in predicting, presenting data, designing experiments, measuring and evaluating results, redesigning etc. They should also be familiar with the method of using references, data books and library. They should be helped to develop the habit of scanning through text-books and journals and find ideas and answers, plan extension of experiments from the initial design provided to them.

The Non-Science Students : It has been estimated that only about 15-20 per cent of secondary school students are interested in science based carrier like engineer- ing, medicines, agriculture, nutrition etc. and the rest which forms the majority have other interests.

The knowledge of chemistry is highly needed even by these non-science students because if they understand advances in chemistry, the advantages and side effects of chemical industries in their nation their lives will be enriched.

There is an increase in literacy and specially in scientific literacy all across the world. In U.S.S.R., U.S.A., Japan and other developed countries about 80-90% of students get their science education which is compulsory upto Class X. The number of students studying chemistry is more than 70% of secondary school students and this number is more than 90% in case of U.S.S.R. The percentage of students undergoing science education is also on the increase in developing countries.

This increase in number of students undergoing chemistry courses is justified because a country cannot have a strong scientific and technological enterprise without a base in chemical education. Each nation needs creative scientists, engineers, science teachers and technologists. Each needs an informed citizen. Each nation needs individuals trained in the process of science and possessing an understanding of science to serve as school administrator, legislator and business and industrial leader.

At the international level, the degree of scientific literacy will help to determine the outcome of global questions related to food, population control, pollution, energy and peace.

CONTENT OF CURRICULUM

Secondary school chemistry in many countries is oriented to inorganic and physical chemistry. However students need an introduction to organic and biochemistry. Environmental chemistry must also be included in the curriculum of chemistry for secondary schools.

With introduction to organic chemistry we will be able to provide the students some understanding of petroleum chemistry, pharmaceutical chemistry and polymer chemistry which are essential areas of importance in economical growth.

Through biochemistry we will be able to introduce some important principles such as catalysis, rates of reaction, types of reactions, mechanism of reaction and chemistry related to human beings.

In environmental chemistry we can include such topics as chemical weathering, pollution, effects of fertilizers on the land and in the water etc. Some attention to colloidal chemistry and surface chemistry, nuclear chemistry will help to keep student interested in chemistry.

ORGANISATION OF CURRICULUM

We have already discussed various approaches such as chemistry as a part of general science, integrated science etc. for study of chemistry. Another view that has been discussed earlier is to have a *core syllabus* and an *optional syllabus.*

Another way of organising the curriculum is to design a two stream course for science students which should be mathematically rigorous, reasonably abstract and the second are a broad interdisciplinary chemistry based on integrating theme such as 'Investigating the chemistry of planet earth'. This may include sectión on cosmo-chemistry, geochemistry, biochemistry, environmental chemistry, nuclear chemistry etc.

The *set of modules* developed under the auspices of American Chemical Society (ACS) is the latest trend to organise chemistry curriculum. The module entitled *Combatting the Hydra* is designed for lower secondary schools. It consists of relevant units which acquaint students with the anticipated side effects for every new development. They use advances in fibres, post control, food additives and energy as examples. These small modules have been field tested and published for possible integration into general science curricula in United States.

Another project funded by National Science Foundation and directed by W.T. Lippincott of University of Arizona will develop a series of consumer-oriented chemistry modules to be class room tested and integrated into existing chemistry curricula.

The very fact that both these programmes are modular make it clear that it is almost impossible to replace existing curriculum and so an effort has to be made to develop material for insertion into existing curriculum.

STRUCTURING OF CHEMICAL KNOWLEDGE

The organisation of knowledge supports learning and retention of knowledge learned. Various theories have been propounded. Gagne's structuralist theory which is based on Blooms *Taxonomy of Educational* objectives has played a major role. *Science, A Process Approach* (SAPA) developed by American Association for the Advancement of Science used this theory to construct learning network of hierchies.

In recent publications written by educational psychologists we come across *cognitive maps* which facilitate learning by helping the learner to incorporate a large volume of information or concepts.

Reigeluth, Merrill and Bunderson recommend the structuring of subject-matter as the basis of deciding how to sequence and synthesise the modules of a subject-matter area.

The interest of chemists in structuring chemical knowledge has increased in recent years. Among the first who developed the structuring of chemical knowledge for chemical education is M. J. Frazer with his example for teaching of Faraday's laws. He presented a paper on this at the International symposium.

A number of other authors have tried to develop examples of structuring chemical knowledge. Basolo and Parry give examples of teaching systematic inorganic reaction without having students memorise specific individual reactions. Instead they should discuss these in terms of general reaction types *i.e.* of a system making extensive use of periodic table of elements. A reaction can be classified as a combination, decomposition, replacement, metathesis and neutralization.

Such structure reactions have existed in organic chemistry since long. Wilson gives an example of classification of electrophilic addition reactions of alkenes and alkynes. Patterns in organometallic chemistry with applications in organic synthesis have been discussed by Schwartz and Labinger.

Hall has proposed for an *organic chemists' periodic table.* Such a table be based on the movement of electrons and defining molecules as donors or acceptors. According to Hall, the periodic table of elements be considered as *Reactivity Map,* when plotting acceptor ability (abscissa) against donor ability (ordinate), the location of the resulting point gives an idea of the tendency for electron transfer to occur. Stronger donors be located down the table and stronger acceptors further across the table of *organic chemists' periodic table.* The more reactive they are, the more likely in the occurrence of transfer. However such a master table would become quite bulky and so construction of limited section of such a table in recommended.

10

BROAD-BASED CURRICULUM

Science Curriculum Programmes at national level began after the establishment of National Council of Educational Research and Training (NCERT) on 1st September 1961 with its headquarters at New Delhi. Besides many functions, NCERT develops curriculum, instructional materials, techniques of evaluation, teaching aids, kits and equipment etc.

In the last four decades, NCERT has developed several National Science Curriculum Programmes at all the school levels—primary, middle, secondary and senior secondary. In this chapter some of the several National Science Curriculum Programmes are discussed.

UN PROGRAMME

With a view to studying the existing science education programme in India a planning mission from UNESCO visited several States and Union Territories in 1964 and made some recommendations for improvement in teaching of science in Indian schools. In order to expedite the implementation of the scheme, it was decided by the Government of India, Ministry of Education and Social Welfare to launch a pilot project from the beginning of the next academic year. The pilot project covered Primary classes (I-V) and Middle classes (VI-VIII), and was funded by UNICEF. This project was called UNICEF-Assisted Science Education Programme (SEP).

PRACTICAL DISCIPLINE

Under this project NCERT developed a national primary science programme, "SCIENCE IS DOING" in 1970. Its adapted, adopted and translated (in regional languages) versions were used in most of the primary schools in the country. This programme was a package of:

(a) Class III-V Text Books;

(b) Class III-V Teacher's Guides;

(c) Primary Science Kit and Kit Guide;

(d) Class I-II Syllabus;

(e) Two 16 mm films for Teacher Training;

(i) Science is Doing; and (ii) Primary Science Kit.

In spite of such a good primary science programme when we went into the classrooms, we found that science was not doing; science was either reading, telling or in very few cases 'science was demonstrating.

SIGNIFICANCE OF RESEARCH

In Delhi Directorate of Education, Siddiqis conducted research studies on cognitive development of primary school children, during 1975-77 on 1206 Delhi Primary school children. It was found that majority of primary school children (95.6 per cent) is either pre-operational or concrete operational, and a very small percentage (4.4 per cent) is at formal operational stage. Similar results could also be obtained in other parts of the country. This shows that working with concrete objects or doing experiments is a very important part of primary science education.

The following recommendations are based on these studies for the purpose of providing guidelines to teachers who teach science to primary school children and to science educators who develop instructional material—textbooks, teachers' guides, audio-visual aids etc., and design teaching techniques:

1. Discourage traditional teaching techniques like book reading and teacher telling.
2. Involve children in activities with concrete objects and doing experiments with their own hands.
3. Encourage children to find out facts of science by doing experiments and not to memories.
4. Delete the science concepts and skills from the existing science texts which are not compatible with the cognitive level of children.
5. Delete the activities from the existing science texts which are not compatible with the cognitive level of children.
6. Introduce only those concepts which are compatible with the cognitive level of children of a particular class and in which use of concrete objects in their immediate environment may be possible.
7. Use local resources and environment which is full of real and concrete objects when teaching science to primary school children.

Similar studies could also be conducted on children at other school levels and the results could possibly have a positive effect on science teaching at all levels. These studies reveal that if our primary school teachers used environment and local resources and teach science through environmental approach, the learning will be more meaningful.

ENVIRONMENTAL EDUCATION

The National Policy on Education (Kothari Education Commission Report 1964-66) adopted by the Government of India recommends that science should form an integral part of general education for the first ten years of schooling. Therefore, NCERT examined the question of what type of science courses should be introduced at various levels of school system of 10+2 pattern. One of the major recommendations of the NCERT is that the child should learn the method of inquiry in science and should begin to appreciate science and technology in the life and the world around him. The NCERT recommends further that in classes I and II science should be taught as Environmental Studies (EVS), which includes both the natural and the social environment. Later on in classes III, IV and V, two subjects, *viz.*, EVS (social science) and EVS (general science) should be taught. There are certain areas where there will be variation depending upon the environment of the child. Hence, it is proposed that the equipment and materials locally available should be used for the teaching of science. Cycle, bullock cart, motor pump etc., available in the village set-up can be used in explaining many important concepts in science. Nature Should be used as a laboratory for science teaching.

On the basis of this (the Kothari Commission Report) NCERT had laid down certain objectives for teaching science through environment. They are stated as follows:

1. The main objective is to enable children to observe their environment and to enrich their experience, thereby developing skills in the processes of science, such as observing, communicating, measuring, hypothesising, and experimenting to test the hypotheses.
2. Besides developing skills in some processes of science, the children, through EVS (General Science) if given knowledge of scientific facts and principles, have a better understanding of the phenomena taking place in the environment around them.
3. The understanding of the environment through application of scientific method (the processes of science will help children to develop a scientific attitude in life which may comprise such components as rational outlook, open-mindedness, a positive inclination fo

democratic, secular, and socialistic outlook to situation in life, opposition to the prejudices based on sex, caste, religion, language or region.

4. Children will be helped to develop their creative faculties — their imagination and independent thinking for locating problems, suggesting solutions and trying out their ideas.

BASIC CURRICULUM

'Science is Doing' syllabus for classes I-V was revised. Environment which is full of concrete objects was taken into consideration when the revised science syllabus was framed, and the instructional materials were developed based on the revised Environment Studies (EVS) syllabus. The new curriculum, 'EVS Programme' developed by NCERT has the following materials:

(i) EVS class I-II (science and social studies) Teacher's Guide;

(ii) EVS (science) textbooks for class III, IV and V.

This programme is to be adopted or adapted by the States and Union Territories depending upon their own environment and local resources.

UNICEF also funded the interested States and Union Territories for developing 'Handbook of Activities Using Environment and Local Resources' for the use of primary school teachers teaching science, so that they could use NCERT developed EVS textbooks more effectively when teaching science with environmental approach.

Science Branch, Directorate of Education, Delhi also took this project. According to the findings of the Siddiqis' Research studies on the "Cognitive Development of Primary School Children (1975-77)" majority of primary school children (95.6 per cent) are either pre-operational or concrete operational and they need concrete objects to learn science concepts and skills. Our environment is full of real and concrete objects, which the children can use to learn science. Based on the findings of these research studies and their implications a "Handbook of Activities Using Environment and Local Resources" was developed by Science Branch, Directorate of Education, Delhi for the use of primary school teachers teaching science and social studies to classes I and II and science to classes III, IV and V. This UNICEF assisted programme consists of an Environmental kit and a package of seveit booklets:

(i) Class I Activities;

(ii) Class II Activities;

(iii) Class III Activities;

(iv) Class IV Activities;

(v) Class V Activities;

(vi) Environmental Kit Guide;

(vii) Class I-II (science and social studies) and classes III-V (science) syllabus.

This is the bank of activities for use of teachers. For one minor idea several activities have been developed to be fit in different environments. This programme was tried out and revised according to the feedback received from experimental schools. Its English version is also available which might be useful for those who are interested or engaged in developing such materials in other States and Union Territories of the country as well as in other countries.

Upto early sixties science at middle level was a general science course. It had a little content and in it no importance was given to science processes. Learning science was a book reading process with no emphasis on experimentation and demonstration. Only once a while some very innovative teachers used to do some demonstrations when teaching science. This process continued till 1964 when UNESCO came into picture, and a new disciplined science course came into existence for middle classes.

This was a package of physics, chemistry and biology courses at the middle stage. These courses were introductory in nature and helped the students to familiarise with the basic concepts and processes compatible with the cognitive levels of students at this stage.

The main objectives of the science course were:

(i) to develop scientific knowledge;

(ii) to develop processes of science such as observation, experimentation, problem-solving and investigatory approach;

(iii) to develop scientific attitude;

(iv) to develop mechanical, experimental and mental skills;

(v) to develop the interest of science in children; and

(vi) to appreciate the role of science in everyday life.

Based on these objectives NCERT developed disciplined science courses in physics, chemistry and biology in mid-sixties. These courses were oriented in such a way that teaching of science was based on first hand experiences, practical experiments, which might be in the form of demonstrations by the teacher and individual laboratory exercises and up-to-date facts of science with suitable examples and illustrations from everyday life.

Physics Course. The physics course was a 3-year programme (VI, VII and VIII). The main objectives of physics teaching were:

To enable the child to:

(i) obtain the knowledge and understanding of the basic concepts and laws of physics;

(ii) acquaint themselves with the application of laws in everyday life;

(iii) obtain the understanding of the physical phenomena and basic laws governing them;

(iv) develop skills in solving problems, handling equipment and performing experiments;

(v) develop scientific attitudes and the spirit of scientific enquiry;

(vi) appreciate the laws of physical science in everyday life.

Based on these objectives, the physics programmes developed by NCERT was a package of:

(a) Class VI-VIII Physics textbooks;

(b) Class VI-VIII Physics teachers' guides;

(c) Class VI-VIII Physics test items;

(d) Class VI-VIII Physics kits (3 – one for each class) and kit guides;

(e) teacher training films (Physics kit – Parts I, II and III).

Chemistry Course. The Chemistry course was a 2-year programme (VII and VIII). The main objectives of Chemistry Teaching were:

To provide the children with:

(i) knowledge of the nature of substances, their properties and their atom-molecular composition;

(ii) knowledge and understanding of the nature of chemical changes, their types and basic laws governing them;

(iii) development of power of observation and ability to explain the chemical phenomena involved in the processes studied;

(iv) acquaintance with language of chemistry;

(v) development of skills in solving problems, handling substances and equipments to do experiments;

(vi) development of computational skills;

(vii) development of scientific attitude and spirit of scientific enquiry;

(viii) application of the role of chemistry in everyday life.

Based on the objectives, the chemistry programme developed by NCERT was a package of:

(a) Class VII-VIII Chemistry textbooks;

(b) Class VII-VIII Chemistry teachers' guides;

(c) Class VII-VIII Chemistry test items;

(d) Class VII-VIII Chemistry kit and kit guide;

(e) Teacher training films (Chemistry Demonstration Kit).

Biology Course. The Biology course was a 3-year programme (VI, VII and VIII). The main objectives of Biology Teaching were:

(i) To acquaint the students with the world of living things which surround them;

(ii) To di: cover the main laws and regularities governing the life processes;

(iii) To give an understanding of the nature of biographical science;

(iv) To create interest in pupils in life sciences enabling them in the solution of problems of everyday life;

(v) To give knowledge of:

(a) plants and their functions (Botany);

(b) animals and their functions (Zoology);

(c) the structure and functions of the human body (Human Physiology);

(d) man and his environment.

Based on these objectives, the biology programme developed by NCERT was a package of:

(a) Class VI-VIII Biology textbooks;

(b) Class VI-VIII Biology teachers' guides;

(c) Class VI-VIII Biology test items;

(d) Class VI-VIII Biology kit and kit guide;

(e) Teacher training film (Biology kit—Parts I, II and III). The Disciplined Science textbooks were written in such a way that science teachers in schools would have physics, chemistry and biology kits, but they could not be supplied to all the schools. Thus again, science teaching became a book reading or teacher telling process. Disciplined science curricula developed during sixties were assessed as inappropriate for the eighties.

Isolated disciplines served to cut science off from our common humanity. For this it was decided to seek a curriculum with more attention to integrative system and operations that can interweave diverse disciplines.

VARIOUS PROJECTS

During seventies a number of integrated science teaching projects and programmes were developed in various countries. These programmes embody a wide range of different approaches to integrate science teaching, including processes, concept, units, environment, applied science, thematic projects and patterns. As a part of 10+2 curriculum the NCERT also developed an integrated science programme for middle classes (VI-VIII).

If we review the overall aims and objectives of integrated science programmes, we find these three aspects are reflected, *i.e.*,

(a) the nature of science; (b) the nature of learners, and (c) the nature of society.

The Nature of Science

(i) The simple cognitive skills, such as the ability to recall knowledge, comprehend the basic concepts and themes of science such as the nature of matter, energy and its transformations, the nature and properties of living things, etc., and their application in novel situations.

(ii) The process skills such as the ability to observe, measure, classify and predict. It is these skills that will largely influence the way in which the subject matter is taught.

(iii) The development of attitudes such as honesty and open-mindedness, and the realisation of the tentative nature of science theories. These are unlikely to arise from the courses unless the approach to practical investigation rejects true query.

(iv) The skills appropriate to science: these would include not only the ability to manipulate apparatus, but also to construct and interpret tables, charts and graphs, as well as to be able to find relevant information from sources of reference.

The Nature of Learners. It seems that many integrated science teaching programmes, most of which cover a period of several years of schooling, attempt to reflect the findings of research in the development of science and mathematics concepts in children. It looks, there appears to be considerable awareness in the designers of integrated science schemes that curriculum development should be geared to the thought of the child and not just to be logical structure of the subject.

The Nature of Society

(i) In the selection of aims for the course as a whole greater attention is paid to the overall needs of society. One reason for the widespread popularity of integrated science courses is an awareness that they can better reflect the aspirations of society than courses in single science discipline.

(ii) In the selection of subject matter, the social significance of science has been given prominence and technology has also crept into integrated science courses. Thus, the Integrated Science Project places heavy emphasis on integration of science, technology and society.

Based on these objectives a full curriculum package containing syllabus, textbooks, teachers' guides, kit and kit guide was developed during 1975-80. The process of development includes participation and interaction of more than a hundred people belonging to the category of scientists, subject teachers, method masters, science educators and classroom teachers. All worked to fulfil certain predetermined objectives drawn on the basis of the curriculum frame work prepared by NCERT in 1975.

This integrated science curriculum was finally implemented. Some states have already introduced it and many are contemplating its introduction. In the States and organisations where this curriculum has been introduced, it has been observed that the textbooks are being used as if these are mere amalgamation of physics, chemistry and biology. The curriculum is not being implemented in the intended spirit.

Integrated science teaching covers all those approaches to teaching science:

(a) in which concepts and principles of science (physics, chemistry, biology, etc.) are presented in such a way as to express to fundamental unity of scientific thought,

(b) which emphasis the processes and methodology of the scientific outlook, and

(c) which embody a scientific study of the environment and technological recruitments for everyday life. The NCERT integrated science curriculum can be analysed keeping an eye over the above given definition of integrated science.

SCHOOL LEVEL PROGRAMMES

The Education Commission headed by Professor D.S. Kothari, was appointed by the Government of India in July 1964. It submitted its report in July 1966, recommending guiding principles and working policies for the development of Indian Education at all stages and in all respects. Based on its recommendations 10+2+3 Education Scheme started in Delhi Schools, Central Schools and other schools under Central Board of Secondary Education (CBSE) throughout the country in July 1975, in which science was compulsory (as a part of general education) like other subjects upto class X. The first Secondary School Examination was conducted by CBSE in 1977. The same year the new Science Course was introduced at +2 stage in class XI in Senior Secondary Schools, and in 1979 the first batch of class XII students appeared in Senior Secondary Examination conducted by CBSE. NCERT developed secondary and senior secondary science curricula were used in the schools under CBSE.

This programme developed by NCERT in 1975 was a package of three textbooks—physics, chemistry and life science. These textbooks after being written were placed before a group of selected science teachers for review. Only after minor changes these textbooks were in the market for the use of students.

This secondary science course lived for four years and in 1979 it split up into two courses—Science A-Course and Science B-Course, according to the recommendations of Ishwarbhai Patel Review Committee.

A-Course. The syllabus of the programme was framed by CBSE, and the books were written by private publishers. This was a package of the following nine books:

(i) Physics Theory Part I for Class IX

(ii) Physics Theory Part II for Class X

(iii) Physics Practical for Classes IX and X

(iv) Chemistry Theory Part I for Class IX

(v) Chemistry Theory Part II for Class X

(vi) Chemistry Practical for Classes IX and X

(vii) Life Science Theory Part I for Class IX

(viii) Life Science Theory Part II for Class X

(ix) Life Science Practical for Classes IX and X.

B-Course. This course was developed by NCERT in 1979. This was a package of two textbooks:

(i) Science Part I for Class IX

(ii) Science Part II for Class X

For science practical, private publishers published science practical books (Physics, Chemistry and Life Science all in one) based on CBSE prescribed syllabus.

These NCERT developed science textbooks were written on integrated approach, and not as separate textbook of physics, chemistry and life science, as it is clear from the sequence of chapters in the two textbooks.

Science Part I (for Class IX)

1. Our Universe
2. Living World: An Introduction
3. Motion
4. Moments and Couples
5. Work and Energy
6. Atomic and Molecular Masses, Mole Concept and Chemical Equation
7. Behaviour of Gases
8. Flotation
9. Elasticity of Solids
10. The Structure of the Atom
11. Chemical Bonding
12. Oxidation and Reduction
13. Periodic Classification of Elements
14. The Halogens
15. Oxygen and Sulphur
16. Nitrogen and Phosphorus
17. Organisation of Life
18. Man and his Environment

Science Part II (for Class X)

19. Wave Motion
20. Reflection and Refraction of Light
21. Carbon
22. Compounds of Carbon—Organic Chemistry
23. Life Processes
24. Genetics and Evolution
25. Electricity

26. Magnetism
27. Solutions and Electrolytic Dissociation
28. The Rates of Reactions and Chemical Equilibrium
29. Combustion and Fuels
30. Human Biology, Health and Nutrition
31. Metals and Metallurgical Processes
32. Some Applications of Science.

If we look at these two science courses, we find that Science A-Course consists of a vast syllabus as compared to Science B-Course. Science A-Course includes nine books (three in each Physics, Chemistry and Life Science), while in Science B-Course all the three subjects (Physics, Chemistry and Life Science) are amalgamated in one book (in two parts), plus book for science practical.

According to the Ishwarbhai Patel Review Committee on the curriculum for the ten year school, published by the Ministry of Education and Social Welfare (1978) the aim of framing Science A-Course was "to develop special interest in students for the science subjects," while Science B-Course aimed at imparting in students a broad based knowledge of science along with other subjects.

This means that the study of Science A-Course demanded an intensive teaching and teachers are expected to put in some more work, and show extra interest in the teaching of this course. But the number of periods allotted per week (usually 9, each of duration 30-40 minutes) to the teaching of Science A-Course remained the same as are allotted to the teaching of Science B-Course. There were only 3 periods per week allotted to each subject physics, chemistry and life science (theory and practical).

Under these conditions it was proposed that in order to make Science A-Course more useful and popular among the students the following recommendations (the first two of the Review Committee, 1978) may be considered by the curriculum developers and educational administrators:

1. The main concepts should be studied and unnecessary details which overload the syllabus should be avoided.
2. The content of the course should be capable of being taught or studied within the time allotted.
3. The Science A-Course should cover the pre-requisites of the senior secondary (XI-XII) science.

GENERAL SCIENCE

One of the recommendations of the Education Commission under the chairmanship of Dr. D.S. Kothari was that the science should be made a compulsory subject in school education.

The recommendation was accepted and science was made compulsory up to class X in several States and Union Territories, creating a lot of problems. In the old 3 years Higher Secondary Scheme (IX-XI), a selected number of students (about 33 per cent) who were really interested in science used to take science in class IX. But now like other subjects science is also a required course upto class X. Therefore all students including a big majority of those who perhaps do not have any interest and aptitude for science have to take science. Now the question arises, must every student be forced to learn the same science for which he has no aptitude and interest or may a special curriculum in science be developed for such students so that science may be interesting even for them.

NEW COURSES

The Science A and B Course started in 1979 finished in 1984 after living for five years. The Central Board of Secondary Education, New Delhi started one science course from 1984. It is 3 in 1 – Physics, Chemistry and Biology.

This programme was developed by NCERT in *1977-78,* starting with textbooks in Physics, Chemistry and Biology for Senior Secondary (XI-XII) students. Afterwards teachers' guides and test-items were also written on these texts. This programme was introduced at +2 stage in class XI in Senior Secondary Schools in

July 1977, and in 1979 the first batch of class XII students appeared in Senior Secondary Examination conducted by CBSE.

After visiting hundreds of schools, observing science classes, interviewing science teachers, students, principals and parents some key problems regarding science education at +2 stage have been identified. They are as follows:

1. There seems to be a big gap between senior secondary science (Physics, Chemistry and Biology) and secondary science courses.
2. It looks that there is no co-ordination between theory and practicals in science Specially in physics at +2 stage.
3. The science laboratories at +2 stage are not equipped enough with all the needed facilities for all the experiments, investigatory projects as well as demonstration experiments.
4. Students, teachers, administrators and parents seem to be not satisfied with the science courses at +2 stage.
5. Science courses at +2 stage do not fulfil the basic admission test requirements of some professional courses like engineering and medicine, as students seeking admission to these courses need extra content coaching.
6. At +2 stage in class XII besides experiments in Physics, Chemistry and Biology students are also to work on one investigatory science project (in each Physics, Chemistry and Biology). It looks that many science teachers are not clear as to what the difference between a science project and investigatory science project is, and they need orientation in guiding their students on some investigatory science projects.

Senior Secondary Science courses were revised afterwards but solutions to such problems (mentioned above) were not taken into consideration satisfactorily when revising these courses.

The responsibility of drawing up science curricula, writing of textbooks and designing of teaching aids for the introduction of science in schools has been given to NCERT. The curricula has been drawn up and textbooks written by those who perhaps have never taught in schools (Indian Express, May 5, 1981). They have tried to compress in the textbooks, a variety of topics some of which have little utility or relevance. What students upto the secondary stage (in general education) should learn, is the application of science to everyday life and not theoretical science. Better science perhaps was taught before as Raman, Saha, and Bhabha were products of pre-independence science. In spite of the Ishwarbhai Patel Committee Report on Curricula Reform for the ten years school submitted in 1978, the curricula have not been updated. Even the Minister of Education presiding over the annual general meeting of the NCERT on March 11, 1981 regretted that attempts at improving the quality of education in terms of upgrading curricula were not heartening.

Morarji Desai, the then Prime Minister, while addressing the members of the Ishwarbhai Patel Review Committee on the curriculum for the ten year school at New Delhi stated, "the books that I did carry in college are being carried by school students today. The students are burdened by how many books, I do not know."

Knowledge of science doubles every decade. We are to keep pace with the new development. The problem is how much knowledge in science should be given to a child at a particular level, so that he is not burdened.

Is the capacity of a child to absorb knowledge limited? Professor V.N. Wanchoo, President, All India Science Teachers Association, in his Presidential Address in the 22nd All India Science Teachers' Conference at Trivandrum in December 1978, has tried to answer this question:

"Research on theory of learning and the development of brain during the last two decades indicate that a child is capable of learning any amount of knowledge at his level. What is really lacking in this country, are the management and transmission technique of information and the process and the channels through which such information should be imparted at different school levels. The exploration of knowledge is affecting all the countries uniformly. Others deviate their attention to the problems of management of information, and we appoint committees which end up by making some marginal changes in the syllabus. Deleting an information in one class and adding an item of information in another class, will not serve any purpose; and this is what exactly Ishwarbhai Patel Committee has done in recommending changes in the Ten-Year School Curriculum proposed by NCERT".

Questions

1. (a) Describe 'Science is Doing' programme?

   (b) How is EVS programme different from 'Science is Doing'?

2. 'Handbook of Activities Using Environment and Local Resources' is based on the findings of the Research Studies on the Cognitive Development of Primary School Children. Discuss.

3. What is the difference between:

   (a) Disciplined Science Programme, and

   (b) Integrated Science Programme? Discuss.

4. What is the difference between:

   (a) Science A-Course and

   (b) Science B-Course. Which course do you think will be a better course as a prerequisite of senior secondary science? Discuss.

5. What are some key problems regarding science education at +2 stage? What do you think will be the possible solutions? Discuss.

6. In the past two decades several national science programme came up, but people seem to be dissatisfied. Discuss.

11

Enrichment of Contents

Since pupils have to learn chemistry and thus content of chemistry is to be given to the students. Thus for chemistry learning the content should be as good as the method of teaching. It is with this view in mind that some content portion is assigned to the syllabus for teaching of chemistry. In the pages to follow we will take up certain concepts in chemistry.

OXYGEN

It is present in the air (atmosphere) in the free (native) form and it is about 20% of air by volume. Lavasior detected the presence of oxygen in atmosphere. Sheele obtained the gas in laboratory and studied its properties.

Preparation : In the laboratory oxygen gas is prepared by heating, a mixture of potassium chlorate (4 parts) and manganese dioxide (1 part), in a hard glass test tube fitted with a delivery tube. The. other end of the delivery tube is placed under beehive shelf kept immersed in a through of water. Over the beehive shelf is placed an inverted gas cylinder filled with water (Fig). On heating test-tube gently the gas bubbles can be seen rising in the gas and the gas is collected by downward displacement of water. The chemical reaction taking place can be represented as under

$$2\,KClO_3 \xrightarrow[\text{(catalyst)}]{MnO_2} 2KC1 + 2\,O2\uparrow$$

Precautions

(i) Always use pure manganese dioxide.

(ii) Before removing the flame remove the delivery tube from the beehive shelf or water as the water may rush into the test-tube resulting into its breakage.

(iii) The test-tube should be clamped in the stand in a slanting position to avoid breakage of the tube by the condensed vapour.

(iv) Test-tube should be heated gently and slowly.

(v) A glass lid should be placed on the mouth of the jar after filling it with the gas. It may be made air tight by applying a little glycerine or vaseline on its surface.

Properties of Oxygen Gas (Physical Properties)

(i) It is a colourless, tasteless and odourless gas.

(ii) It is slightly soluble in water. The dissolved gas is used by the animals living in water for respiration.

(iii) It is slightly heavier than air.

(iv) It can be liquified by lowering the temperature and increasing the pressure.

Chemical Properties

1. It is neutral to litmus.
2. It is not combustible but it is a supporter of combustion.

3. It reacts with hydrogen under the influence of an electric spark and produces water

$$2H_2 + O_2 \xrightarrow[\text{Sparks}]{\text{Electric}} 2H_20$$

4. It reacts with metals its form their oxides.

$$2\ Mg + O_2 \rightarrow 2\ MgO$$

$$4\ Na + O_2 \rightarrow 2\ Na_2O$$

$$4\ Fe + 3O_2 \rightarrow 2Fe_2O_3.$$

5. It oxidises ammonia to nitric oxide.

$$4NH_3 + 5O_2 \xrightarrow{\text{Pt, 800°C}} 4NO + 6H_2O$$

6. It can be converted to ozone (ozonised oxygen) by passing electric sparks at ordinary temperature and pressure.

$$3O_2 \xrightarrow[\text{Discharge}]{\text{Electric}} 2O_3$$

7. A mixture of acetylene and oxygen when burnt produces a very hot flame which is used in welding metals.

$$2\ C_2H_2 + 5O_2 \rightarrow 4CO_2 + 2H_2O$$

Uses

1. It is used as an oxidising agent.
2. It is used in welding.
3. It is used in artificial respiration.
4. It is used in preparation of ozone.

HYDROGEN GAS

It is the lightest element and also the lightest gas. It was discovered by Heavy Cavandish in 1663. The name hydrogen was given by Lavasior in 1783.

Preparation : It can be prepared from acids, alkalies, water etc.

In the laboratory hydrogen gas is prepared by the action of zinc with dilute HC1 or dil $H2SO_4$. The chemical reactions taking place can be represented as

$$Zn + H_2SO_4 \rightarrow ZnSO_4 + H_2 \uparrow$$

$$Zn + 2HC1 \rightarrow ZnCl_2 + H_2 \uparrow$$

A Woulfs bottle is taken and some pieces of granulated zinc are placed in it. Then a thistle funnel is fitted in one mouth and in the other mouth a delivery tube is fitted. Some water is added to cover the zinc pieces. Then conc. H_2SO_4 or HCl is through the funnel. The hydrogen gas coming out of the Woulf's bottle through delivery tube is collected by downward displacement of water.

Precautions

1. The appartaus should be made air tight.
2. The lower end of thistle funnel must be under water in the Woulfs bottle.
3. No flame be allowed near the apparatus.
4. Pour the conc. acid slowly in the Woulfs bottle.
5. Gas is always stored in inverted gas cylinders.

Properties (Physical Properties)

1. It is a colourless, odourless and tasteless gas.
2. It is lighter than air.
3. It is insoluble in water.
4. It can be liquified by decreasing the temperature and increasing the pressure.

Chemical Properties

1. It is a combustible gas.
2. It explodes in presence of air.

3. It is neutral to litmus.
4. On being burnt in oxygen, it forms water.

$$2H_2 + O_2 \rightarrow 2H_2O$$

5. It combines with halogens to yield the corresponding halides.

$$H_2 + Cl_2 \rightarrow 2HCl$$

$$H_2 + Br_2 \rightarrow 2HBr$$

$$H_2 + I_2 \rightarrow 2HI$$

6. It is a strong reducing agent.

$$CuO + H_2 \rightarrow Cu + H_2O$$

$$Fe_3O_4 + 4H_2 \rightarrow 3Fe + 4H_2O$$

Uses

1. It is used as a reducing agent.
2. It is used in preparation of ammonia, methyl alcohol, hydrochloric acid etc.
3. It is used in preparation of Vanaspati Ghee.
4. It is used in welding (Oxy-hydrogen flame)

CARBON-DI-OXIDE GAS

CO_2 is produced during the respiratory by all living beings including vegetable kingdom. During the day in the presence of sunlight plants absorb carbon-dioxide and give out oxygen gas. In this way carbon cycle is formed to keep its balance in nature.

Preparation of Carbon-Di-Oxide : It can be prepared by the action of an acid on a carbonate or a bicarbonate.

In the laboratory carbon-dioxide is prepared by the action of marble or chalk ($CaCO_3$) with dilute HCl or H_2SO_4.

$$CaCO_3 + 2HCl \rightarrow CaCl_2 + H_2O + CO_2 \uparrow$$

A Woulf's bottle is taken and some pieces of marble, chalk or shells are put in it little of water is added to cover the marble. A thistle funnel and a delivery tube bent at-right angles is fitted.

Acid is added through the thistle funnel. The reaction occurs. The gas is collected by upward displacement of air. The gas is not collected over water because the gas is highly soluble in water. The gas can be tested with the help of a burning splinter. It extinguishes a burning splinter or a match stick.

Precautions

1. The apparatus should be air tight.
2. The lower end of the thistle funnel should remain dipped in the acid contained in the Woulfs bottle.
3. The marble pieces should be completely immersed in dilute hydrochloric acid.
4. Use dry cylinders for collecting the gas.

Physical Properties

1. It is a colourless gas.
2. It has a characteristic smell.
3. It is heavier than the air.
4. It is soluble in water.
5. It is acidic in nature.

Chemical Properties

1. It is neither combustible nor a supporter of combustion. Burning objects get extinguished in carbon-dioxide gas.
2. Some metals such as magnessium, sodium, potassium continue to burn in carbon dioxide gas while carbon is set free

$$2Mg + CO_2 \rightarrow 2MgO + C$$
$$4Na + CO_2 \rightarrow 2Na_2O + C$$

3. When carbon-dioxide dissolves in water, it forms an acidic solution which turns moist blue litmus paper red.

4. It reacts with alkalies to form carbonates

$$2NaOH + CO_2 \rightarrow Na_2CO_3 + H_2O$$

$$CaO + CO_2 \rightarrow CaCO_3$$

5. When CO_2 is passed through lime water *i.e.*, $Ca(OH)_2$, it turns it milky

$$Ca(OH)_2 + CO_2 \rightarrow CaCO_3 + H_2O$$

If we continue passing CO_2 gas in lime-water in excess, it again turns colourless

$$CaCO_3 + H_2O + CO_2 \rightarrow Ca(HCO_3)_2.$$

6. On being passed over red hot coal, it is reduced to carbon mono-oxide.

$$CO_2 + C \rightarrow 2CO\uparrow$$

7. Carbon-dioxide gas is absorbed by green plants in the presence of chlorophyl, sunlight and water to form glucose, starch, sugar or cellulose. This process is called photosynthesis

$$6CO_2 + 6H_2O \xrightarrow[\text{Sunlight}]{\text{Chlorophyl}} C_6H_{12}O_6 + CO_2\uparrow$$

Uses

1. Carbon-dioxide is used in preparing aerated water.
2. It is used in the manufacturing of solid carbon dioxide called dry ice.
3. It is used in the manufacturing of baking soda and washing soda.
4. It is used to neutralize the effect of lime in sugar industry.

ACIDS, BASES AND SALTS

Important concepts (theories) of acids and bases are proposed by:

(i) Arrhenius (1887)

(ii) Bronsted-Lowry (1923)

(iii) Lewis (1923)

Arrhenius Concept : Arrhenius (1887) defined acid as a substance that will dissociate to yield a hydrogen ion while base in one that will dissociate to yield a hydroxyl ion in aqueous solution.

Thus:

$HCl\,(aq)$ $H^+\,(aq) + Cl^-\,(aq)$

Acid

$NaOH\,(aq)$ $Na^+(aq) + OH^-\,(aq)$

Base

According to this concept HNO_3, HCl, H_2SO_4, CH_3COOH etc. are acids and NaOH, KOH, NH_4OH etc. are bases.

This definition is of limited application and is applicable in aqueous solution only. It does not cover those substances which fail to give H^+ or OH^- ions but behave as acids or bases.

Bronsted-Lowry Concept : According to this concept an acid is a substance that can donate a proton and a base is a substance that can accept a proton *e.g.*

$HC1\,(aq) + H_2O(1)$ $H_3O^+\,(aq) + Cl^-\,(aq)$

Acid Base Acid Base

$NH_4 + (aq) + H_2O\,(1)$ $H_3O^+(aq) + NH_3\,(aq)$

Acid Base Acid Base

$H_2O\,(1) + NH_3\,(aq)$ $NH_4^+\,(aq) + OH^-\,(aq)$

Acid Base Acid Base

$H_2O(1) + CO_3^{2-}\,(aq)$ $HCO_3^-\,(aq) + OH^-\,(aq)$

Acid Base Acid Base

It may be noted that an acid after losing a proton becomes base where as a base after accepting the electron becomes an acid.

A base formed by the loss of proton by an acid is called *conjugate base* of the acid. An acid formed by the gain of proton by a base is called *conjugate acid* of the base. Acid-base pairs such as H_2O/OH^-, NH_4^+/NH_3 etc. are called *conjugate acid-base pairs.*

Those substances which can act both as an acid and a base are called *amphoteric substances.*

It is important to note that (i) all Arrhenius acids are Bransted acids but all Arrhenius bases are not Bransted bases, and (ii) Bransted-lower concept is not limited to molecules to act as acids and bases but ionic species may also be considered as acids or bases.

This concept serves well in protonic solvents like water, ammonia, acetic acid etc. but fails in case of some obvious acid-base reactions *e.g.* it can not explain how acidic oxides such as an hydrous carbon dioxide, sulpher dioxide, sulphur trioxide etc. neutralize basic-oxides like calcium oxide and barrium oxide even in the absence of solvent.

Lewis Concept : According to this concept an acid is a substance (molecule or ion) that can accept an electron pair to form a covalent bond and base is a substance that can supply an electron pair to form a covalent bond. Thus an acid is electron pair acceptor and a base is an electron pair donor. An acid need not contain hydrogen.

Lewis acids are of several types:

(i) Compounds having a central atom with incomplete octet.

(ii) Compounds containing multiple bonds.

(iii) Simple cations.

(iv) Compounds in which the octet of the central atom can be expanded.

The acids and bases according to this concept are interrelated by the equation

$$\underset{\text{Acid}}{HA} + \underset{\text{Base}}{H_2O} \rightarrow \underset{\text{Acid}}{H_3O^+} + \underset{\text{Base}}{A^-}$$

Classification of Acids : The acids can be classified as (i) Hydra acids and (ii) Oxy-acids

Hydra acids are those acids in which we find no oxygen, *e.g.* HC1, HBr, HI etc. They contain only two elements *i.e.* hydrogen and some non-metal.

Oxy-acids always contain oxygen as one of the elements. They contain hydrogen, oxygen and a third element. *e.g.* HNO_3, H_2SO_4, H_3PO_4, H_2CO_3 etc.

Relative Strengths of Acids and Bases : The relative strength of an acid and a base depends upon their relative capacity to liberate H^+ and OH^- ions in aqueous solution. The higher the $[H^+]$ in aqueous solution, the greater is the strength of the acid. Similarly greater the $[OH^-]$ is aqueous solution greater is the strength of base.

ALKALI AND BASE

As already discussed all those substances which give OH^- in aqueous solution are called bases. Out of these *only those bases which are soluble in water are called alkalies.*

Salts : Salts are the compounds formed by the neutralisation reaction between an acid and an alkali.

$$NaOH + HC1 \rightarrow Nacl + H_2O$$

alkali (base)	Acid	Salt	Water

NaCl is a neutral salt.

$$NaOH + H_2SO_4 \rightarrow NaHSO_4 + H_2O$$

Base	Acid	Salt	Water

$NaHSO_4$ is an acidic salt because in it hydrogen of the acid has been partly replaced.

CONCEPT OF OXIDATION AND REDUCTION

Oxidation might be defined as a chemical reaction. Wherein oxygen is gained or hydrogen is lost.

Reduction may be defined as a chemical reaction wherein oxygen is lost or hydrogen is gained.

For example when hydrogen is passed over heated Coptic oxide (CuO) the following reaction occurs.

$$CuO\ (s) + H_2\ (g) \rightarrow Cu\ (s) + H_2O(g)$$

CuO loses oxygen and so is reduced to Cu. Hydrogen gains oxygen and is oxidised to H_2O.

The hydrogen which is required to reduce CuO is called *reducing agent* and CuO which is required to oxidise H_2 is called *oxidising agent.*

Definition of oxidation and reduction in terms of electron loss or gain is more useful because all reactions do not involve oxygen and hydrogen. According to this concept.

Oxidation is a process which involves loss of one or more electrons by some atom or group of atoms. For example

$$Cu \rightarrow Cu^{2+} + 2\ e^-.$$

$$Zn \rightarrow Zn^{2+} + 2\ e^-.$$

$$Ag \rightarrow Ag^+ + e^-.$$

$$H \rightarrow H^+ + e^-.$$

The substance which loses electron is said to be oxidised and the one which gains electron is said to be reduced.

Reduction is a process which involves gain of one or more electrons by some atom or group of atoms. For example

$$Cu^{2+} + 2e^- \rightarrow Cu$$

$$H^+ + e^- \rightarrow H$$

$$Ag^+ + e^- \rightarrow Ag.$$

Oxidation and Reduction Occur Simultaneously : We have already studied the electronic concept of oxidation and reduction. If some substance loses electrons (*i.e.* undergoes oxidation) then the electrons lost by it must be accepted by some other sabstance. The substance that accepts electrons undergoes reduction. Hence it is clear that oxidation and reduction occur simultaneously. For example in the reaction.

$$Zn + Cu^{2+} \rightarrow Zn^{2+} + Cu \text{ (redox reaction)}$$

Zn is oxidised to Zn^{2+} and Cu^{2+} is reduced to Cu. The reactions involving simultaneously oxidation and reduction are called *redox-reactions.* A redox reaction can be split into two *half reactions* are representing oxidation and the other representing reduction. For example the above redox reaction may be represented as

$$Zn \rightarrow Zn^{2+} + 2e^- \text{ (oxidation half reaction)}$$

$$Cu^{2+} + 2e^- \rightarrow Cu \text{ (reduction half reaction)}$$

In such reactions the substance that loses electrons is called *reducing agent* and the substance that accepts electrons is called *oxidising agent.*

In a redox reaction the total number of electrons lost by reducing agent is equal to the total number of electrons accepted by the oxidising agent.

Oxidation State : The system of oxidation states (or oxidation numbers) has been devised to give a guide to the extent of oxidation or reduction in a species the system is without direct chemical foundations, but is extremely useful being appropriate to hope ionic and covalently bonded species.

The oxidation state can be defined simply as the number of electrons which must be added to a positive ion to get a neutral atom or removed from a negative ion to get a neutral atom *e.g.* Fe^{2+} (aq) has oxidation state of + 2 and Cl^- has oxidation state of –1.

For covalent species the oxidation state is found using the following rules:

(i) The oxidation state of all elements in uncombined state is taken as zero.

(ii) The algebraic sum of oxidation states of elements in a compound is always zero.

(iii) The algebraic sum of oxidation states of elements in an ion is equal to the charge on the ion.

(iv) The oxidation state of oxygen is – 2 (except in oxygen gas and peroxides).

(v) The oxidation state of hydrogen is +1 (except when combined with group I and II metals as hydrides).

ATOMIC STRUCTURE

John Dalton (1808) proposed that matter is composed of small indivisible particles called atoms.

Particles in an Atom : Atoms are composed *of protons, neutrons* and *electrons.* These are known as fundamental sub-atomic particles. The following table compares the properties of these particles.

Name of particle	*Mass*	*Charge*
Proton, p	1 amu	+ 1
Neutron, n	1 amu	0
Electron, e	negligible	–1

A neutral atom contains equal number of protons and electrons in it. This number of protons or electrons present in an atom is called its *atomic number* (Z).

The total number of neutrons and protons present in an atom gives the *mass number (A)* of the atom.

So

Atomic Number (Z) = Number of protons

= Number of electrons

and

Mass Number (A) = Number of protons + Number of

Neutrons = Number of Necleus

Rutherfords' Atomic Model : According to this model atom consists of two parts (i) nucleus and (ii) extra-nuclear part.

Nucleus. The protons and neutrons in each atom are tightly packed in a positively charged nucleus and the electrons move around the nucleus. Nucleus is a small positively charged part of atom and is situated at the centre and carries almost entire mass of atom. The diameter of nucleus is of the order of 10^{-12} – 10^{-13} cm which is only about 1/100,000 part of the diameter of an atom. In chemical reactions nucleus remains unchanged.

Extra-nuclear Space. This is the empty part of the atom. In this part electrons revolve at very high speed in fixed path called *orbits* or *shells*.

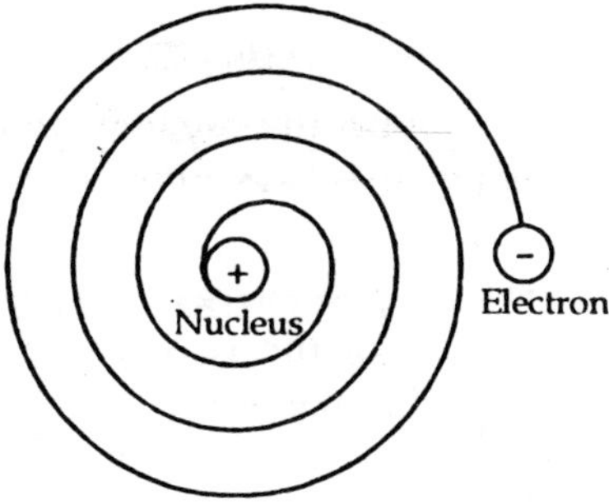

Fig. Gradual decrease in the radius of orbit.

Drawbacks of Rutherford's Model. Following serious objections against the Rutherford's model were reported:

(i) When an electron revolves around the nucleus, it will radiate out energy, resulting in the loss of energy. This loss of energy will make the lectron to move slowly and consequently it will be moving in a spiral path and ultimately falling inside the nucleus Fig. Thus, the atom remains unstable. Fortunately, the atom is stable.

(ii) If an electron loses energy continuously, the observed spectrum would be continuous and have broad bonds merging into one another. But most of the atoms give line spectra. Thus Rutherford's model could not explain the origin of spectral lines.

Bohr's Theory. In order to overcome the drawbacks of Rutherford's model and to account for the line spectra of hydrogen, Niel Bohr in 1913 put forward a theory called Bohr's theory. The main postulates of Bohr's theory are as follows:

(a) That within an atom an electron can move in certain specific orbits without radiating out energy. Such orbits were termed as stationary orbits. These orbits are numbered as 1, 2, 3, 4 etc., or K, L, M, N, etc., starting from the nucleus.

(b) The mathematical condition for stationary orbits is that the angular momentum of the moving electron is an integral multiple of $h/2\pi$, where h is the Planck's constant.

$$mvr = n\,(h/2\pi)$$

where mvr denotes the angular momentum and *n* is called principal quantum number and is equal to 1, 2, 3 ....

(c) When an electron gets energy, it will go to higher energy orbits. Similarly in the reverse process, the excited electron jumps down to lower energy level by emitting absorbed energy in the form of radiations of suitable wave length. The frequency of this radiations (v) is given by the difference in the energy between initial and final orbits.

$$E_1 - E_2 = hv$$

Simple representation of sodium atom on Bohr's model.

A sodium atom consists of 11 electrons ($^{23}Na_{11}$) and they are arranged as 2, 8, 1. It may be represented as

Electrons partly because of their very small size are impossible to locate at any particular time. It is however possible to locate a region or volume where the electron is most likely to be found. This region is called *Orbital.* Each orbital can hold a maximum of two electrons. Orbitals can be divided into *s⁻, p⁻, d⁻, f⁻* types. Each type of orbital has its own characteristic shape.

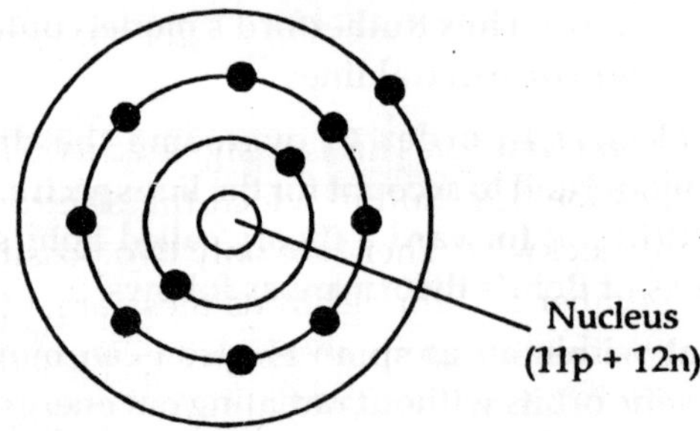

Fig. Simple representation of sodium atom

Quantum Number. The term quantum number is used to identify the various energy levels that are available to an electron in an atom.

Types of Quantum Numbers. Four quantum numbers are necessary to characterise completely any particular electron in a particular orbit. These are as follows:

Principal Quantum Number. This is designated as n and gives the number of principal shell in which the electron is revolving around the nucleus. It designates the average distance of the electron from the nucleus. Hence this quantum number represents the size of electron orbit.

Azimuthal or Subsidiary or Orbital Quantum Number. This is designated as l. This determines the orbital angular momentum and the shape of the orbital. l can have value ranging from 0 to n – 1, *i.e.,*

$$l = 0, 1, 2.... (n - 2), (n - 1)$$

The orbital with $l = 0$ is called s-orbital, that with $l = 1$, is called p-orbital, that one with $l = 2$ is called *p*-orbital and the one with $l = 3$ is called *f*-orbital.

Magnetic Quantum Number. This quantum number is designated as m. This quantum number determines the direction of the orbital relative to the magnetic field in which it is placed. m can have values from – l to + l through zero, *i.e.,*

$$m = + l, l - 1, l - 2 .... 0. - 1, - 2, ... - (l - 1), - l.$$

In other words, the number of m values for a given values of l is $2i + 1$ through zero.

Spin Quantum Number. This is designated as s. This quantum number indicates the direction in which the electron is spinning clockwise or anticlockwise. There are only two possible values for this quantum number and for electrons these are +1/2 and –1/2 according to the direction of spin being clockwise and anti-clock wise respectively.

Table : Electronic Configuration of the First 20 Elements

At. No.	*Element*	*Orbital Electronic Configuration*			
1.	Hydrogen	$1s^2$			
2.	Helium	$1s^2$			
3.	Lithium	$1s^2$	$2s^1$		
4.	Beryllium	$1s^2$	$2s^2$		
5.	Boron	$1s^2$	$2s^2\ p_x^{\ 1}$		
6.	Carbon	$1s^2$	$2_s^{\ 2}\ 2p_x^{\ 1}\ 2p_y^{\ 1}$		
7.	Nitrogen	$1s^2$	$2s^2\ 2p_x^{\ 1}\ 2p_y^{\ 1}\ 2p_z^{\ 1}$		
8.	Oxygen	$1s^2$	$2s^2\ 2p_x^{\ 2}\ 2p_y^{\ 1}\ 2p_z^{\ 1}$		
9.	Flourine	$1s^2$	$2s^2\ 2p_x^{\ 2}\ 2p_y^{\ 2}\ 2p_z^{\ 1}$		
10.	Neon	$1s^2$	$2s^2\ 2p_x^{\ 2}\ 2p_y^{\ 1}\ 2p_z^{\ 2}$		
11.	Sodium	$1s^2$	$2s^2\ 2p_x^{\ 2}\ 2p_y^{\ 2}\ 2p_z^{\ 2}$	$3s^1$	
12.	Magnesium	$1s^2$	$2s^2\ 2p_x^{\ 2}\ 2p_y^{\ 2}\ 2p_z^{\ 2}$	$3s^2$	
13.	Aluminium	$1s^2$	$2s^2\ 2p_x^{\ 2}\ 2p_y^{\ 2}\ 2p_z^{\ 2}$	$3s^2 3p_x^{\ 1}$	
14.	Silicon	$1s^2$	$2s^2\ 2p_x^{\ 2}\ 2p_y^{\ 2}\ 2p_z^{\ 2}$	$3s^2 3p_x^{\ 1} 3p_y^{\ 1}$	
15.	Phosphorous	$1s^2$	$2s^2\ 2p_x^{\ 2}\ 2p_y^{\ 2}\ 2p_z^{\ 2}$	$3s^2 3p_x^{\ 1} 3p_y^{\ 1} 3p_z^{\ 1}$	
16.	Sulphur	$1s^2$	$2s^2\ 2p_x^{\ 2}\ 2p_y^{\ 2}\ 2p_z^{\ 2}$	$3s^2 3p_x^{\ 2} 3p_y^{\ 1} 3p_z^{\ 1}$	
17.	Chlorine	$1s^2$	$2s^2\ 2p_x^{\ 2}\ 2p_y^{\ 2}\ 2p_z^{\ 2}$	$3s^2 3p_x^{\ 2} 3p_y^{\ 2} 3p_z^{\ 1}$	
18.	Argon	$1s^2$	$2s^2\ 2p_x^{\ 2}\ 2p_y^{\ 2}\ 2p_z^{\ 2}$	$3s^2 3p_x^{\ 2} 3p_y^{\ 2} 3p_z^{\ 2}$	
19.	Potassium	$1s^2$	$2s^2\ 2p_x^{\ 2}\ 2p_y^{\ 2}\ 2p_z^{\ 2}$	$3s^2 3p_x^{\ 2} 3p_y^{\ 2} 3p_z^{\ 2}$	$4s^1$
20.	Calcium	$1s^2$	$2s^2\ 2p_x^{\ 2}\ 2p_y^{\ 2}\ 2p_z^{\ 2}$	$3s^2 3p_x^{\ 2} 3p_y^{\ 2} 3p_z^{\ 2}$	$4s^2$

Pauli's Exclusion Principle. This is the most important principle which cannot be derived from any fundamental concept. Pauli's exclusion principle states that no two electrons in a single atom can have all their quantum numbers identical. By this principle it means that if two electrons possess the same value of n, l and m, they must have different values of s.

Hund's Rule of Maximum Multiplicity. This rule has a spectroscopic basis and is mainly concerned with the situation when two orbitals of a sub-group are incompletely filled. This rule can be stated as:

"When electrons enter a set of orbitals in a given shell, electrons will pair up, when all the available orbitals have one electron each". Hund's rule is energetically possible.

Aufbau's Principle. The word Aufbau is a German expression which means build up or construction. This Àufbau principle is mainly concerned with the building up process in which extra electrons are. being added to the various available orbitals so as to balance the nuclear charge. Broadly speaking, this principle states that every electron enters the lowest possible energy state available.

Isotopes. These are the atoms of the same element with same atomic number but different atomic mass (mass number) *e.g.* $^{12}_{6}C$ and $^{13}_{6}C$, $^{1}_{1}H$ and $^{2}_{1}H$.

Isobars. These are the atoms of different elements having different atomic numbers but same atomic mass (mass number) *e.g.* $^{210}_{32}Pb$ and $^{210}_{83}Bi$.

Isotones. These are the atoms having same number of neutrons but different mass numbers *e.g.* $^{30}_{14}Si$, $^{31}_{15}P$, $^{32}_{16}S$. All these have 16 neutrons in their nuclear.

12

PLANNING THE LESSONS

Though a syllabus is prescribed for each class yet the teacher is at liberty to draw up his own teaching syllabus. It is best to organise the teaching syllabus around a few broad areas of experience of pupils. For this purpose the syllabus is divided into a number of units.

UNIT PLANNING

A *unit* is a related learning segment made up of a few lessons along with an outline of its actual execution in the class room. Thus a unit will consist of both the subject matter and methodology of its delivery to students.

Hoover defines unit as, "The teaching unit is a group of related concepts from which a given set of instructional and educational experiences is desired. Unit normally range for three to six weeks long".

In view of Preston, a unit is a large chunk or a block of related subject matter as can be over viewed by the learner.

After having divided the prescribed syllabus into a number of teaching units the teachers will decide the time that could be allotted to each unit. After that he can break up each unit in a number of lessons and each lesson should be complete in itself. After this the teacher will enter in his diary the scheme of work under various headings.

Some of the advantages of unit planning are as under:

(i) It provides a basic course structure around which specific class activities can be organised.

(ii) It enables the teacher to integrate the basic course concepts and those of related areas into various teaching experiences.

(iii) It provides an opportunity to the teacher to keep a balance between various dimensions of the prescribed course.

(iv) It enables the teacher to break away from traditional textbook teaching.

Unit No..................................

Date	*Course content*	*Demonstration*	*Equipment material*	*Student's activities*	*Remarks/ References*

If the prescribed course has to be course has to be covered in a number of years then it is unwise to distribute the course in units spread over a number of years.

Unit Planning Proforma for Chemistry

Grade Level...

Unit Level...

Behavioural Objection......................................

(i) ....

(ii) ....

(iii) ....

Sr. No.	*Major concepts from the content*	*Number of periods and lessons*	*Teaching Method to be used*	*Teaching aids to be used*
1.				
2.				
3.				
4.				
5.				

LESSON PLANNING

A proper planning of the lessons is key to effective teaching. The teacher must know in advance the subject matter and mode of its delivery in the class room. This gives the teacher an idea of how to develop the key concepts and how to correlate them to real life situations and how to conclude the lesson. Lesson planning is also essential because effective learning takes place only if the subject matter is presented in an integrated and correlated manner and is related to the pupil's environment. Though lesson planning requires a hard work but it is rewarding too. L.B. Stands conceives a lesson as 'plan of action' implemented by the teacher in the class room. According to G.H. Green, "The teacher who has planned his lesson wisely related to his topic and to his class room without any anxiety, ready to embark with confidence upon a job he understands and prepared to carry it to a workmanable conclusion. He has foreseen the difficulties that are likely to arise, and prepared himself to deal with them. He knows the aims that his lesson is intended to fulfill, and he has marshalled his own resources for the purpose. And because he is free of anxiety, he will be able coolly to estimate the value of his work as the lesson proceeds, equally aware of failure and success and prepared to learn from both".

The Advantages : Some of the advantages of planning a lesson are as under:

(i) Lesson planning makes the work regular, organised and more systematic.

(ii) It induces confidence in the teacher.

(iii) It makes teacher quite conscious of the aim which makes him conscious of attitudes he wants to develop in his students.

(iv) It saves a lot of time.

(v) It helps in making correlation between the concepts with the pupils environment.

(vi) It stimulates the teacher to ask striking questions.

(vii) It provides more freedom in teaching.

Main Features : Some Important features of a good lesson plan are as under:

Objectives: All the congnitive objectives that are intended to be fulfilled should be listed in the lesson plan.

Content: The subject matter that is intended to be covered should be limited to prescribed time. The matter must be interesting and it should be related to pupil's previous knowledge. It should also be related to daily life situations.

Method(s): The most appropriate method be chosen by the teacher. The method chosen should be suitable to the subject matter to be taught. Suitable teaching aids must also be identified by the teacher. Teacher may also use supplementary aids to make his lesson more effective.

Evaluation: Teacher must evaluate his lesson to find the extent to which he has achieved the aim of his lesson. Evaluation can be done even by recapitulation of subject matter through suitable questions.

Formal steps in lesson planning are:

(i) Introduction (or preparation)

(ii) Presentation

(iii) Association (or Comparison)

(iv) Generalisation

(v) Application

(vi) Recapitulation

Introduction : It pertains to preparing and motivating children to the lesson content by linking it to the previous knowledge of the student, by arousing curiosity of the children and by making an appeal to their senses. This prepares the child's mind to receive new knowledge. This step though so important must be brief. It may involve testing of previous knowledge of the child. Some times the curiosity of pupil can be aroused by some experiment, chart, model, story or even by some useful discussion.

Presentation : It involves the stating of the object of lesson and exposure of students to new information. The actual lesson begins and both teacher and students participate. Teacher should make use of different teaching aids to make his lesson effective. Teacher should draw as much as is possible from the students making use of judicious questions. In chemistry lesson it is desirable that a heuristic atmosphere prevails in the class.

Association : It is always desirable that new ideas or knowledge be associated to the daily situations by citing suitable examples and by drawing comparisons with the related concepts. This step is all the more important when we are establishing principles or generalising definitions.

Generalisation : In chemistry lessons generally the learning material leads to certain generalisation leading to establishment of certain formulaes, principles or laws. An effort be made that the students draw the conclusions themselves. Teacher should guide the students only if their generalization is either incomplete or irrelevant.

Application : In this step of lesson plan the knowledge gained is applied to certain situations. This step is in confirmity with the general desire of the students to make use of generalisation in order to see for themselves if the generalisations are valid in certain situations or not? No lesson of chemistry may be considered complete if such rules, principles, formula etc. are not applied to life situations.

Recapitulation : In this last step of his lesson plan the teacher tries to ascertain whether his students have understood and grasped the subject matter or not. This is used for assessing the effectiveness of the lesson by asking students questions on the contents of the lesson. Recaptulation can also be done by giving a short objective type test to the class or even by asking the students to label some unlabelled sketch.

One most important point to remember is that the six steps given above for lesson planning should not try to follow these very rigidly. These are only guide lines and in many a lessons it is not possible to follow all these steps.

There is another way of lesson planning which is gaining currency these days. It is known as *Glover Plan.* This plan has four steps as follows:

Questioning. Teacher must introduce and develop his lesson through related and sequential questions. Start the lesson by asking questions about previous knowledge of the students. The questions should then lead to new knowledge under consideration.

Lesson can also be introduced with the help of some teaching aid like a picture, chart or model etc. the introduction can also to made by describing a situation or by telling a short story.

However teacher should hear in mind that the introduction is brief and interesting.

Discussion. For discussion the class be divided into smaller groups and in such groups students be encouraged to express their ideas and opinions freely. This helps the students in removal of their difficulties.

Investigation. The students are encouraged to do a project or investigation on the lesson topic either individually or in small groups by processing information or by laboratory work.

Expression. It concerns the strategy in which the student's and teacher's communication of ideas through observation and listening (passive expression) or through doing (active expression) or through fine and performing arts (artistic expression) or by arranging learning situations (organisational expression).

In developing a lesson a teachers must keep in mind the following psychological principles.

Principle of Selection and Division. The teacher should wisely select and divide the learning material into smaller segments. It is also for the teacher to decide about the quantum of subject matter to be covered by him and that which has to be illicited from the students.

Principle of Successive Clarity. It is for the teacher to see that the different learning segments of lesson are well structured, sequenced and connected. Teacher must ensure, at each segment, that students have grasped the subject matter given to them.

Principle of Integration. Teacher should conclude his lesson only after combining various learning segments to produce some generalisation.

DESIGN FOR WRITING A LESSON PLAN

Lecture-cum-Demonstration Method : The style given below is generally followed for writing a lesson plan.

Class: Date:

Subject: Duration:

Topic: of period:

Instructional Matrial ....

....

General Objectives ....

Specific (Objectives ....

....

Previous Knowledge. ....

....

Questions

1. ....?
2. ....?
3. ....?

Introduction

Questions

1. ....?
2. ....?

Announcement of Aim ....

....

Presentation

Matter	*Method*	*B.B.Summary*

Generalisations ....

....

Applications ....

....

Recapitulation ....

....

Questions

1. ....?
2. ....?
3. ....?

House Task ....

....

SPECIMEN LESSON PLAN

Class-X

Subject – Chemistry

Topic – Composition of Air

Date:

Duration: 40 minutes

Instructional Materials

1. Chalk board, duster, coloured chalks.
2. Trough, jar, match box, phosphorus etc.
3. Candle, glass tumbler, house hold plate, baby feeder etc.

General Objectives

1. To develop scientific attitude amongst the pupil.
2. To develop lower of observation and sense of enquiry amongst the pupil,
3. To develop reflective thinking in the pupils.

Specific Objective

To tell the students that air contains one part of oxygen and four parts of nitrogen by volume.

Previous Knowledge

It is presumed that students know that air contains oxygen and nitrogen. They also know that oxygen is a supporter of combustion and that a burning candle goes out in nitrogen.

Introduction

To introduce the lesson teacher will pick up a coin in his fist and will ask the following questions while taking away the coin,

1. What is in my fist? (A coin)
2. When the coin has been taken away? What is now in my hand? (Air)
3. It is possible for us to live without air? (No)
4. Name the gases present in Air? (Oxygen, Nitrogen and some CO2, inert gases etc.).
5. What is the proportion of oxygen and nitrogen in the air?

Presentation

	Matter	Method	Black-board Summary
1.	Yellow phosphorus in air at 307K.	Showing phosphorus, teacher asks what is this? Does phosphorus burn in air?	Yellow Phosphorus It is kept under water. It burns in air.
2.	Yellow phosphorus is kept in water.	What is yellow phosphorus stored water?	
3.	Yellow phosphorus burns in air.	What happens if a piece of yellow phosphorus is kept in air?	
4.	Fitting up the apparatus for the experiment as shown in fig.	What is this? What is this? What is this?	
5.	Phosphorus piece is allowed to burn by touching it with hot iron rod.	What happens? Why does phosphorus burn? What is this cloud like substance?	
6.	Water rises upto mark No. 1.	Why has water risen up in the bell jar?	
7.	Phosphorus pentoxide is soluble in water.	What does it signify? Where has phosphorus pentoxide gone?	
8.	No more oxygen is present in the bell-jar now.	Absence of oxygen in the bell-jar can be tested by taking in burning match stick inside the bell-jar.	Air contains one part of oxygen and four parts of nitrogen. It is soluble in water.

Announcement of Aim

On out receiving a proper reply to question 5 teacher will announce the aim "Today we will try to know about the proportion of oxygen and nitrogen in air".

Generalisation

From the above experiments we conclude that oxygen and nitrogen are present, in the ratio of 1 : 4 by volume, in air.

Recapitulation

Teacher will ask the following questions for recapitulation. Does phosphorus burn if exposed to air?

Home Task

Students will be asked to perform a similar experiment using a candle instead of phosphorus.

SOME SPECIMENS

Sodium and its Chief Compounds

Aim: To teach the physical and chemical properties of the metal sodium, and the names and common uses of some of its important salts.

Previous Knowledge: Students know the distinctive features of metals. They are also familiar with the names and know the common uses of washing soda, caustic soda and common salt.

1st Stage: Introduction. Following questions will be asked to test previous knowledge:

(i) Name the chief characteristics of metals.

(ii) Give some important properties that distinguish metals from non-metals?

(iii) Name an element which though lighter than water is yet a metal. Why do you suppose it to be a metal?

(iv) To what use do we put caustic soda, washing soda and common salt?

Teacher will then declare the aim: 'We shall learn more about the metal sodium and substances like caustic soda, washing soda, etc. today'.

2nd Stage: Some Properties of Sodium. Teacher will put a freshly cut piece of sodium on a filter paper and pass it round the class to show its metallic lustre; a student will be asked to cut another piece and its soft waxy nature will be brought home. Similarly its lightness and the effect of exposure to air will be shown and reasons for storing it under kerosene oil will be explained.

Blackboard. Sodium is a light, soft metal. When freshly cut it shows a metallic lustre. When exposed to air it soon gets tarnished. It floats on water and soon disappears, so it is kept under kerosene oil.

3rd Stage: Action of Sodium on Water. Experiment, to show that hydrogen is given out when sodium react with water, and that an alkali is also formed which turns red litmus solution blue, will be shown. A glass tubing of slightly wide bore will be supported in a beaker containing red litmus solution. One or two small pieces of sodium will be dropped inside the tube. The gas coming out of the tube will be ignited with a match. The litmus solution inside the tube will be seen to have turned blue.

Blackboard. When a piece of sodium is thrown into water it swims around with a hissing sound, reacts with water, giving hydrogen and forming an alkali which turns red litmus blue.

4th Stage: Some Common Compounds of Sodium and their Uses. Samples of common salt, caustic soda, washing soda, and sodium bicarbonate will be shown, and the class will be told that all of them are compounds of metal sodium. Students will be asked some of the uses of these salts and other uses will be told to them. Their chemical names will also be given to the students.

Blackboard

(i) Common salt—sodium chloride is used for (a) eating, (b) curing hides and fish, (c) preservative in achars and other things (d) in the making of washing soda and caustic soda, and preparation of hydrochloric acid.

(ii) Washing soda—sodium carbonate is used for (a) washing, (b) softening hard water and (c) making caustic soda.

(iii) Sodium bicarbonate is used in (a) medicine and (b) baking powders.

(iv) Caustic soda—sodium hydroxide is used in making soap and paper.

5th Stage: Recapitulation.

(i) Why is sodium not stored under water or in an empty bottle?

(ii) Give some physical and chemical properties of sodium.

(iii) List the uses of common salt, soda and caustic soda.

Blackboard Summary. Main properties, uses etc. as above will form B.B. Summary.

Preparation and Study of the Chief Properties of Carbon Dioxide Gas in the Laboratory

Aim: To get pupils to fit up the apparatus for the preparation of carbon dioxide in the laboratory, prepare the gas and study its chief physical and chemical properties.

Previous Knowledge: The preparation and properties of the gas has been demonstrated in demonstration period.

Procedure: The students will be asked the following questions:

(i) How was carbon dioxide prepared in the laboratory?

(ii) Was it heavier or lighter than air?

(iii) Was it soluble in water?

(iv) How can you collect the gas?

A sketch of the apparatus will be drawn on the blackboard and teacher will ask them to fit the apparatus accordingly.

The following precautions will also be emphasized:

(i) The apparatus should be tested to be air-tight.

(ii) The thistle funnel should dip in the liquid.

(iii) Water should be just enough to cover the pieces of marble.

(These will be written on blackboard)

The boys will then be asked to fit up the apparatus. The teacher will go round giving individual help. While the boys are busy collecting the gas, he will put down on the blackboard a list of experiments to be performed and properties to be tested by the boys as given below:

(i) Colour and smell.

(ii) Action on litmus solution.

(iii) Heaviness.

(iv) Action on a burning taper.

(v) Action on lime water for a short-time and for a long-time.

He will ask them to record their work in the following tabular form:

Experiment	*Observation*	*Inference*

When the boys are busy performing the experiments to study the properties of gas, the teacher will go round, give individual help and tick off portions of written work examined.

At the end of the period he will sign the notebooks and supervise the return of clean apparatus to the cupboards.

Note: In the specimens of lesson notes given above, the apparatus required has not been shown. Pupil teachers should always give in their notes the list of apparatus required. This list may be put below the aim, under the heading 'apparatus'.

13

TEACHING DEVICES

The teaching aids are required by a chemistry teacher, like teachers of other subjects, for effective teaching of subject and to realise various objectives of teaching chemistry. Teaching aids help the teacher to communicate with his students in more desirable and effective way. Some barriers of communication can be overcome by using special aids appealing to the senses of the receiver alongwith managing the communication along certain principles. Class room instructions or teaching a curriculum transaction is also a special kind of communication and it is helpful in achieving the instructional goals of a course of study. Effective communication requires a mastery of managerial skills of handling various teaching aids like audio-visual aids, visual aids, audio aids, activity aids etc.

THE CLASSIFICATION

Teaching aids are classified, for convenience of study, into the following categories:

(i) Audio aids (ii) Visual aids (iii) Audio-visual aids (iv) Activity aids.

Examples of various types of teaching aids generally used to make class room teaching of chemistry more effective are given below:

Audio Aids : In this type of aids fall the teaching aids like radio, tape recorder etc. This type of aids help the process of learning as they help the learner to acquire knowledge through his auditory senses.

Visual Aids : This type of aids are very common *e.g.* charts, pictures, models, film strips etc. These aids the learner to acquire the learning experiences through his visual senses.

Audio-visual Aids : These are sensory aids which help to make teaching concrete, effective and interesting. Examples of this type of aids are television, motion picture, video films, living objects etc. By use of these aids we provide the learner an opportunity to utilise both his auditory and visual senses for gaining the desired learning experiences.

Activity Aids : In this type of aids we include all those teaching aids in which the learner is required to be engaged in some useful activity, *e.g.*

(a) Excusions and visits.

(b) Exhibitions and fairs.

(c) Experimentation in the laboratory and work-shop.

THE IMPORTANCE

Teaching aids make the teaching-learning process interesting and more meaningful as we are required to make use of our senses. While commenting on the desirability of making use of ones senses the Indian Education Commission has remarked, "for acquiring right and proper knowledge and experiences regarding the objects and processes must be gained through one's senses".

The importance of teaching aids can be summarised as under:

(i) Teacher can win the interest and attention of the pupils by making use of teaching aids.

(ii) They are effective motivating agents.

(iii) **They help to bring clarity to the subject matter.**

(iv) **They same time and energy of the students and teachers and make learning more effective and durable. A fact, principle or phenomenon that cannot be understood properly with verbal explanation or experience can be easily comprehended by use of teaching aids. In this way the time and energy of both the students and teacher is saved.**

(v) Proper use of teaching aids helps to develop in the pupils scientific attitudes and provide them with a training in scientific method.

(vi) They provide the pupils with the first hand experience by looking at concrete things and actual demonstrations.

(vii) They provide a solution to a number of educational and administrative problems.

(viii) They provide permanent and effective learning.

The importance of teaching aids can be summarised as under in the words of Edgar Dale—"Because audio-visual materials supply of concrete basis for conceptual thinking, they give rise to meaningful concepts—the words enriched by meaningful associations. Hence they offer the best anti-dote available for disease of verbalism".

SELECTION PROCESS

Following principles be kept in mind while making a selection of teaching aids for use in teaching a particular topic:

(i) The aid should have a relevance to the topic to be taught.

(ii) The aid must be such so as to suit the topic and helps to make the study of the topic interesting.

(iii) Any teaching aid used should not only be interesting and motivating but it also have some specific educational value.

(iv) The aid to be used should be a beat possible substitute in terms of reality, accuracy and truthful representation of object or the first hand experiences.

(v) The ad should be simple.

(vi) The aid should suit the physical, social and cultural environment of the pupils.

(vii) The teaching aid be easily available.

(viii) The teaching aid must help in proper realization of stipulated learning or instructional objectives of topics in hand.

EFFECTIVE USE

Teaching aids should be used properly to make teaching more effective. Teaching can because more effective if such aids are used widely but the use of such aids cannot provide a guarantee of good teaching. Following points are important for a proper use of teaching aids:

(i) Teaching aids should be woven with class-room teaching and these aids should be used only to supplement the oral and written work being done in the class.

(ii) While making use of any teaching aid an effort be made that the teaching aids being used in any class are in confirmity with the intellectual level of the students and is in accordance with the previous experience of the students.

(iii) Only such aids the preferred which provide a stimulus to the students for greater thinking and activity.

(iv) If possible actual specimens be preferred to a photograph or a slide of a specimen.

(v) The teaching aid used should be exact, accurate and real as far as practicable.

(vi) The Teacher should use a teaching aid only when he is quite sure about handling a specific teaching aid. For handling some aids (*e.g.* operating a projector etc.) training is provided by various authorities. For this purpose more information can be obtained from local SCERT or directly from NCERT, New Delhi.

(vii) Teaching aids used be such as are closely related to pupils experiences.

(viii) The teacher should use a teaching aid only after a proper planning so that the aid is used exactly at the point; in the process of teaching, where it best fits in the process of teaching.

(ix) Teacher should see that a follow up programme follows the lesson wherein a teaching aid has been used.

(x) Teacher should carry out occasional evaluation about the use, function and effect of a teaching aid on the learning process.

VARIOUS TYPES

For convenience of discussion the teaching aids may be grouped as under:

(i) Visual aids

(ii) Aural aids

(iii) Audio-visual aids

(iv) Activity aids and

(v) Memory aids

VISUAL AIDS

Under this head we will take of following types of teaching aids:

(a) Displayboards such as Chalkboards or Blackboards, Flannelboards, Bulletinboards, Magneticboards etc.

(b) Charts, pictures and models.

Visual aids are those which can be appreciated and understood by seeing them only.

Displayboards. It is any flat surface that can be used to white information to be communicated. At present for this purpose the use is made of *blackboard* or *chalkboard, bulletinboard, flannelboard, magnetic-board* etc.

Though material for display on such a board can be collected from any source even from a text book but for being effective the material should be displayed in such a way that it is eye catching, colourful and purposeful.

Blackboard or Chalkboard. It is one of the most common visual aids in use. It is a slightly abrasive writing surface made of wood, ply, hardboard, cement, ground glass asbestos, state, plastic etc. with black, green or bluish green paint on it. Details of various types of chalkboards and their arrangement for a science laboratory have been given in the lessons dealing with these topics. A chalkboard is generally installed facing the class which is either built into the wall or fixed and framed on the wall and provided with a ledge to keep the chalk sticks and duster. Portable chalkboards are also available these days. Such chalk boards can be placed on a stand with adjustable height. Generally white chalk sticks are used for writing on the blackboard or chalkboard but some times coloured chalk sticks are also used. The coloured chalk sticks are used for better illustration.

Characteristics of a Good Chalkboard. Some of the characteristics of a good chalkboard are as follows:

(i) Its surface should be rough enough so that it is capable of holding the writing on the board.

(ii) Its surface should be dull so that it can eliminate glare.

(iii) Its surface should be such that the writing on the board can be easily removed by making use of a cloth or a foam duster.

(iv) Its height should be so adjusted that it is within the easy reach of the teacher and is easily visible to the students.

Effective Use of Chalkboard. We find that chalkboard is the most common teaching aid used by the teacher for writing important points, drawing illustrations, solving problems etc. The chemistry teacher should keep the following points in mind to use the chalkboard effectively.

(i) Write in a clear and legible handwriting the important points on the chalkboard but avoid over crowding of information on the chalkboard.

(ii) The size of the words written on blackboard should be such that they can be seen even by the back-benchers. The letters should not be less than one inch in height. The recommended height of letters on a chalkboard in between 6 cm to 8 cm. For this the teacher should frequently inspect his own chalkboard writing from the view point of the back-bench on a corner seat.

(iii) There should be proper arrangement of light in the class room so that the chalkboard remains glare free.

(iv) To emphasise some points or parts of a sketch or a diagram coloured chalks be used.

(v) Rub off the information already discussed in the class and noted down by the students.

(vi) Draw a difficult illustration before hand to save the class time.

(vii) Stand on one side of the chalkboard while explaining some points to the students.

(viii) Make use of a pointer for drawing attention to the written material on the chalkboard.

(ix) Students may be allowed to express their ideas on chalkboard, or to make alterations or corrections. Some times teacher may intentionally draw some incorrect diagram and ask the students to make necessary correction, alteration etc.

(x) For maintenance of proper discipline in the class the teacher should always keep an eye on his class while writing on the blackboard.

(xi) For proper writing on chalkboard the chalk stick be broken into two pieces and the broken end of the piece be used to start writing.

(xii) While writing on a chalkboard keep your fingers and wrist stiff and move your arm freely.

Advantages of Chalkboard. Some of the advantages of chalkboard over other visual aids are as follows:

(i) It is a very convenient teaching aid for group teaching.

(ii) It is quite economical and can be used again and again.

(iii) Its use is accompanied by the appropriate actions on the part of the teacher. The illustrations drawn on the blackboard captures students attention.

(iv) It is one of the most valuable supplementary teaching aid.

(v) It can be used as a good visual aid for drill and revision.

(vi) These boards cart be used for drawing enlarged illustrations from the text books.

(vii) It is a convenient aid for giving lesson notes to the students.

Limitations of the Chalkboard. Some of the important limitations of a chalkboard are as under:

(i) The use of chalkboard makes students very much dependent on the teacher.

(ii) It makes the lesson teacher paced.

(iii) It makes the lesson dull and of routine nature.

(iv) It gives no attention to the individual needs of the students.

(v) Due to constant use chalkboards become smooth and start glaring.

(vi) While using chalk-sticks to write on chalkboard the teacher spreads a lot of chalk powder which is inhaled by teacher and students and it may affect their health.

Bulletinboards. It is a display board on which learning material on some scientific topic is displayed. It is generally of the size of a blackboard but some times even bigger depending on the wall space available. It is generally in the form of a framed softboard or strawboard or corkboard or rubber sheets. Such bulletin boards can be specified for individual branches of chemistry or even for some specified chemistry topics *e.g.* chemistry puzzles, chemistry news, chemistry cartoons etc. such a board can also be used for displaying the best work of students. However for a all purpose bulletinboard the following type of display material in recommended:

(i) Interesting science news.

(ii) Book Jackets of recently published chemistry books.

(iii) Brochures.

(iv) Cartoons.

(v) Poems.

(vi) Sketches.

(vii) Pictures.

(viii) Photographs.

(ix) Thoughts.

(x) Announcements etc.

An effort be made to change the material on bulletinboard as frequently as in practicable. Whenever the teacher starts a new topic he may ask the students to display the concerned material on the bulletinboard and the teacher should specifically mention to the students the display material on the bulletinboard while teaching a topic to the class. Students be asked to take the charge of bulletinboard by rotation'.

How to Use a Bulletinboard. To make use of bulletinboard as a useful teaching aid the bulletin board be used for creating interest amongst students an specific topics. For effective use of bulletinboard as a teaching aid following points be kept in mind:

(i) Effort be made jointly by the teacher and the students to procure material from various sources on a given subject or topic.

(ii) Before displaying the material on the board sort out the material relevant to a specific subject or topic.

(iii) Make best use of your aesthetic sense to display the material on the bulletinboard.

(iv) Do fix a title for the specific subject/topic of display material on the top.centre of the bulletinboard.

(v) It is desirable if a brief description about the specific subject or topic is fixed below to title.

(vi) The height of bulletinboard from ground level be about 1 m.

(vii) The bulletin board be fixed in an area where enough lighting can be provided.

(viii) The material displayed should be large enough and should be provided with suitable headings.

(ix) Over crowding of material on bulletinboard be avoided.

Advantages of Bulletinboards. Some of the advantages of bulletinboard as a teaching aid are as follows:

(i) It is a good supplement to class room teaching.

(ii) It helps in arousing the interest of students in a specific subject/topic.

(iii) It can be effectively used as a follow up of chalkboard.

(iv) Such boards add colour and liveliness and thus also have decorative value in addition to their educational value.

(v) Such boards can be conveniently used for introducing a topic and for its review as well.

Limitations of Bulletinboard. Some limitations in the use of bulletinboards as teaching aids are as follows:

(i) They cannot be used for all inclusive teaching.

(ii) They can be used only as supplementary aids to some other teaching aid.

(iii) At times it becomes very difficult to make proper selection of the display material for certain topic.

Flannelboard. It is also some times referred to as *flannel graph* or *felt board*. It is made of wood, cardboard or strawboard covered with coloured flannel or woolen cloth. It is one of the latest devices effectively used for science teaching. Display materials like cut-outs, pictures, drawings and light objects backed with rough surfaces like sand paper strips, flannel strips etc. will stick to flannel-board temporarily.

For display purposes a flannelboard of 1.5 × 1.5 m is generally used. It can be fixed next to the blackboard or can be placed on a stand about one metre above the ground.

How to use a Flannelboard. Following points be kept in mind for effective use of flannel board as a teaching aid:

(i) The teacher should collect a large number of pictures or wall cut diagrams etc. and back them with sand paper pieces. He may then make use of these by displaying there on the board one by one, after proper selection.

(ii) Display the material on the flannel board in a sequence to develop the lesson.

(iii) Make proper use of flannel board for creating proper scenes and designs relevant to the lesson.

(iv) Change the display material on the board as frequently as required.

(v) Flannel board can be used quite effectively for showing relationship between different parts or steps of a process.

Advantages of Flannelboard. Some of the advantages of using flannelboard as a teaching aid are as follows:

(i) It is quite economical and easy to handle and operate.

(ii) The pictures or cuttings can be easily fixed and removed when required, without spoiling the material. Thus same material can be used for display many a times.

(iii) Any display material on the board holds the interest of students and arrests their attention.

(iv) Such boards enable a teacher to talk along with changing illustrations to develop a lesson.

Magnetic Chalkboard. It is a framed iron sheet having porcelain coating in black or green colour. Such a board can be used either to write with chalk sticks, glass marking pencils and crayons or to display pictures, cut-outs and light objects with disc magnets or magnetic holders.

Thus such a board functions both as a chalkboard and as a flannelboard. We can display visual learning material on such a board while writing key points on it. Such a board provides the flexibility of movement of visual material. It is possible to display even a three dimensional object on such a board using magnetic holders.

Since the magnetic chalk-board functions both as a chalkboard and as a flannelboard so various points discussed for the effective use of these boards be kept in mind while using magnetic chalkboard as an effective teaching aid.

Advantages of Magnetic Chalkboard. Some of the advantages of magnetic chalkboard are as follows:

(i) It is a versatile teaching aid that combines the advantages of both a chalkboard and a flannelboard.

(ii) It is possible to move visual material by sliding it along the surface of the board such a movement is not possible on a flannelboard.

(iii) It is very light and can be easily taken from one place to another.

(iv) Such a board can be easily got prepared in the school from an iron sheet and painting with some good paint.

Charts, Pictures and Models. Charts, pictures and models also are an important teaching aids.

Charts. Some times charts are needed by the teacher to supplement his actual teaching. There are certain charts where in the interior of some thing is depicted *e.g.* various systems of human body, internal combustion engine, motor car etc.

Following points be kept in view while using charts as teaching aids:

(i) An effort be made to use charts prepared by students under the guidance of the teacher, however some charts may be purchased.

(ii) Duly such charts be purchased which have bold lines and in which such colours are used as could be seen and distinguished even by the back-benchers.

(iii) Charts should give only the essential details.

(iv) Charts should be properly and clearly labelled in block letters.

Sources for Procurement of Charts

(i) Charts can be prepared by students and teacher.

(ii) Charts can be purchased.

(iii) Charts can be procured on a very normal cost from the following sources:

(a) Ministry of Education, Govt. of India, Delhi.

(b) NCERT, New Delhi.

(c) Director, Extension Service of College of Education in the State.

(d) SCERT of the state.

(e) District Public Relation Officer.

Advantages of Charts

(i) They can be made quickly.

(ii) They have a better appeal.

(iii) Only bare essentials can be shown in the chart and unnecessary details can be avoided.

(iv) Charts are available from various sources.

Pictures. Pictures of gas-works, steamships, and locomotives and portraits of great men of chemistry—chemists will be of great help in teaching of chemistry provided a reference in made to them. Portraits of great scientists if displayed in chemistry room give it the proper scientific atmosphere. These pictures, portraits etc. can be used as teaching aids and they are quite useful in a demonstration lesson. Everything a child learns can be presented graphically with the aid of pictures and brightly coloured diagrams which will excite his interest.

Following points be given due consideration while using pictures as teaching aids:

(i) Pictures should be bold, direct and sufficiently large.

(ii) Pictures should not be over loaded with information rather they should stick to the maxim, *one picture, one idea.*

Models. In teaching of science models are very frequently used. Various costly models are available and some of these may be available and in school laboratory. However the cost of such models should not be any hindrance to the use of models as teaching aid because a science teacher can prepare almost all types of models by making use of ingenuity. It is also possible to take some very costly models on loan or such models can even be hired. Models are very helpful in making the subject clear to the students and they also give the student an idea of the actual shape/size etc. of the article under discussion.

In using charts, pictures and models as teaching aids the teacher should be careful to plan their proper display. These should be displayed in such a way and at such a height that each student can have a detailed view of it.

Following is the list of some firms from whom scientific charts and models can be procured:

1. M/s Scientific Instruments Stores, J-355, New Rajinder Nagar, New Delhi.
2. M/s Educational Aids and Charts, 20, I Block, Kumara Park, West Extension, Bangalore-20.
3. M/s Variety Teaching Aids, Bagalkot, Distt. Bijapur.
4. M/s Educational Emporium, 15-A, Chittranjan Avenue, Calcutta-7.
5. M/s Oxford University Press, Apnollo Bunder, Bombay.
6. M/s School Aids Manufacturing Co., 12-Gun Boat Street, Fort, Bombay-1.
7. The Director, Survey of India, Hathi Barkala Road, Dehradun (UP).
8. M/s Hobby Centre, Mount Road, Madras-2.

AURAL AIDS

In this type the following aids are considered:

(i) Broadcast talks,

(ii) Gramophone lectures, and

(iii) Tape recordings.

Broadcast Talks. All India Radio has in its regular feature some programmes meant for school children. In such a programme generally talks on educational matters or on scientific topics are broadcasted. Such a talk in quite useful for students as also for chemistry teacher. The topic, date and time of broadcast of such talks are given an advance by All India Radio. A school can take benefit of such talks only if it possesses a good radio set and a period is provided in the school time-table for listening such talks. Such an arrangement can be worked out by the school authorities and then teacher can refer to such talks while teaching his class. It is also possible to synchronise the broad cast talk an some topic with the actual teaching of that topic in a class.

Some handicaps of such broadcast task are listed here:

(i) Sometimes when the receiving set is not working satisfactorily there prevails a sense of strain in the class room.

(ii) Some students are poor listeners and may not be benefited by such talks although they benefit by normal teaching through questions, demonstrations and reading.

For the maximum utility of such talks following points be kept in view:

(i) The students with bad hearing be seated on front seats.

(ii) To keep students interest alive in such talks teacher should tell his students in advance a few questions which they have to answer after the talk.

(iii) Only short duration talks be arranged.

Such talks cannot be a substitute to the actual teaching and such a talk is only to help in teaching.

Gramophone Lectures and Tape Recordings. Another teaching aid available to a science teacher is records of short talks an interesting scientific topics by eminent scientists, doctors etc. Magnetic tapes of such recorded talks are now available and the talk can be easily reproduced in the class room. These talks provide an inspiration to the students and such a talk once recorded can be used again and again. Such recording can either be used to introduce a topic or to develop a topic.

AUDIO-VISUAL AIDS

In this category those teaching aids are included which involve the use of two of our senses *i.e.* hearing and seeing. These are classified as (i) optical aids and (ii) Television.

Need for A.V. in Teaching

Audio-visual aids are very important in teaching of chemistry because of the following reasons:

(i) Sensory experience is the foundation of intellectual activity. Verbal symbol, which is meaningless becomes meaningful when it is associated with visual symbols. For example meaning of precipitate is understood only when it is seen in test-tube.

(ii) A.V. aids are needed to stress facts and concepts in chemistry teaching.

(iii) Mental growth is the outcome of two antithetical processes i.e. differentiation and integration. Differentiation develops out of integration. Audio-visual aids are more useful in process of differentiation.

(iv) Generalisation attains a meaning and it becomes concrete experience only with the help of A. V. Aids.

(v) A. V. aids also help in increasing the vocabulary of pupils.

OPTICAL AIDS

Some such aids are discussed here. *Magic Lantern (or Glass slide projector).*

Psychologists have now confirmed that a child grasps abstract facts slowly and can only remember a name which recalls some definite reality. Thus he should be confronted with visual teaching aids to broaden his experience.

A *magic lantern* is a simple device used to project pictures from a glass slide on a screen or wall. Teacher can make use of this device when he intends to show some small figure or illustration to whole class. Many a schools have a *magic lantern* in their laboratories as it is not very costly slides are readily available in the market on various chemistry topics. These can also be got prepared on demand and the cost of such a slide is quite reasonable. Such slides can even be prepared by science teacher himself after some practical training which can be provided by extension service department of training colleges. colleges. Epidiascope

Epidiascope is a more costly instrument but it can project opaque objects as well as transparent objects. The pictures projected by epidiascope are much brighten and need, a less powerful light so that room need not be absolutely dark. Epidiascope can be used to project any picture, map, diagram, photograph or small object. No slide is needed for projection with an epidiascope.

The name *epidiascope* is given to this machine because of the tact that it works, as an *episcope* when it is used to know the image of an opaque object. This machine can be used to project slides and this is possible just by moving a lower provided for the purpose. When it is used to project a slide then at serves as a *diascope*. Thus *epidiascope* is a combination of these two *i.e. episcope* and *diascope*.

Advantages of Epidiascope. In comparison to other projection machines *epidiascope* has some advantages. Some of these are as follows:

(i) It can be operated in a room which may not be absolutely dark.

(ii) With the help of this machine original colours of the picture or photograph can be projected.

(iii) The projection on the screen can be kept for some time during which teacher can explain and discuss it in the class.

(iv) It provides teacher an option to handle the lesson according to himself.

Following points provide useful hints for the proper handling of an epidiascope:

(i) The apparatus works well in a dark room.

(ii) While projecting with an epidiascope an effort be made to keep exposed to the head of the lamp for minimum time delicate pictures, photographs or other such objects.

(iii) The person handling the apparatus must be given some practical training before he is allowed to handle the machine.

Film Projector, Micro-Projector, Film-Strip Projector

There are further improvements on the teaching aids discussed so far. These have brought about a revolution in teaching of science. Science films are shown to the students to illustrate various applications and uses of science as also to supplement the class room teaching. Both type of films have some basic objectives to serve.

Film Strip-Projector

It is an improvement on magic lantern and this machine can be used to project many a topics on a single strip. One such strip generally consists of 40-100 separate pictures and such film strips are available on loan from Central Film Library, NCERT, New Delhi. On such a film strip pictures concerning one topic are arranged in a definite order.

This machine can be easily handled by the chemistry teacher. The machine is operated by hand and thus can be stopped at the discretion of the teacher whenever he wants to explain some aspect of a topic being shown on machine.

Micro-Projector

This is less commonly used in chemistry teaching. This projector is generally operated in a dark room. The projection can be taken on vertical screen if whole class is expected to see it. However such a film cannot be distinctly seen by a student if he is sitting at a distance more than 12 feet from the screen.

Film Projector

This machine is used for showing chemistry films. Some good science films on various topics are available and there can be had an loan some times even free of charge from the source, given below:

(i) Central Film Library, NCERT, New Delhi.

(ii) U.S. Information Service, New Delhi.

(iii) British High Commission Office, New Delhi.

(iv) Some Other Embassies, New Delhi.

For projecting this films in school generally 16 mm projector ('RCA', 'Bell and Havell') are used. These 16 mm projectors are less costly and easier to transport as compared to a 35 mm projector.

Advantages of Motion Pictures. There are some definite advantages of motion pictures to be used as teaching aids, some of these are as follows:

(i) They draw attention of the students.

(ii) They help to bring past to the class-room.

(iii) It is possible to reduce or enlarge the size of the object by using the machine.

(iv) They can be used to show a process which a naked human eye cannot see without its aid.

(v) They can be used to show a record of an event.

(vi) They can serve a large class at a time.

(vii) They provide a good aesthetic experience.

(viii) They help in understanding relationship between things, ideas and events.

Precautions. The teacher should take the following precautions whenever he wants to use a film projection as a teaching aid:

(i) He should satisfy himself about the lighting management and seating arrangement in the room where such a film show is to be given.

(ii) He should himself see the film before hand.

(iii) He should give a complete background of the film to the students before the actual screening of the film.

(iv) He should see that complete calm and peace is maintained during the screening of the film.

(v) Immediately after the film show, he should invite comments, questions etc. from the students and try to answer all the quarries of the students.

(vi) He should encourage some of his students to write articles etc. based on the film show and such articles etc., may be shown on well magazine, may be printed in school magazine.

Television : The role of television in the present day world is becoming more and more important and it is one of the most important teaching aids. It combines the advantages of a radio (broadcast) and of a film. This can be used for mass education and now U.G.C. programmes are a regular feature on "Door Darshan". The topics of discussion are announced in advance and lesson from well qualified reasons and specialists in their fields are shown on TV. Teacher can easily plan his work accordingly and in this way he can make use of TV as a teaching aid.

Limitations : The use of A.V. aids in teaching of chemistry has the following limitations:

(i) The use of A.V. aids is not a guarantee of successful teaching.

(ii) A.V. aids are not a clear substitute for oral or written methods of gaining knowledge.

(iii) Visual instructions are sometimes confused with entertainment.

(iv) Visual aids vary in their effectiveness in direct proportion of their degree of reality.

14

AUDIO-VISUAL AIDS

In an introductory class of audio-visual education from B.Ed. students it was asked some of their earliest school experiences. Following were some of their answers:

(i) "The earliest school experience was when I made things out of plasticine."

(ii) "When in class 3rd we made a model of iglu out of sugar cubes."

(iii) "When I went to see a zoo in my 2nd grade."

(iv) "When we did gardening in a small comer of the school."

(v) "When I played the role of little red riding hood in kindergarten."

(vi) "The puppet show I saw in the school."

Dozens of similar experiences were reported by these (college) students. All these are varied experiences but we see one similarity, they could remember the experiences where they are involved in doing something, when they were active, when more senses were involved. These are some of the experiences where effort was not made to memorise them, on the other hand we do not always remember the facts or concepts that we try hard to memorise. From this we can generalise that learning becomes comparatively permanent when concreteness is there in the experiences. The various experiences help in developing concepts.

The process of building concepts operates naturally from the time a child begins to draw certain conclusions from his experiences and applies these conclusions to new situations. It continues thereafter as he makes new generalisations from new experiences and experiences in which new and old experiences are combined. The overall activity of building concepts, therefore is a realistic definition of Education. Now we can say that two elements are involved in building concepts: (1) Certain amount of concrete experiences, and (2) Combining and recombining these concrete experiences in many ways. When we apply this to classroom teaching, audio-visual aids play a very important role in concept formation and therefore in permanent learning.

THE SIGNIFICANCE

If we see teaching of science in schools of our country by and large we will find teachers lecturing or even reading out from the books and explaining few things on the blackboard. Some teachers use some demonstrations, charts and models but not very frequently and many a times students memorise things without understanding. Audio-visual aids if properly used help in teaching learning process in many ways (as given below) and can ensure quick and effective learning.

(i) The timely use of proper aids compels attention, develops interest and motivates students.

(ii) They break the monotony of teacher's talk, reduce verbalism, save time (of long verbal explanations) and give a better idea of the real things.

(iii) Audio-visual aids can make learning experiences far more concrete; therefore clarification of concepts, better understanding and long lasting learning are possible.

(iv) Great many teaching problems can be solved partly or wholly by the proper use of rich experiences (through audio-visual aids); therefore they offer great opportunities for improved learning.

The Kinds

Variety of audio-visual aids can be used in science teaching. They can be classified in various ways.

(a) One way of grouping them is as follows:

Visual Aids—charts, photographs, diagrams, static and working models, etc.

Auditory Aids—radio, recordings on tapes, and cassettes.

Audio-visual Aids—films, T.V. etc.

(b) Another way of classifying can be:

Graphic Aids—diagrams, photographs, charts, play cards.

Three-Dimensional Aids—models, specimens, real objects, apparatus, dioramas etc.

Projected Aids—slides, films, etc.

Aids Through Activity—excursions, projects setting and maintenance of aquarium, vivarium, botanical garden etc.

VARIOUS EXPERIENCES

Some of these aids are more concrete in nature and some of them are comparatively more abstract. Edger Dale has arranged the various audio-visual aids in pictorial form which he called "Cone of Experiences" as shown in (Fig.).

This is a kind of visual aid to visualise and explain the inter-relationship of various types of audio-visual material as well as their position in learning process.

At the top of the Cone are verbal symbols which are most abstract and at the base are the direct purposeful experiences which are most concrete form of experiences. This is only a pictorial form where all sorts of aids and experiences are arranged in a Cone. The various bands of the cone representing various experiences and aids, should not be considered as rigid divisions or watertight compartments. They overlap and blend with each other. For example you can be a viewer of an exhibit or a person who made it, you can observe a demonstration or can demonstrate it yourself. It is also not being suggested that the various aids and materials are arranged in the form of their effectiveness but they are arranged from most abstract to most concrete. As a teacher we should also know that abstract ideas, concepts, or generalisations are not possible without rich meaningful concrete experiences. A science teacher has to pick and choose the aids according to the maturity levels of the students and the topic to be studied. We will discuss the strengths and limitations of each in teaching sciences.

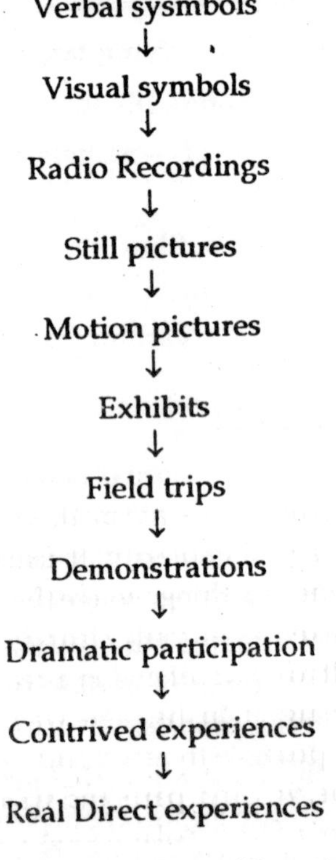

Fig. *Edger Dale Cone of Experiences*

The base of the Cone of experiences represents "direct purposeful experiences." Here the word 'purposeful' is very important. Every direct experience may not be very meaningful, therefore, it may not be purposeful. We have to see the direct experience in terms to learning outcome. In cases where the real things are too small or too big to comprehend, direct experiences are not very effective and therefore are not purposeful. For example, "structure of atom," "working of a factory," "water supply in a city" etc., can be understood better by some indirect experiences like models, maps or charts, etc.

In teaching science many direct experiences can be given to the students for effective comprehension. Some examples are: observing real flowers, leaves, plants, insects; dissecting animals; taking a walk through woods; going to the seashore and observing marine animals; doing salt analysis in the lab; setting and maintaining an aquarium, etc. In such cases learning is by direct participation.

The science teacher has to decide what direct experiences will be purposeful for his classes and then try to give them as many experiences as possible because direct and concrete experiences soon become associated with abstractions and help in developing more difficult concepts.

What are Contrived Experiences? Next in the hierarchy towards abstraction are contrived experiences. Examples of contrived experiences are static models, working models, specimens, dioramas, etc. Contrived experiences may differ from the original in size (big things are made smaller and smaller things are made bigger) and complexity. It usually is a simplified and edited version of the real thing, where the unnecessary details can be removed to make the learning clear. For example a petroleum refinery is difficult to comprehend in a real situation but its model will be more meaningful. In the same way models of places where it is difficult or impossible to reach and see can give a clear idea, like models of globe, volcano, parts and systems of the body, bottom of the ocean, view of a forest, polar region, etc. Sometimes we imitate the whole natural habitat in the form of dioramas and keep in museums. Cut-away or half cut models are extremely useful in teaching internal structure of eye, ear, stem, root and automobile, etc.

There are some examples where nobody has seen the real thing, the models are made on the basis of indirect evidences like model of atom, DNA structure. Here the whole concept is developed on the basis of these imaginary models.

While teaching through the models, teacher should give the idea of the real thing, regarding their size and complexity. All models are not correct reproduction of their originals, they are only simplified versions.

Objects and Specimens. Objects and specimens are very common in science laboratories. These are also examples of contrived experiences. We collect rocks from various places. Different kinds of plants and animals are collected; pressing, preserving and sniffing are done for storing and study purposes. The objects and specimens are taken from the real settings. They are samples of real things minus real settings. The specimens are collected and stored so that they are readily available for study purposes. Another most important advantage of objects and specimens which is not otherwise possible in direct experience is that they can be arranged into groups and classes.

DIFFERENT KIND OF AIDS

This has been placed on the 3rd band of Cone of experiences. Dramatisation means substitute for real experience of reconstruction of the original reality. There are many things we cannot possibly experience at first hand. There is a great value of dramatisation in education. Students can participate in a dramatisation or watch some kind of dramatisation. Both are valuable experiences but participation is much more meaningful and closer to reality than only watching.

The question is "What is the scope of dramatisation in science teaching?" Dramatic acts are quite popular in languages and social sciences. In sciences also the scope is not limited.

The films made on the work of various scientists are only possible because of dramatisation. Such films are quite effective as such experiences are otherwise not possible.

Students of primary and middle classes participate in scientific dramatised act in schools, such activities are also brought to science fairs etc. Some very abstract and uninteresting ideas are taken for dramatisations, for example, different students act as various components of solar system with proper costumes, dialogues, songs, music and dance, and the abstract concepts become clear and leave a long lasting impact on participants and viewers; students act as various petroleum products and explain how they are formed and utilised like coal, petrol, vaseline, synthetic rubber and plastic etc. Functions of vitamins and other components of food can also be taught through dramatisation.

It is also possible to use dramatisation in classroom teaching where costumes are not necessarily required but different students can remember their parts and act out in the classroom.

Interdependence of various components of an ecosystem and balance of nature can also be explained interestingly through dramatisation. An imaginative science teacher can think of many such topics which can be taught more effectively through such activities. Thus dramatisation can become an effective teaching aid in teaching science.

Demonstrations : Demonstrations are quite familiar activities in science class-rooms. Their merits and demerits have been discussed at length in the Cone of experiences they have been placed on the fourth band from the base because it is essentially a process of observing. It differs from the first three bands, which are essentially doing. Demonstrations are used to show how something is done or not done. When demonstration is followed by doing on the part of students, it becomes very much meaningful.

Demonstrations are used to clarify ideas, and help to develop skills, processes and attitudes. They are not limited only to demonstrations through apparatus only. They can be used to clarify abstract ideas on the chalkboard, through slides or motion picture also.

Demonstrations can be improved to a great extent if certain points are kept in mind while planning and doing a demonstration.

- Plan all steps of demonstration in advance.
- Rehearse the demonstration before going to the classroom.
- Keep the demonstration simple as far as possible.
- Keep the students involved.
- Make it sure that all the students can see it.
- Outline various points on the board.
- Keep summarising various steps.

What is Field Trip or Excursion? A field trip or excursion is a planned visit to a point outside the regular classroom. It may be in the school, out in the community or it could be a long trip to far away places. Usually in field trips to places like visits to a factory, observatory, agricultural institute, poultry farms, museums etc., we often see other people doing things. As spectators we are not involved but we directly watch it and get a first hand knowledge. Therefore field trip is an excellent bridge between the work of the classroom and the work of the outside world. The chief difference between a field trip and other educational experiences is that the student get their experiences in the field and not in the classroom. Because of its nature to be mostly observation it is kept on the 5th band of the Cone of experiences as less concrete than other experiences discussed before. But if the field trips are planned and arranged in such a way that they go beyond observation, for example of a sea-beach, on a pond where they can also touch, feel and collect things, it becomes a *direct experience* for them. Such a variation in the field trip indicates again how the bands of the Cone interlap and blend into one another.

Importance of the Field Trips. Excursions or Field Trips are of great educational value especially in science subjects. The classroom is a limited place, bounded normally by four walls and meagrely equipped for the task or providing students with worthwhile experiences. The environment outside the classroom has no bounds; it has almost every conceivable situation that a teacher might wish to utilise. In school corridor students may study writing system for supply of electricity to different rooms and laboratories, may determine the power (in watts). On school grounds there may be various types of plants, birds, insects, different kinds of soil, sunshine and shadows, building materials, bicycles, scooters and cars. And just beyond the school boundaries lie the unlimited resources of community.

Contributions of an Excursion or Field Trip

(i) Field experiences are first hand experiences. They arise from direct learning situations. Sometimes they play the same role or even better in the learning of science as do experiments and demonstrations.

(ii) Field experiences tend to be much more meaningful and permit easier transfer of learning to solutions of real life problems.

(iii) Fieldwork if properly organised awakens many interests that classroom work cannot arouse. Fieldwork is the study of actual objects which stimulate more curiosity than to ideas. Out of almost any situation encountered in the field can develop into some challenging problems.

(iv) Fieldwork permits first-hand study of many things that cannot be brought into the classroom because of size and other inconvenience, *e.g.*, it is only outside the class that the students can be acquainted with the flora and fauna of the area.

(v) Fieldwork permits a class to engage in activities that are too noisy or too violent to be used in the classroom, *e.g.*, a model airplane, gasoline engine if demonstrated in the classroom would disturb the other neighbouring classes too.

(vi) Outdoors, students are able to work with large size materials, *e.g.*, an iron piece pipe makes a more impressive lever than a routine stick and erosion is better demonstrated from a garden hose than with a tiny trickle from a yet drawn in a glass tube.

Some Special Experiences of Field Trips. Fieldwork brings students in contact with many objects. The observation and manipulation of objects in the environment are bound to arise questions. Attempts to answer questions give rise to new problems.

Field trips can be used for review and drill. Ideas learnt in classroom can be better fixed in mind in actual situations, *e.g.*, by visiting factories the ideas of running a plant and the products manufactured can be better fixed in students' minds, or visiting a zoological park or a botanical garden, more abstract ideas about animal and plant life can be more clarified to students.

Difficulties Experienced in Arranging Field Trips. Lack of availability of good inventories regarding field experiences, school policies, and transportation problems create hurdles in arranging field trips. Therefore the teacher will have to take a key role if he wants to arrange the trip.

Procedure to Arrange Field Trips

1. Survey of the place of excursion should be taken before going to the field trip, so that the teacher knows beforehand what their students are to see there; or what relevant literature should be studied if places are far away.
2. Objectives of the field trips should be very carefully identified to make a field rip a success. If this is done teacher knows what he is going to teach and the students know what they are going to learn there.
3. Permission from the authorities and parents of students should be taken well in advance.
4. Appropriate activities compatible to the identified objectives should be listed and given as well as discussed with the students beforehand.
5. If there is a need for transport and place to stay they should be arranged in advance.

Preparation of Students/or Excursion

1. It is essential to brief students after arriving at the area. This should be as minimum as possible. A long lecture may deprive the students of an opportunity to explore the place.
2. Students should be divided into small groups appointing a group leader for each group. Group leaders may help in running fieldwork smoothly and quickly.
3. You as a teacher should be aware of the fact that there are slow as well as rapid learners. Activities and responsibilities should be so divided among the students as to be equally shared by both type of students without any feeling that they are slow learners or rapid learners.
4. Students should be made aware that there may be some difficulties like: (a) noise while visiting any working plant in a factory, (b) listening to the guide due to distance while standing around him, or (c) technical language used in explaining particular process; and they should try to solve such difficulties themselves as far as possible.
5. Students may be advised to take notes and draw diagrams, whenever they think it is necessary.

Teacher's Role. The teacher's role is very important for a successful field trip. Some of them are listed below:

1. Watches students closely and gives specific help as and when needed.
2. Recognises student's achievement.
3. Avoids frequent interruption in student's work but occasionally if it is justified.
4. Does not lecture while in field ?
5. Avoids loud voiced comments.
6. Acts as a guide, resource person or consultant.
7. Does the relevant follow-up activities of the trip ?

Follow-up Activities. Follow-up activities are very important in any kind of field trip, it may be a short trip just outside the classroom or a long excursion to various far away places.

Follow-up activities vary accordmg to the nature of excursion. If the field trip is taken just outside the classroom in the school lawns to find the population densities of various species of plants, the follow-up activity will include the pooling up of data collected by each student or each group of students and discussion on the result. If the field trip is an observational trip to places like factories, mills, observatories or hospitals, discussion about what they have learned is important. Field trip can also be taken to study the fauna and flora and collection of specimens from seashore, hill stations or any other places. If such field trip is taken by the students follow-up activities will include pressing of plants, preservation of animals, drying of insects, classification and displaying of material. If proper care has not been taken just after or during the trip (in case of long trips) the materials collected cannot be utilised properly and goes to waste. Sometimes the students and teachers are quite enthusiastic while planning and taking the field trip, but forget about the material after the big excitement or do not do the follow-up activities properly, therefore, the field trip is not as effective as it should be.

In short we can say that follow-up activities should be planned according to the objectives of the field trip. Science teachers should plan their objectives for the field trip well and do the follow-up accordingly for better understanding.

Exhibits : There is a big variety of exhibits. Sometimes they are three-dimensional working models, sometimes a series of photographs or photographs mixed with charts, models and real objects. But exhibits are essentially something one sees as a spectator. Usually one is not involved in handling any thing or working with the material. Science teachers take their students to show the science fairs where different kinds of exhibits can be seen. They are also of great educational value. Sometimes they may also influence the attitudes.

When students are involved in making exhibits, it becomes a direct experience for them. Investigatory science projects done by students can be displayed as exhibits. Exhibits can also be used by the science teachers to teach subject matter.

Museum. Museums are places where items and exhibits of knowledge are assembled, protected and studied. In big cities there are public museums of various kinds like art museums, history museums, science museums, and natural history museums etc. Here we are concerned with science and natural history museums. In our country there are not very many science and natural history museums. But if they are available in your cities, advantage should be taken from them.

Mostly Science and Natural History Museums (Science museum in Bangalore, Natural History Museum in Darjeeling and New Delhi) have two functions: (i) presentation and display of the materials, and (ii) to work with classroom teachers on specific curriculum unit. If this facility is given by the public museums, science teachers should take full advantage of such arrangements.

The other kind of museums are college and school museums for various subjects. Biology museums are quite common museums established in some form or the other in many schools and colleges. Museum should not be considered as a collection of various items and objects. It is more than that, it must be viewed with an idea, a process, and an objective. Therefore science museums should not emphasise only on the product of science but due importance should also be given to science processes.

There is a big scope of displaying of specimens and objects collected by students. Models and projects made by students could also be displayed there. In fact development of museum can be taken as one of the science club activities.

Motion Pictures and Television : Next on the cone towards little more abstraction comes the TV and motion pictures because we are only the viewers of these audio-visual aids. First we will discuss the motion pictures.

Motion Pictures 16-mm Educational Films. It is not possible to learn everything by doing or first-hand viewing. We have to get some of our experiences indirectly, 16-mm films play a very important role in giving this indirect experience. Motion pictures present an abstracted version of the real events omitting unnecessary and unimportant details, they can, sometimes dramatised events so effectively filmed that we feel as though we are present at the reality itself. No other medium has brought so much information and scientific knowledge to the classrooms as the educational sound motion pictures.

There are various kinds of motion pictures. Here we are concerned with the *educational films*. Educational films include *documentary* and *instructional films*. Though some documentary films can be used in classroom teaching but they are especially planned for classroom teaching purposes. On the other hand *instructional films* are specially planned to achieve certain educational objectives and are made in specific subject areas tor teaching purposes. These films can be background films or direct teaching films. They help to promote to achieve a skill, an attitude or to convey certain facts, information, phenomenon or theory. As a science teacher we will be mainly concerned with the instructional films in our areas.

Though we are only spectators before a motion picture but the learning outcomes are quite effective because of certain specific values of motion pictures.

For 16-mm films, 16-mm movie projectors are needed. Now video cassettes of 16-mm films are available, which can be seen on TV. with V.C.P. or V.C.R.

Strengths of Motion Pictures

(a) Motion pictures motivate the students and compel attention.

(b) Movement can very effectively be shown by motion pictures which is not possible in any other aid except direct experience.

(c) It's is an edited version of reality, the editing involves manipulation of time, space and by eliminating distractions; it gives relationships of things, ideas and events that might well be overlooked in real life. For example, food web, food chain, etc., can be seen as continuous processes which is not possible in reality.

(d) Time can be controlled in a motion picture with the help of slow motion photography, "movements in animals, insects, flight of birds" can be understood very easily. With the help of time-lapse photography it is possible to see the blooming of flowers, germination of seeds, growths of plants, etc.

(e) Motion pictures can enlarge or reduce the actual size of the objects for better compensation. By means of microscopic lens attachments microscopic organisms like algae, fungi, protozoas, and blood circulation in capillaries etc. can easily be seen and understood by students.

(f) By X-ray cine photography techniques movements of internal organs of animals—action of arms, legs, movement of the heel, swallowing of food, heart-beating/living movements, etc., can be shown.

(g) Motion pictures can bring past and distant present into the classroom.

(h) With the help of animation techniques motion pictures can show processes which cannot be seen by human eye even with the help of microscope or telescope. For example, behaviour of molecules in solids, liquids and gases, phenomenon of nuclear fission and fusion, etc.

(i) Motion pictures can reproduce the record of events like lunar and solar eclipses, etc. which are not always possible to see. Complicated techniques can be filmed and reproduced when required.

(j) Motion pictures promote understanding of abstract relationship, offer a satisfying aesthetic experience, influence and even change in attitudes.

With so many values, motion pictures not only expedite the rate of learning but they also increase the scope of teaching. This is an important consideration in the field of science where mass of learning and the learning processes are expanding so rapidly that it is to keep hand up with them. Motion pictures enable the teacher to clarify the difficult concepts in less time than with any other technique.

In order to get the most effective use of films or video tapes, the following necessary information and skills should be acquired:

(i) Where to obtain appropriate films or video tapes?

(ii) How to use such films and video tapes in your teaching?

(iii) How to operate the 16-mm film projector, V.C.R;, V.C.R.?

School, college and university teachers have to spend some time to find films or video cassettes which they can integrate into their courses. It is possible to find suitable films or video cassettes on various science subjects. Securing catalogues will be important for this purpose.

For an effective use of films or video cassettes, preparation and follow-up are two very important steps to be taken by a teacher. Teacher should select the film or video cassette which goes along with the topic. The film or video cassette should be previewed and important points to be covered in the lesson should be outlined.

It will be advisable to frame few short answer questions. These questions can be given to the students before showing the film or video. During the follow-up activity unanswered questions and other important points should be discussed. Such activities help in coordinating the film or video with the topic. In the absence of such coordination sometimes the film or video becomes a wastage of time and effort.

The next point is to learn to operate the 16-mm projector and V.C.P./V.C.R. which is not very difficult to learn. Ordinarily only a few hours instruction followed by a brief practice results in satisfactory operation. Simple threading and operating instructions are given somewhere on the projector, which should be followed carefully. The possibilities of error should not discourage the teacher but it should be taken as challenge. The thrill of this educational device will compensate for minor disappointments.

Caution to be Observed in Using Films or Videos. Motion pictures may not necessarily be effective for teaching everything. As a teacher you have to be cautious about certain things.

- You have to think about the *effectiveness* of the film or video. If other experiences like direct or contrived are more meaningful, film or video should not be used.
- Sometimes the film or video gives a wrong idea about the *time notion* and *size notion*. It should be clarified to the students by comparing it with a known object or by giving a familiar example.
- If inexpensive devices are available with the *same effectiveness* as motion pictures, then less expensive devices should be used.
- Teacher should see that the film or video is adequate for the comprehension of his/her students.

School T.V. Programmes. Television has all the potentialities of motion picture with a little more concreteness because of the "on the spot coverage" and the nature of the TV programmes, as most of them are specially produced for a particular audience. This is more so for educational TV programmes. In many countries educational TV programmes include series of science programmes.

Educational TV in India. Experimental TV Service was inaugurated on September 15th, 1959. This programme was planned for educational and cultural values of community and designed for community viewing. In the meantime Ford Foundation in India was approached to assist in the development of educational TV. Ford Foundation team of TV experts visited India in February 1960. In 1961 Television was started in India as an educational TV project. The project was launched in close collaboration with the Delhi Directorate of Education and with the financial assistance of the Ford Foundation in 1961.

The educational TV programmes were integrated with the school syllabus based on the principle of direct teaching. Direct teaching implied that the TV programmes were directly related with the school syllabus. They were proposed to help in classroom teaching by bringing into classroom additional resources through the medium of TV. The students were benefited from talented teachers, best and expensive equipment and other audio-visual aids which were not usually available in schools. In the project the teachers were also fully involved from the planning to evaluation. This arrangement of instructional TV was working well in Delhi schools because there was a set prescribed syllabus. In some other advanced countries there is not any set syllabus for all but they have different syllabi choosen by teachers and students. Their educational TV programmes are not strictly integrated with the syllabi.

In Delhi the educational programmes started in General Science, Social Studies, Physics and Chemistry. Later Biology Maths and Geography were also included.

For proper functioning of educational TV and better coordination between Doordarshan and Schools a Television Branch was set up in 1967 in Delhi Directorate of Education. The TV branch used to divide the syllabus term-wise and week-wise, and select lessons for TV teaching. To ensure close relationship between TV and classroom teaching, a package of a uniform time-table, set examination days and working hours, and a uniform weekly syllabus in the form of a TV booklet was to be distributed to all viewing schools in the beginning of the school session. Such TV booklets used to be prepared for each subject taught on TV. But now we do not have such school TV programmes in Delhi or elsewhere in the country.

This kind of educational TV programme if started again can solve several problems of science teaching in our schools.

Merits

1. It solves the problem of unequipped laboratories to certain extent. Students are able to see effective

demonstrations and expensive apparatus which is otherwise not possible for them to see.

2. TV teachers prepare and rehearse a lesson, spend enough time to collect relevant material and up-to-date information.
3. It has all advantages of films plus being a live presentation seems more natural. Only relevant portions of films are shown, along with teacher's explanation and other visual material.

Demerits

1. It is a one way process and students are passive viewers.
2. There is no opportunity for an active participation of the learner during TV lesson.

Better Utilisation of Educational TV. The disadvantages can be removed if some preparation is done and precautions are taken by the classroom teacher.

For effective use of any mass media three things are important: proper reception, proper seating arrangement, carefully planned preparation and follow-up.

Good reception is one of the basic important things for effective viewing. The television branch in Delhi had the responsibility of installing and maintenance of TV sets. The coordination had to be done by the teachers and administration of the school. Classroom teacher was also be familiar with proper handling and minor adjustments of a TV set.

Next important thing is the proper seating arrangements. If a big crowd is sitting on the floor (without any discipline) in an auditorium or classroom, not sure of proper viewing, this kind of arrangement will be a waste of time. The classroom teacher was to see that there was proper seating arrangement.

TV presentation is only one part of the learning procedure. Preparation for the TV lesson or the pre-telecast activities and the follow-up or post-telecast activities by the classroom teacher are equally important without which the TV lesson may not be very much meaningful.

Pre-telecast activities included the preparation by the subject teacher. Preparation varied with class to class and also depended on the topic, the classroom teacher could see the topic of the TV lesson in advance from the TV booklet. During pre-telecast activities his job was to make the students ready to receive the TV instructions. He could ask motivational questions. If some background knowledge was needed it was to be given at this time. The time-table was arranged in such a way that there were about 10 minutes before and after the actual telecast, usually the presentation was of 20 minutes duration, and class periods varied from 35-40 minutes.

After the TV presentation follow-up activities included clarification of points of doubts raised by students. Recapitulation questions could also be asked to see how much they have grasped. With little encouragement by the classroom teacher many activities could be followed by students as continuation of the TV presentation for better understanding.

The TV branch of Delhi also tried to evaluate the lessons. They used to send a printed pad of evaluation check sheets to each school for the constant feedback of TV lessons. If various people connected with educational TV production do their jobs consciously the E.T.V. programmes can be quite effective. You as a science teacher has to play an important role. During your practice teaching you can observe some science lessons on video tapes, evaluate them according to the evaluation check sheet developed by you and give suggestions for further improvement.

Radio Recordings and Still Pictures : Next stage on the cone of experiences after motion pictures is the number of those devices which can be called as one-dimensional aids. We will take the scope of each in teaching science one by one.

Kinds of Still Pictures. Various kinds of still pictures can be used in teaching science. They include photographs, illustrations and slides. These visual materials are of great importance in teaching learning situations.

Photographs and illustrations can be used without projection, slides can be projected on the screen with slide projectors. Therefore pictures can be divided into two kinds: (i) unprojected, and (ii) projected.

Unprojected Pictures. Photographs, illustrations and clippings of photographs from magazines and newspapers can be collected for teaching purposes. Pictures give a correct impression of the object or situation and motivate and enrich teaching. It is good to have relevant pictures on the walls of science rooms—pictures of great scientists and some of their apparatus, etc. Pictures can also be used in teaching for motivation, introduction, presentation or recapitulation as the need may be.

Pictures and illustrations with some theme can be displayed on a bulletin board.

Bulletin Board. It is a place for posting "bulletins", as the name suggests. Bulletin boards can be used in many different ways and as an effective "teaching device". Bulletin boards inside and outside the science rooms and laboratories can be used for putting visual materials (pictures, illustrations) with relevant heading and some labelling for supplementing the teaching. It should be of scientific interest and importance. With proper teacher guidance and motivation bulletin boards can provide opportunity of developing creativity, responsibility and interest among • the students. Other than displaying the photographs and illustrations, bulletin boards can also be used for displaying reports of science projects done by students, science news and cuttings from science magazines, collected and presented by them.

Projected Pictures. Projection of visuals have certain advantages. For example, projection magnifies the material, therefore, a bigger group can easily see it. It is somehow motivating, therefore, compels attention.

Different kinds of projectors aroused in classrooms for projecting still pictures. They all are very easy to use, with little planning on the part of the teacher, teaching can be quite effective.

Opaque Projector of Episcope. The opaque projector projects and simultaneously enlarges material directly from original books, magazines, etc. All kinds of written, printed or pictorial matter in any sequence can be projected for teaching purpose. It can also project opaque thin objects like leaves, shells, sample of fabrics, butterflies, moths, etc.

Designs for posters, maps, pictures for displaying on bulletin boards etc., can be projected in the desired enlarged forms and then traced. The opaque projector though has many unexplored possibilities but is not being used much because of its bulk, weight and requirement of a very dark room.

Slide Projector. Such projectors usually project 35 mm slides. It is essentially a simple machine, easy to operate, inexpensive and light weight. It has most of the points of practical importance.

Slides can be shown individually in any desired order.

(i) Slides are of great value in visual teaching situation, when motion is of little or no importance, for example, in teaching structural details.

(ii) Great variety of visual material such as pictures, charts, graphs, diagrams, maps, tables, anything that can be photographed can be put on a slide.

(iii) Slides are available in black and white and coloured forms on many science subjects covering a wide range of topics and levels.

(iv) Slides are comparatively inexpensive.

(v) Slides require only a slight darkening of the room.

(vi) In some little more expensive projectors the slides can be moved automatically either from a master control or from a synchronising device on a sound track. This arrangement of slide-tape programme is an effective device as the well prepared commentary makes it more meaningful.

The use of this visual aid will be more meaningful if following points are considered while using them:

(i) The science teacher has to explore if suitable slides are available on the particular topics.

(ii) Second step is the careful preview. The preview helps in deciding on how to use the material to the best advantage. Is it stimulating enough for introduction on the whole lesson could be developed with it or only suited for summarising the lesson.

(iii) Teacher has to think about the purpose also. If showing of motion is necessary for understanding, then slide is not the best medium.

(iv) If teaching involves a series of step by step development, one leading to the next logical sequence the slides are well suited.

Showing slides is only one part of the process. Good discussion and further activities could be developed from it.

The Micro projector. One of the more specialised types of projection equipment is the micro projector. As its name indicates it shows enlarged images of stained sections of microscopic slides or other biological material mounted on microscopic slides so that the bigger group can see it.

The advantages of micro projector are that:

(i) It presents an enlarged picture of the object on the slide for common view.

(ii) It assures the teacher that his students are seeing precisely what he wants them to see.

Some manufacturers make low power projection attachments for slide projectors. Some are simple extensions of a microscope using a more powerful illumination system with a small view screen. This can be easily shown in small groups. But the full scale micro-projectors are quite expensive.

Projectors of any kind are a boon to classroom teachers. These technological tools, if coordinated wisely make the classroom teaching quite effective, because of the novelty of presentation, students become motivated and interested.

Radio and Recordings

Language and Voice Modulation. These are primarily auditory aids. If the speaker on radio or recordings uses simple everyday language with meaningful associations with familiar examples the listening can become quite concrete. On the other hand if the language is difficult without any associations, it could be an abstract thing for listeners. Being only an auditory aid language and voice modulation etc, play a very important role in the effectiveness of these programmes

Values of Radio. Immediately we are able to get the news of important events from all over the world, which is not possible from any other media except vedio or TV. Many events are of great importance for science classes, some of which are mentioned below :

(i) Radio brings reality to the classroom The spectator who describes the events with his tone and description can brings sense of participation amongst listeners.

(ii) Radio programmes if well rehearsed and well presented in the form of stories bring the personal feeling of the actor, different sound effects and voices make them more realistic and meaningful.

(iii) It brings variety to the classroom and helps in teaching

(iv) Though in a well prepared programme enough expenses may be involved but radio being a mass media technology, on the whole it is inexpensive.

Limitations

(i) It is still a one way communication

(ii) Availability and maintenance of radio set may be a problem.

(iii) Radio broadcast timings always do not coincide with the class timings. Provision of radio broadcasts in the school time table is made only in a very few schools.

Educational Radio Programmes in Our Country. Educational broadcasts for schools in the AIR were regular features from the last few decaues. These programmes included science lessons for students and teachers at various levels. Teachers' programmes were on content as well as on methodology. Before the board examinations revision lessons on various science subjects were quite popular. These were used to be given by experienced science teachers and educators

The school broadcast was a separate unit of AIR in New Delhi. The unit tried to coordinate between various agencies to improve the effectiveness of the broadcasts. Meetings were held where people were invited from Directorate of Education Delhi, Municipal Corporation Delhi, New Delhi Municipal Council and Delhi University to plan future programmes and give suggestions for their improvement

Radio broadcast schedule in the form of a chart was prmted and sent to the schools in the beginning of the year. Teachers could utilise the relevant broadcast in their classes. Radios and transistors were or could be easily available in the schools. If the teachers are conscious of the radio programmes students can be benefited Pre- and post-broadcast activities improved the effectiveness of the programmes as discussed in TV programmes.

Recordings. All the values of radio can be applied to recordings also. But the disadvantages can be eliminated like timing, administration and one way communication problems. Recordings from many sources can be utilised in the classrooms, like spool-tape records and cassette records.

Advantages of Recordings

(i) Recordings can become two way communication as it can be stopped, discussed and replayed wherever it is necessary, it can be controlled by us.

(ii) Recordings on cassette or spool-tape-recorder can be made in the school also. A commentary can be written and recorded on the available slides in your subject in the school for effective use and re-use.

(iii) Good radio programmes can be recorded and replayed in class whenever needed.

(iv) Scientific talks by eminent personalities can be taped and reproduced in the class.

DIFFERENT SYMBOLS

Kinds of Visual Symbols. They include the abstract representation of real pictures. Various kinds of visual symbols used in communication are drawings, sketches, diagrams, graphs, cartoons, flat maps, etc. They all can be projected on screen, and can also be shown on the blackboard or on the overhead projector.

Diagrams and charts etc., are part of everyday work for most of the science teachers. Almost all the science teachers use blackboard to show in the structure and happenings of various things in their subjects.

Commercially made charts are available in various subjects. Charts and other graphic aids are also made by various Governmental agencies. Central Institute of Educational Technology (CIET) of NCERT New Delhi develops various kinds of graphic aids for school purposes. Charts are also made in schools by teachers and students and can be utilised in teaching science quite effectively.

Chalkboard. Blackboard now is usually called a chalkboard because of variations in colours. It is one of the very important but quite neglected aid of the classrooms. If it is properly used can become a valuable aid in teaching science.

It should not be taken for granted that you already know the use of chalk board, but the techniques should be learned and practised especially as a trainee teacher.

Importance of Chalkboard

(i) This aid is used with all other aids for better clarification, for example, the main points of a demonstration planning and summarising of a field trip, questions for a motion picture and so on can be written on the board.

(ii) It gives a concrete form to abstract and vague statements and ideas.

(iii) It helps in developing the skill of drawing a particular diagram..

(iv) It is less time consuming and comparatively cheaper.

(v) It can be used for some students activities like quizes, competitions and discussions, etc.

(vi) Some chalkboards can be used for permanent outlines of maps, graphs, tables and other special materials where some filling up can serve the purpose.

(vii) If properly used chalkboard becomes an attractive point and holds students attention.

Effective Use of Chalkboard

(i) Clean the board properly before using it.

(ii) Try to write neat and bold so that it is legible.

(iii) Do not write too much on the board. Start writing from top left hand. Give headings and sub-headings in the written summary.

(iv) If diagrams are used for referring or introduction, they can be made beforehand. If you want the students to draw the diagrams then it should be drawn in front of them and they should be asked to draw side by side. In the same way a complicated process should not be drawn beforehand, but it should be developed before them for clarification and better understanding.

(v) If necessary, some tools can be used to draw on the board.

(vi) Coloured chalks should be used for making complex diagrams.

Overhead Projector. Any thing which is written or drawn on a chalkboard can also be projected by an overhead projector with some additional advantages.

An overhead projector projects material overhead or over shoulder the teacher using it on to a screen behind and above him. They generally have 25 cm x 25 cm writing area which is big enough for writing. What is required to be shown on the screen is written on a glass plate covered with sheet or roll of transparent plastic. Variety of fabrics tipped pens or china marking pencils are used for writing and drawing. Wet cloth can be used for erasing and re-using the sheets.

Advantages of Overhead Projector

(i) It is very simple and convenient to use the machine.

(ii) This projector unlike any other projectors is operated from the front of the room and the teacher faces class as he or she writes or points on already made transparencies.

(iii) Plastic roll attachment is quite useful. Diagrams, points of the lesson, assignments, tests and similar material can be effectively presented gradually with a minimum of time and effort.

(iv) An important feature of overhead projector is the provision of "overlays" or 'build ups," which have successive layers of transparencies in black and white coloured or both showing cumulative stages of development, sequences and sectional views, which is quite effective in many scientific processes and phenomenon.

Limitations

(i) Though it is not very heavy but a voluminous projector.

(ii) It is quite expensive and needs some planning.

This is the most abstract and one of the most important forms of experience we get and give to our students. Our job as a teacher is to make sure that the various terms, ideas, words, principles and other abstractions used should be meaningful for students. The ideas and concepts which can be translated into verbal symbols come by getting other concrete experiences. Rich experiences gained by students help them to understand the verbal symbols meaningfully and therefore they can read and understand the textbooks also. Ability to speak or read the word does not mean that one also understands the object, process or phenomenon.

If from the very beginning science is taught by reading books or abstraction only, students usually acquire the habit of memorising and accepting verbal formulation given by others. This is no way of teaching science.

Various kind of experiences discussed on the core of experience from direct purposeful experience to visual symbols, all help in the development of verbal symbols meaningfully. Then reading is not only the process of reproduction of verbal symbols but also involves a thinking process, which includes meaning of words.

Textbooks and other reference books provide the most to the students, because all teaching is not possible by any one particular aid or experience. But the textbooks should be written in understandable vocabulary of that level. Sometimes in primary classes the language of science textbooks is much more difficult than the language in the language textbooks of that particular class. Another important aspect is also the style of writing and format. In writing and specially in teaching if references and examples are given from their environment and known things learning will be more meaningful.

UTILITY IN EFFECT

A variety of teaching aids has been discussed in this chapter with some details. It is difficult to select few aids and to say that they are more important than others, or mis should be used more often than others etc. The value of an aid does not depend wholly on its quality itself but it also greatly depends upon the way it is used and the particular time it is used.

The qualities of various aids have also been discussed. No matter how perfect the aid may be, if it is irrelevant to the occasion of its use then it is of little value and an ordinary aid with not too many qualities becomes indispensable if it is used relevantly at the right time. For example, there is film which shows the animals under the sea or life in a desert in relation to their ecology. Neither the materials nor this relationship could be shown in a class by any other media or field trip as effectively as the film could. But always it should not be used as a substitute for other materials of the classroom.

Questions

1. What is the importance of audio-visual aids in teaching science?
2. What are various kinds of audio-visual aids which can be used in teaching science?
3. How will you use the following activities or aids effectively in your teaching? Explain with examples.
   (i) Direct experiences
   (ii) Contrived experiences
   (iii) Demonstration
   (iv) Science museum
   (v) Still pictures.
4. Identify some places where field trips can be arranged for meaningful learning in your teaching subject. Explain how will you arrange and carry out this activity.

5. What is the importance of 16 mm films? Identify five topics in your teaching subject where films can be effectively used.
6. Discuss the role of the following in teaching science:
   (i) Slide projector
   (ii) Overhead projector
   (iii) Micro projector
   (iv) Opaque projector.
7. As a science teacher how will you utilise educational TV for your classes?
8. How will you use the bulletin boards in your laboratory or classroom?
9. What precautions should be taken while selecting audio-visual aids in your teaching?
10. What audio-visual aids would you like to have in your science laboratory? Justify your answer.

15

Role of Laboratory

Chemistry is essentially a practical oriented subject. No course in chemistry can be considered as complete without including some practical work in it. For proper understanding of chemistry, it should be taught using a large number of demonstration experiments. For carrying out demonstration experiments and for the performance of practicals by the students, a chemistry laboratory is a must for every school offering chemistry as a subject. Like any other science subject a chemistry laboratory is justified on the following grounds:

(i) In chemistry laboratory the required apparatus and other apparatus etc. can be safely stored.

(ii) As in other science subjects so also in case of chemistry laboratories are helpful in creating and promoting scientific attitude in the pupils.

(iii) Laboratory provides a proper and congenial place for performing experiments and is helpful in developing a sense of cooperation and spirit of healthy competition among the students.

IMPORTANCE OF PRACTICAL WORK

No course in chemistry can be considered as complete without including some practical work in it. The practical work is to be carried out by individual in a chemistry laboratory. Most of the achievements of modern chemistry are due to the application of the experimental method. At school stage practical work is even more important because of the fact that we 'learn by doing' scientific principles and applications are thus rendered more meaningful. It is a well known fact that an object handled impresses itself more firmly on the mind than an object merely seen from a distance or in an illustrations. Centuries of purely deductive work did not produce the same utilitarian results as a few decades of experimental work. Practical class room experiments help in broadening pupil's experience and develop initiative, resourcefulness and cooperation. Because of the reasons discussed above practical work forms a prominent feature in any chemistry course.

ORGANISATION OF PRACTICAL WORK

Out of the various teaching methods discussed earlier *the Assignment method* is the only method that combines theory and practice in a harmonious manner and can be easily practiced in our schools. The *Heuristic method* is predominently a *laboratory method*. However from this it should not be concluded that practical work in laboratory is impossible if the teacher makes use of any other teaching method. Thus irrespective of the method adopted by the teacher for teaching of chemistry in the class, practical work in laboratory must be attempted. The following guide lines will help the chemistry teacher to make his practical work effective.

GUIDELINES FOR TEACHERS

For smooth working in the laboratory teacher should give due consideration to the following points:

(i) If teacher follows the demonstration method to teach theory, he should remember the most important principle that practical work should go hand in hand with the theoretical work. Thus if a class is doing theoretical work in chemistry it should also do practical work in chemistry during the practical periods.

(ii) An attempt be made to arrange the practical work in such a way that each student is able to do his practical individually. Thus for practical work individual working be preferred in comparison to working in groups.

(iii) In case of a large class, it is convenient to divide the class in a suitable number of smaller groups, for practical work. A practical group in no case should have more than 20 students. The limit on practical group is essential otherwise teacher will not be able to devote individual attention to the students.

(iv) To save time on delivering a lecture about do's and don'ts in laboratory, card system is used. This card which contains certain amount of guidance printed on it is given to each pupil. In some laboratories where card system exists each student is given a card containing instructions about the experiment that he has to perform. This card also contains the details of the apparatus required. Student can complete his practical work according to instructions given in the card.

(v) The apparatus provided should be good so that students get an accurate result particularly in those experiments in which the student is likely to compare the numerical value of his result with some standard. However, every chemistry teacher should gaurd against 'Cooking' of results by his pupil. If this bad habit of cooking is not checked in the beginning it persists through out the students career.

(vi) A true and faithful record of each and every experiment be kept by pupils. The record should be complete in all respects.

(vii) To check the habit of 'cooking' teacher should see that students enter all their observations directly in their practical notebook. The teacher should insist that the pupils do not go to the balance room without first entering the data in their notebooks.

(viii) Students should not be allowed to erase any figures. To change any wrong entry the same be crossed and correct figure entered only with the permission of the teacher.

(ix) Students should not be allowed to calculate results or write data on scrap papers.

(x) In practical notebook the right hand page be reserved for record while the left hand page be left for diagram and calculations. This practice be followed for Assignment method. For any other method the laboratory work be done on left hand page of practical note book and procedure etc. on right hand page of practical note book.

(xi) Teacher should see that students complete their practical note book in all respects and get it signed before they are allowed to leave the laboratory. Incomplete practical note books be kept in the laboratory and students be asked to complete it in their spare time.

(xii) Teacher should thoroughly check and critically examine the account written by students.

(xiii) Whenever a student is required to make use of a piece of apparatus for the first time it is the duty of the teacher to explain to his students the working of the apparatus. He should also explains reasons for necessary care and accuracy.

(xiv) Teacher should see that students find no difficulty to get apparatus and chemicals needed by them. In the absence of provision for laboratory assistants it is for the teacher that he arranges the apparatus in such a way that things frequently needed by students are easily accessible to them. Teacher should also emphasise proper and economical use of apparatus and chemicals.

(xv) While working with larger groups and with limited apparatus teacher can act as under:

(a) He may use assignment method.

(b) He may allow students to work in groups.

(c) He may devise alternate simple experiments and work with improvised apparatus.

(d) He may allow use of home made apparatus.

(xvi) Whenever the teacher is required to draw up suitable laboratory directions or instructions for practical work by pupils, be should keep the following points in mind:

(a) Beginner be given detailed directions.

(b) He should not tell the students what is actually going to happen.

(c) The main aim of the experiment should be made clear.

(xvii) During a practical class teacher should observe all children from his desk otherwise chances of accidents are there.

Even when teacher has to move from his desk his power of control over the class should be such that students continue their work satisfactorily.

CHEMISTRY LABORATORIES

Combined Lecture room-cum-Laboratory : Laboratory is a spacious room where in a group of students carry out their practicals. The work of designing and building a science room (laboratory and lecture room) is that of the architect but science master should collaborate with the architect in planning for what is best from the educational point of view. The plan of a combined lecture room and laboratory for use in schools upto matriculation standard, devised by Dr. R.H. Whitehouse, formerly principal of the Central Training College, Lahore, has been adopted as the official standard plan by Punjab Education Department.

The plan combines laboratory and class room for science teaching. The suggested size of the room is 45' × 25' and it is meant for a class of 40 students which is sub-divided in two groups of 20 each for practical work.

The size of the room is most economical. Though the length of the room is 45' but it should not be considered as disadvantageous because the teacher is expected to address a class of 40 students who will be occupying only about half the room.

For constructing such a room walls are to be of 1' 6" thick keeping Indian conditions in view, use of distemper be preferred to white wash for the walls. A perfectly smooth floor is preferable to one exhibiting any roughness. Such a floor is easier to clean of the two doors, one is used for lecture room and the other is reserved for laboratory part. To provide side lighting three large windows (6' × 8') are provided. One of these is provided near practical benches and two near seating accommodation. Doors as also windows sills may be used as shelves for carrying out experiments. To avoid flies wire gauze screens be provided to the windows. If necessary, in such a case, the windows be constructed with an upper and a lower half. The lower half is fixed so that the inner sills of windows could still be used as shelves.

FURNISHINGS AND FITTINGS

In the area meant for lecture room a wall black board 10' × 4 is provided. About 3' away from this black board is the teachers table which is about 6' long and 2.5 feet high. Such a table can be conveniently used both as a writing table as also a demonstration table and causes no disturbance or in convenience to the students in watching the demonstration or observing the black board.

For seating dual table and chairs are most economical. Thus by providing twenty tables and forty chairs sufficient seating arrangement could be made. Dual tables should be of the size 3.5' × 1.5' × 2'. They may be provided with shelf. The top of these tables should be flat and plain having grooves for pen/pencils. The chairs are 1.5' high in the seat, which in case of an iron chair, may be covered with a small mat. The area necessary for a dual table and two chairs is a square of 3.5'. Passages of 1.5' are sufficient for single file and 2.5' to 3.5' at the sides.

A sink is provided for use of the teacher. The size of the sink generally used is 18" × 12" × 6".

The advantages of table and chair system are as under:

(i) They are quite economical.

(ii) They provide quite natural seats.

(iii) They allow enough space for easy passage of the students.

(iv) They can be easily moved while cleaning the room.

(v) They can be used for other purposes such as accommodating guests at various school functions.

***Laboratory*:** In the laboratory part of the room are provided six laboratory tables which are made of wood and are perfectly plain. A black board is also provided on this side of the room. The laboratory tables are of the size 6' × 3.5' and are provided with a shelf on the working side just below the top. Four students can work on each table. The whole of each table except top should be stained dark. The top should be treated with wax ironed with a hot flat iron in order to fill the pores of the wood and to prevent the easy penetration of the liquids. The space between 3' and 4' and passage-way at the end of the tables is 2' wide. At school level the laboratory tables are not provided with any sink. Some of the reasons for not providing the sinks are as follows:

Economy: A large economy is observed because much plumbing and a network of drains is avoided. Cost of sinks is also saved. For most of the experiments at school level a trough can serve the purpose.

Usefulness: The table is quite useful for both physics and chemistry. In absence of sinks more space is available for use as working space. Such a table can also be used for other purposes.

Appearance and cleanliness: The floor of the room is not broken for providing drains etc. It gives a better look.

Tidiness: The tables if provided with sink would make the room untidy because such tables invariably allow splashing of water which is likely to interfere with experiments and is likely to create problems.

As shown in the plan there are only three sinks, one for the teacher and two for the students. Of the two sinks for students one is placed in the window recess and the other in recess in the wall. Each of the sinks is provided with a drawing board having grooves arranged to drip over the suits. It is used for placing beakers, flasks, etc. for drying.

For placing balances, recess in walls may be used. They may be about a foot wide at a height of about 3', 3". Such recess has the following advantages over wooden or stone shelf:

(i) It is very economical because only very small masonry is needed.

(ii) It is more substantial as compared to a bracket shelf.

(iii) It does not project into the room and so space economy can be made.

For providing ample accommodation for balances a length of 7' to 7.5' is sufficient.

In the plan provision has also been make for the storage of apparatus, equipments etc. For this purpose there is a provision of eight almiras (each with 7' × 5' dimensions). Each almirahs provided with shelves 1.5' deep, of this 1' is recessed in the wall and only 6" projects out. These almirahs provided sufficient space for the storage of not only the apparatus, equipment etc. but can also serve the purpose of storage of science library.

Reagent shelves can be very conveniently placed on either side of the recesses for balances space can also be found, for placing notice boards for assignments of work, results of tests, etc., on the wall between the windows or just inside the doors.

The Advantages

The combined lecture room-cum-laboratory discussed in previous pages has the following advantages:

(i) It is very economical.

(ii) It is compact and provides enough space for seating, working, storage etc.

(iii) It can be furnished easily and with meager resources.

(iv) It provides enough and comfortable seating space for the students.

(v) In this room science atmosphere prevails.

(vi) It provides an opportunity for better control. For a better control following points be kept in view by a teacher:

(a) Every student has his assigned place which is indicated by his name written on a card placed in a brass card holder fixed on the leg of the table.

(b) The four boys working on any table be allotted number 1, 2, 3, 4 and number 1 of each table be asked to collect four sets of articles required for each table. Number 2 be asked to remove the dirty apparatus, after the period, to drain board and number 3 will remove clean apparatus. Number 4 will wipe down the table with a duster.

(c) Class monitors be named for cleaning dirty apparatus after school hours or during recess period.

(d) Students be made responsible for the correct alignment of their tables. For this black and white lines be pointed on the floor.

LABORATORY PLANNING

In a senior secondary school the arrangements are made to provide education in chemistry as elective subjects in addition to teaching of general science. In senior secondary school a provision has to be made for a chemistry laboratory. The laboratory in senior secondary schools is almost the same as in colleges. Each laboratory is provided with a preparation-cum-store room attached to it. The size of the laboratory will depend on the number of students likely to work in it at a time. About 30 sq. feet. If space be provided for each student. The structural details are generally provided by the architects but the following points be kept in mind.

Planning: It would be better if chemistry teacher is consulted and for this there should be frequent conferences between the chemistry teacher and the architect. Various points be thoroughly discussed. Some of the points of consideration are as under:

(i) Laboratories and class rooms should not be mixed on the same corridor.

(ii) Laboratories be situated, as far as possible, away from crafts room, music room, play fields, main gate etc.

(iii) The consideration be given to proximity of stores, preparation room, balance room, green houses etc.

Following points be given due consideration while planning individual laboratories:

(i) Each student is easily accessible to the teacher.

(ii) There is minimum of movement.

(iii) Each student has a cupboard, bottles, heating point and a sink near him.

(iv) Teacher can easily watch each student.

(v) Black board is visible to each student.

(vi) Each student can easily see the demonstration.

(vii) There is enough space between two laboratory tables.

(viii) Master switches be provided to control electricity, gas, water etc. in each laboratory.

Lighting : Proper lighting arrangements be made for laboratory tables and class rooms. Special attention be given to the lighting of demonstration table and black board. It would be preferred if a provision could be made for electrical lights over tables through pulleys so that their height may be varied from 2 to 8 ft. Two way switches be provided for controlling the main lighting from doors and preparation rooms. Dark blinds or curtain must be provided for each laboratory.

Ventilation : It possible each laboratory should be surrounded by a 6' verandah on all sides to keep away the direct heat of the sun. Ventilators be provided as usual. In case of chemistry laboratory ceiling should be high and exhaust fans must be provided.

For laboratory ventilation full height windows are desirable. To avoid direct draughts even when the windows are open windows should be designed in Fig.

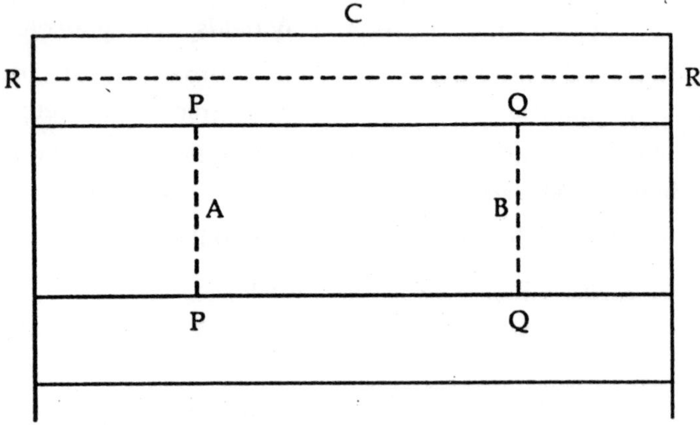

Fig. Design of a window to avoid draughts.

Windows A and B are side lung or pivoted along the axis PP and QQ. Window C is pivoted along RR. If this plan is used them windows can open in different ways depending on the wind direction. In dark room the ventilation can be provided by deflecting incoming and outgoing air by opaque partition. A no door arrangement as shown in Fig. may made.

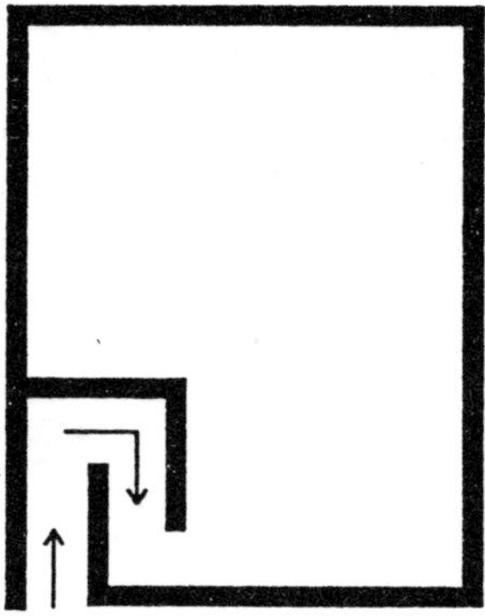

Fig. A 'no-door" Dark Room

Water Supply : Provision of water supply must be made in every laboratory. Water supply is most essential item and for this purpose proper arrangement of water laps and sinks is a must in every laboratory. In case of non-availability of adequate water supply from municipal/local sources alternate arrangements have to be made. For making alternate arrangements suggestion given below be considered.

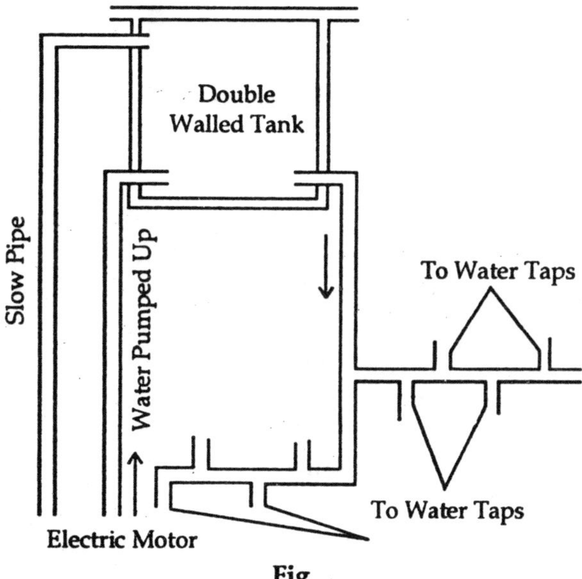

Fig.

A water storage tank having a capacity of 1000 to 5000 litres be constructed with concrete and cement or a readymade tank of synthetic material be purchased and such a tank be then placed at the roof of the room. Water be then lifted using electric pump for filling this tank. The water supply is then provided from this storage tank to the laboratories. A tentative scheme for storage and supply of water is shown in Fig.

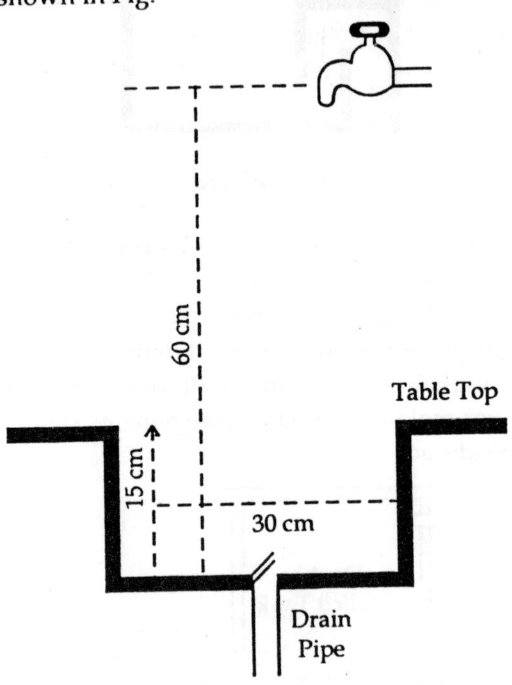

Sinks : Provision of sinks in each laboratory is one of the essential requirements. For a laboratory of ordinary size generally four sinks of 15" × 12" × 8" or 20" × 15" × 10" are sufficient. These sinks be fitted on side walls. These sinks are in addition to the one provided with the demonstration table. Waste water from these sinks is carried to the drains with the helps of the lead pipes fitted with the sinks. In laboratories kitchen type sinks are preferred to wash basis type. Fig gives a sketch of sinks and drainage for water.

Waste Disposal : In laboratories two types of wastes (*i.e.* liquid and solid) are often encountered. Arrangements have to be made for disposal of these wastes. For disposal of liquid wastes use of lead pipes or earthen ware pipes is considered most suitable. However care be taken to avoid the flow of solids like pieces of filter paper, cork, broken glass pieces etc. through these pipes, otherwise these pipes get chocked. For disposal of such solid wastes metal boxes or wooden boxes be provided. Such boxes be placed in the corners of the laboratory and students be asked to put all solid wastes in these boxes. Such waste boxes can even be placed under the sinks as shown in Fig.

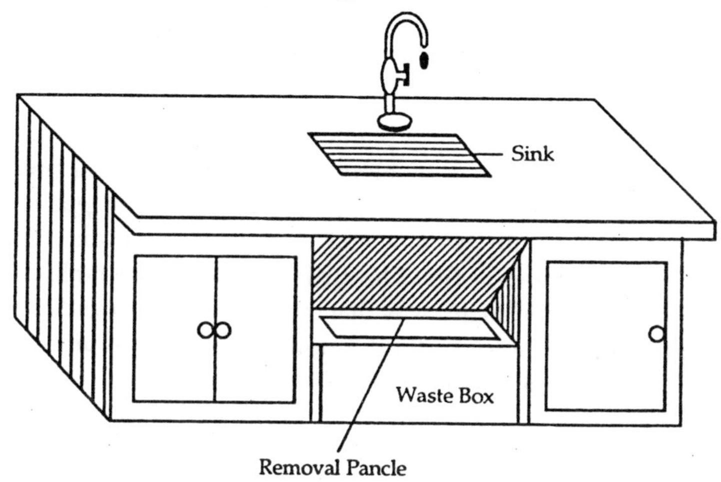

Fig. A space saving position of a disposal box

Pipe Lines : Installation of water pipes and gas pipes is another important aspect for furnishing a science laboratory. While installing pipes some of the points that be given due consideration are given below:

(i) Not more than 4 or 5 half inches pipes be led from any pipe for purpose of supply of water or drainage of water.

(ii) In case of physics laboratory all efforts be made to avoid iron pipes.

(iii) Pipes should never be placed on the laboratory tables.

(iv) It is convenient if the pipe fittings are not underground.

Gas Supply : For adequate supply of fuel gas to the laboratory generally any one of the following arrangements is made:

(i) Kerosene oil gas plant is installed.

(ii) Coal gas plant is installed.

(iii) Petrol gas plant is installed.

(iv) Gobar gas plant is installed.

The petrol gas plant is preferred as such a plant is economical and such plants are available in various capacities. A moderate capacity plant can feed 10-20 gas taps. Petrol gas plants are readily available and such plants are also manufactured at Ambala (Haryana). These plants can be easily operated.

For housing a petrol gas plant we need only a small room. The gas can be distributed to the practical tables using a 2" main gas pipe with further distributaries of 1/2" pipe. Each practical table is provided with gas taps and these taps should be of the rigid nozzle type and be fitted towards the back of the table. The gas tables be fitted in such a way that the point upwards and are at an angle of 45° from each other. If double benches are provided them taps should be fitted along the centre line of each bench. In most of the laboratories iron pipes are used but it would be preferable, in case of physics laboratory, if we use brass pipes. For controlling the supply of gas in addition to main control valve provision be made to control the supply of gas to each group of tables. These controls should be easily accessible to teacher and should not be easily accessible to students.

Laboratory Tables : The provision of laboratory tables as a must for each laboratory. The taps of laboratory tables be preferably made to teak wood. However other hard wood such as sheesham or deodar can also be used for making tops of laboratory tables. These tops are generally 1" thick. Other parts of the table *i.e.* legs, drawers etc. may be made of any other type of locally available wood. Plywood or hardboard can also be used for drawers. In chemistry laboratory such drawers are provided with the laboratory tables.

In addition to these provision for boards be made in the laboratories. For this either wall blackboards be provided or movable wooden blackboards with stands can be used.

The organisation of laboratories in secondary schools was also discussed at a seminar (All India) on the teaching of science in secondary schools. This seminar was held at Tara Devi (Simla) and it made some recommendations. Its recommendations are given below:

Layout

(a) Provision be made for one laboratory for chemistry in every higher secondary school.

(b) A floor space of 30 sq ft per student be provided in each laboratory.

(c) Adjacent store room be provided with each laboratory.

(d) A part of store room may be earmarked for use as a preparation room.

(e) In science wing, some suitable place for work benches with tools, be provided.

(f) A minimum of two class rooms provided with galleried seats be provided in each school.

EQUIPMENT FOR LABORATORY

The equipment for chemistry laboratory as recommended at the Tara Devi (Simla) Seminar is as under:

(i) Almirahs (wooden and steel).

(ii) Wallboard or blackboard.

(iii) Demonstration table (8' × 4') with cupboards, water and gas points.

(iv) Working tables with cupboards, shelves, water and gas points.

(v) Balance room should be attached to the laboratory.

(vi) Sinks on each working table or at least two large sinks at the corners of the laboratory.

(vii) A fume cupboard.

(viii) A wooden box half filled with sand for use as waste material box.

(ix) Acid proof drainage system.

(x) Shelves for reagent bottle on each working table and wall shelves for storage of reagent bottles.

LABORATORY INSTRUCTIONS

Instructions to Pupils : When a group comes to laboratory for practical work it should be given a guidance for the experiment to be performed. Such guidance can be given by (i) Laboratory instructions *(ii)* Laboratory manuals or *(iii)* Instruction cards.

Laboratory Instructions : Laboratory instructions should be given in a clear and simple language. It should give a precise but systematic method of performing the experiment. Special emphasis be given on how the record is to be kept and number of observations to be taken. Calculations be clearly explained and precautions to be observed be specifically emphasised.

Laboratory Manuals : Any good laboratory manual should contain the following:

(a) It should contain full and complete directions about the experiment. Such directions should clearly give the procedure to be followed and the precautions to be observed.

(b) It should give the method of recording of observations. Tables if needed for recording observations be clearly given.

(c) It should give clear directions about the writing and completing of practical note book. Important equations, diagrams etc, be given in it.

Instruction Card : In some laboratories instruction cards are used for providing guidance for laboratory work. Each student is given a card containing instructions about the experiment he has to perform.

The use of cards saves time as also wrong of the teacher. By this system different students can perform different experiments but the system is stereo typed and makes no allowance for individuals.

Usually cards of 6" × 4" are used.

PRACTICAL NOTE BOOKS

For keeping a true and faithful record of practical work done by him each pupil is required to have a practical note-book. An effort be made to avoid printed note-books and plain note-books be encouraged. By using plain note-books teacher can make his students to follow any suitable method of keeping record of the experiment.

As a general practice description is given on the right hand page and observations are recorded on the left hand page. In case assignment method is used them the left hand page is reserved for preparatory work and laboratory record is kept on right hand page which contains description as also the observations.

The record of the method should be brief and in the first person singular. A three column system be used for keeping a record of experiments about the properties of gases etc. The three column be headed *Experiment, Observation* and *Inference.*

The precautions that have been observed while performing the experiment be recorded at the end in the first person singular (past tense).

All records in practical note-book be made with lead-pencil. The diagrams should be simple and will labelled.

COMMON ACCIDENTS AND REMEDIES

Burns : Burns by Dry Heat (*i.e. by* flame, hot objects etc.). For slight burns apply *Burnol* and *Sarson oil.*

In case of blisters caused by burns apply *Burnol* at once and rush to dispensary.

Caution. Heat bums should never be washed.

Acid Burns : Wash with water and then with a saturated solution of sodium bicarbonate and finally with water. Even after this if burning persists, wipe the skin dry with cotton wool and apply *Sarson oil* and *Burnol.*

Caution. In case of conc, sulphuric acid, wipe it from the skin before giving the above treatment.

Alkali Burns : Wash with water and then with 1% acetic acid and finally with water. Dry the skin and apply *Burnol.*

Cuts : In case of a minor cut allow it to bleed for a few seconds and remove the glass piece if any. Apply a little methylated spirit or *Dettol* on the skin and cover with a piece of leucoplast.

For serious cuts call the Doctor at once. In the mean while try to stop bleeding by applying pressure above the cut. The pressure should not be continued for more than five minutes.

Note. Minor bleeding can be stopped easily be applying concentrated ferric chloride solution or alum.

Eye Accidents

Acid in Eye. At once wash the eye with water a number of times. Then wash it with 1% sodium carbonate solution by means of an eye-glass.

Alkali in Eye. At once wash with water and then with 1% boric acid solution by means of an eye-glass.

Foreign Particles in Eye. Do not rub the eye. Wash it by sprinkly water into the eye. Open the eye and remove the particle by means of a clean handkerchief or cotton wool. Again wash freely with water.

Poisons : It a solid or liquid goes to the mouth, but is not *swallowed,* spit it at once and repeatedly rinse with water. If the mouth is scalded, apply olive oil or *ghee.*

Acids. Dilute by drinking much water or preferably milk of magnesia.

Caustic Alkalies. Dilute by drinking water and then drink a glass of lemon or orange juice.

Arsenic of Mercury Compounds. Immediately give an emetic *e.g.* One table spoon full of salt or zinc sulphate is a tumbler of warm water.

Inhalation of Gases : Pungent gases like chlorine, sulphur dioxide, bromine vapours etc. When inhaled in large quantities often choke the throat and cause suffocation. In such a case remove the victim to the open air and loosen the clothing at the neck. The patient should inhale dilute vapours of ammonia or gargle with sodium bicarbonate solution.

Fire

Burning Clothing. It clothes have caught fire then lay the victim on the floor and wrap a fire-proof blanket tightly around him. The fire in the burning clothes will thus be extinguished. *Never throw water on the person* as it will cause serious boils on his body.

Burning Reagents. In case of fire on the working table at once turn out the gas taps and remove all things which are likely to ignite. Following methods be used to extinguish the fire:

(i) If any liquid in a beaker or flask has caught fire, cover the mouth of the vessel with a clean clamp cloth or duster.

(ii) Most of the fire on the working table can be extinguished by throwing sand on them.

(iii) If any wooden structure has caught fire it is put up by throwing water on it.

(iv) Never throw water on burning oil or spirit. Since it will only spread the fire. Throwing of a mixture of sand and sodium bicarbonate on the fire is most effective.

FIRST AID BOX

A first aid box should be provided in every laboratory. It should contain the following materials.

Bandages (3-4 rolls of different sizes), gauze, lint, cotton wool, leucoplast.

A pair of forceps, a pair of scissors, safety pins. Glass dropper, two eye-glasses.

Vaseline, boric acid powder, sodium bicarbonate powder, a tube of Burnol.

Sarson oil, olive oil, glycerine.

Picric acid solution, Tannic acid solution 1% acetic acid, 1% boric acid, 1% sodium bicarbonate, saturated solution of sodium carbonate.

Methylated spirit, rectified spirit. Dettol.

STORAGE OF CHEMICALS

In storage of chemicals the following methods are normally adopted:

(i) Grouping the chemicals in a systematic way.

(ii) Arranging the elements in alphabetic order.

(iii) Arranging the elements and their components in which they occur in periodic table.

(iv) Grouping all elements and their similar components together.

(v) Numbering each bottle and jar and keeping and index book.

(vi) Keeping reagent bottles in definite places on the bench and the cupboard.

(vii) Storing similar types of solutions at one place.

(viii) Using coloured bottles or bottles with spots of coloured paint.

(ix) Using same type of bottles for a particular type of reagent.

(x) Always store large bottles on floor and not on shelves.

(xi) While storing Winchester bottles of concentrated acids, they be kept in brackets with sand.

(xii) Bottles containing inflamable liquids be stored in a cool place outside the laboratory.

(xiii) White phosphorus be stored under water and sodium be stored under kerosene oil.

(xiv) Hydrogen peroxide be stored in an air light tin.

LABORATORY ASSISTANT

Each laboratory be provided with a laboratory to perform the following duties:

(i) Keeping benches and laboratory clean.

(ii) Oiling benches with linseed oil.

(iii) To draft orders for chemicals and apparatus.

(iv) To receive the supplies of chemicals and apparatus after proper checking.

(v) To prepare solutions for volumetric analysis.

(vi) To prepare the solution for reagents shelf and to keep the reagent bottles full.

(viii) To set up apparatus for demonstration and experiments.

(viii) To maintain apparatus (burette, pipette etc.) in proper working conditions.

(ix) Keeping reagent bottles and chemicals at proper places.

(x) Periodic cleaning of iron stands, balances etc.

(xi) Keeping the first aid box replenished.

(xii) For repair of apparatus and glassware.

(xiii) Periodic checking of chemistry books in library and reference books in the laboratory.

REFERENCE BOOKS

Books containing following type of details be kept in the chemistry laboratory as reference books:

(i) Books containing physical constants of common substances.

(ii) Books which give the details of preparation of solutions for reagent bottles as also for volumetric analysis.

(iii) Recipes for cleaning glass ware and metals, removing stains, freeing glass stoppers, fire proofing etc.

LABORATORY DISCIPLINE

Maintaining discipline in laboratory is more difficult as compared to maintaining discipline in the class room. This is so because, pupils doing the same work wish to talk and discuss with others. Modest talking is inevitable in the laboratory. Yet talking and walking in the laboratory may cause accidents. Following rules will help to avoid any such accidents:

1. Admission to the laboratory in the absence of teacher should be avoided.
2. Teacher should not be late unduly.
3. Students should silently go to their places after entering the laboratory.
4. Before beginning his lesson teacher should wait for silence.
5. The teacher should adress the whole class.
6. Teacher should see that a complete silence is observed during his talk.
7. Teacher should change his pitch at times to add interest to his talk.
8. Teacher should make adequate preparation to keep class busy.
9. The teacher should for see and remove all possible causes of trouble.

10. Adequate apparatus be made available.
11. The teacher should try not to produce rigid discipline.

Following rules should be observed by students working in a chemistry laboratory:

1. Nothing should be taken out of the laboratory without the permission of the teacher.
2. Apparatus and chemicals be used only for specific purposes.
3. Any mistake be brought to the notice of the teacher, immidiately.
4. Breakages be reported to the teacher.
5. Before returning the apparatus to its original place it should be thoroughly cleaned.
6. Wastage of water, petrol gas etc. be avoided.
7. Make economical use of chemical reagents and chemicals.
8. All doubts be cleared with the help of the teacher.

Following rules if observed will help to avoid accidents:

1. Never use concentrated acids unless specifically instructed.
2. Do not mix chemicals aimlessly.
3. Do not taste chemicals without permission.
4. Pour liquids only down the sink.

16

A Rich Laboratory

Laboratory work is an essentiàl component of chemical education. However, schools in most developing countries are ill equipped for practical work, and even where laboratories have been built the problems of servicing the laboratory as well aş equipment are more acute. The basic problem is of funding the purchase of consumables and equipment, together with the associated maintainance cost.

In one area at least, in the provision of equipment, solutions are possible. Hakansson has pointed out, if the selection of equipment for school science is based upon 'principles' rather than upon obtaining accurate results, very simple and quite in expensive equipment can be used.

THE PLANNING

Teacher should be very careful while planning the purchase of equipment for the laboratory. He should carefully weigh each item to be purchased with its educational worth. He may classify his requirements as under:

(i) Apparatus required for laboratory work.

(ii) Apparatus required for demonstration purposes.

(iii) Apparatus required for general use.

While determining the quantity of apparatus to be purchased, he should keep the following points in mind.

(i) Financial resources at his disposal.

(ii) Demonstration and laboratory work that has to be done during the year.

(iii) Scheme of work including the method of teaching to be used.

(iv) Storage facilities available.

Before making actual purchases a list be prepared of experiments to be informed by students and principles to be demonstrated by the teacher. For demonstration only one set will do but for experiments to be carried out by the students the number of sets required will be equal to the member of students working at a time. Some additional sets be purchased to cover up for the breakages etc. only such articles which are really required should be purchased.

If only limited funds are available then the purchases of beakers, flaskes, funnels, files etc. should be accorded first priority. These are the articles which are required by students while doing experiments. When ample store of such articles has been made then only the apparatus needed for demonstration be purchased. Another important point which must be considered is that there is enough accommodation for the proper storage of articles likely to be purchased. While ordering for purchases scheme of teaching, method of teaching and knowledge and ability of teacher must also be given due consideration.

Keeping in view the points discussed above the teacher should prepare a list of articles to be purchased. While selecting apparatus teacher must not be tempted by attractive descriptions given in catalogue. While preparing an indent the teacher should give full specifications of the article required. In the absence of such specifications it is just possible that you make purchase of items which you never intended to purchase. For selecting a good firm the list of apparatus with complete specification be sent to some competing and reputed firms and they be asked to quote their lowest rates. A specimen for inviting quotation in shown below.

After receiving quotations a reliable firm quoting the lowest rate be asked to make the supplies.

The UNESCO designed apparatus for tropical schools is very satisfactory. The government of India is considering an arrangement for the manufacture of such instruments and making supplies of these to schools in lieu of cash grants.

S. No.	*Articles*	*Quality*	*Size*	*Quantity*
1.	R.B. Flasks	Pyrex glass	250ml	10 doz.
2.	Titration flasks	Pyrex glass	100ml	10 doz.
3.	Troughs	Pneumatic glass	12"dia	2 doz.
4.	Nitric acid	Commercial		51
5.	Sulphuric acid	B.D.H.		11

Chemistry teacher should carefully check the items received and then arrange them properly after making entries in the stock register.

METHOD OF PROCUREMENT

After preparing the list of items to be purchased the chemistry teacher should make purchase from the firms approved by the controller of stores or from some other approved source. However if no such source is available then he should send a list of his requirements to reputed firms for quotations. After receiving quotations, the teacher can select the dealers and firms for placing orders – the criterion being lower price and better quality.

It is desirable to patronise local and neighbouring firms. This provides the teacher a chance to select personally the items required and get them packed in his presence. Many a times it is better to go to a firm of repute and make the selection and purchase, and have the apparatus packed in one's presence. It is always wise to get insured against breakage and loss of the fragile apparatus ordered from out station firms.

On receiving the apparatus it should be carefully unpacked and after proper checking all the items of the purchase be catalogued and recorded in stock register then the goods received be properly stocked.

ARRANGEMENT AND CARE

The apparatus received be arranged in almirahs provided with glass fronts and preferably be fitted with mortise locks to avoid dust getting in. Apparatus should be arranged in such a way that each and every item could be easily located. Items which are frequently required be stored at such places that they are readily available. The apparatus should be arranged one deep of shelf; several rows of same articles may be placed on one shelf. The apparatus may be arranged either subject wise or alphabetically. If we arrange the apparatus subject-wise we find that some articles fall under more than one heading and if we arrange them alphabetically we find that glass and metal articles are coming together in which there is more likely hood of breakage. Thus it is always better to reserve a few almirahs for apparatus required for individual practical work in which the apparatus be arranged alphabetically. The chemicals can also be stored alphabetically.

A list be pasted on the almirahs showing the names of articles stored in it.

The apparatus needed only for demonstration purposes may be stored in separate almirahs subject-wise.

Chemicals can be stored even on open shelves. For this purpose two open shelves can be provided on either side of the recess for balances. However dangerous and costly chemicals like phosphorus or sodium or salts of mercury, bismith or cadmium be stored separately in an almirah. The containers or bottles containing chemicals should be neatly labelled.

To effect economy in space some items of common use such as stands, holders, clamps etc. many be stored outside almirahs. Two possible arrangements for storage of iron stands are shown on next page.

CARE OF EQUIPMENT AND APPARATUS

Care of equipment and apparatus is one of the important functions of the chemistry teacher. For this the apparatus kept in almirahs must be checked at regular intervals. During this checking operation the apparatus should not only be inspected but it should also be dusted, cleaned and polished if necessary. If proper care is taken the life of the apparatus will increase. For proper upkeep and maintenance the following points be kept in mind.

(i) After use the apparatus should be properly cleaned before it is returned to its proper place. Never return dirty apparatus to its proper place. This is specially applicable in case of glass apparatus used in chemistry laboratory. For proper cleaning of glass articles we can make use of soap, pumice stone, hot alkali solution, acidified potassium dichromate solution etc.

(ii) For cleaning items made of brass we can use *Brasso*. *Brasso* be applied to the article with finger covered with a piece of muslin, allowed to dry and then rubbed off with a clean duster.

(iii) Iron articles are generally polished. For polishing such articles use Black Japan thinned with a little turpentine or kerosene oil. Aluminium paint can also be used. If the article to be painted has any rust it should be removed, by rubbing with an emery paper, before painting the article. Use of kerosene oil can also be made for removal of rust. Take care to apply vaseline on screws and hinges of iron articles during rainy season.

(iv) Wooden articles be left in the sun after being polished with spirit polish. Spirit polish can be made by dissolving shellac in methylated spirit. One or two coatings of it are then applied on the article.

(v) The top of each laboratory table is unpolished but it should be waxed (specially in case of chemistry laboratory) to avoid the action of acids. For waxing either paraffin wax or candles can be used. Wax is coated over the table with the help of painters brush and is then spread over and smoothened using the hot iron of washerman. It is then allowed to dry and any excess of wax is scarped off with a blunt knife. It is then polished with a coarse duster.

(vi) Special attention be paid to keep sinks clean. For cleaning sinks use vein powder or some other cleaning powder. Use special chemicals for removal of stains if they persist.

(vii) In chemistry laboratory special attention be paid to the fact that stoppers of bottles are not lost or get changed. For this they should be tagged to the bottle either using a copper wire or a rubber band.

(viii) The apparatus which is frequently used by students may go out of its proper adjustment and a good chemistry teacher must find time for its proper adjustment and must also be able to carry out minor repairs. For this the chemistry laboratory must be equipped with a tool kit containing usual hammer, wrenches, pliers, screw drivers, forceps etc.

(ix) Glass panes of almirahs should also be cleaned occasionally. For cleaning glass panes use monkey brand soap. Rub a wet sponge over the soap and then over the pane and clean off with a duster. Pumice stone dipped in water is in methylated spirit and rubbed over the panes will remove all dirt.

(x) For cleaning of glass apparatus in general and burette and pipette in particular, use a solution of potassium dichromate acidified with dilute sulphuric acid.

THE RECORD

Maintaince of a proper record of the apparatus, material etc. in the laboratory is one of the important duties of the science master. For this after receipt of articles they should be thoroughly checked and then they be entered in the stock register. A specimen page from a stock register is shown on next page.

Seperate stock register be maintained for consumable and non-consumable items, permanent articles, glass articles etc. Following stock registers are generally maintained in schools:

(i) Stock register for non-breakable articles.

(ii) Stock register for breakable articles.

(iii) Stock register for consumable articles.

(iv) Stock register for permanent articles.

In addition to various stock registers following registers should also be maintained.

Order Register : This Register is meant for orders sent for the purchase of new apparatus. Entries in this register should indicate the serial number and date of the order, name of the firm to whom the order has been placed, details of articles ordered, articles received, cost of articles received. For convenience a copy of the order be posted on the left hand page of this register and a copy of supply under be pasted on the right hand page.

Requirement Register : This register if maintained makes the task of placing orders easier. Teacher will enter in this register the items whose absence is felt by the teacher at the time of demonstration of an experiment or during the practical class. If such entries are not made them there is every likelihood that some of the items needed by the teacher may be left out while placing the order for purchase *of* material and equipment. The requirement register should invariably be consulted by the teacher whenever be places orders for the purchase of materials or other requirements of the laboratory.

Specimen Page from Page............

Stock Register

Stock Register of....................................Department

Name of the article..............................

Month & Date	*Particulars (Name of the Firm, Bill No. and Date)*	*Receipt written of*			*Consumed/*		*Balance*		*Initials of Tr. incharge*
		Qty.	*Rate*	*Amt.*	*Qty.*	*Amt.*	*Qty.*	*Amt.*	

Stock Register for Science Club : Organising science clubs is quite useful in creating a scientific atmosphere and each secondary school is expected to have a science club. For organising various activities of science club the teacher needs different types of apparates, equipment and materials. It is desirable to maintain a separate stock register for the science club. In this register all the apparatus meant for science club be entered. Entries of models, charts and collections made by students should also be made in this register.

Maintainance of Stock Registers. Following points should be given done consideration while maintaining any stock register:

(i) The outer cover of the stock register should indicate the name of the register, name of the school, date of opening and closing of the register, etc.

(ii) A certificate be given on the first page of the register indicating the total number of pages in the register. All the pages be numbered serially and the above certificate be countersigned by the head of the institution.

(iii) Either seperate stock registers be maintained or the same stock register be divided into a number of portions under various heads such as Mechanics, Heat, Light, Sound, Electricity, Magnetism etc.

(iv) An effort be made to make entries alphabetically.

(v) An Index be given at the beginning of the stock register.

(vi) Each receipt entry should be entered with date of receipt and the items consumed or broken be shown in the columns meant for this purpose. All these entries be initialled by chemistry teacher and countersigned by head of institution.

HOME MADE APPARATUS

It is expected that science teacher is capable of devising and making apparatus for some simple experiments, modify apparatus and carry out simple repairs. The apparatus devised and made in school work shop or laboratory by the teacher or student is known as home-made apparatus. A science teacher with a little thought and ingenuity can make a number of valuable and serviceable models making use of cheap materials such as Jam-Jars, bits of wire, corks, motor parts etc. Some of the advantages of using home-made apparatus are as under:

(i) Such an apparatus is economical.

(ii) Use of such an apparatus makes more obvious the application of science to life and things around us.

(iii) It provides an encouragement to the student to make such an apparatus and adopt it as a hobby.

(iv) It helps to correlate science with manual training.

(v) It creates extra interest in the subject.

(vi) It provides training in manual skill, resourcefulness and ingenuity. These qualities are quite useful for life.

A *word of caution* for teacher in using house-made apparatus is that he must not sacrifice efficiency just for his over enthusiasm for using house-made apparatus.

LOCALLY PRODUCED LOW-COST EQUIPMENT

Such equipment can be made by individual teachers for their own use in schools or made available from a production centre. This type of equipment can serve the needs of the teacher, the student and the curriculum more effectively. As already pointed out such an equipment can be produced by individual teachers or can be procured from production centres.

EQUIPMENT MADE IN SCHOOLS

The UNESCO source book for Science Teaching contains a number of suggestions for simple teacher-made equipment in addition to a wide variety of experiments. One chapter has been specially devoted, in UNESCO Handbook for Science Teachers, to facilities, equipment and materials. The Guidebook to Constructing. Inexpensive Science Teaching Equipment, which have been produced at the university of Maryland (United States).

A phamphlet has been produced by the Junior Engineers/ Technicians/Scientists (JETS) based in the school of Engineering, University of Zambia. It is intended to help schools produce equipments such as wooden racks and stands for pipettes, burettes and test-tubes, and metal clamps, clamp holders and retort stands.

In India similar work has been undertaken by the National Council for Educational Research and Training (NCERT). Details for a mobile laboratory unit has been published in India.

The *Manual de quimica experimental,* produced in Bolivia contains a number of experiments which illustrate most of junior secondary level chemistry course. *e.g.* preparation and properties of common gases; acids, bases and salts; laws of chemical composition. In this manual instructions are written for teachers with little or no workshop experience, on how to make simple balances, various supports, an alcohol burner and some items of electrochemical equipment. It also provides a list of chemical that can be procured locally from market or pharmacy.

EQUIPMENT MADE IN PRODUCTION CENTRES

The production of equipments by teachers in their own schools and its advantages were taken up in the previous section. However many a teachers find it burdensome because of the fact that they are faced with day-to-day difficulties of teaching. Really speaking it is too much to expect teachers to be the sole providers of equipment. From their efforts we can develop local production units and the teachers can then be expected to maintain the equipment supplied to them. Warren and Lowe's. *The Production of School Science Equipment* provides an insight into developments in various countries. A summary of experience in Bangla Desh, Figi, Pakistan, India, Hongkong, Japan, Indonesia, Philippines, Singapore, Vietnam and Republic of Korea has also been published.

There are some large-scale projects, in developing countries, for production of locally based equipments. The concept of centres is not new, a prototype being set up in chile in 1964. Other production centres are NCERT (New Delhi), IPTST (Bangkok), the Science Education Production Unit (SEPU) in Kenya and the National Educational Equipment Centre (NEEC) in Pakistan.

NCERT (New Delhi) makes batches of 1500 lots for primary and middle schools and is under contract to UNICEF for 50,000 kits.

SEPU produces teaching aids (*e.g.* Slides and Photographs) and chemistry, biology and physics kits for secondary schools which are designed to meet all the practical requirements associated with East African Certificate of Education. Kits are accompanied by manuals for teachers and students. The emphasis is on pupil participation and small-scale experiments thus the kits are not suitable for demonstration work.

Some of the most essential points that must be kept in mind while establishing production centres for low-cost equipment are summarised below:

(i) The centre must have *expertise in design, in management* and *distribution.*

(ii) To overcome the *shortage of technicians,* the training of management staff and training of technicians is of vital importance. The committee on the Teaching of Science of International Council of Scientific Unions (ICSU-CTS) in conjunction with UNESCO, is endeavouring to discover the extent of the shortages and find ways of alleviating them.

(iii) *Realistic Budgeting.* The production centre must work to realistic budgeting. To lower the cost of production the production centre must be cost-concious. Making as large a range of apparatus as possible from a given item of equipment will help to lower production costs.

(iv) *Effective Marketing and Distribution.* For effective marketing and distribution it is essential to make an infra-structure between the production centre and the educational establishments. In small countries production centres may be set up to serve both the schools and the institution of higher studies.

(v) *Cooperation with Teachers and Curriculum Designers.* The production centres should design the equipment, to be produced, in conjunction with teachers and curriculum designers and only such equipment as needed in view of the requirements of prevailing text-books be only produced.

(vi) *Quality Control.* Before supplying the equipment to schools it must be checked for the quality including reliability. Only good quality equipment be marketed.

(vii) *Facility for Repairs and Maintainance.* The production centre must have an efficient system for repairs and maintainance.

THE CHEMICALS

It is possible to reduce the cost of teaching a laboratory-based chemistry curriculum by using small scale techniques. It is also important to consider how much and what chemicals are to be used.

Small-scale techniques are generally more safe and they also help to improve the manipulative skills of the students. Texts indicating how small-scale work can be used through out a school course have been published in many a countries.

To further reduce the cost of materials it is desirable that locally available chemicals are put to maximum use *e.g.* geochemical minerals, disused dry cells, scrap metal, vegetable oils, orange peel, root extracts, soap and baking powder.

In Thailand, IPTST[1] has oroduced a detailed list of chemicals readily available in local markets. The production of similar lists by institutions in other countries would be of much use.

COMPUTERS IN TEACHING

We find that in new programmes in chemistry teaching the computers are used increasingly. Many articles that have appeared in literature also point to the increased use of computers in teaching of chemistry. The applications of micro-computers in school chemistry can be classified as under:

Direct Teaching. In this type are included the use of computers for simulations, instructional games, revision questions and exercises.

Data Handling. This includes word processing, data base management and data collation and display in the laboratory.

Computer Assisted Learning. From the survey of literature we can easily find that most commonly the micro-computers are used in teaching of chemistry are used for handling of experimental data, *e.g.* interfacing with a gas chromatograph, monitoring and controlling clock reactions and the calculations of numerical constants.

Though micro-computers are quite expensive yet their education potential is considerable and they offer chemistry teachers an opportunity to experiment with imaginative and innovative ways of teaching chemistry.

CHARTS, DIAGRAMS AND PICTURES

Charts, diagrams, pictures etc. if displayed in the laboratory provides right scientific atmosphere to the place various details about these have been discussed in chapter on *Teaching Aids*. Here the topic is discussed just as a reference.

Charts : An all out effort be made to avoid display of printed charts available in the market because these charts are quite costly and are not fully representative. Such charts are also sacrifice simplicity and directness to details.

Following type of charts be preferred for display in chemistry room:

(i) Charts showing diagrammatic sketches of different pieces of apparatus generally used by students in their practical work. e.g. beaker, flask, gas-jar, retort, spirit lamp etc.

(ii) Charts depicting diagrammatic sketches of different important experiments from various branches of chemistry e.g. chart showing the preparation of oxygen, hydrogen, carbon di-oxide etc. Such a chart should be fully labelled and should be drawn in lead pencil.

(iii) Some charts for use in demonstration lessons.

(iv) A progress chart depicting the progress of each student be prominently displayed. Such a chart should show the complete record of work of the student.

(v) Some important do's and don'ts be also displayed on a chart placed at some prominent place in the laboratory.

(vi) A chart of common accidents and first aid be also depicted in the laboratory.

In addition to various types of charts given above, the following types of *pictures* and *illustrations* are quite useful if depicted in the laboratory:

(i) Portraits of great Indian and world chemists.

(ii) Pictures of scientific interest *e.g.* pictures of Nangal Fertilizer Project.

(iii) Pictures showing progress of chemistry, *e.g.* pictures of atomic power stations.

(iv) Maps indicating sources of ores, of metals and chemical products.

(v) Weather charts, maps and graphs prepared by students after observing and collecting data from weather reports.

(vi) Various types of demonstration models preferably prepared by students.

BULLETIN BOARDS

Each laboratory is expected to have at least three boards to be used as bulletin boards. These are to be used as under:

(i) One of the boards is reserved for display of newspaper cuttings, sciences news and pictorial illustrations of scientific interest.

(ii) One of the boards is reserved for putting up notices about science club activities.

(iii) One of the boards may be used for indicating the assignments.

IMPROVED APPARATUS

For teaching of chemistry availability of good apparatus and well equipped laboratories is a must. However it should lead us to a wrong conception that teaching of science cannot be carried out in the absence of expensive apparatus. One of the reports by NCERT observes that from among various factors that stand in the way of science education in our country one is lack of adequate resources for laboratory building, purchase of good and adequate apparatus and equipment. This lack of funds and resources makes improvisation of apparatus almost a necessity in India.

Need for Improvisation : India is a poor country and so we have only limited financial resources. For imparting effective and efficient science education, due to this financial constraint we require the production of improvised and inexpensive learning aids. A teacher with some ingenuity and manual skill can make a number of valuable and serviceable articles from discarded things all around him. For this purpose every science room should be equipped with a work bench and a kit of tools that may be used by students and teacher in making and improvising equipment for chemistry teaching.

Definition of Improvisation : Some of the definitions of improvisations are given below:

It refers to a make shift arrangement for accomplishing the intended learning task.

It refers to contrived situation that is created from reading available material for sake of convenience.

It refers to a stimulating situation for demonstrating and imparting learning is respect of controls and operations making use of low cost materials.

It refers to those learning aids which are prepared from simple and readily available cheap material by students and teacher.

Significance of Improvisation : Improvisation is quite significant and has many values as the process of improvisation needs resourcefulness and ingenuity on the part of the chemistry teacher. It is based on the concept of solving some problem by a make shift or alternate arrangement given below are some significant values attached with the process of improvisation:

(i) It splashes the cost of apparatus and is quite helpful in making the school self-reliant.

(ii) It has instructional value as well. When we are carrying out any improvisation we do get a proper feeling for the scientific process and designing. Thus we learn by doing.

(iii) It help develop the dignity of labour and also satisfies the urge of creative production.

(iv) It helps to develop the habit of cooperation and coordination.

(v) It provides training in thinking skills through the process of looking for low-cost substitutes or alternatives.

Process of Improvisation : It refers to a systematic way of constructing a piece of apparatus or designing an experiment. It involves the following steps:

(i) Making a careful study of the conventional apparatus or experiment.

(ii) Thinking of some low cost substitute that may be available in the market.

(iii) Designing the improvised apparatus or experiment.

(iv) Putting the improvised apparatus or experiment to test.

(v) Making further improvements in the improvised apparatus keeping the test results in mind.

(vi) Making use of the improvised apparatus in the laboratory for demonstration or practical work.

Examples of Improvised Apparatus : Some examples of improvised apparatus are given below.

Simple Tripod Stand : To make a simple tripod stand we have only to cut away A or n shaped piece from the sides of a discarded tin can. We can remove the lid and bottom of the tin can completely or we can simply make holes in the bottom. If holes are made it also serves the purpose or wire gauze.

Beehive Shelt : An improvised beehive shelf can be obtained from empty tin can. The tin can to be used for the purpose should be rust free and its inner and outer surfaces are either galvanised or varnished. To make a beehive shelf drill a hole of 1/2" diameter in the centre of the bottom of tin can and cut a V-shaped notch on one side of it. This can now be used as a beehive shelf.

In this boiling water from a kettle is allowed to condense in a jam jar which is immersed in a pan containing ice cold water. A simple glass tube fitted with a rubber tubing can be fitted to the mouth of the kettle and another glass tube is fitted to serve as outlet for condensed steam.

There are many more such items which can be easily obtained. Some such items are:

(i) Spring balance.

(ii) Spirit lamp.

(iii) Water voltameter.

(iv) Fire extinguisher.

Advantages of Improvised Apparatus : Some of the advantages of improvised apparatus are:

(i) These are quite cheap and economical.

(ii) They have great educational value. While devising such apparatus students gains more familiarity with the underlying principles of the apparatus.

(iii) It helps to develop the creative and constructive instructs of the child.

(iv) It inspires young students to explore and invent new things.

(v) It develops the lower of initiative and resourcefulness in the student.

(vi) It helps to develop power of scientific thinking.

(vii) It helps to inculcate the habit of diligency in the students.

(viii) It galvanises dignity of labour.

(ix) It solves problem of leisure time.

CHEMISTRY KITS

A chemistry kit is a container or box in which are stored some special apparatus/material and so these are readily available for experimentation and demonstration work.

The central science work shop, a wing of NCERT, New Delhi, has prepared kits for teaching of chemistry to various classes along-with manuals and detailed guidance for the use of these kits by the teacher and the students.

The material stored in these kits is easily available in market and some of the items of these kits can be improvised or made in work shop by carpenters or black smiths. These kits are of three types:

(i) Kits which are helpful for demonstration of certain specific facts and principles.

(ii) Kits which help the students in performing experiments and draw inferences so as to study facts and principles.

(iii) Kits which are useful for both teachers and students.

The *demonstration kit* devised for chemistry by NCERT can serve the purpose of demonstration kit for classes VII and VIII. It contains chemicals, glass apparatus etc. required for demonstration of various experiments. In it there is a total of 63 items of apparatus, 67 chemicals and it contains 12 types of containers. Apparatus stored in the kit is mostly improvised apparatus and the containers are bottles and ink phials. All the items of the kit are arranged in a suitable manner and are packed in a box made of wood. Such a box can be easily transported. This kit contains no liquid chemicals and these have to be arranged locally whenever the need arises.

Chemistry pupil's kit is meant for use of students in their practicals and it can serve as a 'mini laboratory' for village schools. The front covers of the kit can be hinged to serve as a table. It contains 37 different items, 40 chemicals and 10 types of containers for chemicals. It is also provided with two test tube stands, one on each side of the box. These can also be used as handles for lifting the box.

The Advantages : Some of the important advantages of the science kits are summarised below:

Low Cost. These kits are very economical and a primary science kit costs only around rupees one hundred. All the kits for a middle school are not likely to cost more than Rs. 3000/-

Use of Indigenous Resources. Majority of items stored in chemistry kits are indigenous and no import or foreign collaboration is required.

Easy Replacement of Items. Various items stored in chemistry kit can be easily replaced in case of loss or breakage etc.

Easily Portable. The kits are easily portable and can be easily used for demonstration in classes being met in open or under trees.

Economy of Time. Being planned in a very systematic way, minimum time is needed for setting up an experiment by using such kits.

Consolidated Material. All the essential items of apparatus, equipments, chemicals etc. are arranged in such a way that any item can be put to multipurpose use. In this way material is consolidated in a chemistry kit. Moreover all the material needed for an experiment is consolidated in the kit.

Economy in consumption. In a science kit the items stored are in mini size and so the consumable items such as chemicals etc. are consumed in small amounts.

Teacher's Innovation. The science kits can serve to motivate and inspire an innovative chemistry teacher to work out new ideas and he can encourage his students to improvise new apparatus and experiments.

Students Involvement. Since the various items stored in science kits are quite simple so they can be easily handled by the students. It encourages the students and they become active participants in the teaching-learning process.

TEXT BOOKS

In the present educational set up the role of text-book is of prime importance. However we find that little attention is paid to this important aspect of education. Most of the text-books in chemistry are not of good standard. They follow the prescribed syllabus too rigidly and no attention is paid to develop the topics according to the need and interest of students. A good text book is one which is a source of knowledge arranged systematically ands it enables the reader to acquire the needed information quickly. It inspires the student to invent, to discover and to inculcate scientific methods. However teacher should not depend solely even on the best of the text books because even such a text book omits many details which teacher wants to tell to his students.

The use of a text-book is made by the students for completing the preparatory part of an assignment. They also use their text-book for doing revision of course. Some students also consult and use their text books to study at home, the demonstration lesson given to them by their teacher in school. In this way text-books are used to supplement the class work. Text books also provide a help to students in correct understanding of basic concepts and principles of science.

Generally a numbei of books are prescribed by board or university to be used as text books. NCERT prepared text books are available upto class XII. While recommending a text-book to his students the teacher should consider the following points to assess the worth of the book:

(i) Correctness of matter.

(ii) Purity of languages.

(iii) Simplicity of diagrams.

(iv) Quality of printing and binding.

Correctness of Matter : In this correction the standing of the author and the reputation of publishers should be considered. The books written by well known author having a long teaching experience of teaching the subject and possessing requisite qualifications be recommended. It would be much appreciated if certain minimum qualifications and experience for authors is laid down by authorities.

Purity of Language : A text book that presents the subject matter in a simple, clear and lucid language should be preferred. For text book in a regional language, the scientific terminology should also be given in English with in brackets. In such books only standard terminology evolved by the Central Ministry of Education and State Governments should be used.

Simplicity of Diagrams : Only simple and well labelled diagrams be given in text books. Such diagrams are self explanatory and help the student in properly-understanding the subject matter.

Quality of Printing and Binding : It is desirable that a text book makes use of a good quality paper and the quality of printing, and type of letters in fine. It should be so bound that its binding is appealing to the student.

In addition to the above a good text book is expected to select and arrange the subject-matter in a psychological sequence. The book should follow the aims of teaching chemistry and should serve as a guide for demonstration lesson as also for individual experiments. Each chapter should start with a brief introduction and a summary of the subject matter be given at the end of the chapter. Some assignments should also be given at the end of each chapter and the assignments should cover such areas as applications to life situations, numerical questions, suggestions for experimental work and projects, objective type tests etc. Heading and sub-headings be given in bold type. A table of contents be provided at the beginning and a subject-index be provided at the end. Glossary of some important scientific terms be given at the end of the book.

In most of the school still the traditional school chemistry text books are in use. Such books are used for reading, revision, to follow instructions for some laboratory exercise etc. However traditional chemistry text books have been abandoned in those countries in which 'process' has become a significant feature of school chemistry courses. In such countries generally well illustrated work-books that contain exercises for fostering the development of such 'process skills' as observing, hypothetising and inferring. These are accompanied by data books and books of questions for pupils and teacher's guides.

Text books also communicate to pupils various assumptions about the nature and purpose of scientific activity.

17

New Trends

Science education forms an integral part of our school curriculum upto the secondary level in the process of Universalisation of Science Education. The National Policy on Education (NPE)-1986 has laid considerable emphasis on strengthening the science education in the school education system. The current situation of teaching of school science content is as Environmental Studies at the lower primary level (classes I – V). Integrated approach of teaching science is followed at the upper primary stage (classes VI – VIII) and secondary stage (classes IX – X) by integrating all disciplines of Science in a natural fashion. The NPE-86 envisages extension through every effort of Science Education not only to those who are in the formal school system but also to those who have remained outside the system under non-formal and adult education programmes. The qualitative improvement in science education depends on many vital components. The teacher is considered as a crucial factor in the teaching-learning process, developing positive attitudes in the learners for better achievement and the formulation and implementation of science education programmes. The teachers have to discard their traditional methods and usual practices in relying entirely on textbooks. The teaching has to be integrated with environment based on real life situations using local experiences, expertise and resources. The classroom territory has to be expanded over the whole environment so that the activities become supplementary to classroom teaching. If such an approach is systematically implemented with mobilisation of needed resources, it is very much likely that there may be an improvement in our science education at the school stage. Several attempts are being made to improve science teaching in our country, both at the formal as well as non-formal sectors of school education. Some of the innovative experiences in science education at the school level include Nehru Science Exhibition, Science Museums and Mobile Science Vans, Vikram Sarabhai Science Centre Ahmedabad, Kerala Shastra Sahitya Parishad and Ekalavya Project etc. In such innovative experiences and science activities, the learning is fitted to the abilities and interests of learners as there exists an opportunity for individuals initiative, independent or collective study and creativity. A large number of such activities are organised in India. A few of the major activities are listed and described briefly here.

EXHIBITION FOR SCIENCE

November 14 is the birth anniversary of Pandit Jawahar Lal Nehru, our first Prime Minister. Children call him Chacha Nehru, as he used to love them much. We celebrate Children's Day on November 14. On this occasion Science Exhibition is also organised by the NCERT. This exhibition is Science Exhibition. To start with, this exhibition used to be organised at New Delhi where Pandit Nehru used to live, when he was our Prime Minister. Now this exhibition is organised in different states. Children from country, from all States and UTs participate in this exhibition. Nehru Exhibition is organised at the national level.

Every year NCERT announces a main theme and sub-themes for Nehru Exhibition. Children make their exhibits on these sub-themes.

Main Theme: Science in our Environment

(i) Agriculture, Horticulture, Farming and Animal Husbandry.

(ii) Conservation of the Environment

(iii) Health

(iv) Energy Conservation and Needs

(v) Astronomy

(vi) Town and Village Planning

(vii) Machines in the Service of Rural Areas

(viii) Teaching Aids for Science and Mathematics

(ix) Innovations.

This information along with the last date of submitting the entry with the dates of exhibition reaches every school of the country, from States and UTs and from States and UTs to all schools. On information children start working on their projects—static or workin investigatory science projects under the guidance and supervision of the teachers. If a school has a Science Club, it becomes quite active after information under the supervision and guidance of the Science Club.

ROLE OF TEACHER

Very often in Nehru Science Exhibition we see some static work or some noble experiments demonstrated by the students with lines and graphs. These are projects but not Investigatory Science Projects. Students should be encouraged and motivated to work on some of science projects, and bring them to Nehru Science Exhibition.

A project may be any purposeful activity. It may be a model working, or experiment.

A project which involves investigation, discovery and finding out which was not known to the student before, is an investigatory investigation is much more than the repetition of a standard

Experienced student is to decide what experiments are necessary. He may have to design his own apparatus, if that is not available in the laboratory. He has to search for the appropriate principles, laws, formulae, apparatus and data, and originate a solution to a problem. The student has to behave like a scientist.

Working on an investigatory science project is the way a student can learn science by project method which involves some steps of scientific method like Problem, Hypotheses and Experiment.

Every year more and more investigatory science projects are being seen in Nehru Science Exhibition. It is very encouraging. You should also encourage your students to work on investigatory science projects under your guidance and send it to Nehru Science Exhibition through District and State Science Exhibitions and Fairs.

THE MUSEUMS

You must have seen science museums. They are very effective and interesting sources of learning science. What experiences do you get from a science museum ?

Objectives of Science Museum. Main objectives in establishing science museums are:

(i) to help young science learners in understanding concepts of science by play way method.

(ii) to provide a glimpse of past as well as an insight into the future.

(iii) to help schools in their class activities by providing them with a number of equipments and specimens which are otherwise difficult for a single school to procure.

(iv) to arrange extension activities such as field trips, lectures, film shows and exhibitions for the students as well as public.

During the last decade or so, a couple of science museums have been set up in the country including one at Delhi, the Natural History Museum. In Delhi's Pragati Maidan, National Science

Centre (National Council of Science Museums) has also been set up few years back. It has several units. 'FUN GAMES' and 'ENERGY' units are very interesting for students. Delhi also has two Primary Science Museums:

(i) Municipal Corporation Children Resource Centre (MCCRC) at R.K. Puram, Sector VI.

(ii) New Delhi Municipal Council (NDMC) Science Centre at Lakshmibai Nagar.

There are good science museums in various parts of the country – Bombay, Bangalore, Calcutta. All these science museums are doing very good Job, carrying out various innovative activities, in science for the improvement of science education. Let us discuss some science museums a little bit in detail.

Nehru Science Centre. The Nehru Science Centre (NSC) is established in Bombay by the National Council of Science Museums. The most important and attractive part of the NSC is a 'Science Park' for children. With green surroundings, the Children's Science Park has exhibited on time, motion, energy, power and work. Also, there are models of railway engines, tram cars, aeroplanes, steam lorries, a windmill and a sun dial. There are birds, animals and fish to acquaint children with nature. While children enjoy the Science Park the most, it also helps them to understand 'what' 'why' and 'how' of the queries, questions and problems haunting their minds.

Nehru Science Centre, Bombay is basically multi-disciplinary in character. Collection of antique exhibits of historic value, presentation of the same through permanent and temporary exhibitions on selected themes, extension activities offering multiple avenues of learning, enjoyment and training to the student community as well as the public, taking science to rural areas through mobile science vans, aiming towards interacting mode of presentation of themes are some of the ways in which the NSC operates. The Science Centre also offers a gallery on 'light and sight'. It presents different principles involved in file process of 'seeing and the vision.' A survey is made of vision, its defects, its importance, its complexities and varieties. Nehru Science Centre also organises extension activities such as science extension in rural areas, film video shows, science seminars for schools, films, video cassettes loan service, amateur weather station, amateur radio classes for children, sky observation programme, astronomical camps, popular science lectures, special science film festivals, aeronautic modelling programmes and training camps for under-privileged children.

Visvesvaraya Industrial and Technological Museums. The Visvesvaraya Industrial and Technological Museum is established in Bombay. It organises various activities and programmes such as motive power gallery (science museum), teacher training, hobby centre, student's science seminars, science quiz, science fair, temporary science exhibitions, science demonstration lectures, mobile science exhibitions, film shows, popular science lectures, etc. The museum has also a regional science centre at Gulbarga.

If you have a science museum at the place where you teach, plan a visit to that museum. If your students go to some places, where there are science museums, ask them to visit them with their parents or if you arrange a field trip to any place, where there is a science museum, take your students there, and see how much science they learn—the science which is not there even in their science books.

Mobile Science Vans. Some science museums have mobile science units, museums on wheel. They are usually sent to the places, where there are no science museums. They are not as big as a science museum. They do not have as many science exhibits as a science museum has. But even this is a very effective source of learning science for students at upper primary level.

Natural History Museum, New Delhi, National Science Centre, New Delhi and Nehru Science Centre, Bombay have Mobile Science Vans. You try to find out whether there is some science museum, not very far from the place you are teaching, and whether that science museum has the facility of mobile science vans. You can ask such museums to send that unit to your school. If you are successful to bring it, your students may visit the science museum even in their school, and can learn a lot of science.

VARIOUS INSTITUTIONS

For improving the quality of science learning in non-formal system of education, Vikram Sarabhai Community Centre was established in Ahmedabad in 1963. The Centre is one of the pioneer organisations in the country providing a variety of out-of-school activities in science for students, teachers and community. It has a team of highly skilled staff which acts as a nucleus and catalyst for various programmes undertaken by the Centre.

The Centre conducts research and innovative programmes for improving education and community life. These programmes include studies on science and mathematics, environmental studies, integrated science and science learning improvement programmes through enquiry approach, mathematics laboratory, teacher orientation, designing and development of teaching and learning material packages.

The Centre also organises programmes for rural as well as urban community. These programmes are related to the problems of pollution, health, security, population, communication, settlement and values. The Centre is basically a community centre where people come with their children and learn science where interested teachers and scientists experiment new ideas in teaching and learning. The Centre organises science seminars, film video shows, popular lectures, exhibitions, sky-gazing through a telescope, etc. The Centre has a library, laboratories, science museum, workshop, science playground, mass media and A.V. facilities for the community. The Centre provides facilities in rocketry and electronics hobbies to children. In science playground, the children get a glimpse of science through play toys, colour filter towards musical pipes, sand, pits, water pond and evolution pillar.

The centre has also started some small extension centres to the rural areas. A mobile van equipped with a laboratory and A.V. materials tours different villages. Science club activities are organised in rural areas based on emphasis on the environmental awareness.

The Kerala Shastra Sahitya Parishad (KSSP) is a voluntary organisation. It was established in 1963. KSSP has around 10,000 members comprising scientists, doctors, engineers, social scientists, teachers, students, workers, peasants and technicians. It has 600 units all over Kerala.

Objectives

1. To popularise science amongst society.
2. To generate science literacy amongst people.
3. To increase community involvement for developing scientific temper in the society.
4. To develop rural technology in the field of energy.
5. To organise health camps, classes and audio-visual campaigns on a wide scale.

Activities. The society has about eight major areas of activities –

(a) Publications, (b) Non-formal Education, (c) Formal Education, (d) Environmental Bridge, (e) Research and Development Wing, (f) Rural Science Forums, (g) Health Brigade, (h) Art and Science.

The details of these activities are as follows.

Publications. KSSP prints a variety of scientific periodicals and books meant for popularisation of science and generation of science literacy amongst the people. These include:

(i) Eureka – monthly magazine for primary classes.

(ii) Sastrakeralam – monthly magazine for secondary School children.

(iii) Sastragathy – monthly magazine for adults.

(iv) Parishad Vartha – monthly bulletin for members.

Non-formal Education. These activities cover a wide spectrum, the main ones being 'Science Campaign' and 'Science Centre.'

Formal Education. KSSP promotes a number of activities aimed at improving science clubs, talent tests and promotion of awareness about the education system amongst the public. The talent tests are:

(i) Eureka Talent Tests—at elementary level.

(ii) Sastrakeralam Quiz—at high school level.

(iii) Sastragathi Talent Tests—at college level.

Environmental Bridge. KSSP was involved m Silent Valley Campaign, Social Forestry Programmes and campaigns against industrial pollution.

Research and Development Wing: Its responsibility is to develop appropriate rural technology in the field of energy, environment etc. A high efficiency *Chulha* (Stove), developed by them has been widely propagated.

Rural Science Forums: KSSP has initiated these forums to prompt villagers to think on their own about their problems and solutions.

Health Brigade: KSSP organises health camps, classes and audio-visual campaigns on a wide scale.

Art and Science: It organises Sastra Kala Jatha and Bharat Kala Jatha.

Ekalavya Science Teaching Project (ESTP) started in 1972 in sixteen rural middle schools of district Hoshangabad in Madhya Pradesh for teaching science through environment based discovery approach. This project was started by Kishore Bharati, in collaboration with Friends Rural Centre, Rasulia with the support of the Department of Education, Government of Madhya Pradesh. A large number of teachers and scientists from various institutions and organisations such as the All India Science Teachers Association, Physics Study Group; Bombay Municipal Corporation; Gandhi Vidyapeeth, Vedehi, Surat District; Lok Bharti, in Gujarat; The Space Application Centre, Ahmedabad; Universities of Delhi, Rajasthan and Indore; The Tata Institute of Fundamental Research, Bombay; Indian Institute of Technology, Kanpur; NCERT, DAV College of

Education, Abohar (Punjab) etc. participated in the development of curriculum, workbooks, science kit, other materials and training of teachers.

In 1978 this programme of science teaching was extended to all the 206 middle schools of District Hoshangabad.

Objectives

1. Implementation of introducing innovations as envisaged in Ekalavya Project within the given framework of the Government school system.
2. Encouraging science teaching through discovery approach in Indian schools.
3. Providing science education experiences through environment.
4. Developing ability among students for applying scientific methods in different situations.
5. Developing scientific attitude (scientific temper) among the students.

Curriculum. Keeping in view the objectives of this Ekalavya experiences the curriculum of science teaching has been on process approach rather than product approach. The process approach of learning science provides numerous opportunities to children to explore scientific phenomena of their local environment. Most of the curricular contents have been taken from their environment. Advanced scientific concepts, such as abstract chemical symbols, theoretical concepts of atomic and molecular structure, and human anatomy etc. have not been included in the curriculum because these concepts are beyond the students direct interaction with the environment.

The selection of curricular content is dependent upon:

(a) relatedness to environment, (b) relatedness to the needs, interests and mental level of the students, and (c) possibility of the application of discovery approach.

Through the above mentioned procedure the curricular contents for classes sixth, seventh and eighth was developed. Some of the examples of the curricular contents for various classes are given below:

Class VI	Kuchh Khel Khilwar
	Samuh Banana Sikho
	Hamari Phaslen aur Samuhikaran
	Vidyut
	Ganak Ke Khel
	Jeev Jagad me Vividhata
	Mini, Pathar aur Chattane
Class VII	Ek Majedar Khel
	Jar aur Patti
	Keeron Ki Duniya
	Phaslon Ke Dushman
	Apni Haddi Pahachano
	Aakash Ki Or
	Taraju Ka Sidhant
Class VIII	Jantuon Ka Jivan Chakkar
	Phool aur Phal
	Paudho me Prajanan
	Vargikaran Ke Niyam
	Jantuon ka Vargikaran
	Gasen

Work Book and Science Kit Materials. In this programme, the workbook is introduced in place of textbooks, which is process based. Principles of science are discovered through experiments.

Science Kit is very conducive for discovery approach to science teaching.

Teaching Method. Discovery approach of science teaching is the main teaching method followed in this programme. Students learn science through inquiry approach especially by experimentation, discussion and field trips. The whole class is divided into subgroups of four students each known as a Toli. This Toli pattern is also followed in their teacher training programmes. The students perform experiments in their respective tolies, collect and analyse data and draw conclusions on the basis of the guidelines given in the workbook.

Examination. In this Eklavaya Experience the examination is not based on rote memory or recall etc. Independent observation, data collection, data analysis and drawing conclusions have been given due weightage. It also seeks to test the extent of a pupil's readiness to innovate through physical experimentation.

The examination is conducted to test three basic elements of science teaching, namely, scientific skills, scientific attitude (scientific temper) and understanding of scientific concepts and principles.

Questions

1. When is the Nehru Science Exhibition organised? Who organises it? Where is it organised? Who participate in it? What is the nature of exhibits displayed in it?
2. What is the difference between a 'science museum,' and a 'mobile science unit'? How will you use them in science teaching?
3. Name the science museums you have seen. Where are they located? What did you see in them?
4. Name the city and State where "Vikram Sarabhai Community Science Centre" is situated. What are its activities?

5. What do you mean by "KSSP"? When was it established? What are its activities?
6. What do you mean by "ESTP"? When and where was it started? What are its objectives? What materials were developed under this project?

PLACE AMONG OTHER DISCIPLINES

In many countries of the world, the primary school curriculum bears little relation to that of fifty years or so ago. Then the subjects were reading, writing and arithmetic. Now the curriculum is achieved much more as a whole. The primary school curriculum has to a considerable extent become integrated and a large number of good primary school teachers possess a broad background, which enables them to guide their pupils' learning on a variety of topics as often based as the surroundings of the school.

However secondary school curriculum generally consists of a number of separate subjects having little or no coordination between them. This may largely be due to the training received by secondary school teachers and to the public examination system which a strongly subject bounded. An attempt has been made in recent years to bring about an integrated curriculum which has helped to bring various science subjects closer but no effort has been made to consider other areas such as languages, mathematics and social sciences.

IMPORTANCE OF CORRELATION

No subject can be taught in isolation and so is the case with teaching of chemistry. For an effective learning full advantage must be taken of various correlations and applications of chemistry. In addition to correlation of chemistry with other school subjects and daily life, a lot of correlation is possible with other science subjects. Artificial division of science into various branches is a matter of convenience and not of necessity. Based upon this premise, many educators advocate the implementation of curricula based upon the correlation between various subjects. These kinds of curriculum give more meaning to our class room instructions. Various inventions in chemistry have contributed a lot to the social and physical advancement of our society. Chemistry has contributed a lot to development of some other subjects. In the following pages we will take up the correlation of chemistry with other subjects.

CORRELATION BETWEEN CHEMISTRY AND LANGUAGE

Chemistry in closely related to language in which it is taught. This correlation arises because of the fact that language provides not simply a way of communicating with others but it is also the vehicle of thought. A student can not grapple with a scientific problem without the use of words. This brings about the importance of encouraging the student to master a language both in its spoken and written forms.

Practical work in science provides a very good opportunity for development of a language. It can be developed by discussion between the student and the teacher and also by discussion amongst students themselves. The written form of the language can be developed by encouraging the students to make their own record of practical work, may be in the form of a diary, instead of copying it from the book or black board.

CORRELATION BETWEEN CHEMISTRY AND MATHEMATICS

Mathematics and chemistry are closely related to each other. Actually speaking mathematics is considered as the mother of all sciences. A thorough knowledge of some fundamentals of mathematics is very useful in understanding certain concepts of chemistry. A closer coordination between the chemistry teacher and mathematics teacher makes the job of teaching chemistry easier.

In physical chemistry such topics as thermodynamics, chemical kinetics, radioactivity etc. Can only be properly understood by using certain mathematical equations. For derivation of such equations the students must be familiar with various sign used for representing certain mathematical operations.

Thus we conclude that there is a close relationship and so there is a correlation between chemistry and mathematics.

CORRELATION BETWEEN CHEMISTRY AND SOCIAL SCIENCES

Chemistry is a highly useful subject for the present day society. Many an inventions in chemistry have a lot of social implications and influences the social thinking of individuals. Knowledge of chemistry is quite useful in dispelling superstitions. The contribution of chemistry in development of society is visible in all walks of our life. Many a luxuries which have now become essential for comfortable living owe their origin to knowledge of chemistry. Teacher can refer to such contributions of chemistry while teaching the social sciences. In history reference can be made to various inventions in chemistry which were used to fight or win wars. Geography depend highly on chemistry for some of its aspects. The two subjects geography and chemistry overlap in various areas particularly in areas of study of rocks, atmosphere, hydrosphere, lithosphere, minerals, rain etc. Present day geography is considered as one of the science subjects.

CORRELATION BETWEEN CHEMISTRY AND PHYSICS

Chemistry and physics both are branches of science and they have a large number of common concepts. Many a laws of chemistry can be quite useful for explanation of certain important concepts in physics. The illustration of common topics in chemistry and physics is given by topics such as nuclear physics, thermal physics, atomic physics etc. Many a methods of chemistry are used for carrying out the experiments in physics. This points to a scope of great cooperation between chemistry and physics teachers.

CORRELATION BETWEEN CHEMISTRY AND BIOLOGY

The correlation between chemistry and biology is so large that at present we came across such subjects a "biochemistry". There are many a topics in biology which are quite dependent on knowledge of chemistry, *e.g.* biomolecules, working of various human systems such as blood circulation, digestive system etc.

The knowledge of chemistry is helpful in understanding various diseases and in helping to cure/prevent such diseases.

From the above we find a lot of correlation between chemistry and biology. For a better teaching there should be close cooperation between the chemistry teacher and biology teacher.

CORRELATION BETWEEN CHEMISTRY AND WORK EXPERIENCE

There is a lot of correlation between chemistry and some of the work experience subjects. It is due to this that in many schools chemistry-teachers are assigned the duties which require them to take some work experience subjects. A few such subjects are:

(i) Candle making.

(ii) Itching.

(iii) Engraving.

(iv) Chalk making.

(v) Preparation of shoe polish and nail polish.

(vi) Preparation of soaps and detergents.

(vii) Preparation of antiseptics, cosmetics etc.

CREATIVITY AND CHEMISTRY TEACHING

Chemistry like physics is an experimental science and so it has grown through inventions and discoveries. These require a lot of creativity. It is possible to fulfill the creative urge of students if chemistry is taught to them using the method 'learning by doing'. For this the teacher is expected to impart chemistry instructions in such a way that students are actively involved in all activities and it places a good deal of responsibility on chemistry teachers.

Creativity has been defined in various ways, however there is one thing in common in all these *i.e.* creativity is a process of change, of getting away from main track, of sensing gaps or disturbing missing elements.

A definite correlation has been shown between creativity and intelligence. A high intelligence does not mean high creativity. According to Guilford, creativity represents patterns of primary abilities, patterns which can vary with different spheres of creative ability. It is generally believed that creativity consists of about 120 abilities, the most important of these being sensitivity to problems, fluency of ideas, originality and redefining.

Some of personality characteristics found in creative persons are:

1. Curiosity
2. Ambition

3. Drive
4. Independence of Judgement
5. Self assertion
6. Imagination
7. Initiative
8. Concern for basic problems
9. Openness
10. High ego strength
11. Emotional stability
12. Less talkative
13. Abstract thinking
14. Non-conformist attitude
15. Capability to take risk.

It is possible to foster creativity, through chemistry, in children if we make use of scientific methods in teaching of chemistry. The important of such methods are problem solving method, project method, laboratory method etc.

We can say that most chemists were creative because they relied on method of discovering new knowledge. For fostering creativity in children the chemistry teacher is expected the perform varied roles. He is expected to perform the following roles:

(i) He should give due consideration to questions and ideas of his students.

(ii) He should put provoking questions in class.

(iii) He must be able to recognise originality and should value such an originality.

(iv) He must foster in his students an ability to elaborate a given point.

(v) He should set more questions and problems for experimentation.

(vi) He should help in developing creative ideas.

(vii) He should have guided and planned experiences.

(viii) He should emphasise for research of truth through experimental research.

(ix) He should choose same investigatory projects in chemistry which give his children an opportunity of self-direction.

(x) He should encourage his students to improvise chemistry apparatus and experiments.

Muslims, Nation and the World

Life and Thought of Abul Hashim, Leader of the Bengal Muslim League

Muslims, Nation and the World

Life and Thought of Abul Hashim, Leader of the Bengal Muslim League

Sho Kuwajima

LG PUBLISHERS DISTRIBUTORS

First Published, 2015

ISBN 978-93-83723-05-8

Price: ₹ 595

Published by
LG PUBLISHERS DISTRIBUTORS
49, Gali No. 14, Pratap Nagar
Mayur Vihar Phase I, Delhi 110 091
Tel: 011 2279 5641 email: lgpdist@gmail.com

Printed at
Mudrak, 30 A, Patparganj, Delhi 110 091

Contents

Preface

This is a revised and enlarged work of my earlier article on Abul Hashim which appeared in a book edited by me, *Life, Freedom and War-Twentieth Century South Asia* (Aakar Books, Delhi, 2010).

Abul Hashim, the Secretary of the Bengal Provincial Muslim League in 1943-47, was a political leader and thinker. He has attracted less attention compared with Fazlul Huq and H. S. Suhrawardy, both Chief Ministers of undivided Bengal. Hashim did not show any interest in ministerial posts. He liked reading even after he lost his eyesight, and stressed on the importance of 'ideology' in politics, but tried to keep aloof from 'power politics'.

At the beginning of the 1940s there was a trend of thought and action called the Left or the Progressives inside the All-India Muslim League. Mian-Iftikhar-ud-din represented this trend in western India. His shift from the Indian National Congress to the Muslim League in September 1945, and his idea of Hindu-Muslim unity was criticized as fanciful by the Congress leaders. But it was also true that Mian-Iftikhar-ud-din's rather isolated battle produced a stream of thought represented by Faiz Ahmad Faiz, a poet, and Mazhar Ali Khan, a journalist, both of whom fought against political corruption and military regime in Pakistan. In Bengal the Muslim League grew into the mass organization, or correctly speaking, a middle class-based organization under the dynamic leadership of Abul Hashim after he was elected as the Secretary of the Bengal League in November 1943. The Bengal League's remarkable results in the 1946 provincial elections could not be conceived without the role of Suhrawardy and Hashim. But the position of Abul Hashim and his Left was not so strong both among the League members of the Bengal Legislative Assembly, and also in their relations with the central League leadership. In the depth of despair Hashim was forced to request his leave from the post of the Secretary on February 14, 1947, though he later tried to realize his idea of 'Independent Bengal' in co-operation with Suhrawardy and Sarat Chandra Bose from April to June in the same year.

Here I tried to find out from the limited materials why Hashim and his followers were once called the Progressives or the Left, why Hashim's idea was shared by the Muslim educated youth, and why they seemed to have disappeared from the political scene in the critical pre-partition period. In this connection I spared some pages for Hashim's work during one year in Bengal after the formation of the Suhrawardy ministry in April 1946. Also I tried to understand what message Abul Hashim wanted to send to the world on the controversial issues throughout his checkered career full of hope and despair, and under the condition of loss of his eyesight in later years, while the eyes in his heart were widely open and simultaneously his political life was sometimes circumscribed by his own 'ideology'.

In preparing this work I own much to the help and co-operation extended to me by my friends for many years.

I would like to express my grateful thanks to Professor K.M. Mohsin who kindly helped me since I visited his office of the Department of History, Dhaka University in September 1978. He has become a real guide to the history of Bangladesh, providing me with related literature and introducing me to several scholars in Bangladesh.

Professor Harun-or-Rashid, a political scientist, not only took trouble to locate some books written by Abul Hashim, but kindly clarified some points described in his pioneering work first published in 1987.

I obtained useful information on Abul Hashim from Mr. Badruddin Umar, a political scientist and the author of *The Language Movement in East Bengal*. In addition to many letters which answered my questions, he kindly provided me his view of the political life of his father, Abul Hashim observed from the closest position at our meeting in November 2012.

I am also thankful to Mr. Syed Mansur Ahmed, the editor of a collection of essays on Abul Hashim, for kind clarification in connection with his paper written for it.

Both Mr. Umar and Mr. Ahmed helped me to understand colloquial Bangla expressions which appeared in their writings.

In Burdwan, with the kind guide of Mr. Noaman Zahedi I could get first-hand knowledge of the location where Hashim and his family lived.

Professor Amalendu De, the former President of the Asiatic Society, Kolkata, always encouraged my work since we first met at the beginning of the 1980s, and also found related studies for me.

In the 1960s I first took an interest in the life of Abul Hashim in the process of working on the Bengal Famine of 1943. How the growth of the Muslim League organization was made possible in the midst of the famine was one of my main concerns since then. Therefore I attached as Appendix 4 a short paper on the Famine which I read at the Department of History, Burdwan University in February 2008. This is a slightly revised version of the paper sent for the felicitation volume in honour of Professor Amalendu De.

I could read a copy of the *Millat,* a Bangla weekly founded by Abul Hashim, courtesy of Mr. Hiroshi Sato, one of the pioneers of modern Bengal studies in Japan. Reading the *Millat,* I could cover the critical one year after the birth of the Suhrawardy ministry, which I could not discuss in detail in my earlier monograph on Abul Hashim.

As usual, Mr. Shahabuddin Ansari, the former Chief Librarian, Dr. Zakir Husain Library, Jamia Millia Islamia, New Delhi, and a good friend of mine since 1962, helped me to locate out related literature.

There is no need to mention that only I am responsible for the views expressed in this work.

Lastly I thank to Mr. Rahul Saxena of LG Publishers Distributors for his careful support in bringing out my work in this present form.

1

Introduction

Abul Hashim: Political Life at a Glance

Abul Hashim (1905-1974) is a less known political leader despite his remarkable role in the political history of South Asia, and particularly in Bengal of the 1940s.

One of the main reasons is that he was politically active as the Secretary of the Bengal Provincial Muslim League during the limited period from November 1943 to February 1947. We may also add that he was one of the main players who worked for the 'Independent United Bengal' from April to June 1947.

Another reason is that when Hashim shifted to Dhaka in April 1950, he was sidelined by the colleagues and co-workers of the Bengal League in 1943-47, and was forced to act in an isolated way. This was an unexpected position as he believed that he contributed extensively to the making of a strong League branch in Dhaka under his leadership before the partition of Bengal in 1947.

Thirdly his political philosophy, which was once discussed in connection with the concrete political and economic situation in Bengal, began to walk alone after the formation of the League Ministry in April 1946, and particularly after his resignation as the Secretary of the Bengal League in February 1947. The complete loss of his eyesight by 1947 may have promoted the inclination to his own philosophy, though he never talked about this aspect of his idea.

He became known outside South Asia by the work of Wilfred Cantwell Smith, *Modern Islam in India,* revised edition, published in 1946. There he writes that since 1942 the Muslim League has become 'a Muslim-nationalist organization first by the adherence to it of the Muslim bourgeoisie and more recently by the adherence of peasants.'[1] Depending mainly on the *People's War*, organ of the Communist Party of India, he mentioned the growth of the Bengal Muslim League under the leadership of Abul Hashim.

> Bringing Muslim peasants under the influence of the League has been a remarkable achievement, and one entirely of the years since 1942. By the end of 1944 the Bengal Muslim League claimed half a million members, enabling its young left-wing secretary (Abul Hashim) proudly to call it "the biggest political body that Bengal has ever seen."[2]
>
> The Bengal Muslim League's 1945 draft Manifesto, published immediately after the Bengal ministry was overthrown, was still more radical (than that of the Punjab Muslim League in 1944), looked forward still more clearly to a people's rule.[3]
>
> In Bengal, the progressives, under the leadership of the able provincial secretary, Abul Hashim, fought the millionaires, represented by the Nazim al-Din ministry. At the annual Congress (Council?) meeting in November 1944, the former group, though powerful, was still unable to move beyond a subordinate position. In March 1945, the ministry fell—caught between popular pressure (some of it Muslim League) particularly for cloth rationing and against livid corruption, on the one hand, and the powerful, corrupt commercial magnates on the other.[4]

Abul Hashim was at the height of his political activities. However, Smith had not yet examined the thought of Abul Hashim in detail. As for W. Cantwell Smith's view on the Muslim League, D.D. Kosambi expressed his comments at the earliest stage.[5]

> The OM (Indian Official Marxists) thesis at this time was that the British would never transfer power to the Indian National Congress. The OM solution was that the Hindus and Muslims somehow equated to the Congress and the Muslim League, should unite to throw out the foreign imperialists. The question of the class structure behind the two parties was never openly raised, perhaps because the writings of W. Cantwell Smith led the OM to believe that the Muslim League was, in some mysterious way, at

> heart anti-British and on the road to socialism. One sure test of effective anti-imperialism, namely how many of the leaders were jailed or executed by the rulers of the empire, was not applied. The intransigence and the open alliance with the British, so profitable to the leading personalities in the League, and the insistence on the "two nation" theory were dutifully ignored. No emphasis has been laid on the total disruption of advanced peasant movements in the Punjab and in Bengal by the 1947 separation of Pakistan. For that matter, the OM dismissed the Satara peasant uprising (*patri sarkar*) of 1942-43 as pure banditry.

It is true that Abul Hashim maintained friendly relations with the Communist Party of India which carried a slogan of 'National Unity' and responded positively to the Pakistan movement in 1942-47. He continued to stress that the Pakistan movement was not against the Hindus, but against British imperialism. Also the peasant movement in Bengal, in which the *bargadars* (share-croppers) participated with the slogan of *'Tebhaga chai'* (We want a two-third share) was seriously affected by the negative response of the Bengal League leadership which considered the interests of the *Jotedars* (tenure holders) who were the League supporters in the rural areas. However, unlike most of the Muslim Leaguers, Abul Hashim did not accept the 'Two Nation Theory', though he thought that the basis of the Pakistan movement was the Lahore Resolution adopted at the annual session of the All India Muslim League in March 1940, which assumed two independent Muslim majority states in the eastern and western parts of undivided India. Hashim welcomed in 1946 the release of political prisoners who joined the Chittagong armoury raid of 1930, and did not deny the importance of the Quit India movement of 1942. He did not go to jail before 1947, but was arrested owing to his role in the Language Movement in East Pakistan of 1952. Why Hashim kept his independent thinking and action while maintaining discipline as a member of the Muslim League before the partition of India needs a separate analysis.

After partition in August 1947, Abul Hashim remained in India, and acted as the opposition leader in the Bengal Legislative Assembly. Since 1947 he was more interested in the study of Islamic thought and the philosophy of Rabbaniyat[6] on the basis of which his earlier political activities had been developed.

In February 1950 his house in Burdwan (West Bengal) was set on fire by the students and refugees. It was a relatively 'small' communal riot, but a heart-rending experience for Abul Hashim. He was forced to cross the border into East Bengal with his family, and settled in Dhaka in April. In this year Hashim's first book, *The Creed of Islam or The Revolutionary Character of Kalima* was published in November.[7] Azad Subhani, who initiated Hashim to the philosophy of Rabbaniyat writes in the foreword of the book: "The philosophy of 'Rubbaniyat' runs throughout the book from cover to cover although there is a direct mention of it only in one place, viz. the article on the conception of religion."[8] Hashim's own world outlook can be noticed in many parts of the book. Simultaneously we find in the book the conspicuous lack of his concrete analysis of the situation he faced in Bengal of 1943-47, while discussing the political, economic and cultural revolution.

Thus Hashim's political isolation after his move to Dhaka was caused by the standoffish attitudes of the erstwhile colleagues and co-workers and partly by his own philosophy. The latter aspect of Hashim's life is recognized by Kamruddin Ahmad, once a leader of the Dhaka branch of the Bengal Muslim League.[9]

In 1952 Abul Hashim was one of the main leaders in the Language Movement in East Pakistan against the compulsion of Urdu as the state language of Pakistan, and protested against the reckless police firing on the unarmed students and youth on February 21.[10] In his statement of February 23 he showed his deep sympathy with the students and youth who lost their lives, just as in his messages of 1943-47. He joined the movement in his personal status, but did not lose sight of what people tried to express. Later, in 1954 his party, the Khilafat-e-Rabbani Party (Divine Sovereign Party) fought the election for the East Bengal Legislative Assembly mainly outside the United Front against the Muslim League, though Abul Hashim called for the need of the United Front at the earliest stage. He not only lost his communication with his erstwhile colleagues, but soon felt it difficult to initiate a dialogue with new adherents in East Pakistan.[11] He found himself a voice crying in the wilderness after 1954.

It was Ayub Khan who saved Abul Hashim from his despondency in East Pakistan. After his military coup in 1958, Ayub Khan met Abul Hashim twice, and courteously received him as a learned Islamic scholar and political thinker.[12] After the first meeting Abul Hashim was appointed as the first Director of the Islamic Academy in Dhaka on November 8, 1960, and remained in this post till 1970.

He contributed a lot to the study of Islamic thought including the translation of the Quran into Bangla. Simultaneously Abul Hashim had to play the tragic role as a part of the military regime of Ayub who tried to curb the resurgence of Bangla nationalism under the ideal of Islam, though Hashim's attachment to the culture of Bengal so often forced him to protest against the repressive policy of the Pakistan Government. One of the serious shadows of his co-operation with the Ayub regime can be observed in the delicate change in his theory of nation which moulded the main framework of his idea since 1943. What this change means needs to be examined in detail.

However, Abul Hashim never made any statement in support of the military action by the Pakistan Government since 1971, and expressed his disagreement by his silence.

Bibliographical Introduction

For a long time since Wilfred Cantwell Smith's writing, Abul Hashim's thought and action was discussed mainly in connection with his role in the growth of the Bengal Muslim League before the Partition of 1947. In 1987 the first edition of Harun-or-Rashid, *The Foreshadowing of Bangladesh: Bengal Muslim League and Muslim Politics 1906-1946* appeared. This well-documented and systematic study made it much easier to trace correctly the history of the organization and movement of the Bengal League in its critical period 1940-47. The historical role of the Suhrawardy-Hashim group inside the Bengal League, and the later fissure between both leaders is also carefully observed.[13]

In 1974, Abul Hashim's autobiography, *In Retrospection* appeared. He writes vividly how he shifted his residence from Burdwan to the party office in Calcutta and 'democratized' the Bengal League on the basis of the strong district branches he built, getting rid of the organization depending financially on a few business magnates and League parliamentary members. In this sense, his comment on Mr. Fazlul Huq who resigned as the Chief Minister of Bengal in March 1943 is quite pertinent.

In his view, Fazlul Huq "spent the best part of his career as a politician in a socio-political environment in which leadership of the people lay in one's personal merits and personal service to the people who needed sympathy and support of reputed politicians for securing jobs and similar other favours. In this respect, Mr. Fazlul Huq was fairly generous and efficient. Every outstanding leader was then an institution by himself. Parliamentary party politics was in the making but was not strong enough to compel obedience of members to their Party. This is one of the reasons why Mr. Fazlul Huq was not loyal to any party."[14] Also Fazlul Huq was 'a typical Bengali', and "never submitted himself to the discipline of non-Bengali leadership. Mr. Suhrawardy and Khwaja Nazimuddin were tied to the apron strings of Mr. Jinnah. This made Mr. Fazlul Huq uncomfortable as the head of the Government of Bengal. This is the second reason why he could not remain loyal to the Muslim League for long."[15]

Abul Hashim's memoir ends with the description of his meeting with Gandhi in Calcutta on the day of India's independence, August 15, 1947. However, under the turbulent winds of the people's movement for the independence of Bangladesh in the first half of the 1970s, Abul Hashim seems to have confirmed the return to his original idea in his political life. The memoir was the product of the 1970s.

By the way, Kamruddin Ahmad noticed the change in Hashim's thought before the partition of 1947, and found that he could not accept what Hashim told him soon after his migration to Dhaka in 1950. Kamruddin Ahmad's two stimulating books cited earlier, succinctly writes about it as a political worker who was close to Hashim in 1943-47.

In 1990 Mafidul Hoque, *Abul Hashim–1907-1974* appeared as a most detailed study of the political life of Abul Hashim.[16] He followed the thought and work of Abul Hashim critically without losing sympathy with his physical handicap and the circumstantial adversity he faced. Mafidul Hoque appreciated Hashim's attachment to Bengal culture and his rational approach to Islam while maintaining critical view of his cooperation with the Ayub regime in 1958-68. Now, with the help of this thought-provoking work we can cover the whole of Hashim's life within the same field of vision.

After a decade, a collection of reminiscences of Abul Hashim edited by Syed Mansur Ahmed was published.[17] Besides a biography of Abul Hashim by the editor, Left intellectuals, Communist leaders, Islamic thinkers, journalists, scholars and other writers are recollecting their days with Hashim. Mohammad Toaha, who joined the Muslim League from the Communist Party of India, assesses critically the theory of the nation and the slogan of Hindu-Muslim unity carried by the CPI. Mohammad Abdul Gafur, who came to know Hashim after his shift to Dhaka, examines Hashim's position in the Tamaddun Majlis (Cultural Organisation) and the Khilafat-e-Rabbani Party in the 1950s. Badruddin Umar, Abul Hashim's son, writes in his "Amar Pita" that Abul Hashim was so seriously affected by the communal riot when his house was set on fire, and was never free from this dumb despair in his later life. We are forced to consider a life of Hashim beyond the segmental approach whether Hashim was an Islamic thinker or a political leader.

Finally I have to mention Badruddin Umar's three-volume autobiography.[18] This should be read, above all, as an autobiography of Badruddin Umar who taught at the universities in Rajshahi, Dhaka and Chittagong for some years, and also spent some years as a political activist. It is like a long novel by the author who acted as Amal in Rabindranath Tagore's drama, *Post Office* in his boyhood. He observes various aspects of human activities including politics and the academic world sometimes critically and at other times with sorrow or sympathy. His description of the familial background and a student life in Burdwan helps us to understand how

Hashim was attached to his life in Burdwan city and his village Kashiara. The story of his family's move to Dhaka in 1950 throws light on the unexpected difficulties Hashim faced both in his life and ideas.

ENDNOTES

1. Wilfred Cantwell Smith, 1969. *Modern Islam in India,* Lahore: Sh. Muhammad Ashraf, reprinted from London (1946) edition, p. 332.
2. Ibid., p. 334.
3. Ibid., pp. 336-7.
4. Ibid. p. 339. Smith wrote a comment on his book later, "This youthful work has many defects; among them, those of which the writer is most conscious—chiefly the inadequate understanding of Islam and also of the crucial role played in history by ideological and moral factors—are corrected as far as possible in the present study. The account of the sociological factors at work in the development, though one sided, is perhaps not invalid so far as it went, and may still be significant. But those factors, although valid, did not themselves add up to explain adequately what happened subsequently; neither the full cataclysm of 1947, nor the mood of vibrant stamina and creativity of Pakistan in the initial years of its existence, nor the subsequent disillusionment. The writer, it is now clear, had failed adequately to comprehend the integration of these mundane factors into significantly Islamic history" (Wilfred Cantwell Smith. 1959. *Islam in Modern History,* Mentor Book edition, New York: The New American Library of World Literature, pp. 212-3, fn. 5). It may be due to this reason that there is no reference to Abul Hashim and his thought in this later work.
5. D.D. Kosambi, "The Bourgeoisie Comes of Age in India (1946)" in D.D. Kosambi, 1957. *Exasperating Essays: Exercises in the Dialectical Method,* Poona: People's Book House, p. 18, endnote. This supplementary remark was added to the paper contributed to the *Science and Society,* New York, Vol. X, 1946. As for my view on the *Prati Sarkar* movement in 1942-46, see Sho Kuwajima. 1998. *Muslims, Nationalism and the Partition: 1946 Provincial Elections in India,* New Delhi: Manohar, pp. 73-9.
6. Abul Hashim writes, "Rabbaniyat in concrete terms means physical, mental, intellectual and spiritual development of man according to the divine way of creation, sustenance and evolution of the universe visible in nature, Al-Quran and in the life of the

Holy Prophet Muhammad (peace be on him)", Abul Hashim, 1974. *In Retrospection*, Dhaka: Subarna Publishers, pp. 31-2.

7. Here I use, Abul Hashim, 1985. *The Creed of Islam or The Revolutionary Character of Kalima*, 4th edition, Dhaka: Islamic Foundation Bangladesh, as my text.
8. Ibid., p. vii.
9. Kamruddin Ahmad, 1975. *A Socio-Political History of Bengal and the Birth of Bangladesh*, 4th edition, Dhaka: Zahiruddin Mahmud Inside Library, pp. 74-5.
10. Badruddin Umar, 1985. *Purva Banglar Bhasha Andolan O Tatkalin Rajniti, 3*, Chittagong: Bohi Ghar, pp. 361-2.
11. Kamruddin Ahmad, 1382 (Bengal Calendar). *Banglar Madhyavitter Atmavikash*, Dvitiya Khand, Dhaka: Zahiruddin Mahmud Inside Library, p. 158, and Mohammad Abdul Gafur, "Amar dekha Darshanik Rajnitivid Abul Hashim", in Syed Mansur Ahmed, 2007. *Abul Hashim: Tanr Jiban O Samaya*, 2nd edition, Dhaka: Jatiya Sahitya Prokash, pp. 369-70.
12. Badruddin Umar, 2008. *Amar Jiban*, Vol. 2, Dhaka: Jatiya Sahitya Prokash, pp. 251-3.
13. Here I am using, Harun-or-Rashid, 2003. *The Foreshadowing of Bangladesh: Bengal Muslim League and Muslim Politics 1906-1947*, Revised and enlarged edition, Dhaka: The University Press Limited.
14. Hashim, op. cit., pp. 26-7.
15. Ibid., p. 27.
16. Mafidul Hoque, 1990. *Abul Hashim 1905-1974*, Dhaka: Bangla Academy.
17. Here I use its second edition, Syed Mansur Ahmed (ed.), 2007. *Abul Hashim —Tanr Jiban O Samaya*, Dhaka: Jatiya Sahitya Prokash.
18. Badruddin Umar, 2004, 08, 09. *Amar Jiban*, Vol. 1 (1931-1950), 2 (1950-1968), 3 (1968-1971), Dhaka: Vol. 1, Sahitiika, Vols. 2 and 3, Jatiya Sahitya Prokash.

2

Background

Familial Background

Abul Hashim writes about his familial background as follows;[1]

> I was born and bred in a feudal environment. The family did not belong to the landed aristocracy. They were, however, landlords of their own village and they had a small estate yielding an annual income of 10 to 12 thousand rupees. Their main profession was government service.

His maternal grandfather, Nawab Abdul Jabbar Khan Bahadur was a Deputy Magistrate, and spent the greater part of his life in Bihar. After retirement he was appointed Prime Minister of Bhopal. Moulvi Mohammad Abdullah, the eldest son of Nawab Abdul Jabbar, was a Deputy Magistrate. Khan Bahadur Abdul Momin, the second son, retired as Divisional Commissioner of Chittagong. Moulvi Mohammad Abdul Hafiz, the eldest son of Moulvi Mohammad Abdullah, was an Accountant-General in the Indian Financial Service, and retired as Chief Auditor of the North West Frontier State Railways.[2]

Hashim's paternal grandfather, Moulvi Abdul Majeed, was a Class I officer of the Government of India, and was posted in the United Provinces of Agra and Oudh. His great grandfather, Khan Bahadur Gulam Asgar, was also a Subordinate Judge under the East India Company.[3]

Moulvi Abul Kasem, Hashim's father was the first child of Moulvi Abdul Majeed, and Mokarrama Khatoon, the youngest daughter of Nawab Abdul Jabbar.[4]

Abul Hashim recollects, "The family had not much attraction for town and city life. According to them towns and cities were good for working and earning but not for living, they preferred their village home. They spent much of their resources in building comfortable houses in the village.... My grandfather Nawab Abdul Jabbar died in 1918 when I was a boy of 13. So long as he lived, his children had to spend their holidays with him in the village. Thus from my childhood I had developed an attraction for village life. When I entered life as an earning member of the family, I also built a decent house with garden and tanks in the village."[5] This familial background delicately influenced the young life of Abul Hashim. He did not enjoy his student life in Calcutta and Aligarh, though he finally passed Law in Calcutta in 1931. He returned to Burdwan very often when he could not adapt to his student life, and later, to his political life. He also invited political leaders and followers to his village Kashiara.

The English education the family members received from the earliest days led them to government jobs. Khan Bahadur Gulam Asgar sent his children to English schools. Later, Abul Kasem started a Hostel for Muslim students in a big garden house belonging to a member of the family of the Maharaj Bahadur of Burdwan, and Abul Hashim was also sent to this Hostel. Moulvi Abul Qasim, the Superintendent of the Hostel initiated students to manual labour in the field. This also strengthened Hashim's attraction for village life. After Hashim had built his village home, he acquired some agricultural land and often worked in the field with labourers.[6]

His positive interest in various aspects of human life can be found in a wide range of hobbies he enjoyed; drama, photography (still photography to cinematography), dogs, animal husbandry and poultry. Hashim started studying Biology and read Darwin's *Origin of Species*. This again led him to the study of Sociology, Economics, Political Science, History and Law. He writes:[7]

> Study of Sociology led me to the study of Philosophy. From these studies I saw that for proper understanding of the Quran a fair knowledge of Philosophy, Sociology and Biology was necessary. I then devoted myself to a comparative study of Islam and Communism.

Abul Hashim's wide interest is observed in his first book, *The Creed of Islam or the Revolutionary Character of Kalima,* though the philosophy of Rabbaniyat narrowed it on the other hand. Most of his hobbies were given up after Hashim entered the political world and soon lost his eyesight. However, his broad outlook and concern lay beneath his thought in his later days too. Rabindra Sangeet was one of those 'hobbies', for which Hashim struggled in the 1960s.[8]

Inversely, his unconcern with the accumulation of his own wealth can be seen in the following episode he recollected.[9]

> During the infancy of my father (Abul Kasem), my grandfather Abdul Majeed disposed of the property left by his first and second wife. Thus my father did not inherit any property from his mother and from his aunt Nazrunnessa Khatoon. My grandfather Abdul Majeed was a sincere devotee of Islam. He personally lived a very simple life but was extremely generous to others. His generosity exceeded limits and consequently he incurred heavy debts. On one occasion, when one of his creditors attached his village house and put it to auction, his elder brother Nawab Abdul Jabbar paid his creditor's dues. My grandfather Abdul Majeed was advised by elders of our family to transfer his property including his homestead in favour of his third wife. This was meant to be a formal transaction necessitated by the extravagant generosity of my grandfather. But after the death of my grandfather his children by his third wife appropriated the whole property depriving my father and his sister A'fia Khatoon (two children by his first wife). My uncles Abul Khairat and Abul Hasanat (two of seven children by his third wife) were minor children when my grandfather died. My mother died in the lifetime of her father. I, therefore, did not inherit any property from my maternal and paternal ancestors. My maternal grandfather, Nawab Abdul Jabbar, however, gave me a nice house on the Grand Trunk Road, Burdwan. When my father died I received a leather portfolio, an eye glass and a fountain pen which he left under his pillow. I do not think I shall leave any property for my children to inherit.

This last 'promise' proved true. Hashim was consistent in his unconcern with his private wealth and ministerial post since he entered political life.

Abul Kasem and His Age

The family had their own land and small Zamindari, though they could not be called a big Zamindar.[10]

Abul Kasem (1871-1936), Hashim's father, is well-known as a full-time political leader who worked with Surendranath Banerjea and joined the Swadeshi and boycott movement against the partition of Bengal in 1905. He did not adopt the political line of the Nawab of Dhaka and was a Moderate and secular minded Congressman. After the dissolution of the partition of Bengal, when the Bengal Provincial Muslim League was founded in 1912 with Nawab Salimullah as President, Abul Kasem, a Congressite, was elected as Joint Secretary[11]. In 1913, Abul Kasem was selected as a member of the Bengal Legislative Assembly, though the election results were disappointing to Banerjea's group of Moderates.[12] In 1917 he was the president of the annual session of the Bengal Provincial Muslim League.[13] This was the period when Muslims could join both the Congress and the League. Abul Kasem later again joined the Khilafat and Non-Cooperation movement, but when Surendranath Banerjea's group fought the Council election and Banerjea took his ministerial post in 1921, both Banerjea and Kasem left the Congress. Also, with the radicalization of the Khilafat movement, the group headed by Fazlul Huq and Abul Kasem, who participated in the Council election, was expelled from the Bengal League. It was after the communal riots in Calcutta in 1926[14] that Abdul Rahim tried to use the long experience of Abul Kasem as a legislator before he formed a Council party before 1926 Council election.[15]

As for the change of fundamental importance in the drama of Bengal legislative politics after 1927, Broomfield wrote as follows:[16]

> Because of the determination of the Muslims to stand apart from nationalist politics, there was a decisive shift in power in the Council away from the Hindu bhadralok. Henceforth the ministries were invariably led by Muslim politicians and supported in the Council by Muslims, low-caste Hindus, Europeans, Anglo-Indians, and a handful of 'responsivist' Hindu bhadralok members. Moreover, despite their instability, these

> ministries pursued a common aim: the enactment of legislation to benefit the Muslim masses. Agrarian reform and the extension of education became the main planks on which all ministries were formed in Bengal up to 1947.

Suranjan Das also takes notice of the appearance of a 'Muslim bloc' inside the Bengal legislature after 1927 despite factionalism observed among Muslim legislators. This was demonstrated clearly in discussions on economic issues:[17]

> To mobilize support from the community's subordinate social groups the Muslim leaders voiced in the Legislative Council and other bodies an unequivocal support for the overwhelmingly Muslim *praja* (tenant) against their predominantly Hindu zamindars. In the process a linkage was established between elite and popular Muslim communalism. This could be noticed during the Tenancy Act debates in the Council in 1928. While the Muslim members with few exceptions voted for all clauses in favour of the *bargadars* (sharecroppers), under-raiyats and tenants, the Hindu members—Swarajists and non-Swarajists alike—sought to protect the interests of the controllers of land. In the popular Muslim perception, the Hindu politicians came to be viewed as allies of the Hindu rentier class.

Abul Kasem died as a member of the Bengal Legislative Council. He was one of the leading zamindars in Burdwan district and was trusted by the Muslim peasants of the district. He organized the Burdwan Mohammedan Association.[18] In his age the confrontation between zamindars and peasants had not yet come into the open, and if necessary, Kasem could take the complaints of the peasants to the notice of the Council where they developed their argument against Hindu zamindars.[19] In this connection we should also note Kawai's view that in western Bengal, "political movements since the 1920s were primarily aimed against the government. Forging a unity of the entire peasantry against the zamindar was extremely difficult. For the peasantry was highly differentiated. Therefore, it was never possible to demand the abolition of the Permanent Settlement in western Bengal", though he adds we have to consider other factors like commercialization of agriculture, the government policy and the attitudes of the zamindars too.[20]

Abul Kasem, Fazlul Huq and Abul Hashim

Fazlul Huq (1873-1962) was a contemporary of Abul Kasem, and lived in the age of Abul Hashim, Kasem's son, too. Huq, who knew Hashim from his youth, called him 'Hash'. Unlike Kasem who joined the Anti-Partition movement in 1905-08, Huq started his legislator's life with his protest against the revocation of the Partition of Bengal in 1911. Huq said at the end of his speech for the Budget for 1913-14:[21]

> There is a very strong and widespread feeling that, in spite of their loyalty and devotion, the Muhammedans have fallen on the frosty side of official pleasure, and that somehow or other, Muhammadan interests are not receiving proper attention. Let the officials judge for themselves whether recent events have not contributed to the existence of these feelings in the minds of the Muhammadan community. But as far as we are concerned, our policy is perfectly clear. We will no longer be satisfied with pious wishes expressed eloquently in Government Resolutions. For the present we, in Calcutta, are very particularly keen about a Muhammadan College and a hostel in College Square. We will not consent to see the removal of our grievances in these two vital matters to be deferred, on the score of expense or any other considerations whatsoever. And generally we demand that all other considerations should be subordinated to the necessity of affording the fullest relief to Muhammadans in the matter of education. This will be some compensation for all that we have patiently and loyally borne, even under the greatest provocations which human nature can bear. Hitherto, Muhammadans have so completely confided in the sense of justice of officials in all cases, that now it almost does violence to their feelings to be compelled to adopt the more modern and effective method of popular agitation. But in spite of their aversion to agitation, Muhammadans are drifting, owing to sheer force of circumstances, into the area of political warfare. We feel that we have got to move with the times or else we are doomed.

In this part of his speech Fazlul Huq declared that he was forced to start his long time 'political warfare', for the furtherance of the Muslim education and by the 'modern and effective method of popular agitation'.

His concern with the Muslim education is fully expressed

in his many later speeches at the Legislative Council of Bengal. In August 1918 Huq even proposed the resolution on the voluntary tax on Muslims in Bengal to raise funds for Muslim education, and said, "We have all felt for several years past that one of the chief difficulties in the way of Muhammedan students is not merely the want of accommodation in existing colleges, but also the obstacles that naturally arise from the fact that Muhammedan students belong to a very poor community".[22] Though this unique resolution was put to vote and lost, it discloses his strong will to develop the Muslim education by all possible means. Therefore he strongly objected to the boycott of educational institutions by Muslim students during the period of the Khilafat and Non-Cooperation movement in 1920-22. In this connection the role of Fazlul Huq in the establishment of the University of Dhaka in 1921 should be recollected here.[23]

In 1924 Fazlul Huq was Education Minister of Bengal for six months. In this year a Muhammedan College by the name of Islamia College was founded in Calcutta. It had been earlier prepared by Syed Shamsul Huda,[24] Secretary of the West Bengal Muslim League which was formed in 1908.[25] Earlier Huq ironically said at the Legislative Council of Bengal on March 14, 1918: "This question of the establishment of a Muhammadan Arts College is really a very old one and in one respect it is even older than the Legislative Council. It was so long ago as the year 1784 that a committee was appointed by the first Governor General, Mr. Warren Hastings to consider the advisability of the establishment of two Colleges in Calcutta, one for Hindus and the other for Muhammadans."[26]

When the first Huq ministry was formed in 1937, he took the post of Education Minister too. In his concern with the Muslim education in the Legislative Council and the Cabinet since 1913, there was his strong will to rectify unusually low percentage of administrative and judicial posts distributed to the educated Muslims. The emergence of the educated Muslim middle class in Bengal cannot be conceived without the role of Fazlul Huq.[27] However, we should note that he had a 'non-communal' view of education in general. Fazlul Huq said at the meeting of the Legislative Council in 1930: "I for one cannot understand how the cause of Primary Education can be the issue either of the Musalmans or of the Hindus. I feel, Sir, that the cause of Primary Education is as sacred a cause of the Musalman as of the Hindu".[28] His concern with primary education was also the reason he stuck to the post of education minister as the political leader who carried a slogan of the politics of *Dal Bhat* (*dal* soup and rice, or bread and butter).

Like Abul Kasem, Fazlul Huq was not a peasant himself. Abul Mansur Ahmad, who worked together with Huq, and joined the Muslim League in 1944, writes about him in his recollections: "He was from the upper middle class. He received all the facilities of feudalism. He personally managed all kinds of work for his own zamindari. But, despite that, in his time no discrimination was observed in his land. He never wished that peasants were in difficulties or oppressed."[29] Fazlul Huq started the *Krishak Praja* (Peasant) movement when he presided over the public meeting against the zamindars and moneylenders in Jamalpur subdivision, Mymensingh district in 1914, and spread the movement within a short period to Barisal, Faridpur, Chittagong, Khulna, Dhaka, Comilla and other areas of Bengal.[30]

After the discussion over the Bengal Tenancy (Amendment) Bill earlier mentioned, Fazlul Huq formed the Council Praja Party, which became the 'nucleus of the Nikhil Banga Praja Samiti that was founded sometime later in 1929 with Sir Abdur Rahim as President'.[31] Harun-or-Rashid appraises the foundation of the Samiti as 'the first political party founded by a section of Bengali Muslim leaders on non-communal and economic lines'. Some of the office bearers like Abdul Rahim, had 'a previous record of being communally vocal', but "they did not hold a dominant position within the new organization". Leaving 'gentlemen politics', it indicated 'the necessity to mobilize the peasantry around economic issues'.[32]

With the emergence of the Samiti as 'the body of rural Bengal with a large following', the young radical elements became rapidly vocal. On July 11-12, 1936 Fazlul Huq was elected as the President and the party was re-named as the Krishak Praja Party.[33]

On the basis of the recognition of this overall direction of the Praja movement and his own class analysis of the leadership and support base of the KPP before the 1937 elections, Harun-or-Rashid concluded that the *praja* movement was 'predominantly a movement of middle class Muslims against Hindu feudalism'.[34] The men of the middle class background—lawyers, doctors, journalists, teachers, *jotedars* were at the apex of the KPP leadership, while the occupancy *ryots* constituted its major support base in the rural areas. He adds that progressive Muslim students of colleges and universities also supported the KPP, but they were not many, and were not formally organized into any student body.[35] Abul Mansur Ahmad himself admitted that the critical view that the KPP was the Muslim *jotedar* party was not totally unfounded.[36]

Abul Mansur Ahmad, who worked as the KPP leader, takes notice of the gap between Fazlul Huq and other leaders in their thinking, and also between the professed and the real position of the KPP:[37]

> *'Langal jhaar Mati tanr'* (Land belongs to the man who ploughs) was a slogan carried by the left group of the Krishak Praja Party. Leaders did not believe in these words. Their view was different. They thought the *praja* movement was the Muslim movement. Acharya Ray rightly said that Krishak Praja leader Huq Sahib was a Musalman from the top of his head to the tip of his toes. Therefore he was not purely a leader of the peasants, but a leader of the Muslims....
>
> The Congress and the Kisan Sabha workers said that the Praja movement in Bengal was the Muslim *jotedar* movement. Their accusation was not totally unfounded. Even when the Krishak Praja movement was a strong popular movement, and when the Krishak Praja Samiti was a powerful organization, the discussion on giving occupancy rights to the *Bargadars* threw many Praja leaders into an uproar.... Plainly speaking the Praja movement was the middle class movement against feudalism. As the predominant majority of the feudal Rajas were Hindus, the Muslim middle class could not enjoy any facilities of feudalism, and therefore the *Praja* movement was so popular among the Muslims. The anger of the Muslim educated class against feudalism may be understood from the fact that, far from the Hindu feudal Rajas who occupied the government services, the

> young sons of the Muslim feudal lords could not get these jobs. Besides feudal Rajas paid an unmeasured amount of money for judicial courts, festivities and amusements, and the Hindus earned it. Therefore the *Praja* movement in Bengal was basically and primarily the Muslim middle class movement against Hindu feudalism. ... Among the middle class leaders, Fazlul Huq was the only 'man of the masses'. ... He advised people in their words. He could make his words understood by the people. There was 'emotion' in his words and work and sympathy is his heart. (translated by Kuwajima)

While the Krishak Praja Party was a 'non-communal' and 'rural-based' party, it represented the demands of the emerging Muslim middle class in both the rural and urban areas. However, in the idea and work of Fazlul Huq there was something which could go beyond its limit, and absorb the expectation of the various classes into the will of the people of Bengal. This was the reason Fazlul Huq played a leading role in the politics of Bangladesh even in the 1950s, though in the meantime he was in rivalry with the British Governor of Bengal, the central leadership of the All India Muslim League and the Bengali leadership of the Bengal Provincial Muslim League too. What Abul Hashim inherited from Fazlul Huq's idea and movement, and what Hashim refused to accept needs to be observed carefully. In the election campaign for the Bengal League, Abul Hashim confessed that he spent most of his time in Bakarganj district where Fazlul Huq came from.[38]

ENDNOTES

1. Hashim, op. cit., p. 3.
2. Ibid.
3. Ibid., p. 1.
4. Ibid.
5. Ibid., pp. 3-4.
6. Ibid., pp. 8-9.
7. Ibid., p. 9.
8. Also see, Badruddin Umar, "Amar Pita", in Syed Mansur Ahmed, op. cit., pp. 261-2.
9. Hashim, op. cit., pp. 5-6.

10. Umar, *Amar Jiban,* Vol. 1, p.13.
11. Harun-or-Rashid, op. cit., p. 11.
12. J. H. Broomfield, 1968. *Elite Conflict in a Plural Society: Twentieth-Century Bengal,* Berkeley and Los Angeles: University of California Press, p. 57.
13. Sarahuddin Ahmad, "Abul Hashim Smarane", in Syed Mansur Ahmed, op. cit., p. 170.
14. Suranjan Das, 1991. *Communal Riots in Bengal 1905-1947,* Delhi: Oxford University Press, pp. 81-102.
15. Broomfield, op. cit., pp. 279-80.
16. Ibid., p. 280.
17. Das, op. cit., p. 30.
18. Hashim, p. 16.
19. Ashok Mitra, "Tanr Samaya aar elo na", in Syed Mansur Ahmed, op. cit., pp. 164-5.
20. Akinobu Kawai. 1986. *'Landlords' and Imperial Rule: Change in Bengal Agrarian Society C1885-1940,* Vol. 1, Tokyo: Institute for the Study of Languages and Cultures of Asia and Africa, p. 87, note 69.
21. Sirajul Islam (ed.), 1976. *Fazlul Huq Speaks in Council 1913-1916,* Dhaka: Bangladesh Itihas Samiti, pp. 27-8. Also, see Sirajul Islam, Introduction, pp. 1-3.
22. The National Archives of Bangladesh (comp.), 1986. *Speeches of Sher-e-Bangla A. K. Fazlul Huq at the Legislative Council of Bengal Vol. 1 (1918-1937),* Dhaka: The National Archives of Bangladesh, p. 42.
23. Muhammad Abdul Khaleque, "Fazlul Huqer Ganashiksha Bistar" in: Muhammad Abdul Khaleque (ed.), 1395(Bengal Calender). *Mahapurush Fazlul Huq,* Dhaka, Sher-e-Bangla Jatyo Gabeshana Kendra, p. 216. Also see, M. Nazrul Islam, "The Political Role of Dhaka, 1905-1971" in Sharif Uddin Ahmad, 1991. *Dhaka: Past, Present, Future,* Dhaka: The Asiatic Society of Bangladesh, pp. 198-9.
24. Syed Murtaza Ali, "Shiksha Bistare Shere Bangla", in Khaleque, op. cit., p. 74, and Khaleque, "Fazlul Huqer —", Ibid., p. 211.
25. Official name is "The Bengal Provincial Muslim League". See, Harun-or-Rashid, op. cit., p. 7, footnote 26.
26. National Archives of Bengal, op. cit., p. 9.
27. K.M. Mohsin, "Fazlul Huq O Bangali Musalman: Dui Dashaker Samiksha", in Khaleque, op. cit., p. 41.
28. National Archives of Bangladesh, op. cit., p. 93.
29. Abul Mansur Ahmad, "Shere Bangla O Banglar Krishak", in Khaleque, op. cit., p. 45.

30. Muhammad Abdul Khaleque, "Fazlul Huqer Krishak Andolan", in Khaleque, op. cit., pp. 217-8.
31. Harun-or-Rashid, op. cit., p. 30.
32. Ibid., pp. 30-1.
33. Ibid., p. 44 and footnote 194.
34. Ibid., p. 60.
35. Ibid., p. 61.
36. Ibid., p. 60. See, Abul Mansur Ahmad, 1975. *Amar dekha Rajnitir Panchash Bachar*, Dhaka: Nawroze Kitabistan, 3rd edition, p. 182.
37. Abul Mansur Ahmad, *Amar dekha ...*, pp. 182-3.
38. Abul Hashim, "Muslim Chatra O Yuva Shakti Zindabad – League Secretarir Abhinandan", *Millat*, March 22, 1946.

3

Organizational Reforms of the Bengal Muslim League

AS THE SECRETARY OF THE BENGAL PROVINCIAL MUSLIM LEAGUE

Maulana Azad Subhani

Maulana Azad Subhani (1873-1957), who was an Islamic thinker, wrote a small leaflet on his philosophy of Rabbaniyat when he visited America in 1946. Abdullah Uthman Al-Sindi, a Ph.D. student, Columbia University, referred to Subhani's 'characteristic faith in the ability of the youth', and said that he was encouraged to write an introduction for this brochure.[1] Subbani was a thinker who initiated Abul Hashim to Rabbaniyat, and led him to active politics in Bengal. When Abul Hashim met Subhani for the first time, he was in his middle thirties.

Subhani was born in Sikandarpur, Ballia district, UP. He was educated in the *Madrasa,* but revolted against the traditional education. He founded Madrasa-e-Ilahiyat (School of Divinity) in Kanpur, and taught philosophy in general and philosophy of religion in particular for seventeen years.[2] Later he was known widely as a local agitator in the Kanpur Mosque affairs in 1913–4 when the Muslims protested against the demolition of a washing place of the Machhli Bazar Mosque on July 1, 1913.[3] He left the Madrasa-e-Ilahiyat, and joined the Anjuman-i-Khuddam-i-Kaaba (The Society of the Servants of the Holy Place) and became one of its major preachers.[4] In 1920-22 he was one of the leading Ulama in the Khilafat movement. When the third All India Khilafat Conference was held in Bombay in February 1920, the Ulama session was chaired by Subhani, and there it was decided under the inspiration of Abdur Bari that it was *haram* (forbidden) for Muslims to belong to the Indian army.[5] Subhani was the president of the UP Provincial Khilafat Committee.[6] With the growing confidence of the Ulama, writes Robinson: "By 1921 some Ulama were ready to set up organizations to administer the Sharia. In Bihar, for example, a conference dominated by Abul Kalam Azad and Azad Subhani set up a system of religious courts in the districts, each headed by an Amir-i-Shariat, which were to administer the Sharia. These were subject to a provincial council, which was also headed by an Amir-i-Shariat, ..."[7]. This is an interesting description when we examine the Manifesto of the Bengal Provincial Muslim League published in 1945.

The Ulama's demand in the Khilafat movement reached its peak when they proposed the resolution for India's complete independence in the sessions of both the Indian National Congress and the All India Muslim League in January 1922. The resolution put forward by Subhani in the subjects committee of the League session, was defeated by 36 to 23.[8] Then he became vice-president of the UP Congress Committee, and after the decay of the Khilafat movement, abandoned his Muslim orthodox line in favour of a secular and political approach.[9] He was involved in the labour movement in Kanpur.[10]

When the Communist Party of India was founded in Kanpur, December 26-28, 1925, Subhani was selected as a member of the central executive, and also as the vice-president for the coming year.[11] As in the case of many communist Muslims, Subhani observed there was something in common between Islam and communism in their idea of equality. When Abul Hashim met Subhani first in 1942, the latter was no longer a communist, but a philosopher of Rabbaniyat. At that first meeting they were 'deeply attracted towards each other'.[12]

Hashim Enters Politics

In his youth Abul Hashim liked his house at 2, Parker Road, Burdwan city and his village Kashiara. He did not enjoy his student life in Calcutta and Aligarh, though he finally passed Law in Calcutta in 1931. Hashim was not interested in politics during his student days and during the period as a lawyer. But he was interested in social service, and formed the Young Men's Muslim Association with his classmates in 1928. He organized its first Provincial Conference, inaugurated by Abdur Rahim. There a resolution was passed for the abolition of the practice of seclusion of Muslim women.[13] In fact, after Hashim was married to Mahmoodah Akhter Meher Banu Begum, a cousin of the later Chief Minister of Bengal, Hussain Shaheed Suhrawardy, in 1928, he sent his wife to school, but had to give up this plan due to his father's strong objection. Since the 19th century, Social Reformers in Bengal so often excluded their family from the orbit of their reforms.[14] At this stage, the characteristic of the Muslims' political thought was that, while feeling the necessity of a separate Muslim organization, they did not want to part from the nationalist trend.[15]

On October 11, 1936 Abul Kasem died. Under the Government of India Act, 1919, he was a member of the legislature, Provincial or Central, till his death. Immediately after his funeral, thousands of people in the village and the town decided that Abul Hashim should lead the Muslims of Burdwan in place of his father and should be elected in the general election from the Burdwan Mohammedan Constituency.[16] Thus Hashim entered politics, and was elected to the Bengal Legislative Assembly as an independent candidate in November 1936.

Joya Chatterji writes that, described in the past as 'a stronghold of Hinduism', Burdwan was one of the last bastions of the Hindu bhadralok in Bengal, and 'the epitome of the bhadralok order which the Permanent Zamindari Settlement had introduced' but the "sense of security and self-congratulation which characterized the bhadralok of Burdwan was shaken in the following decade (1930s), when middle class Muslims began to play a prominent part in Burdwan's public life".[17] Along with his father's long years of service to political life, the strong movement of the emerging Muslim middle class cultivated by Fazlul Huq during the inter-war period, promoted the appearance of a young lawyer first as one of the local representatives of its class.

The Macdonald Award or the Communal Award of 1932

also gave impetus to this trend. Earlier only one seat was allotted to the Muslims of the three districts, Burdwan, Birbhum and Bankura. Under the new award each district was allotted one seat. Hashim's cousin, Mohammad Abdur Rashid was elected from Birbhum.[18]

Between 1936 and 1943 Abul Hashim met two key figures in his political life, Mohammad Ali Jinnah and Maulana Azad Subhani, and attended the historical Lahore session of the All India Muslim League in March 1940 which contributed to the formation of his basic political line.

Abul Hashim writes about his first meeting with Jinnah in Calcutta in 1937:[19]

> Mr. Jinnah said, 'Young man, come under my banner'. In reply I said, 'why me alone, Sir, every man and woman will come under your banner if you can provide sufficient cause for that. Youths want thrill, sensation and romance. Congress, by its anti-imperialist movement, proves sufficient thrill and romance; there is much romance behind prison-bars'. Mr. Jinnah said, 'Come, let us organize ourselves in such a way that we can give 24 hours' notice to the job- hunters of Bengal and the Punjab. I thought by job-hunters of Bengal and the Punjab, Mr. Jinnah meant Khwaja Nazimuddin and Sir Sikander Hayat Khan. I left him with the impression that Mr. Jinnah wanted to organize the Muslim League as a broad-based democratic and progressive political party. Believing in what Mr. Jinnah said, I joined the Muslim League. But I was deceived. Later I found that to Mr. Jinnah, persons other than nawabs, knights and business magnets were of no consequence.

This is a recollection by Hashim in the 1970s. If this recollects correctly his thought in 1937, three points should be noted here. One is his will to 'democratize' the League organization. Second is the recognition of the role of the Indian National Congress in the Indian anti-imperialist movement. Last he puts his hope in the political action of the youth. Actually these three were the integral parts of Hashim's thought in 1943-47, irrespective of his leaning to the philosophy of Rabbaniyat.

At the meeting of the Muslim leaders of Burdwan, the Burdwan Mohammedan Association which Abul Kasem founded was converted to the Burdwan District Muslim League, and Abul Hashim was elected its president.[20]

A recollection of his early political life provides two other interesting episodes, which will help us understand his rational thinking in later years.

One occurred when Hashim attended the annual session of the All India Muslim League (Allahabad, 1938) for the first time. When Maulana Hasrat Mohani opposed the resolution, which Jinnah placed, as inconsistent with the ideal of Islam, Hashim argued in the League Council that Jinnah was in perfect harmony with the principles of Islam.[21] In later years Hashim and Mohani often acted in the same line, but Hashim inclined more to the rational interpretation of Islam. Since then Jinnah called Hashim 'Maulana Sahib'.

Abul Hashim's political activities in the earliest years were confined within Burdwan district except the Legislative Assembly. He recollects this was the result of a lesson he learned from Sardar Vallabhbhai Patel, who, after his victory in the Bardoli satyagraha, arrived on the all-India political scene.[22] Hashim emphasizes that the District Muslim League was thoroughly organized. The details of its organizational change are not written though he referred to a peasant meeting and a conference of Muslim leaders attended by Fazlul Huq and H.S. Suhrawardy, which demanded that the canal tax after the construction of the Damodar Canal Project should be paid by the landlords.[23] In 1942 he was elected a member of the Working Committee of the Bengal Provincial Muslim League.

This political stance of Abul Hashim partly comes from the liberal familial background. His Burdwan residence was the centre of politics of the district, and among his relations were leaders and workers of all political parties except the Hindu Mahasabha.[24] Therefore, though he was a new comer to the political world, he already had some experience in political training, how to develop his cherished view, and how to learn from political opponents. Badruddin Umar recollects that in this atmosphere the father's affiliation to a particular party did not affect the political stance of his children.[25]

The Lahore Resolution and Hashim

Abul Hashim attended the Lahore session of the All India Muslim League. Fazlul Huq, Chief Minister of Bengal, moved the Pakistan Resolution. The resolution demanded, "geographically contiguous units are demarcated into regions which should be so constituted, with such territorial readjustments as may be necessary, that the areas in which the Muslims are numerically in a majority as in the north-western and eastern zones of India should be grouped to constitute 'Independent States', in which constituent units shall be autonomous and sovereign". Also it clarified, "adequate, effective and mandatory safeguards should be specifically provided in the Constitution for minorities in these units and in these regions for the protection of their religious, cultural, economic, political, administrative and other rights and interests in consultation with them."

The Lahore Resolution adopted at the annual session of the Muslim League became the guiding principle for the political action of Abul Hashim. It complied with the history of Bengal or India which he had conceived so far. He interpreted the resolution as follows while he disagreed with the two nation theory (Hindus and Muslims are different nations) expounded by Jinnah.[26]

> The Lahore Resolution was the basis of our movement for carving out of India, independent and sovereign states as homelands for the Muslims of India. It did not contemplate creation of a single Pakistan State but it contemplated two independent sovereign states as homelands for the Muslims of India. One in North-West India consisting of the Punjab, Sind, Baluchistan, North-West Frontier Province and Kashmir and the other in North-East India consisting of Bengal and Assam. In the Lahore Resolution I saw my complete independence as a Muslim and as a Bengali and for this I supported the movement based on the Lahore Resolution of 1940. Mr. Jinnah preached the two-nation theory and this was the burden of his song. I never believed in Mr. Jinnah's two-nation theory and I never preached this in Bengal. I preached the multi-nation theory. I maintain that India is a subcontinent and not a country. India consists of many countries and many nations.
>
> ...The Muslim League did not contemplate partition of any

> country of India or partition of the Punjab or of the Punjabis and partition of Bengal or of the Bengalis. Thus there was nothing communal in the Lahore Resolution of 1940.

It is true that Hashim was critical of Jinnah's two-nation theory, and preached the multi-nation theory. There was no change in his basic stance. However, delicate changes occurred in his theory of nation and also in his view of the Pakistan state between 1947 and 1971 according to the situation he faced in both his own life and political history of Bengal.

Meeting with Azad Subhani

After the 1937 elections, Huq's first ministry started. In October 1937 Huq rejoined the Muslim League on the occasion of the Lucknow session of the All India Muslim League. This session authorized Jinnah to organize a Muslim League branch in Bengal.[27] While Huq was Chief Minister in 1937-43, the Krishak Praja Party declined from the political scene of Bengal, while a strong branch of the AIML was emerging in the province.[28] The second Huq ministry, coalition ministry which included Shyama Prasad Mukherjee of the Hindu Mahasabha, started in December 1941. Huq already had a serious conflict with Jinnah over the membership of the National Defence Council and was expelled from the League. Though Huq tried to solve political tangles through Hindu-Muslim communal amity, "the middle class Muslims of Bengal, who benefited from various enactments during the previous Ministry, cast their lot with the Muslim League."[29]

Abul Hashim's first appearance at a public meeting outside the Burdwan district was realized when a mammoth meeting was held in Calcutta against the coalition ministry.[30] However, Hashim appreciates Huq's later plan expressed in his letter to Jinnah:[31]

> The idea of a National Government in Bengal under the leadership of a Muslim League Chief Minister was not congenial to Mr. Jinnah's political outlook. So Mr. Fazlul Huq's plan failed. Mr. Fazlul Huq had never been consistent in his political thinking, but it must be admitted that his decision to constitute a National Government under his leadership after his reentry into the Muslim

> League fold was perfectly correct. If Mr. Fazlul Huq succeeded in implementing his plan, partition of Bengal could be avoided.

Fazlul Huq's ministry was forced to resign on March 28, 1943. It was tantamount to a dismissal by the Bengal Governor, Sir John Herbert.[32] Huq complained: "Administrative measures must be suited to the genius and traditions of the people and not fashioned according to the whims and caprices of hardened bureaucrats to many of whom autocratic ideas are bound up with the very breath of their lives. It is to your own Ministers and not to this class of officers that you should turn for advice if you desire to avoid pitfalls which have always been responsible for administrative disaster."[33] He resigned under the isolated position caused by the loss of support from the Muslim League and the intransigence shown by the Governor and bureaucracy.

On April 24, 1943 the League Ministry under the Chief Minister Khwaja Nazimuddin was formed. Unlike Fazlul Huq, the Bengal Provincial Muslim League had a man of the organization, H.S. Suhrawardy. Now what the Bengal League needed was the appearance of a leader who can develop its organization on a broader basis, and simultaneously can understand the ethos and demands of the people of Bengal though in a way different from Huq. However, impetus was given from an unexpected direction.

Abul Hashim writes about his meeting with Subhani, 'a philosopher and an analytical thinker of repute', whose 'scholarship in Islamics was profound and his approach was rational'[34].

> In October 1943, Moulana Azad Subhani visited Burdwan and put up with me. The Moulana told me that he had come to me with a mission. He said, "You must be elected General Secretary of the Bengal Provincial Muslim League and utilize the Muslim League platform in Bengal for preaching the pragmatic values of Islam." This suggestion of the Moulana appeared fantastic to me. It was, therefore, unthinkable that the members of the Council of the Bengal Provincial Muslim League, with whom I had no personal contact, would vote for me. As to the pragmatic values of Islam, I did not consider myself competent for that. I had no

> respect for my private life and I was fully conscious of my limitations. I frankly conveyed this to the Moulana. After a little pause, the Moulana said, "In spite of that I repeat, you must be elected General Secretary and preach Islam from the platform of the Muslim League. ... I know something of Islam and I can tell you this much that I am not backing a wrong horse."

Subhani's 'characteristic faith in the ability of the youth' may have spurred him on to this 'mission'. It is not so clear whether his 'mission' was promoted by the collective will of some religious leadership as in the years of the Khilafat movement or by the individual initiative of Subhani as a philosopher of Rabbaniyat. If it was the latter case, why did Subhani stick to the post of the General Secretary of the Bengal League? To what extent did Subhani exert his influence on the thought and activities of Abul Hashim after he was selected as the General Secretary? Hashim writes that Subhani never left Bengal without seeing him, and they used to spend nights discussing the Islamic way of life.[35] Irrespective of who was behind this meeting of destiny, Hashim's finally positive response to Subhani's proposal had an unmeasured impact on Hashim's later life and the activities of the Bengal Provincial Muslim League.

In October 1943 Hashim met H.S. Suhrawardy and offered to work as the General Secretary of the Bengal Provincial Muslim League. The vacancy of the position of the General Secretary was created by the formation of Khwaja Nazimuddin's government in Bengal on April 24, 1943 and the entry of Suhrawardy as Minister for Civil Supplies. In the same year the Working Committee of the All-India Muslim League adopted a resolution to the effect that both the parliamentary office, like ministers and parliamentary secretaries, and the office of the League organizations would not be occupied by the same person.[36] Though Suhrawardy worried about the failure of Hashim's eyesight, he later agreed to it. Hashim recollects, "In 1943 I was not completely blind; I could see things, read and write but I could not freely move about at night without a helper".[37] It was the support of Suhrawardy that made a rather unknown Hashim elected as the General Secretary in the Provincial League Council meeting on November 7 by an overwhelming majority against Abul Qasim, the nominee of the Khwaja family, who got only eleven votes.[38]

In his address of thanks Hashim declared that he would do his best to organize the Muslim League as a broad based democratic and progressive political party of Bengal.[39] The following day at the general session of the Council, Abul Hashim said that the Muslim League in Bengal was mortgaged in three sectors. One was the mortgage in 'leadership', which was imposed by the Nawab family of Dhaka or the Ahsan Manzil from the time of Sir Salimullah. The second was the mortgage of 'propaganda', which was brought by Maulana Akram Khan's newspaper, *Azad*. The third was the mortgage of 'economy', which was forced by M.A.H. Ispahani, a business magnate who was the Treasurer of the Bengal Muslim League. Hashim promised to liberate the League from these three mortgages, and provide a suitable place for the Muslim middle class. Though the old leaders understood that these words came from a person who did not know politics, it encouraged young Muslim activists in Dhaka where the League was in the grip of the Nawab family or the Khwaja family.[40]

Preliminary Steps for the Organizational Reforms

Here, Abul Hashim's activities from November 1943 to March 1946 can be divided into four periods; (1) November 1943–January 1944: reorganization of the Provincial League office in Calcutta, (2) January 1944–November 1944: setting up of the District and Sub-divisional League branches in Bengal and Hashim's extensive tour for it, (3) November 1944–July 1945: League as the mass organization, Draft Manifesto of March 1945 and 'Long March', (4) July 1945–March 1946: election campaign and 1946 Provincial Elections.

Abul Hashim first shifted his residence to Calcutta, leaving his family in Burdwan. Unlike earlier citations, Hashim writes in another page of his autobiography: "I was then not blind but my vision had very much deteriorated and I needed an assistant for my movements. By the middle of 1943 I lost the power of reading and writing and since then I needed others to read and write for me. I consulted Colonel Kirman, a reputed eye surgeon.

He said that I suffered from *retinitis pigmentosa,* an incurable disease of optic nerves. He advised me not to read and write but to keep a secretary for reading and writing."[41] Abdus Samad, who was related to Hashim, acted as his honorary personal secretary. Though Abul Hashim does not talk much about this aspect of his life, Mafidul Hoque, a biographer of Hashim, writes that in his political life he had to pay the price for his physical handicap.[42] It seems that both Hashim's deep attachment to the philosophy of Rabbaniyat and his daring action to reform the Bengal League organizations were prompted by his stubborn will to overcome this handicap.

The Provincial Muslim League office, which had been used as the family residence of Suhrawardy, was a mixture of public and private life. Now at the suggestion of the new General Secretary, the office was not only furnished, but began to function as the real head office of the Bengal League. Previously the meetings of the Working Committee used to be held at the residence of Khwaja Nazimuddin, but for the first time Hashim convened its meeting at the Muslim League office at No. 3 Wellesley First Lane, Calcutta.[43]

The Provincial Muslim League had a Treasurer, Mirza Hasan Ispahani. There was a Treasurer, but no Treasury.[44] The influential figures of the League collected funds individually, and used them as they liked. Now, collection of the membership fees was systematized. Everyone had to take receipt books from the provincial office after payment of the provincial quota of the membership fee. The district Muslim League was duly informed of the names of persons who collected receipt books from the provincial office. By the way, Hashim writes that, with the help of a Communist friend, he had to purchase the quantity of papers he needed at the black market price from the daily *Azad,* whose office had surplus stock.[45] The connection between a League stalwart Akram Khan and a Communist may show one of the 'friendly relations' between the Bengal League and the Communist Party of India. The default of payment of a monthly subscription of Rs 5 by the members of the Muslim League Parliamentary Party, who were ex-officio members of the Council of the Provincial League, came to be strictly subjected to penalty.[46] The organizations at every level were directed not to depend solely on any individual or a group.[47]

Abul Hashim also started issuing periodical circulars and bulletins giving instructions as to how the Muslim League should be organized in their districts.[48]

Thus was completed the preliminary work for the organizational reforms of the Bengal League by January 1944. Hashim was now prepared for the extensive tour for his discussion with the district League leaders and workers. In this month Maulana Akram Khan, President of the Bengal Provincial Muslim League and his son Khairul Anam took Hashim to the provincial office of the Communist Party of India. There Hashim met P.C. Joshi, General Secretary of the CPI, for the first time. Hashim writes: "The leaders of the Communist Party of Bengal offered their services to us for organizing the Bengal Muslim League as a broad based, democratic and progressive political party. We thankfully accepted their offer. Thus began my association with the Communist Party."[49]

In 1944, P.C. Joshi was inclined to recognize the right of self-determination to the 'Muslim nationalities'.[50] He applied this view to 'culturally and economically unified' Bengal.[51] On this basis he made contact with Abul Hashim and the Bengal League leaders:

> Bengal is more unified, both culturally and economically, than any other province of India. The Bengalis as a nationality are also perhaps the most developed. ...
>
> In this whole contiguous territory (inclusive of Sylhet district in Assam), the Bengali Muslims have a right to form their separate and sovereign state—their Pakistan State.
>
> But by the same right by which they demand Pakistan, they cannot claim as a right that the western Hindu districts be also included in their Eastern Pakistan state.
>
> The question can be solved on the basis of the Congress-League agreement if the right of entire Bengal, together with Sylhet, to form its own sovereign and independent state through its own Constituent Assembly, is recognized.

While recognizing the Muslims' right of self-determination, P.C. Joshi found that the final solution should be in the realization of United Bengal on the basis of Congress League Unity.

Hashim's response to the Communists' both friendly and critical approach was thus; "I knew with precision where Islam agreed with communism and where it differed from it. I was quite friendly with the Communists. As a Muslim I could not be intolerant of other views. My attitude towards communism was 'support where you can and oppose where you must'."[52] Friendly relations between Hashim and the CPI survived despite occasional friction till the beginning of 1947.

As for the organizational reforms of the League, Harun-or-Rashid clarifies that Hashim wanted the Bengal League 'to develop as a broad organization such as Congress' unlike the restricted membership of the Communist Party.[53] Hashim's role in the 'democratization' of the League reminds us of the appearance of the Indian National Congress as the mass organization after its Nagpur annual session in December 1920.

Hashim's Extensive Tour to North and East Bengal

After the preliminary work in Calcutta, Hashim went outside from February 3, 1944 for organizing the Muslim League at the district and sub-divisional level. So far there were no district League offices in any of the districts in Bengal, though there were some well-organized city offices like Calcutta under Raghib Ahsan.

It is symbolic that Hashim selected Dhaka as the first destination where the district League was in the grip of the Khwaja family, and Khwaja Shahabuddin in particular, President of the District League. There was no official invitation from the District League, but Kamruddin Ahmad arranged Hashim's stay at the house of his friend, Dr. Moizuddin, a physician and President, Dhaka City Muslim League.[54] Hashim met Shamsul Huq of Tangail and Shamsuddin Ahmad of Munshiganj, both students in this tour. He found in them 'qualities of leadership' and marked them well.[55] During his stay for a few days, he discussed the 'ideology of Islam' and the 'democratization' of the Dhaka District Muslim League with a number of youths of Dhaka and Narayanganj. As for the organizational matter, Hashim advised them to set up the

District League office and a Party House. He recollects he was able to organize a small army of honest and efficient Muslim League workers.[56] On this ground work the leftists defeated the Khwaja family in the Distict Council election held at Ahsan Manzir on September 24, 1944. Khan Bahadur Awlad Hussain of Manikkganj was elected President and Shamsuddin was elected Secretary of the Muslim League of the district of Dhaka. "Dhaka District Muslim League was liberated from the prison of the Khwajas."[57] Two days earlier, it was decided at a meeting in Narayanganj that to keep their plan in secrecy Kamruddin Ahmad, Shamsul Huq and Shamsuddin would act as dictators of the leftist movements till the Council meeting was over. Tajuddin Ahmed, later Prime Minister of the exile government in 1971, was also one of the young workers who joined the Narayanganj meeting.[58]

Young Muslim workers had to face strong opposition from the Khwaja group in other districts too. Hashim writes about the case of Comilla and Faridpur, where two later Presidents of Bangladesh worked:[59]

> In May, June, July and August I frequently went out of Calcutta on lecture tours in the districts of East and North Bengal. By this time, young Muslim League workers were fairly organized in East and North Bengal. With the exception of the districts of Faridpur and Comilla the leftist workers of the Muslim League had the full support of people in their campaign for democratization of the Muslim League. ... Sheikh Mujibur Rahman was deputed to organize a strong leftist group of the Muslim League in the district of Faridpur. Sheikh Mujibur Rahman had a very difficult task to form. ... Khondakar Mustaq Ahmad, then a student, was the leader of the leftists of the district of Comilla. The rightists in Comilla conducted their opposition to the leftists in a peaceful and constitutional method but in Faridpur, ... the reactionaries indulged in unconstitutional and violent methods. Sheikh Mujibur Rahman had of necessity to meet violence with violence.

Harun-or-Rashid explains that the college and university educated middle class romantic youths, born in the 1920s, largely constituted Hashim's cadre of workers, and Calcutta and Dhaka—the seats of the two universities—were the main centres of their activity, although Hashim was able to organize cadres in several districts.[60] Sheikh Mujibur Rahman, born in 1920, was a student of Islamia College, Calcutta.[61] In the eyes of the Khwaja group they were Communists, but Harun-or-Rashid clarifies that, though under the direction of the CPI a number of its workers like Mohammad Toaha and Shamsuddin had infiltrated into the League organizations, the majority of Hashim's workers like Sheikh Mujibur Rahman, Shamsul Huq, Tajuddin Ahmed and Khondakar Mustaq Ahmad were innocent of any such connections.[62]

Simultaneously it may be admitted that Hashim learnt a lot from the thought and action of socialism, though the impact of Islam that he comprehended on his idea is quite discernible. For instance, in his tour he discussed the ideology and organization of the Muslim League with young workers for hours at night. He presented before them 'four principles of political war'.[63]

> I advised them to place their case before the people positively without offending the sentiments of others who did not agree with them. The four principles of political warfare I taught were, 'Consolidate yourselves, seek as many allies as you can, if you can not make some your allies, try to make them neutral and thus single out your enemies and beat them in a pitched battle'. Any movement based on hatred may have immediate benefit but it can never secure abiding results conducive to the welfare of the people. I wanted Muslim League workers to make themselves lovable and for that I advised them to render social service to all, irrespective of religious or political persuasion.

Two aspects of Hashim's idea, Islamic thought and approach to social and economic problems, are not always harmoniously internalized. However, so long as he was ready to observe the situation in Bengal carefully, he could influence young workers persuasively.

In his tour 'Islam ideology' or 'social and economic fundamentals of Islam' was one of the main themes of Hashim's talk with young workers and his speech at a public meeting. Kamruddin Ahmad found something different in Hashim's speech at Siraj-ud-Daulah Park. In Hashim's view, Islam was not only religion, but also the way of economic and social liberation, while the older people thought that Islam was the religion of God, which left no room for talk from a scientific point of view.[64]

In April 1944 Abul Hashim visited Faridpur for the training programme of the League workers in the Muslim League Civil Defence Training Centre. Every morning he studied the Al Quran and prepared his evening lecture. Abdus Samad of Burdwan, who accompanied him, read out to him selected passages from the Al Quran. In a week Hashim delivered seven lectures on the 'pragmatic values of Islam'.[65] The contents of his lectures are not known from his autobiography, but the details of his philosophy of Rabbaniyat seem to have been prepared first in this tour. His tour programmes were carried according to the schedule kept in the Muslim League office, and he never missed any engagement. On one occasion, Subhani, who came to Calcutta to see him, could know his tour schedule precisely, and went to Chittagong where Hashim was busy at the League office. Even after his election to the General Secretary of the Bengal Provincial Muslim League, close relations between Hashim and Subhani continued.[65] Subhani could confirm that his mission in 1943 was in the process of fruition. Simultaneously, to what extent young Muslim League workers were impressed by the philosophy of Rabbaniyat was a different matter. They also positively reacted to Hashim's 'socialistic' approach to social and economic problems according to their own interests. However, all workers had no doubt as to his indomitable will and action to reorganize the Muslim League.

Reforms in the Council and the Working Committee of the Provincial Muslim League

Towards the middle of 1944 Abul Hashim suggested to the Working Committee the change in the composition of the members of the Council and the Working Committee. In consultation with Khwaja Shahabuddin, he could draft a new constitution of the Provincial Muslim League, and got it approved at the meeting of the Working Committee.[67]

Under the new constitution, every district irrespective of

the population was entitled to have 25 delegates in the Council.

Also, the number of the members of the Working Committee was fixed at 27, and two-thirds of the members were elected by the Council. The President was entitled to nominate one-third.

Thus, as the results of Hashim's whirlwind tour for the organizational reforms, the Bengal Provincial Muslim League came to have the apparatus as the political party cum mass organization on the basis of the newly formed District League offices.

ENDNOTES

1. Subbhani Rabbani, 1947. *The Teachings of Islam in Light of the Philosophy of Rabbaniyyat (sic) for Beginners*, First Series, Book 1, New York: Academy of Islam International, p. 1.
2. Ibid.
3. Yuvaraj Deva Prasad, 1985. *The Indian Muslims and World War I : A Phase of Disillusionment with British Rule 1914-1918*, Patna: Janaki Prakashan, pp. 34-6.
4. Francis Robinson, 1993. *Separatism among Indian Muslims: The Politics of the United Provinces' Muslims 1860-1923*, Delhi, Oxford University Press, pp. 214-5. For a short life sketch of Azad Subhani till the middle of the 1920s, see, Ibid., pp. 426-7.
5. Ibid., p. 306. Abdul Bari was the founder of Firangi Mahal, School of Ulama. Ibid., pp. 419-20.
6. Ibid., p. 325.
7. Ibid., p. 329.
8. Ibid., p. 332.
9. Ibid., p. 426.
10. Ibid., p. 427.
11. G. Adhikari (ed.), 1974. *Documents of the History of the Communist Party of India, Vol. 2, 1923-1925*, New Delhi: People's Publishing House, p. 667.
12. Abul Hashim, op. cit., p. 31.
13. Ibid., p. 15.
14. Umar, op. cit., p. 24.
15. Syed Mansur Ahmed, "Abul Hashim: Bangali O Musalman", in Syed Mansur Ahmed, op. cit., p. 302.
16. Hashim, op. cit., pp. 15-6.
17. Joya Chatterji, 1995. *Bengal Divided: Hindu Communalism and Partition, 1932-1947*, New Delhi: Foundation Books, pp. 213-4.

18. Hashim, op. cit., p. 16.
19. Ibid., pp. 17-8.
20. Ibid., p. 18.
21. Ibid., p. 20.
22. Ibid., pp. 20-1.
23. Ibid., p. 18. Also, see Umar, *Amar Jiban 1,* p. 53.
24. Hashim, op. cit., p. 16.
25. Umar, *Amar Jiban 1,* p. 20.
26. Hashim, op. cit., pp. 22-3.
27. Harun-or-Rashid, op. cit., pp. 93-4.
28. Ibid., p. 83.
29. Ibid., 131-2.
30. Hashim, op. cit., p. 24.
31. Ibid., p. 27-8.
32. Harun-or-Rashid, "Ministries of Bengal 1937-1947", in Sirajul Islam (ed.), 1992. *History of Bangladesh 1704-1971, Vol. 1, Political History,* Dhaka: Asiatic Society of Bangladesh, p. 387.
33. A. K. Fuzlul[sic] Huq, "Why I Resigned", in A.K. Fuzlul Huq, 1977. *Bengal Today,* Chakhar: Fuzlul Huq College, reprint (originally published in 1944), pp. 12-3.
34. Hashim, op. cit., pp. 30-1.
35. Ibid., p. 31.
36. Ibid., p. 30.
37. Ibid., p. 32.
38. Ibid., p. 34. Also see, Hoque, op. cit., p. 37.
39. Hashim, op. cit., p. 34.
40. Kamruddin Ahmad, *Atmavikash,* pp. 21-2.
41. Hashim, op. cit., p. 35.
42 Hoque, op. cit., pp. 31-2.
43. Hashim, op. cit., p. 42.
44. Ibid., p. 36.
45. Ibid., p. 39.
46. Ibid., pp. 47-8.
47. Ibid., p. 47.
48. Ibid., pp. 38-9.
49. Ibid., p. 40.
50. P.C. Joshi, 1945. *They Must Meet Again,* Bombay: People's Publishing House, 4th ed., p. 31.
51. Ibid., pp. 35-6.
52. Ibid., p. 54.
53. Harun-or-Rashid, *Foreshadowing,* p. 154.
54. Kamruddin Ahmad, *Atmavikash,* p. 23.

55. Hashim, op. cit., pp. 50-1.
56. Ibid., p. 52.
57. Ibid., p. 70.
58. Ibid., p. 67.
59. Ibid., pp. 57-8.
60. Harun-or-Rashid, *Foreshadowing*, p. 155.
61. Ibid., p. 155n.
62. Ibid., pp. 159-60.
63. Ibid., p. 59.
64. Kamruddin Ahmad, *Atmavikash*, pp. 24-5.
65. Hashim, op. cit., p. 57.
66. Ibid., p. 50.
67. Ibid., p. 62.

4

New Message to the Bengali Muslims

TOWARDS THE MANIFESTO OF THE BENGAL PROVINCIAL MUSLIM LEAGUE

Council Meeting, November 1944

The Council meeting of the Bengal Provincial Muslim League, which started on November 17, 1944, provided Abul Hashim a rare chance to demonstrate the results of his year's activities as the Secretary of the Bengal Provincial Muslim League. However, his position in the Council still lacked stability because of the opposition from the Khwaja group who had experienced a fatal defeat in the Dhaka district. The meeting was also the place of both stock-taking and tightrope walking on the left and the right of the League.

In his report of the activities of the Bengal League, Abul Hashim declared that it had more than half a million formal members in 1944; 160,000 from Barisal, 105,500 from Dhaka, 60,000 from Faridpur, 50,000 from Noakhali, 44,700 from Tippera, 41,000 from Mymensingh, 40,000 from Chittagong, 24,500 from Dinajpur, 13,470 from Rangpur, and 2,000 from Jangipur subdivision, Murshidabad district.[1] As is well known, Barisal was Fazlul Huq's home district. The League successfully absorbed the Krishak Praja Party excluding Fazlul Huq.

Nikhil Chakravarty, a communist who followed the growth of the Bengal League with sympathy, wrote: "It is almost unbelievable but it is true that this phenomenal growth of the Bengal League has been achieved in the course of a single year", and explained how it was possible.[2]

> First it has grown out of the old shell of mere communalism into a powerful organ of freedom. It is no accident that the bulk of the enrolment was done during the three months from July to September when the country as a whole was expectantly waiting for the Congress and the League to unite for freedom. The usual impression that the League thrives by pampering to the communal prejudices of the Muslims is completely discounted by this as also by the other fact that none among the new leaders spoke in the old communal vein, which was supposed to be the main capital of League propaganda.
>
> Second, the terrible experience of the famine, in the course of which the League Ministry played a timid role, has convinced the younger generation of the Muslims that the only way to make the League strong is to go out among the people and not to exhaust one's energy in the precincts of the Legislature.

At this Council meeting, Abul Hashim's position as the General Secretary was intact despite the serious attack from Khwaja Nazimuddin and others that Hashim preached communism under the cover of Islam and that his design was to convert the Muslim intelligentsia of Bengal to communism.[3] However, the 'democratic upsurge' failed to affect the 'upper echelon' of the Bengal League. Suhrawardy could pose to be a balancer and peace maker between the Left and the Right, and maintain the unity of the League by forcing Hashim to swallow a list of the members of the Working Committee, in which Khwaja Shahabuddin, a member of the Khwaja family was included. At that stage of the drama Suhrawardy was still an effective leader of the rising middle class, and Hashim was his choice.[4] In his autobiography Hashim compares his position to that of Subhas Chandra Bose who was re-elected as the President of the Congress on the occasion of the Tripuri session in March 1939, but Gandhi and his followers in its Working Committee adopted non-cooperation with Bose.[5]

The above mentioned report by Nikhil Chakravarty wrote about the unity of the Bengal League leadership as follows:

> There were scenes of great enthusiasm when Hashim himself proposed Maulana Akram Khan for presidentship, and the Maulana himself proposed Hashim for re-election to Secretaryship. Sir Nazimuddin seconded Hashim's re-election and

embraced him in congratulation. With great emotion, the President said, 'We may have differences in opinion, that is a sign of breath, but so long as there are Muslims in Bengal, the League shall never split, for our division perpetuates our slavery." Hashim also declared amidst applause, "Muslim Bengal knows how to keep its own house in order."

Hashim knew his own position well, and did not dare to defy the prevailing tide of unity. Instead, Hashim succeeded in making the Council ready to bring out a Manifesto of the Bengal Provincial Muslim League, and to publish an official weekly of the Provincial League in Bengali. Although the Khwajas felt the smell of 'communism' in the word 'manifesto', and the 'Party organ' in the original proposal was altered as the 'Official organ' by Suhrawardy, these two documents published or started in 1945 had a long-term impact on the history of the League movement in Bengal.[6]

In his Secretary's report, Abul Hashim honestly admitted that the League could not make any contact with innumerable illiterate Muslims.[7] In the discussion on the Food Resolution, there were serious confrontations on the enhancing or lowering of controlled prices between the delegates from the surplus districts and those from deficit districts. After informing the delegates that he would try for rationing of the necessary commodities, Suhrawardy proposed the withdrawal of the resolution, and got it supported.[8] Here the opinions of the victims of the Famine of 1943 were not fully used, though the food problem was the most crucial issue that people of Bengal had been facing during the Second World War, and, according to Nikhil Chakravarty's view, this experience made the Muslim youth go out 'among the people'.

Party Houses in Calcutta and Dhaka

In December, 1944, Abul Hashim shifted his residence to the Muslim League Party House at 3, Wellesley First Lane, Calcutta, and started discussions with young leaders and workers. The 'grammar of political warfare' which he taught was the same which he taught in his tour to North and East Bengal, though he advised them to be tolerant of the views of others. Hashim recollects:[9]

> Ever since I took up my residence at the Party House it became the centre of Muslim League Politics of Bengal. Every day I had to interview hundreds of visitors coming from all parts of Bengal. The flow of visitors was almost continuous. At night I discussed with young leaders and workers of the Muslim League the fundamentals of Islam, methods of party organization and political warfare, philosophy and sociology. Generally I retired to bed at 2.30 a.m. Sheikh Mujibur Rahman attended my night classes but he had little or no interest in academic discussion. He often fell asleep and rising in the morning he would ask me what was to be done. I found in him an exceptionally good young man of action and not of thought. He did his duty with precision.

Inspired by Abul Hashim, the Party House of Dhaka was opened on April 1, 1944. Full-time workers in the Party House were Shamsul Huq, Shamsuddin, Tajuddin Ahmed and Mohammad Shaktkat Ali. Among part-time workers were Mohammad Toaha and Khondakar Mustaq Ahmad. They planned to collect books on politics and Islam written from several viewpoints. These included books on communism and books written in English by Maulana Maududi. Kamruddin Ahmad published his first book, *Islam–The Only Solution,* which appeared as the results of his discussion with Abul Hashim in Narayanganj and Dhaka for long hours. Shamsul Huq, *Pakistan-Ki, Keno O Kono Pothe?* (What, Why and How?), which appeared later, was also the results of his discussion with Hashim. Besides, they bought a weekly *Hushiyar* from Mohammad Mohsin, and began to use it as the party organ. Tajuddin Ahmed played an important role in this matter.[10] It can be noted that the philosophy of Rabbaniyat which Hashim preached had a strong impact on some of the leaders including Kamdruddin Ahmad, a leader of young workers.

Mohammad Toaha represented another trend of thought inside the Bengal League, though his activities were also inspired by Hashim. He was a Communist who entered the Muslim League as instructed by the CPI who asked the Muslim Communists to support the Pakistan demand of the League and work for Hindu-Muslim unity.

While recognizing the Bengalis as a distinct nationality on the basis of 'a contiguous territory as its homeland, common historical tradition, common language, culture, psychological make-up and economic life', the CPI resolution (passed by the Enlarged Plenum of the Central Committee on September 19, 1942, and confirmed by the First Congress in May 1943) admitted that "in the case of the Bengali Muslims of the Eastern and Northern Districts of Bengal where they form an overwhelming majority, they may form themselves into an autonomous region in the state of Bengal or may form a separate state".[11] The concept of the 'Muslim nationalities' was already there in 1940. G. Adhikari reported in September 1942 that since 1940, "our Party began to see that the so-called communal problem—especially the Hindu-Muslim problem in India was really a problem of growing nationalities and that it could only be solved on the basis of the recognition of the right of self-determination, to the point of political secession, of the Muslim nationalities, as in fact of all nationalities which have India as their common motherland."[12]

Toaha recollects that, with his reading of Adhikari's *Pakistan and National Unity,* he was convinced of the reasonableness of the Pakistani demand.[13] He also writes that Abul Hashim's interpretation of the Lahore Resolution and his theory of the 'nation' on the linguistic basis made him popular among the young Muslim workers, though other leaders turned towards 'religious communalism'.[13]

Khondakar Mustaq Ahmad was the editor of the *Hushiyar,* but the actual work of editing and managing the weekly was entrusted to Toaha. When the controversy occurred whether an article on the 'Banish Communists' movement should be carried in the weekly or not, Hashim, instead of answering this problem directly, said that the attitudes of the League towards the Communists should be 'absolutely friendly'.[14] Close relations between the League Left and the CPI workers were maintained for some time.

However, in his recollection Mohammad Toaha critically assesses the character of Joshi Adhikari Thesis. According to his later view, the CPI leadership wrongly supported the religion based 'Two Nation Theory' preached by Jinnah, they lacked the independent and class-based view of the Congress and the League leadership, and could not afford a clear perspective of India, a state of multi-nations.[15]

The influence of the thought and action of Abul Hashim on the young League leaders and workers was multi-facetted, and not the straight expression of his philosophy of Rabbaniyat. Anyway, Party Houses in Calcutta and Dhaka were two centres of training for young activists.

Manifesto of the Bengal Provincial Muslim League

Abul Hashim prepared the draft of the Manifesto of the Bengal Provincial Muslim League with the help of Nikhil Chakravarty, a Communist mentioned earlier. However, Hashim recollects that the draft was based on the universal values of Islam preached by the prophet of Islam and his faithful followers.[16] Hashim knew that the Working Committee of the Bengal League would never place their thumb impression on the draft Manifesto, and decided not to place it before the Working Committee for their consideration but to place it before the Council. Hashim published the draft Manifesto on his own, but Suhrawardy questioned his authority to publish the draft and demanded disciplinary action against him. Hamidul Huq Choudhury, a member of the Working Committee, remarked that the word, 'Manifesto' was a Communist term.[17] The draft was published on March 24, 1945.[18]

First of all, the draft corroborates its belief in the goal expressed in the Lahore Resolution of 1940: "The Bengal Provincial Muslim League reiterates, in all solemnity, the declared and unequivocal goal of the All India Muslim League as set forth in the Lahore Resolution of 1940. Thereby it stands for the realization of complete independence for the whole of India together with the achievement of Pakistan for the Muslims in the country. The establishment of Free Pakistan in Free India is therefore the objective, which in concrete terms implies the creation of a democratic state in areas where the Muslims constitute the majority." Also, the Bengal League, while taking upon itself 'its primary responsibility of striving for the political, economic, social and moral uplift of the Muslims who form the dominant nationality of East Pakistan', emphasized that its struggle for Pakistan was not directed against the Hindus or any other non-Muslims, but against the British imperialist domination. It is to be noted that the expression of the 'free state of Eastern Pakistan' was used in the Manifesto.

As Harun-or-Rashid analysed, what was lacking in the Manifesto was 'the ideal of the common nationality of the Bengalis, both Muslims and Hindus, as Hashim himself pointed out that Muslims formed "the dominant nationality of Eastern Pakistan".'[19] Hashim believed in the theory of the formation of the nation based on language, but so long as he was at the important post of the Muslim League, he showed his idea of the nation extracted from his interpretation of the Lahore Resolution. He made his theory of language based nation known widely when he thought it highly pertinent to do so, or could develop his idea freely.

As for the role of the Constituent Assembly, the Manifesto clearly said: "The sovereignty of Eastern Pakistan shall be vested in the people. A democratic state shall be set up in a Constituent Assembly elected through universal adult franchise". Though Hashim was attracted to the philosophy of Rabbaniyat, here was neither negation of democracy nor acceptance of the sovereignty of God. However, the Manifesto placed emphasis on the observance of the laws of the Shariat in Muslim society as their rights: "It shall be the duty of the Muslim League to see that the principles of the laws of the Shariat are applied and observed in Muslim society. The Islamic moral values have to be resuscitated and the tenets of Islam have to be followed. The regeneration of Islamic culture as it has developed through centuries in this land of Eastern Pakistan—its history, its folklore, its art and music—shall be particularly encouraged and popularized."

Besides the rights of Muslims, the draft mentioned the rights of workers, peasants, artisans, women and minorities as well as the rights to defence, work, education and health. The immediate abolition of the Permanent Zamindari Settlement, and also of monopolies, particularly in the jute industries was one of the main demands on the economic front. These policies expressed the thought of Hashim who considered where the 'universal values of Islam' and the thought of socialists and communists met and differed. The fact that the people's sovereignty was so clearly declared in the Manifesto reflects where Hashim's main interest was at that stage of history.

As for the food problem calling for immediate solution, the Manifesto demanded, besides Grow More Food drive, anti-hoarding drive and rationing in all towns and deficit areas. It is to be noted that the draft was conscious of the serious character of the Bengal Famine of 1943 as follows:

> The immediate programme of the Bengal Provincial Muslim League shall aim at the restoration of prosperity in villages. ...
>
> An effort in this direction in the grim context of today must begin with a concerted plan of rehabilitation.
>
> ...The very soldiers of freedom today are in danger of being totally exterminated, thanks to hunger and disease. ...
>
> In this great and urgent task, it is the common pooling of the resources of all that alone can save the victims and save us. And it is only by such a super-human effort that a mighty patriotic upsurge is bound to manifest itself. The common enemy of all is imperialism that binds us all in common bondage, while the common strength to fight that imperialism came to us from the people. ...

While grasping hunger and freedom in the context of imperialism *versus* the people, the draft was cautious not to make an assessment of the Food Policy of the League Government under Khwaja Nazimuddin, which was forced to resign due to the withdrawal of support by some members over the budget in the Provincial Assembly on March 28, 1945.[20]

The draft Manifesto was a milestone in the history of the League Left in Bengal, and tried to connect Islam as the inspiring 'religion' for educated young Muslims with the image of the people-oriented state of Eastern Pakistan. Mafidul Hoque evaluates the meaning of the publication of the Manifesto highly, saying that it neither referred to the communalism based on the two-nation theory, nor to the secularist theory of the nation, but it was an exceptional document during this period of religious political consciousness.[21] The Manifesto was neither a 'communal' nor a 'secularist' document, while carrying the slogan of people's sovereignty.

In his autobiography Abul Hashim wrote: "The Manifesto took the wind out of the sails of all critics of the Muslim League. It broadened and enlarged the outlook of the followers and supporters of the Muslim League and it convinced them that they were struggling for a just cause."[22]

The copies of the Manifesto were sold as one of the League publications on the occasion of the ninth session of the All India Kisan Sabha held at Netrakona (Mymensingh) on April 5-9, 1945.[23]

Before the annual meeting was opened, a notice was issued from the Congress and the League that people should not participate in the Kisan Sabha meeting. Thinking that the order of the League in particular would affect the meeting, Moni Sinha, a Communist who prepared for the annual session, made contact with the League leader and a lawyer, Kaviruddin. Then, he promised not to obstruct the Kisan meeting. The Congress leader also responded to do so.[24] In the open session one lakh kisans participated, and the majority was Muslim peasants.[25] The period from 1943 to the first half of 1945 was in the heyday of the activities of Abul Hashim and the League Left in Bengal, and the Manifesto was its expression.

Bengal Famine of 1943

Abul Hashim writes about the Japanese bombing in Calcutta in 1942-3, and the Bengal Famine of 1943 in his autobiography though he does not discuss these issues in their connection with the growth of the League organization in Bengal.[26]

> In 1942-43 the Second World War was in full swing. The Japanese bombed Calcutta. All who could find shelter at a safe distance from Calcutta left the city. The crowded city of Calcutta looked like a deserted city. People in thousands moved out of the city with all their belongings along the Grand Trunk Road like a retreating army. Unable to feed themselves and their children people in rural areas sold their sons and daughters. Thousands of men, women and children died of starvation. To meet the situation

> a Ministry of Civil Supplies was set up. Mr. Hussain Shaheed Suhrawardy was the Minister for Civil Supplies. The Second World War irreparably damaged human values and lust for immediate material values was let loose. A famine condition was artificially created by blood suckers, hoarders, profiteers and black marketers. The army had priority of all means of communication for carrying army and war materials. Free movement of food became almost impossible. The government organized gruel kitchens all over the country. This was all that a government having no control over the resources of the country could do. For proper sustenance of the people the state must have supreme right to administer the wealth when the state is independent and sovereign and this was a great lesson I learnt from the famine. In our struggle for freedom I preached this with all the emphasis that I could command.

Ashok Mitra, who worked as the Subdivisional Officer in Munshiganj during the days of the famine, writes that colonial policies in Bengal, and the Denial and Evacuation policy in particular were at the root of the famine. His hunch is that "Herbert (John Herbert, Governor of Bengal, 1939-43) probably took Netaji's flight (from his residence in Calcutta on January 27, 1941) as a slap in his face. The failure of intelligence was too much to bear for Linlithgow and even his masters in Whitehall. They were determined not to take further chances, to judge by the steps that Linlithgow and Herbert embarked upon soon after. Not merely the flight, the assistance that Subhas Chandra Bose sought and received from the Nazis and the Japanese must have stoked sentiments of hatred and revenge all along the line".[27] His description of the denial policy was based on the observation with his own eyes.[28]

> The much trumpeted Denial and Evacuation Policies were executed with ruthlessness accompanied by thoroughness in denial of information, so much so that no firm record exists either in the newspapers or in government archives as to the exact dates on which these two policies were launched. But by February 15, 1942, when I joined in Munshiganj, the effect of the Denial Policy was all too visible, in the numerous rice markets and *hats* (fairs) of the subdivision. In the nearly two dozen large wholesale rice markets conveniently spaced all over the subdivision with their

attendant weekly *hats*, I did not see any warehouse in any one of the bigger markets in February-March 1942 which contained more than a hundred to two hundred bags of rice exposed to view. In a normal year, they would have contained at least several thousands each.

The Denial Policy in its turn had two prongs. First, the destruction and/or the forcible removal by the constabulary of the bulk of privately stored rice, not only in merchants' warehouses but also in private households as well (where paddy is stored in *malais*) in the coastal rice growing districts of Midnapur, 24 Parganas, Khulna, Bakarganj, and Noakhali. Anyone who resisted was denied even the money compensation for the rice removed or destroyed. ... Bengal, in spite of its three traditional crops a year, was deficit before 1941. The deficit used to be made up by imports of large quantities of Burma—commonly known as *Pegu*-rice. These imports totally stopped after April or May 1942. I did not see any Pegu rice with any merchant in Munshiganj after November 1942....

The other prong of the Denial Policy was the destruction of rice-carrying barges and boats in the East Bengal districts of Noakhali, Bakarganj, and Khulna and the boats and indigenous goods transport vehicles like bullock carts in southern 24 Parganas and Midnapur. This kind of denial not only destroyed—with little or no compensation in most cases—thousands of crores of rupees worth of investment and rolling stock on the waterways and dirt roads. It wiped out the means of transportation for the supply of vital grain from the surplus districts of Bengal to the deficit and marginal districts. I hardly even saw a large *balam* (a superior variety of rice) boat on the Padma or Meghna during my entire stay in Munshiganj in 1942-44. The *balam* boat—so named because of the rice it carried from Bakarganj, Khulna and Noakhali which in full sail would have won praise from John Masefield—varied in capacity from a few hundred maunds to as much as two or three thousands, but all had an elegance and stateliness in full sail.

No argument to the contrary will shake me from the conviction that it was this two-pronged policy of denial, denial of rice and paddy by forcible seizure, destruction and removal; denial of movement of supplies by forcible destruction of boats and indigenous road transport that caused the famine in Munshiganj. The famine was manmade.

Ashok Mitra was critical of the CPI's policy of 'prevent riots, form food committees and unearth hoardings' as quite unequal to an historic occasion, and concluded, "With the access they enjoyed at that time to information, they should have known that if anyone were hoarding to the point of forcing a famine on the country it was the central and provincial governments and their purchasing agents. Hoarding by petty traders or producers were a mere fleabite beside what the government was guilty of. It is surprising that even Satyajit Ray should have glossed over this startling fact and toed the petty hoarding line in his otherwise moving film *Asani Sanket (Distant Thunder).*"[29]

The administrator who observed the famine and worked for relief recollected that the colonial government policy or the lack of it was thoroughly responsible for the famine, rejecting the prevalent theory that speculators and black marketers also contributed seriously to the catastrophe. Though the flow of grain to the districts had already started under Thomas Rutherford, acting Governor of Bengal who assumed office in September 1943, "The situation took a sudden dramatic turn for the better after Wavell was sworn in on October 20. He and Lady Wavell, ..., came down to Calcutta and on October 26 went round in the streets of Calcutta with Rutherford, visiting some of the areas where the shelterless refugees lay about."[30] He also visited Contai of Midnapur district. Wavell's three days in Bengal are well epitomized in his journal. He writes about the meeting on October 28, 1943 as follows:[31]

> I don't think anyone really knows the whole situation or what is going on in some of the outlying areas, but obviously we have got to get to immediate grips or it may get out of hand altogether. I saw all the Ministers yesterday evening, told them they must get the destitutes out of Calcutta into camps, which should have been done long ago, got them to accept a Major-General and staff to help with the transport of supplies and the assistance of the Army generally. I also urged them to get on with their rationing schemes, and put before them the proposal to take Calcutta out of the Bengal food problem and feed it from outside. This last proposal seemed to meet with some doubts, but I am advised it is the only possible solution that will restore confidence in the rural areas and bring prices down.

> Three pretty hectic and distressing days. I wonder if my intervention will do any good. The Ministry is obviously a very weak one, and the acting Governor (Rutherford) rather disappointed me—no fire in him.

As Wavell hoped, Calcutta, full of destitutes from 24 Parganas, Midnapur and other districts since July 1943,[32] soon recovered its 'normal' scenery, though the death rate caused by hunger and its related diseases in Bengal reached its peak in December 1943, while in Calcutta its peak was in October.[33] As for the removal of destitutes to camps outside the city, Ela Sen describes how they responded: "Fear shook the destitutes as they saw police vans, A.R.P. (Air Raid Precautions) vans with uninformed attendants picking up people at random and taking them away. Where? Rumours were rife, and as a breeze whispers sprang up: "Let us run away, back to our deserted villages, rather to die there than be sacrificed here." Mothers weeping for their children were forcibly picked up and carried away in these vans; when in desperation they tried to escape, rough hands tied them by their hair in their places. .... Then the great exodus began and to escape forceful repatriation nearly 80,000 men, women, and children faced the rigours of the journey back and the probability of starvation at the end."[34]

However, Ashok Mitra mentions Pandit Hriday Nath Kunzru, president of the Servants of India Society, as 'the man who must have moved the authorities in Calcutta with a special plea for Munshiganj'. He "visited Munshiganj on October 20-21 and, despite his age and the frail state of his health, went round with me (Ashok Mitra) visiting a number of gruel kitchens as far as Ṛampal and a number of dispensaries we were setting up as famine relief hospitals. ... For close on his departure came medical supplies and token money along with a representative of the Servants of India Society. Arthur Moore, editor of *The Statesman* after his tour of Munshiganj in the footsteps of Kunzru wrote helpful dispatches."[35] So far as Munshiganj was concerned, Kunzru's persevering observation of the relief work at grass root level moved the authorities in Calcutta to action. Munshiganj, located near Dhaka, was one of the subdivisions 'very severely affected' by the famine[36].

The Famine Inquiry Commission mentions the following six points as the causes of the Bengal Famine.[37]

(1) A shortage in the yield of the winter rice crop (*aman*) of 1942, combined with
(2) A shortage in the stock of old rice carried forward from 1942 to 1943.
(3) The incapacity of the trade operating freely in response to supply and demand.
(4) The absence of that measure of control, by the Bengal Government, over producers, traders, and consumers in Bengal.
(5) The loss of imports of rice from Burma.
(6) The delay in the establishment of a system of planned movement of supplies from surplus provinces and states to deficit provinces and states.

The Commission report added that the remarkable feature of the Bengal famine was that the rise in the price of rice was one of the principal causes of the famine. They said that so far the great majority of Indian famines have been caused by drought and widespread failure of crops over wide areas.[38] While conscious of popular indignation against 'profiteers, speculators and hoarders', and conceding that, "Popular views about large profiteers who speculated and hoarded amidst growing distress, and the inability of the government to control them, were indeed not without foundation, the Commission added, "There were such profiteers, but they were not the only culprits. The fact is that a large section of the community, including producers, traders and consumers, contributed in varying degrees to the tragic outcome. The movement of prices which started in 1942 did not originate in the villages but by the end of the year producers as well as traders were infected by the unhealthy atmosphere of fear, greed, and speculation. At this point the upward movement of prices was resumed. The rise reflected the prevailing mood of producers as well as of traders and consumers. Thereafter every producer who retained his surplus grain or sold it at prices much higher than those prevailing in the autumn of 1942, every trader who held back stocks in the hope of further gain or made a big profit on his sales, every consumer who held larger supplies than usual, helped in accelerating the rise in prices and in precipitating the final catastrophe."[39]

In the chapter on the general conclusions and observations, the Commission wrote, "We have criticized the Government of Bengal for their failure to control the famine. It is the responsibility of the government to lead the people and take effective steps to prevent avoidable catastrophe. But the public in Bengal, or at least certain sections of it, have also their share of blame. We have referred to the atmosphere of fear and greed which, in the absence of control, was one of the causes of the rapid rise in the price level. Enormous profits were made out of the calamity, and in the circumstances, profits for some meant death for others. A large part of the community lived in plenty while others starved, and there was much indifference in face of suffering. Corruption was widespread throughout the province and in many classes of society. ... A million and a half of the poor of Bengal fell victim to circumstances for which they themselves were not responsible. Society, together with its organs, failed to protect its weaker members. Indeed there was a moral and social breakdown as well as an administrative breakdown."[40] In the Bengal Famine of 1943 agricultural labourers suffered most severely in every respect.[41]

In the Famine Commission Report its members recognized that producers, traders and consumers, at least some of them were responsible for the catastrophe besides profiteers. In Hashim's recollection there is also reference to 'blood suckers, hoarders, profiteers and black marketers' who made the famine, while he was also very critical of the colonial policy. Ashok Mitra exclusively attributed the cause of the famine to the reluctance of the British authorities to take up the food problem seriously after the exodus of Subhas Chandra Bose. Conversely this view led him to think highly of Wavell's intervention, though it was true that it occurred at the turning point of famine relief.

The League Ministry which started in April 1943 first reversed the policy of 'de-control' started in the latest days of the Huq Ministry and the succeeding Governor's rule, and in

June launched a provincial wide 'food drive', which was 'to ascertain the actual statistical position, to locate hoards, to stimulate the flow of grain from agriculturists to the markets, and to organize distribution of local surpluses as loans or by sales to those who were in need of foodgrains.'[42] In the first stage Calcutta and Howlah were excluded from the 'Drive', and the food drive showed the enquiries covered stocks held by nearly 10 million families consisting of 56 million members. The stocks held by them were estimated at one million tons. But there was a consensus of opinion that stocks had been under-estimated and that this under-estimation was partly due to concealment.[43] Late in July it was decided that a food drive in Calcutta and Howrah should be undertaken in the nature of a food census, but here also the Bengal Government stated, "as anticipated, there was no large-scale hoarding by consumers and that the stocks held by traders are in close accord with the figures they had declared." Famine Inquiry Commission concluded that the scheme was not a success. The Government of Bengal attributed the most serious cause of this failure to "the widespread reluctance on the part of agriculturists to place their stocks on the market, coupled with the disinclination of the trade to operate under control."[44]

In this connection Greenough writes that Suhrawardy, Minister for Civil Supplies, never defined who was a 'hoarder', beyond pointing to large landlords and big merchants. It seems likely that by 'hoarder' he had no intention to point to 'comfortable tenant farmers (*jotedars*)', who employed their surpluses in ordinary times to hire wage-labourers and to make sales for cash in the market. Greenough surmises, "The principal constituency of the Muslim League lay among the successful Muslim peasant cultivators of central and eastern Bengal, while the large landlords and big merchants were mostly Hindus. Thus there may well have been a political motive behind the whole policy of humbling and intimidating 'hoarders'."[45]

Karunamoy Mukerji, who made a survey of land transfer in the villages of Faridpur district, noticed the discrepancy between the official figures of land transfer and the figures gathered through his personal survey, and explained that the villagers, in many cases, mutually consented to transfer lands on verbal contract or contract written but not registered, so as to avoid delay, expenses and harassment incidental to registration. Moreover, registration was not compulsory in all cases of transfer.[46] He described the situation which forced land transfer in 1943 as follows:[47]

> The hungry needed food, and, therefore, money; the rich hungered for land and they had money. The holding of the poor might be tiny, they had to sell it out, and too many of them competed to sell. The rich knew their game; they displayed deep sympathy in the course of talks, but showed reluctance to purchase; then they bargained, and, again, hung back, but ultimately bought at a nominal price. Even that price was mostly not fully paid. Thus, fraud was added to blackmailing. In many a sense, the situation in the village in question, in the Famine year of 1943, was quite grim, desperate and disgusting.

Mohammad Toaha writes that there were neither the rich Muslims who extended their help to the famine-stricken co-religionists, nor the rich Hindus.[48]

Ashok Mitra, who was critical of the CPI's support to the League's demand for 'secession' at this critical point of the history of Bengal, simultaneously recollects that the CPI as a group and the Students' Wings of the Muslim League 'rendered yeoman's service' in Munshiganj from January 1943 onwards. He says, "They took the lead in all vigilance work and in enforcing accountability of all arrivals, stocks, and distribution. Together with non-political social workers and Congressmen they were responsible for reducing the actual mortality to less than half of what I had feared. Of a total population of nine lakhs I had feared a death toll of about sixty thousand. The death arising from starvation did not exceed twenty-five thousand followed by another five to six thousand who succumbed to the after effects of starvation while under medical ministration."[49]

'To render social service to all, irrespective of religious or political persuasion' was one of the principles that Abul Hashim advised the Muslim League workers to practise. At this critical moment how the idea of the Muslim League workers, and the 'leftists' in particular, who worked for the famine relief, was cultivated, or whether the Pakistan movement was the issue of a different category to be discussed? Many subdivisions or districts 'very severely affected' by the famine (in the Industries Department classification) were also the areas where the rapid increase of the members of the Bengal Muslim League was observed in 1943-44 (See, Appendix 1). However, in this survey the criteria of classification is not clear. Arup Maharatna classified the districts into groups in terms of their proportionate increases in mortality during the prime famine period. According to this criteria, he showed a following classified list of districts;[50]

> *Group A (very severely affected):* Those experiencing more than 150 per cent rise in mortality during the period July 1943 to June 1944: Midnapur, Howrah, Murshidabad, Dhaka and Tippera.
> *Group B (severely affected):* Districts experiencing 100-150 per cent rise in mortality: Birbhum, 24 Parganas, Nadia, Rangpur, Mymensingh, Chittagong, and Noakali.
> *Group C (moderately affected):* Districts experiencing 50-100 per cent rise in mortality: Burdwan, Bankura, Rajshahi, Bogra, Pabna, Malda, Bakarganj and Faridpur.
> *Group D (slightly affected):* Districts experiencing less than 50 per cent rise in mortality: Hooghly, Jessore, Khulna, Dinajpur, Jalpaiguri and Darleeling.

He confirms that, in general, the 'most severely affected' category in both reports (by the Departments of Industries and Revenue) roughly corresponds to his classification (except Murshidabad). But he adds that those districts classed as 'severely affected' do not correspond well between the various classifications. Maharatna finds: "On the whole the impression one derives from the classification made by the Industries Department is that famine severity in eastern Bengal was more widespread and acute than in western Bengal. But neither our classification (based exclusively on excess mortality) nor that of the Revenue Department support such a conclusion." [51] He examines pre-famine malaria death in both parts of Bengal and migration during the post-famine period, and warns against a hasty conclusion. He showed his findings: "The greatest increases in malaria deaths in 1943 and 1944 happened in districts which normally were relatively less affected by malaria. This is consistent with our findings that West Bengal—with a lower overall pre-famine malarial incidence—registered a higher rise in famine mortality."[52]

Here I only want to add that, apart from Fazlul Huq's district, Bakarganj (Barisal), Dhaka, Faridpur and Noakkhali were the districts where the Muslim League had more than 50,000 members in 1944.

P.C. Joshi, who was then Secretary of the Communist Party of India, and spent six weeks in Bengal in crucial days wrote that the stoppage of import of rice from Burma caused by the Japanese occupation there in March 1942 had a limited, but serious impact on the food market in Bengal.[53] He explained, "It shows that Bengal did not carry on with Burma rice to any great extent and that mass starvation did not certainly come because Burma rice stopped. But Burma rice did play a role. It acted as a potential reserve, i.e. the trader within Bengal had always to think of competition from Burma when he fixed his own price." That restraint factor was removed.

However, the impact of the Japanese bombing on Calcutta was more direct. The Famine Inquiry Commission also mentioned its serious impact:[54]

> Air-raids on Calcutta took place on the 20th, 22nd, 23rd, 24th, and 28th December 1942. The first raid had comparatively little disturbing effect, but evacuation began on a small scale on the 22nd and increased in volume until the 24th and 25th, after which there was little further exodus. The most important effect, however, of the raids was the closing down of a considerable number of food grain shops and the consequent interruption to the city's food supplies. At first immediate needs were met from air-raid reserves. The opening of closed shops in the markets was also tried, but this yielded little result as the shopkeepers had either removed or sold their stocks before leaving. Finally, on the 27th December, it was decided to requisition stocks in the city and to distribute them through controlled shops and 'approved' markets.

As for the Japanese bombing on Calcutta on December 5, 1943, the Japanese military authorities were proud of its results, stating that 10 ships were crashed and 19 planes were shot down (five unconfirmed) besides the damages to wharves, warehouses and railway carriages.[55] The meaning of the bombing in the midst of the famine relief was not examined at all by both the military authorities and the Japanese journalism which supported the bombing. Actually the struggle of the people against hunger in Bengal was the people's anti-war, whatever slogans the British and Japanese forces carried for the legitimacy of their war.

ENDNOTES

1. Hashim, op. cit., p. 74.
2. Nikhil Chakravarty, "Secret of Bengal League's Phenomenal Growth", *People's War*, December 3, 1944.
3. Hashim, op. cit., p. 73.
4. Harun-or-Rashid, *Foreshadowing*, p. 162.
5. Hashim, op. cit., p. 75.
6. Harun-or-Rashid, *Foreshadowing*, pp. 163-4.
7. Hoque, op. cit., p. 46.
8. Chakravarty, op. cit.
9. Hashim, op. cit., p. 77.
10. Kamruddin Ahmad, *Atmavikash*, pp. 26-7.
11. G. Adhikari (ed.), 1944. *Pakistan and National Unity*, Bombay: People's Publishing House, p. 34.
12. Ibid., p. 29.
13. Mohammad Toaha, "*Shmritikathae Abul Hashim*", Syed Mansur Ahmed (ed.), op. cit., p. 132.
13. Ibid., p. 131 and p. 135.
14. Ibid., p. 133.
15. Ibid., p. 136. In 1964 G. Adhikari writes about the CPI's stand in 1942; "It is agreed that our slogan of "People's War", our campaign against the fifth column, our rigid anti-strkie attitude—our stand on Pakistan—were all serious errors", and "Our attitude of keeping away from the movement (of 1942) was both theoretically and tactically wrong". (G. Adhikari. 1964, *Communist Party and India's Path to National Regeneration and Socialism: A Review and Comment on Comrade E.M.S. Namboodiripad's Revisionism and Dogmatism in the Communist Party of India*, New Delhi; Communist Party Publication, p. 84).

16. Hashim, op. cit., p. 79.
17. Ibid., pp. 79-80.
18. As for the full text of the draft Manifesto, see, *People's War,* April 15, 1945.
19. Harun-or-Rashid, *Foreshadowing,* p. 178.
20. Harun-or-Rashid, "Ministries of Bengal", pp. 393-4.
21. Hoque, op. cit., pp. 47-8.
22. Hashim, op. cit., p. 82.
23. Hoque, op. cit., p. 55.
24. Moni Sinha, 1983. *Jiban Sangram,* Dhaka: Jatiya Sahitya Prakashani, p. 67.
25. Ibid., p. 70.
26. Hashim, op. cit., pp. 52-3.
27. Ashok Mitra, "Famine of 1943 in Vikrampur Dacca", *Economic and Political Weekly,* February 4, 1989, p. 253.
28. Ibid., pp. 253-4.
29. Ibid., p. 258.
30. Ibid., p. 260.
31. Penderel Moon (ed.), 1977. *Wavell: The Viceroy's Journal,* Delhi: Oxford University Press, pp. 29-30.
32. Tarakchandra Das, 1949. *Bengal Famine (1943)—As Revealed in a Survey of the Destitutes in Calcutta,* Calcutta: University of Calcutta, pp. 56-7.
33. Famine Inquiry Commission, 1984 (Reprint). *Report on Bengal,* New Delhi: Usha Publications, pp. 112-4.
34. Ela Sen, 1944. *Darkening Days: Being a Narrative of Famine-Stricken Bengal,* Calcutta: Susil Gupta, pp. 21-2.
35. Mitra, op. cit., p. 260.
36. P.C. Mahalanobis *et al,* "A Sample Survey of After-Effects of the Bengal Famine of 1943", *Sankhya, Indian Journal of Statistics,* Vol. 7, Part 4, 1946, p. 14. As for the famine in East Bengal, also see Paul Greenough, 1982. *Prosperity and Misery in Modern Bengal: The Famine of 1943-1944,* New York: Oxford University Press, pp. 163-70.
37. Famine Inquiry Commission, op. cit., p. 77.
38. Ibid., p. 96.
39. Ibid., pp. 83-4.
40. Ibid., pp. 106-7.
41. Mahalanobis et al., op. cit., p. 57.
42. Famine Inquiry Commission, op. cit., p. 55.
43. Ibid., p. 57.
44. Ibid., pp. 57-8.

45. Greenough, op. cit., p. 125.
46. Karunamoy Mukerji, 1957. *The Problems of Land Transfer: A Study of the Problems of Land Alienation in Bengal,* Santiniketan: Santiniketan Press, p. 57.
47. Ibid., pp. 64-5.
48. Toaha, op. cit., p. 131.
49. Mitra, op. cit., p. 260.
50. Arup Maharatna. 1996. *The Demography of Famines: An Indian Historical Perspective,* Delhi: Oxford University Press, pp. 188-9 and p. 189, footnote, 12.
51. Ibid., p. 191.
52. Ibid., p. 235.
53. P.C. Joshi, "Where is Bengal's Rice?", *People's War,* November 28, 1943.
54. Famine Inquiry Commission, op. cit., p. 37.
55. *Asahi Shimbun,* December 19, 1943.

5

Towards the Central and Provincial Elections

'Long March'

After Abul Hashim shifted his residence to the Muslim League Party House in Calcutta in December 1944, he planned a 45-day 'Long March'. As usual, Burdwan remained a place for rest after his tour. From the published sources it is difficult to know when the tour started, and which parts of Bengal he covered, and whether any special programme he carried in this tour though in his autobiography Barisal, Noakhali and Jessore are mentioned as the districts he visited. But the details of his tour are not written there. He writes, "The year 1945 was for me a year of extensive tour. Direct personal contact with the people and indoor discussions with the prominent leaders and workers of areas I visited was key to my success in party organization and political warfare. I would remain outside Calcutta on tour lecturing for weeks without any rest. In my long tours I never missed any of my engagements. Once I made a continuous tour programme of 45 days."[1] The first half of 1945 seems one of the periods when Hashim could freely express his idea before the League workers and the Muslim mass, though in the Manifesto of the Bengal League published during this period, he was cautious enough not to refer directly to the common nationality of Hindus and Muslims.

Mohammad Toaha, originally from Noakhali, recollects that as he was brought up in the background of the Indian freedom movement including the salt satyagraha of 1930, he had a 'non-communal' outlook from his childhood and thought of one state composed of Hindus, Muslims and others, and therefore could not easily accept the idea of Pakistan.[2] What brought Toaha closer to Hashim was the latter's objection to the Two Nation Theory and his interpretation of the national self-determination on the basis of language.[3]

During the conference of the Dhaka District Muslim League at Chalakchar, a village near Narshingdi and one of the estates of the Khwajas, Abul Hashim was the main guest, and Toaha observed the violent scene between the Khwaja group on one hand, and the Muslim League and Krishak Samiti (peasant organization) on the other. Shamsuddin, who arrived at Chalakchar with Toaha, was attacked by the *goondas*. The next day, Abul Hashim who was led to the venue by Vinay Bose, a leader of the Communist Volunteer Vahini, made an appeal at the meeting for the removal of the feudal aristocracy and the British imperialists, its protector, and the realization of Pakistan, democratic and free from exploitation. Toaha recollects that the Chalakchar meeting was an ideal one prepared by the joint efforts of innumerable peasants who longed for freedom.[4] Abul Hashim also concluded this was 'a victory of the combined forces of the Muslim League and the Krishak Samiti'.[5] The meeting was held when the relations between the League Left and the Communists were, in Hashim's words, 'absolutely friendly'.[6]

'Let Us Go to War'

On July 15, 1945, the All India Muslim League demanded that fresh elections to the Central and Provincial Legislatures should no longer be delayed and immediate steps should be taken to hold them as soon as possible. On August 21, 1945, the Viceroy Lord Wavell announced at a press conference that the elections to the Central and Provincial Legislatures would be held in the coming cold weather.

On September 6, 1945, Abul Hashim expressed his determination as the Secretary of the Bengal Provincial Muslim League in his press statement, *Let Us Go to War*. There is a noticeable difference between the Manifesto published six months earlier and this document. For the All India Muslim League, the Pakistan scheme was the only election issue to be raised. Since 'in these days the ballot box is the only medium through which the public opinion can be ascertained with the greatest possible accuracy', the League wanted to prove through the elections that "the All India Muslim League is the only representative organization of the ten crore Muslims of India", and "the Pakistan Scheme of the All India Muslim League faithfully represents the views of the entire body of the Muslims of India".[7]

To that extent the view of the Bengal Muslim League, and the idea of Abul Hashim in particular receded to the background in this statement. There is one part where his idea crept in:[8]

> Free India was never one country. Free Indians were never one nation. In the past India was *Akhand* under the domination of the Mauryas and the Mughals and is now *Akhand* under the domination of Great Britain. Liberated India must necessarily be, as God has made it, a subcontinent having complete independence for every nation inhabiting it.

Here Abul Hashim showed his cherished theory that India was a country of many nations, but did not express his support to the 'two nation theory'. Except this part, Abul Hashim tried to express the basic view of the All India Muslim League. Hashim observed, "In Pakistan there will be just and equitable distribution of the rights and privileges of the state amongst all its citizens irrespective of caste, colour and creed", but did not refer to the abolition of landlordism.[9]

Instead, Hashim appealed to all Muslims in Bengal to 'bundle up all their differences and to preserve them if necessary in cold storage during the pendency of our common struggle.'[10] He said:[11]

> Our poets and litterateurs, artists and artisans, youths and students, landlords and peasants, ulema and laymen must answer to the clarion call of the great Leader of Muslim India (Quaid-e-Azam Mohammad Ali Jinnah), sink all their differences, forget the past, and pull all their resources for the winter struggle, the General Election of the Legislatures.

Hashim's anxiety was whether the League could elect the personnel of the Parliamentary Board which would nominate honest and competent candidates, and might inspire confidence among the people. Already prospective candidates had started canvassing votes for themselves. Hashim warned: "The Muslim League calls upon the people not to vote for any individual but to vote for the claims and the ideals of the League."[12]

Election of the Provincial Parliamentary Board

As expected, the process towards the election of the Bengal Provincial Parliamentary Board was full of skirmishes between the Right and Left. The Board consisted of nine members. The President of the Provincial Muslim League, Akram Khan, and the leader of the Provincial Parliamentary Party, Khwaja Nazimuddin, are ex-officio members. One member, Nurul Amin, was elected by the Upper House members. Another member, Fazlul Rahman, was selected by the Lower House members, and Nazimuddin preferred him to Suhrawardy, who believed Nazimuddin would support him. September 29 was fixed for election of the remaining five members by the Provincial League Council. On that date the proceedings were obstructed by the shouting down or by the removal of the microphone followed by hand-to-hand scuffles.[13] Finally, on the following day five members were selected by the Council. They were Lala Miah of Faridpur, Suhrawardy, Raghib Ahsan of Calcutta, Ahmed Hossain of Rangpur and Abul Hashim. The Left composed of Suhrawardy's group 2 and Hashim's group 3 members, got the majority in the Parliamentary Board, and Suhrawardy was selected as its Secretary. This 'victory' certainly symbolized the completion of the increasing trend in the League politics. Harun-or-Rashid evaluates it as follows;[14]

> The election to the Provincial Parliamentary Board was not simply a leadership race between Nazimuddin and Suhrawardy. It was far more significant. The success of the Suhrawardy-Hashim group marked a victory for the Organization against the Parliamentary coterie. The verdict of the League Council heralded the prominence of the middle class whose representatives comprised the majority. Furthermore, it was tantamount to a vote of no confidence in Jinnah's confidants in Bengal.

Simultaneously Suhrawardy knew well how to keep the 'unity' of the League. Later he showed his reconciliatory gesture to Nazimuddin and Hasan Ispahani, Jinnah's right hand man in Bengal, with the provision of the posts of the President and Treasurer of the Election Fund Committee. The nomination of the League candidates by the Provincial Parliamentary Board was also forced to reconsider in favour of the Nazimuddin group by the final decision on the side of the Central Parliamentary Board of the Muslim League.[15]

In this connection the Communists who had been observing the growth of the Left in the Bengal League with sympathy came to observe the same situation critically, saying that the entire propaganda of the Progressives harped on a mere anti-Ministry tirade, which was soon reduced to a factional attack on the Nazimuddin group without harnessing the League to the immediate service of the Muslim people, though two years ago they came forward voluntarily at considerable personal sacrifice. They thought that the League Progressives now did not constitute a unifying force inside the League, more so because of their unfortunate participation in the squabbling at the top, and tragic negligence in serving the millions as such.[16] Not only the candidature of the Communists in the Muslim seats in the provincial elections, but this observation seems to have estranged Hashim and the League Left from the Communists.

The Publication of the *Millat*

As we noted, the publication of a weekly in Bengali as the official organ of the Bengal Provincial Muslim League was decided by its Council meeting in November 1944. The coming elections also needed it at least on the side of the Left. Already the *Dainik Azad* was there as the daily which was owned by Akram Khan, and represented the views of the Khwaja group.[17] When Hashim wrote a letter to Jinnah to give his blessings for the weekly, in his reply Jinnah advised Hashim not to publish the journal in the name of the Muslim League.[18]

The first issue of the *Millat* appeared on November 16, 1945. Its editor was Abul Hashim. From its March 1, 1946 issue, though Abul Hashim remained as the Chief Editor, the name of Kazi Mohammad Idris was added as the Editor-in-Charge. From December 20, 1946 issue, Idris assumed office as the Editor. Later, the name of Moulvi Abul Hashim was added as the Founder of the *Millat* from its issue of January 10, 1947. Mafidul Hoque writes that the person who did practically editing work was Idris. Golam Kuddus, who had just completed his course at a university, worked in the *Millat* office from the start. Kuddus mentions Idris, Benazir Ahmad and himself as the men who worked substantially for the weekly.[19] Hashim's role in the editing work was indirect, though he discussed the main policy of the weekly with its staff. Simultaneously it was Abul Hashim who recruited Mohammad Idris as the competent editorial staff from the *Dainik Azad* office. The *Millat* started, as the editorial of its first issue declared, not as a news-oriented paper, but as a view-oriented paper.

The same editorial stated that the *Millat* was the national newspaper (*jatiya patrika*) of Muslim Bangla, and its owner was not any individual, but all Muslims of Muslim Bangla. It is not clear whether Muslim Bangla indicated any particular demand for the Muslims of Bengal in the Pakistan movement.

But, the editorial clarified that, against Jinnah's advice, the weekly started as 'the official organ of the Bengal Provincial Muslim League'. It was actually the mouthpiece of the Left of the Bengal League. As expected, Jinnah's message of 'blessings' for the first issue was brusque: "No need of saying any more. All of you, do work—that's what I want", though on the front page the *Millat* carried Jinnah's interview with the A.P. correspondent dated November 8, 1945, saying that Pakistan would be a democratic state.

The *Millat* was the site where the Bengal League appealed to Muslims to vote for the League candidates. In its first issue nine members of the Bengal Provincial Parliamentary Board including Suhrawardy and Hashim declared in its appeal that the Muslims were not prepared to be slave *Jati*. In this first issue Abul Hashim appeared not only as the editor of the weekly, but also as a scholar on Islam, writing an article on *Kalima*.

The *Millat* reported in detail on the speeches made in the founding conference of the All India Jamiat-e-Ulama-e-Islam held in Calcutta on October 26-29, 1945. It was attended by the Ulama from all over India. Suhrawardy was one of the League leaders who initiated the formation of a pro-League Ulama organization, though all arrangements for the conference were made through the Jamiat-ul-Ulama-i-Bangal.[20] At the conference Akram Khan, President of the Bengal League, welcomed the birth of the new Jamiat, saying that, after the British rule, the Congress was planning the Hindu rule. The President of the Reception Committee was Abul Azad Subhani who initiated Hashim to the philosophy of Rabbaniyat. Subhani said that the Ulama of India had become the supporters of the Muslim League. A day is not far when the *Muslim Jati* (Muslim Nation) will reach the seat of power. He appealed for the unity of the Muslims. This Ulama association served as a significant mobilizing agency for the League in the election.[21]

The first issue of the *Millat* mentioned the role of the Muslim students as a fountain of power of the Muslim League. Later, Abul Hashim sent his congratulations on the role of the Muslim students and the youth power in the election campaign for the Muslim League. Hashim, who worked in Barisal district where Fazlul Huq stood as a candidate, extolled that the Muslim students in Calcutta, and the students of Islamia College in particular did their duty tirelessly with a smile. He hoped that the students' experiences would be useful in any struggle for the realization of Pakistan, an independent sovereign state of the Muslim *Kaum* (Nation) and the *Millat*.[22] It is to be noted that, according to the *Millat*, Hashim used the word, Muslim *Kaum* here.

Muslim students and the Ulama were the two main forces who worked for the League in the election campaign which Suhrawardy and Abul Hashim organized. Besides, Abul Mansur Ahmad stated that the Muslim League had inherited the Krishak Praja movement in its membership and its programme, demand for the abolition of the zamindari system. Thus the Muslim League had become a mass organization. Demand of Pakistan was the symbol of the people's expectation, and there the unity of the Muslims and the economic emancipation of the people had become one.[23] Sardar Fazlul

Karim reported how the ordinary peasants and day labourers were organizing the League in a remote village of Vikrampur.[24] Karim was an activist who entered the League from the CPI.

Appeal for the Muslim unity in the election campaign made Hashim and Suhrawardy's idea of independent Bengal less discernible,[25] while they allowed the theory of a Muslim Nation to prevail.

This mood seems to have affected the destiny of Abul Hashim's utterance at the Convention of the League legislators in Delhi in April 1946. However, the attachment of the editorial staff of the *Millat* to Bengal culture was clearly expressed by carrying the photo of Rabindranath Tagore on the front page in its issue of May 10, 1946, congratulating him on his birthday.

The League election campaign forced the discussion on the progress of social stratification of Muslim peasant society in Bengal due to the famine to be put into 'cold storage', just as the Communists could not observe the agrarian situation carefully due to their theory of National Unity and 'Grow More Food' campaign. As noted earlier, agricultural labourers were most severely hit by the famine. The elections of 1946 were held under the limited franchise system, and most women, and people of lower classes were deprived of their right to vote owing to illiteracy and lack of property. In the circumstances how the political organizations and voters could listen to the voice of those who had no right to vote is worth examining. Zainul Abedin's paintings began to appear from December 14, 1945 in the *Millat*, which described quietly, but vividly the life and work of common people, peasants, fishermen, labourers, women, children and the old.

Delhi Convention of the League Legislators

In Bengal the mode of campaigning became the main issue of an open controversy between the League and the Indian National Congress. Maulana Azad, Congress President, said in his statement on April 4, 1946 that the elections in Bengal were reduced to a mockery. In his words, they were "hardly an election in the normally understood meaning of the term. It was more in the name of a crusade in which the worst religious passions were excited than an election in the modern age where political parties placed before their constituencies alternate programmes to be carried out through the legislatures." Suhrawardy retorted to this statement, saying that there had not been a single case in which the Muslim League had sought votes or captured any vote by holding up the terror of religious condemnation.[26]

The results in the elections of the central and provincial legislatures in Bengal were very clear. In the Central Assembly elections held in December 1945, the Muslim League won all the six Muslim constituencies, and in the provincial elections held in March next year the League won 114 seats, including all the 4 special seats, 6 urban (out of 6) and 104 rural (out of 111) seats. Fazlul Huq only personally remained popular. The results showed the eclipse of the Krishak Praja Party from the political scene. The Congress failed to secure a single Muslim seat on its ticket, though in the general seats they could win 71 seats out of a total of 74.[27]

On April 2, at the meeting of the Muslim League Parliamentary Party, Suhrawardy was unanimously elected leader of the Parliamentary Party. A way to the Chief Minister of Bengal was opened to Suhrawardy. He said he would welcome a coalition in Bengal with the Congress and the Hindu Mahasabha.[28]

The incident which made the name of Abul Hashim most conspicuous in the history of the Pakistan movement is the point of order he raised at the Convention of the League Legislators, which was held in Delhi on April 7-10, 1946, following the 'victory' in the elections. Abul Hashim declared at the Subjects Committee that the Lahore Resolution of 1940 contemplated two independent and sovereign Pakistan states and homelands for the Muslims of India. Jinnah, who responded first, saying that the plural 's' was an obvious printing mistake, later modified his view after checking the original minutes produced by Nawabzada Liaquat Ali Khan, General Secretary of the All India Muslim League, and clarified that 'independent states' in which the constituent units shall be autonomous and sovereign, stood, and the Convention was not in a position to amend the

Lahore Resolution. However, Jinnah conceded only to the extent that 'one sovereign independent state' in the Resolution of the Convention should be modified into 'a sovereign independent state', which meant, according to Jinnah's explanation, one constituent assembly for the Muslims of India.[29]

Except the letter 'a', the only modification done in the resolution of the Convention was the omission of the preamble of the resolution. According to Kamruddin Ahmad, the preamble was vehemently opposed by Mian Iftikhar-ud-din, G.M. Syed, Abul Hashim and Hasrat Mohani. But he also adds that Suhrawardy, while moving the resolution, used almost the same 'inflammatory' language when he placed the resolution in the open session of the Convention.[30]

So far as the demand for an independent state of East Pakistan is concerned, Abul Hashim's protest was a lonely voice, though there is a different interpretation on the role of Suhrawardy in the Convention.[31] Hashim recollects that he deliberately kept himself absent from the open session of the Convention,[32] but the *Dawn* carries his speech, though his name is misspelled as Abdul Hashim, in which the General Secretary of the Bengal Provincial Muslim League described Jinnah as the world's greatest realist, and said that Bengal was ready for any action that might be taken for the achievement of Pakistan.[33] Later, Mafidul Hoque confirmed that Hashim's speech was carried in the *Millat* dated April 19, 1946. According to the report in this issue, when Abul Hashim rose for his speech in English, he was greeted by the echo of 'Allah Akbar', 'Muslim League Zindabad' and 'Quaid-e-Azam Zindabad' uttered by the participants. Abul Hahim told them, " I am not a leader. I am a humble soldier for Pakistan. With our firm trust in the Quaid-e-Azam and under his leadership, the people of East Pakistan smashed all conspiracies of the enemy of Islam. I support this historic resolution of the Muslim League from the standpoint of a servant and soldier of East Pakistan" (translated by Kuwajima).[34] His own view was reflected by two parts in his speech. He said, "We Muslims have our view of 'independence' different from the Hindu Congress. What we meant by 'independence', each *jati* (nation) has its grand ideal and right of self-determination. This is the basis of our demand for Pakistan." He also clearly stated, "We believe the struggle for Pakistan means the struggle for democracy". He concluded his speech, stating that the Bengal Muslims were ready to follow the instruction from the Quaid-e-Azam. Hoque explained that Abul Hashim was forced to drift in the full flush of the victory of the elections.[35]

When the League campaign for the provincial elections was proceeding in Bengal, Akram Khan, President of the Bengal League, stayed at Madhupur (Santal Parganas), Bihar owing to bad health, and Nazimuddin, Chief Minister of Bengal in 1943-5, went abroad as a member of the Indian Food Delegation. Jinnah paid a visit to Bengal, but did not address any public meetings outside Calcutta. Liaquat Ali Khan visited only Gafargaon constituency in Mymensingh where the League candidate was defeated miserably by a strong opposition candidate, Maulana Shamsul Huda, Imarat Party.[36] Kamruddin Ahmad, one of the League Left workers in Dhaka, recollected later: "Suhrawardy, the Secretary of the Parliamentary Board and Abul Hashim, the Secretary of the Provincial Muslim League with their workers organized the campaign in such a manner that the non-cooperative attitude of the rightists was forgotten by the people."

Despite the League 'victory' in the elections, Abul Hashim had a slightly bitter taste in the Convention of the League Legislators. It seems undeniable that Hashim felt isolated from the prevailing trend at the centre and in Bengal. This isolation drove Hashim to his intensive study of Islamic thought.

The Birth of the Suhrawardy Ministry

On April 24, 1946 the Suhrawardy ministry started after the failure of negotiations between the League and the Congress for a coalition. Harun-or-Rashid evaluates the ministry as it represented the Bengal middle class in general, and did not include any members belonging to the Dhaka Nawab family.[37] The *Millat* congratulated on the birth of the Suhrawardy ministry in its editorial dated April 26, stating: "Bengal is the Muslim majority province. The Muslim League is the *jatiya* (national) organization of the Muslims. The popular government has been formed whose ministers were legislators nominated by the national organization of the major nation. While keeping the democratic norms of policy, the government declared the influential power of the Muslim national organization in and outside the country". The *Azad* and other papers owned by the Khwaja group were critical of the new ministry from its start.

After the formation of the League ministry, Abul Hashim invited young leaders and workers of the Provincial Muslim League to his village Kashiara. At the meeting Suhrawardy and a minister, Shamsuddin Ahmed of Kushtia were present.[38] Among other participating leaders were Kamruddin Ahmad, Shamsul Huq, Shamsuddin Ahmad (Dhaka), Nuruddin Ahmad, Nurul Alam, Sheikh Mujibur Rahman, Mohammad Toaha and Khondakar Mustaq Ahmad.[39] Umar recollects there was a festive mood. Hashim may have wanted to thank young activists for their hard work in the election campaign, and also to lay down some lines of action for them in future. Toaha had thought before that it might be an important meeting, but found there was no sign of it. He remembers that Kamruddin whispered to him that this was a game of 'pressure politics' to demonstrate to Suhrawardy that he owed the election 'victory' of the League and his status as the Chief Minister to these young leaders and workers.[40]

Hashim writes in his autobiography that it was decided at the meeting that leaders and workers of the Muslim League must not seek personal favours from the ministry and that they must approach the ministry concerning matters of public interest through their organizations, the Muslim League of their districts, or the Provincial Muslim League.[41]

Soon friction began to be observed between the League Government and the League organization. Also, a serious change in the thought of the League Left came to be noticed. Simultaneously, while dealing with the daily work as the Secretary of the Bengal Provincial Muslim League and as the editor of the *Millat*, Abul Hashim came to be more inclined to the philosophy of Rabbaniyat. Kamruddin Ahmad writes about this change as follows:[42]

> Most of the followers of Abul Hashim, who were supposed to be leftists, made Calcutta their center of activity. After the resounding victory in the general election in Bengal the leading workers of Abul Hashim inclined more towards metaphysical discussions than to organizational work. They talked about 'Rabubyat' and 'Rabbanyat' and held philosophical discussions under the guidance of Allama Azad Subhani. The rank and file were not interested in those learned debates but would not say so because they did not want to displease Abul Hashim. The leaders of the workers who made their mark as organizers of great ability soon began to function as a pressure group on the Government. They would ask for the transfer of any officer from any place if that officer would not listen to their requests. Ministers were very often threatened with dire consequences. They did not even spare the Chief Minister. Gradually misunderstanding began to grow between Abul Hashim and Suhrawardy. Most of the so-called star workers lost their ideals and were after money, and they knew of no other business except selling permits, especially the Civil supply permits. They began to float companies over night. One such company was named 'Darul-Islam Syndicate'. They wanted to guide the destiny of the nation from Rippon Street in Calcutta (where the *Millat* office was located). They were no more the same political workers, who had organized the democratic fight against the reactionary forces in Bengal. The student community as a whole began to lose confidence in Abul Hashim and his followers.

In the meantime, Abul Hashim had to face many critical views and actions from both inside and outside the Muslim League, and to respond to the critical 'communal' situation in the later half of 1946 sometimes with his independent judgment despite his inclination towards the philosophy of Rabbaniyat. In a sense, this was the time of his most serious trial though his activities in 1943-5 are relatively well-known.

ENDNOTES

1. Hashim, op. cit., p. 78.
2. Toaha, op. cit., p. 131.
3. Ibid., p. 135.
4. Ibid., p. 130.
5. Hashim, op. cit., p. 87.

6. Toaha, op. cit., p. 133.
7. Hashim, op. cit., pp. 170-1.
8. Ibid., p. 176.
9. Ibid.
10. Ibid., p. 172.
11. Ibid., p. 175.
12. Ibid., p. 174.
13. *People's War,* October 28, 1945.
14. Harun-or-Rashid, p. 185.
15. For details, see Sho Kuwajima, 1998. *Muslims, Nationalism and the Partition: 1946 Provincial Elections in India,* New Delhi: Manohar, pp. 55-6.
16. *People's War,* August 28, 1945.
17. Harun-or-Rashid, op. cit., p. 188.
18. Hashim, op. cit., p. 99.
19. Hoque, op. cit., p. 58.
20. Harun-or-Rashid, *The Foreshadowing,* p. 211 and its footnote 157.
21. Ibid., p. 211.
22. Abul Hashim, "Muslim Chatra O Yuva Shakti Zindabad-League Secretarir Abhinandan-", *Millat,* March 22, 1946.
23. Abul Mansur Ahmad, "Banglar Muslim Rajnitir Patbhumi O Parichay", Ibid., November 23, 1945. Also, see Harun-or-Rashid, *The Foreshadowing,* p. 199.
24. Sardar Fazlul Karim, "Banglar Grame Grame Jagiteche", *Millat,* November 30, 1945. Also, see Harun-or-Rashid, *The Foreshadowing,* p. 160 and pp. 199-200,
25. Harun-or-Rashid, *The foreshadowing,* p. 203.
26. Kuwajima, *Muslims, Nationalism* , pp. 143-4.
27. Harun-or-Rashid, *The Foreshadowing,* pp. 214-21. As for the results throughout India and the class of constituency in the 1946 provincial elections, see Kuwajima, *Muslims, Nationalism,* pp. 166-208 and pp. 221-2.
28. Hashim, *Retrospection,* p. 108.
29. Ibid., pp. 109-10.
30. Kamruddin Ahmad, 1967. *The Social History of East Pakistan,* Dacca: Crescent Book Centre, pp. 71-2 and p. 74.
31. Harun-or-Rashid., *The Foreshadowing,* pp. 236-9.
32. Hashim, *Retrospection,* p. 110.
33. *Dawn,* April 10, 1946.
34. "Dillir sumhan Sammelane Muslim janaganer pratinidhira je vada kariyachen taha vyarth hoite pare na," *Millat,* April 19, 1946.
35. Hoque, op. cit., pp. 61-2.

36. Harun-or-Rashid, *Foreshadowing,* pp. 209-11, and Kamruddin Ahmad, *Social History,* pp. 69-70.
37. Harun-or-Rashid, *Foreshadowing,* p. 227.
38. Hashim, *Retrospection,* p. 111.
39. Umar, *Amar Jiban 1,* pp. 154-5.
40. Toaha, op. cit., p. 145.
41. Hashim, *Retrospection,* p. 111.
42. Kamruddin Ahmad, *Social History,* p. 83.

6

Critical One Year as the Leader of the Organization

Responding to Critical Views from Inside the League

The crack in the Bengal League leadership soon appeared after the Suhrawardy ministry started. Akram Khan, President of the Bengal Provincial Muslim League, suspended the meeting of the Provincial League Council called by Hashim to be held on May 16, 1946 for the reason that the latter did not get his approval according to the rule of the League.[1] Abul Hashim responded to this action in his press statement.[2] The gist of the statement is as follows: The rule of the League that the Council meeting needs the approval of the President in advance was not applied for three years since he assumed the post of the Secretary. This unwritten rule was established when earlier Suhrawardy was the Secretary for seven years. One of the reasons for this rule is perhaps the bad health of the old President. He lived outside Bangladesh, and we could not talk freely. Owing to his bad health the President could not appear in the most stiff struggle for Pakistan, that is, the election campaign for the central and provincial elections. Now he could not even participate in the meetings of the central Working Committee of the League, though the Quaid-e-Azam needed the support of his colleagues. Besides, Nazimuddin Sahib was on his trip to London. There was no representative from Bangladesh in the central Working Committee.

Abul Hashim lamented that our President did not realize the importance of the Working Committee at the centre and the Council meeting in Bengal. Hashim stressed there was the imminent situation which needed the meeting of the Council, the *Jatiya Parishad* (National Assembly) of East Pakistan. He said that in Assam, an integral part of Pakistan, Muslims were suffering relentless persecution, and Maulana Abdul Hamid Khan Bhashani, President of the Assam Provincial Muslim League, was asking Bengal for help. Actually Bhashani started an indefinite hunger strike from the beginning of May.[3] Secondly, Hashim mentioned the work of the British Cabinet Mission, and added that Muslim Bangla had to make a crucial decision. On May 16, 1946 the Cabinet Mission Plan was published, which opened the way to Pakistan after ten years, while keeping a federal structure of India for the moment. Thirdly, Abul Hashim indicated that, since the League ministry had started, popular leaders and local representatives felt it necessary to issue instructions on their governance to the cabinet and the parliamentary party. Later, Abul Hashim informed that the Council meeting of the Bengal League would be held in Calcutta on June 21, 1946.

In the *Millat* dated May 31, 1946 a statement appeared by Farumuzul Huq, a Joint Secretary of the Bengal League, who said that in these weeks Bengali journalism including Muslim papers, *Morning News, Star of India* and *Azad* carried articles in which they insisted that Abul Hashim had lost the trust of the people, and therefore he should not occupy the important post of the League. They made use of recently organized 'communal riots' in Kalna subdivision and tried to prove that Hashim did not show any sympathy to the pitiable sufferings of the poor Muslims in his own district.

In its next issue of June 7, the *Millat* had many pages on the 'communal riots' in Kalna.

First, Abul Hashim as the Secretary of the Bengal Provincial Muslim League, published his press statement. He said so far there was no time to issue his press statement, but after his own survey in the afflicted area he reported its results to Suhrawardy, asking for imminent need of relief. The communal riots had now subdued. The riots which Hashim described were as follows:[4] In the last elections the zamindars in this area put pressure on the Muslim peasants not to vote for the Muslim League. On May 10, Hashim asked the present Bengal Government to abolish the Permanent Settlement immediately. On May 16 there was annual *Puja* (worship) and *Mela* (fair) of the Budo Raj in Jamalpur. Both Hindus and Muslims came to the *Mela* every year. One Muslim sweets shop was near the place of the fair. Some Hindus demanded that a sign board should be put up to indicate that the shopkeeper was a Muslim. Muslims refused it. Then many Hindus attacked that shop, and set fire to the houses inhabited by the Muslims. Muslims took reprisals and plundered the shops opened by the Hindus for the fair. On that day three Muslims were killed. From the 17th to the 19th arson and plunder continued. In all, seven Muslims were killed in the riots. Hashim writes that he was surprised to find that only Muslims were arrested.

Besides the editorial, the same *Millat* carried a report on the Muslim peasants 'under the ruthless tyranny', and cited the pronouncement of Abul Hashim on May 10, who observed that the present government took the abolition of the zamindari system as its first duty. The report said that this led the Hindu zamindars to raise 'communal riots' on the Muslim peasants.

The same issue of the *Millat* also carried a letter to the editor from four local persons including the President and Secretary of Mukashimparha Union Muslim League, and showed how mistaken was a letter, which appeared in the *Azad*, written by Onnol Hachna Sahiba, Secretary, Haldi-Nauparha Women's Muslim League. They refuted this, saying that such a person did not exist in their village, and Hashim's words, "If you bring sturdy fellows, then disorder will be finished" was a made-up story. They added that actually Hashim met injured and grieved people on May 23, and took immediate steps for their relief.

During this period, Abul Hashim seems to have been occupied in providing relief to the Muslims afflicted by the riots in his own district, while facing all kinds of slander from the 'Muslim papers'.

Outside the circle of the editorial staff of the *Millat*, was the League Left or the Bengal League interested in Hashim's work? Or, did they remain as observers? In his autobiography Hashim says nothing about communal riots in Kalna.

On May 17, 1946, Raghib Ahsan, a member of the Working Committee of the Bengal Provincial Muslim League, and one of the founders of the All India Jamiat-e-Ulama-e-Islam, sent his letter to Jinnah, informing him of 'a very painful and deep feeling of resentment among the Musalmans of Bengal on the League acquiescence, in theory, in a union centre', and questioning, *"Is Pakistan a mere slogan of bargaining for securing Muslim parity in the centre of the one-nation one-state one "sovereign" State of India?"*[5] However, the League Council accepted the Cabinet Mission Plan on June 6, and the Congress Working Committee decided to participate in the Constituent Assembly on June 26. Later, on July 10, Jawaharlal Nehru observed at the press conference: "The first thing is that we have agreed to go into the Constituent Assembly and we have agreed to nothing else. What we do there, we are entirely and absolutely free to determine. We have committed ourselves to no single matter to anybody."[6] This pronouncement finally changed the destiny of the Cabinet Mission Plan. On July 29, 1946 the Muslim League Council decided to withdraw its acceptance of the Cabinet Mission proposals, and appealed to the 'Muslim nation' to 'resort to direct action to achieve Pakistan'.[7]

In the meantime, Farumuzul Huq, Joint Secretary, Bengal Provincial Muslim League, sent Jinnah the cuttings from the *Dainik Azad* dated June 8 with its English translation. The paper reported on the meeting in camera of the All India Muslim League Council, and wrote: "At this meeting in the course of his speech Abul Hashim of Bengal, without expressing any opinion for or against Mission's Proposal, launched an attack on Quaid-e-Azam and the members of the Working Committee".[8] On June 15, Jinnah sent a telegram to Hashim, advising, "Postpone (Bengal League) Council meeting. Maintain complete truce. Hope you will all follow my advice pending enquiry into differences that may have arisen."[9] At this critical stage of history, without Jinnah's intervention the League organization in Bengal did not work properly. After the Council meeting of the All India Muslim League on July 29, Hashim was called to Jinnah's residence in Bombay, where Suhrawardy was also present. There Akram Khan placed before Jinnah a 32-page typed petition of complaint against Hashim. Jinnah's response was "Go to your people, that is the highest court of appeal". Jinnah pushed back the papers to Akram Khan. Then Mohan Miah of Faridpur appealed, "Mr. Abul Hashim is unfair and unjust to us." Hashim retorted, saying that, in spite of his defeat in the election to the Legislative Assembly, he nominated Mohan Miah for the Legislative Council. After the meeting, Jinnah patted Hashim on his back and said, "We have won our battle. Now you go to your people and consolidate them. Bengal has a culture of its own."[10]

Despite their different views of the Pakistan State(s), the Jinnah-Hashim relations were still communicable. Hashim supported the resolution on Direct Action on the condition that the action should be against the British Government and not against any party.[11] Direct Action was called under the name of the Muslim nation.

Mohammad Toaha, who was working in Dhaka, recollects that, when he heard the Cabinet Mission Plan was published, he was happy to find that the way to Pakistan was finally ready, though he was soon disappointed with the pronouncement of Nehru and the destiny of the plan. He writes that, when the League activists found that Hashim was now travelling in search of a new way, the philosophy of Rabbaniyat, they gradually left him, and began to seek their own way of action. When the Cabinet Mission Plan was published, they were at a loss, because so far, when they faced some important problems, Hashim called a meeting of the activists, and after their discussion they decided the guidelines for action. On this occasion, Hashim failed to make such efforts.[12]

As we noted, this was partly caused by his busy schedule to face the slander from the conservatives in the Bengal League who consolidated their positions after the elections, besides providing relief to the victims of the communal riots in his own district. However, despite Hashim's remarkable contribution to the 'victory' in the elections, his position in the Working Committee and among the legislators was not strengthened, though he got strong support from the ordinary members.[13]

Owing to this reason and also as the man of the organization Hashim did not want a direct confrontation with Akram Khan, Bengal League President beyond the necessary limit. To that extent he needed Jinnah's hand. The *Millat* continued to function as the mouthpiece of the Left in the Bengal League, but it can not be denied that the erosion of the 'Left unity' in the Bengal League already started partly with the start of the Suhrawardy ministry, and partly with the inclination of Hashim towards the philosophy of Rabbaniyat. Under this situation the priority of the League organization over the League government, which Hashim wanted, was difficult to be realized.[14]

On June 21, 1946, the *Millat* wrote in its editorial that Bengal was a Muslim majority province, but the Muslims were an exploited class.[15] "The demand of the Muslim League as the organ of the exploited *jati* is to expand its influence in the life of the Bengal Muslims, and to shake the foundation of the bastion of the vested interests in Bengal." Despite its declaration of the struggle against the vested interests, the prospect for the Bengal State on the basis of language could not be found in this statement.

Direct Action Day

A statement issued by S.M. Usman, Secretary of the Calcutta District Muslim League on August 10, which stressed the importance of the mass mobilization in the midst of Ramazan, called forth an unusual echo.[16] However, Abul Hashim stated in his press statement on August 13 that the Muslim League would observe the Direct Action Day to demonstrate their grievances against British imperialism and their target was British imperialism alone. He appealed to everyone to make the day peaceful and not to let it degenerate into strife between people and people.[17] In his witness before the Riot Enquiry Commission later started, Abul Hashim stated that, if the League had any knowledge as to the unprecedented violence on August 16, he would not have taken from Burdwan his two sons, Badruddin Umar, a boy of 15, and Shahabuddin, a boy of 8 to the Calcutta Maidan to show them the great gathering.[18]

The Maidan was full of people. Time allowed for each

speaker was limited. Khwaja Nazimuddin said that their struggle was against the Congress and the Hindus. Hashim pushed him back from the microphone, and pointing to Fort William, asserted that their struggle was not against any people of India, but it was against British imperialism. Umar remembers Suhrawardy also spoke in the same tone as Hashim did. While they were on the platform, news came from all sides that communal riots had started in every area of Calcutta.[19] The riot continued till the 20th. Only on August 21, Suhrawardy called a meeting of all party leaders at his residence, and after the meeting, their procession covered various parts of Calcutta, appealing to the people to remain peaceful and bring about normalcy in the city. Among the participants at the meeting were Sarat Bose, Nazimuddin, Kiran Shankar Roy, J.C. Gupta, S.M. Usman, M.A. Ispahani, Shamsuddin Ahmed, and others besides Suhrawardy and Hashim.[20]

The Viceroy Lord Wavell writes in his journal on August 18: "Calcutta is as bad as ever and the death-toll mounts steadily. Sarat Chandra Bose rang up in the afternoon with a message of protest to me that the police was favouring the Muslims against the Hindus, whereas the Governor tells me the casualties are higher amongst the Muslims. Anyway it is a thoroughly bad business."[21]

After nine months Sarat Bose and Suhrawardy came closer with their idea of a United Independent Bengal. Wavell visited Calcutta on August 25 and returned to Delhi the next day. After a two-hour tour of the places of the recent riots, and speaking to some of the troops, he started a series of interviews, and top leaders of the police, army and administration told him about the 'communal' bias of the Chief Minister Suhrawardy.[22]

The main points he heard from the Commissioner of Police, D.R. Hardwick were Suhrawardy's continual presence in the Control Room on the first day with many Muslim League friends and his 'obvious communal bias'; that the victims were almost entirely goondas and people of the poorest class; there were no attacks on the Police; and that any hesitation of the Police to open fire or take firm action was partly due to the political criticism directed against them after the riots of last

February and November on the occasion of the trial of the Indian National Army officers. However, Wavell found that Hardwick had only held this job for a few months, and perhaps lacked toughness and experience.

Then Wavell met Roy Bucher, acting Army Commander and E.K.G. Sixsmith, acting Area Commander. The Viceroy found that their judgement and action had been correct and they had used the troops at the right time and in the right way. Bucher said the Indian troops behaved very well, and that there was complete harmony between Civil and Military authorities during the disturbances. He also commented on the 'completely communal attitude' of the Chief Minister when he had driven round with the Chief Minister on the 18th.

The Chief Secretary, R.I. Walker and his assistant, O.M. Martin, agreed on the 'communal bias' of Suhrawardy, and said he had made continual allegations against the Chief Commissioner and his police.

Wavell talked to Suhrawardy for 45 minutes. The Viceroy records, "He was polite and not at all aggressive and took in a subdued way a homily I delivered to him on his duties as Premier of Bengal. He suggested that the Chief Justice, Patrick Spens, should head an enquiry into the disturbances."

Army, police and administrative top leaders who met Wavell were unanimous in their view of the 'communal bias' of the Chief Minister Suhrawardy, though its details were not clear. However, Abul Hashim defended Suhrawardy when the motion of no confidence was tabled against the Suhrawardy ministry in the Bengal Legislative Assembly. As we noted before, Hashim earlier opened the way to the Chief Minister for Suhrawardy in September 1945 when the election of the Bengal Provincial Parliamentary Board was held. Hashim later wrote that Suharawardy's declaration of August 16 as a public holiday was a great blunder that he committed, because peace-loving Hindus and Muslims had little or nothing to do with the riot.[23] Suhrawardy made this decision without consulting any member of his ministry or the League Working Committee of Bengal. But, on September 9, Hashim said, "what has happened did happen not due to Mr. Suhrawardy or his Ministry but in spite of them." He attributed its cause to the diplomatic game of Stafford Cripps and his colleagues, and concluded, "Will this public calamity, the blood of our friends, relations and comrades help in levelling our differences and make a united effort to drive out the third party, the British Imperialism from India?"[24]

Hashim deeply appreciated the work of the Chief Minister in the riot days as follows:[25]

> At that time he was seen moving at the risk of his life in the streets of Calcutta day and night. He saw his comrades, friends falling one by one but he never lost that sense of justice which is becoming of a Chief Minister of our country. Our friends of the Congress said that his affiliation and attachment to the Muslim League Party unbalanced him, but nothing can be a greater perversion of truth. We found during those days Muslims in bands and parties coming to us and complaining that Mr. Suhrawardy was attending too much to the Hindus. We found him working restlessly without food, without sleep these three, four days, locking himself up in Lall Bazar control room, passing orders. ... It is true that on the 16th and 17th the ordinary traffic police were found absent, it is true that the Calcutta Police could not cope with the situation, but who can deny this fact that Mr. Suhrawardy at the earliest opportunity called upon the Army to take charge of the city ... but the Army did not obey as hastily and as quickly as they ought to have done, because under the Government of India Act the Chief Minister has no control over them. And if he says anything against the Commissioner of Police he is not making him a scapegoat. Whatever Mr. Suhrawardy may be, I can assure the friends of the opposition and through them the country, he is not a coward. He knows how to take responsibility himself.

As for Suhrawardy's confrontation with the Commissioner of Police and his order from the Control Room, there is a contradictory interpretation between Hashim's speech and the report which Wavell received in Calcutta.

Before August 16, Suhrawardy had placed at the meeting of the Muslim League Parliamentary Party the question of the release of prisoners who were repatriated from Andaman and kept in Dhaka Jail. The League unanimously decided in favour of their release. Suhrawardy met the prisoners at Dhaka on August 14. Shortly after the Calcutta riot all the prisoners were released. Hashim entertained them for lunch at his residence in Calcutta. Abdullah Rasul, a Communist, took them to the residence. Hashim recollects that he saw for the first time the revolutionary leaders of Bengal like Messrs Ananta Singh, Ganesh Ghosh, Ambika Chakravarty and others.[26] Recollecting the Chittagong Uprising in the 1930s, Kalpana Joshi (Dutt) writes, "Who were these boys and girls who had created the epic, the Chittagong uprising? They were both Hindu boys and Muslim boys from the upper class, from the middle and lower class, from the loyalist families and nationalist families, from the peasantry and artisans backed by the sympathy and support of the people in general. ...And, there lay the secret of the success of the Indian Republican Army, Chittagong Branch." Examining the Census data for Chittagong district, she says, "It is gloriously evident that with such an overwhelming majority of Muslims in the countryside and the thickly populated villages the Hindus alone could not go very far without the help and sympathy of the Muslims."[27]

Hashim did not ignore the initiative of Suhrawardy in releasing Andaman prisoners. In his speech, unlike the official stance of the Muslim League, Hashim appreciated the Quit India movement of 1942 led by the Indian National Congress, which 'during recent years held aloft the torch of revolution and independence in India'.[28] For this reason Hashim felt 'a pity' for the Congress which charged Suhrawardy for making the Commissioner of Police 'a scapegoat' and defended 'the bureaucratic machinery of the government'.

On August 1, in his speech at Islamia College Hall, Calcutta, Abul Hashim repeated his view that their struggle was not against any of the parties or the communities in India, but declared that, if any of the parties in India made an alliance with the British imperialism and was involved in the conspiracy to make India remain in permanent servitude, we were forced to wage war with them.[29]

Along with the critical attitudes of the Congress towards the Suhrawardy ministry after the Calcutta killing, the start of the Interim Government headed by Jawaharlal Nehru on September 2, 1946 without the participation of the Muslim

League circumscribed Hashim's idea within limited bounds. The *Millat* dated September 13, 1946, first published after the Calcutta Killing, carried Abul Hashim's speech in Delhi, in which he said that the Indian National Congress had become an Indian agent of the British imperialism, adopting the repressive policy towards the Indian Muslims. He said that the Muslims' demand for Pakistan was for the liberation of all the people in India, but the Congress did not understand its meaning. In this connection the Calcutta Killing is a warning.[30]

Kamruddin Ahmad, who was a leader of the left of the League in Dhaka, recollects the position of the Left after the Killing, as follows:[31]

> As a result of these communal riots the leftist political workers– both Hindus and Muslims, were isolated. They were rendered completely ineffective in the atmosphere which was surcharged with suspicion and revenge. Communal frenzy was raised to such a pitch that no one would listen to reason. Reactionary elements assumed the leadership of both the communities. The idea behind the famous Lahore Resolution was forgotten, and people began to think in terms of Muslims and Hindus.

Mohammad Toaha also says that, on the occasion of communal riots in Dhaka, they were occupied in saving the Hindus from the Muslim majority area, and the Muslims from the Hindu majority area, and could not find what was the basis of the real Hindu-Muslim unity.[32]

The *Millat*, which appeared after about one month since the last issue, said in its editorial that this one month was not just one month, but we entered a new age. Its editor Idris relentlessly criticized the stance of the leadership of the Indian National Congress, the powerful men of the 'Hindu Bharat' who succumbed to the temptation of British imperialism.[33] The editorial of its next issue overlapped the victims of the Calucutta Killing with those who died in the Bengal Famine of 1943.[34]

Both the political development in the centre and the anti-Suhrawardy storm in Bengal forced the editorial staff to converge on the diagram of Hindu Bharat *versus* Muslims, though they tried to open their eyes to the poor and unarmed victims of the famine and massacre.

The situation after the Calcutta Killing forced the League Left workers into a difficult position. For Hashim it was extremely difficult to develop his cherished view that their struggle was against British imperialism alone. In the *Millat* dated October 18 appeared Hashim's article, "The men of the world will be liberated?"[35] Whether this rather 'metaphysical' monologue shows his delusion of judgment or his conviction of his own philosophy is not clear.

Riots in Noakhali

Communal riots in Noakhali, Muslim majority district, came to be widely known to the world with the visit of Gandhi in November. Suranjan Das describes the economic situation on the eve of the riots and the development of the riots in Noakhali and Tippera as follows:[36]

> The violence started in the northern part of Noakhali on 10 October, 1946 and spread to the adjourning district of Tippera on 13 October. Rioting reached its peak on 14 October. No serious incident was reported from Noakhali after 16 October with the exception of two outbreaks on the island of Sandwip. The situation in Tippera became 'quieter' from 20 October....
>
> Neither Noakhali nor Tippera had experienced any major Hindu-Muslim outburst before October 1946. As in other parts of eastern Bengal, the Muslims in Noakhali and Tippera laboured under the economic domination of Hindus—commerce, money-lending and landownership being concentrated in Hindu hands, as were shops selling daily necessities. Certain short-term economic trends in the mid-1940s particularly impoverished the Muslim peasantry. While depressed jute prices depleted their purchasing power, the scarcity and high prices of grain drove them to the brink of starvation. Noakhali and Tippera depended for food supplies on imports from the neighbouring areas of Dinajpur, Bakarganj, Chittagong, Sylhet and Burma. But by September 1946 this supply line had dried up. ... Noakhali and Tippera now had to fall back on the Supplies Department of the Bengal Government which could not meet this demand. In the second half of September the modified rationing system in Noakhali broke down; the price of rice rose to a level far higher than the provincial average. The Muslim peasantry was the section worst hit by this economic crisis which fuelled their resentment against Hindu economic supremacy.

Sugata Bose explains the riots of 1946 in Noakhali and Tippera in their historical background. He writes that, though by and large the pattern of tenure in the agrarian society of these two districts was not different from that of other districts in East Bengal, landlords became increasingly involved with money lending with the expansion of jute cultivation in the early 20th century, and the traders were gradually becoming middlemen in the land system, while the bulk of the peasantry had rights of occupancy raiyats and were not sharply differentiated.[37] Also Bose stressed that religion was an important element in the psyche of the Muslim peasantry. Noakhali and Tippera were under the influence of the Faraizi movement in the 19th century which rose against the landlordism under the name of God. Faraizi comes from the word *farz,* which means religious obligation. In spite of that, till the great depression of 1930 there was little actual violence in Noakhali and Tippera, and the rural interior, by and large, remained unaffected by the troubles in the urban areas. The depression of 1930, which caused an unprecedented slump in jute prices and the drying up of credit from moneylenders, destroyed 'symbolic relationship in a benevolent garb', the justification for the exploitation and 'the very basis of the ties between the peasants and the mahajans (moneylenders)'.[38]

The Indian National Congress under Ashrafuddin Ahmad Chaudhuri tried to mobilize the Muslim peasantry behind the civil disobedience movement, and the Krishak Samiti was closely connected with the local Congress organization.[39] Bose admitted that Krishak Samiti meetings were usually held on Fridays after the customary Jumma prayers, but clarified, "despite the frequent use of mosques, the only real institutional facilities available, and the broad appeal to religion, the conflict in the east Bengal countryside did not, without external interference, flow easily into a communal mould".[40]

In 1937 after the provincial elections, the Krishak Samitis and the Congress had still support among the Muslim peasants in Tippera. It was due to this reason that the third session of the All India Kisan Sabha was held at Comilla, headquarters town of Tippera district on May 11-14, 1938. Abdullah Rasul writes:[41]

> Tripura (Tippera) district had a predominantly Muslim population. The Muslim League, which had by now developed into a very militant organization of the Muslims, claimed to be the sole representative of that community in that district as elsewhere. The reality, however, was that in large parts of the district Congress had a hold on the Muslim kisans as well as the Hindu. So had the Kisan Sabha too. This League would not tolerate and it campaigned against the Kisan Sabha and its conference, asking Muslim peasants, in the name of their religion, not to participate in it. ... But the class sense of thousands of awakened Muslim kisans, mostly poor and middle peasants who were still suffering badly from the persisting economic depression, was strong enough to disregard the League and other hostile forces and their propaganda.

Swami Sahajanand Saraswati, the president of the session, writes in his memoir that people said, "Muslims, and Bengali Muslims in particular do not want the Kisan Sabha", but, despite the obstruction of the Huq Ministry, the objection of the Muslim League and the disposition of the *goondas* in the city, the conference was successful. Sahajanand was fascinated by a Bengali song named 'Ore bhai chasi, satya katha shuno (Hear, Kisans, True Story!)'[42]

In Noakhari Ghulam Sarwar, who belonged to the Krishak Samiti and had a close connection with organized armed dacoity, was elected to the provincial assembly in 1937. While continuing to incite peasants against landlords and money-lenders, he began to use the communal card against Hindus too.[43]

Sugata Bose concluded, "The magnitude and the extended nature of the economic crisis of the 1930s were unprecedented. The old ties snapped once and for all. The period of war and famine that followed hardly afforded an opportunity for repair." He continued: "To the vast mass of small-holding peasants living under similar, yet splintered, conditions of economic existence in east Bengal, religion, seemed to impart a sense of 'community'; so at a critical juncture of history, religion provided the basis of a 'national bond', however stretched, and became the rallying cry of a 'political organization' demanding the creation of a separate Muslim homeland.[44]

In this connection the impact of the Calcutta Killing of August 1946 was beyond any calculation.

On October 10, Ghulam Sarwar, an ex-League member of the Bengal legislature, addressed 15,000 Muslims at the Sahapur English High School at Ramganj police station area. The excited Muslim crowd first looted the local bazaar and then under Ghulam's direction attacked the establishments of the two richest Hindus in the locality; the Narayanpur zamindar and Rai Sahib Rajendra Lal Roy Chowdhury of Karapara. Then followed a general Muslim rising against the Hindu populace of Karapara.[45] Das concludes that the distinctive features of the riots in Noakhali and Tippera were the conversion of non-Muslims to Islam and assaults on Hindu women.[46]

Pethick Lawrence, Minister of State for India, published that the number of deaths in communal riots between September 2 and November 18, 1946 was 133 in Noakhali and Tippera, while in Bihar, a Hindu majority province, where riots started on October 25, 'Noakhali Day', the number was about 5,000. Why Gandhi did not visit Bihar too, was a complaint from the Muslim League. Mahatma Gandhi came to Patna on March 5, 1947, and stayed in Bihar till he attended the Asian Relations Conference in Delhi on April 1. He said, "To me, the sins of Noakhali Muslims and the Bihar Hindus are of the same magnitude and equally condemnable."[47]

Facing Noakhali and Tippera riots, the Bengal League was forced to take defensive response, though they protested against the 'hysterical' exaggeration of the situation by the 'Hindu press' and others.

After criticizing the 'Hindu Press', The *Millat* dated October 25, 1946 analysed in its editorial that the Congress leadership asked the British authorities to intervene, and showed sympathy to the Hindus in Noakhali and visited there without their contact with the League Ministry. While Jinnah and the Muslim League condemned the riots severely, the Congress did not do so in the Hindu majority area. The editorial wrote that they never supported the criminals in Noakhali, and never intended to underestimate the seriousness of those crimes. "What we wanted to say was that a trumped-up story would be useless for anyone, but would only instigate the riots ... Actually, in all communal conflicts there were faults on both sides, and both suffered. But, the Congress supported the Hindus in all riots. This is the lesson which we learned from the communal riots." The editor concluded, "The real (key to the) solution of the riots consists in the true love of the country. The true love of the country is the love of the people."[48] The use of the words, love of the people (*Desher Manusher prati Prem*) may have indicated a sign of the change in the stance of the editor, though there was no change in his basic posture.

The same issue of the *Millat* carried the contents of the report of the Noakhali Enquiry Commission which Abul Hashim published to the press.[49] The committee started by the Working Committee of the Bengal League was composed of Hashim, Shamsuddin Ahmed, Fazlul Rahman and other members. The report stated that riots did not occur in the wide areas; there was no fact to show the violent assault of one community on another community; in the interior parts the *goondas* made use of the spreading riots, and plundered the properties of the other community. The report added that undoubtedly the situation was serious, and the acts of the *goondas* could not get the approval or sympathy of the people. But, it was not true that, as the 'Hindu papers' reported, horrible incidents occurred. There was no assault on women, and there was no organized arson and killing. There were some cases of compulsory conversion or compulsory marriage. Pillage of the houses of a few zamindars and money lenders occurred, but no women and no infants were killed.

On the Direct Action Day, irrespective of men or women, and old or young, people from Noakhali, Tippera and their adjoining districts were killed in Calcutta. It is known that many labourers in Kidderpur area were from Noakhali, and those who survived returned home with their fresh memory of the riots, and the communal hostility against the Hindus. While recognizing the fact, the report pointed out the concealed intention in the exaggerated report by the 'Hindu papers'. According to the report, it was to defame the League ministry in Bengal, and to instigate riots and avenge Muslims in various parts of Bengal and also in Hindu majority provinces.

Abul Hashim concluded, "if the Hindu leaders bring ruin on their community, it is sure to bring ruin on all Bengal (*Samgra Desh*). I believe that the time has come when we should be ashamed to recognize them as the successors to Raja Rammohun Roy, Ishwarchandra Vidyasagar, Surendranath Banerjea, Chittaranjan Das, etc. ... People like the present Hindu leaders can not lead Bengal. I am very happy to say that the situation in Tippera and Noakhali is today completely under control. I expect that, unless riots occur somewhere, Bengal will soon come back to complete peace and order." From this statement it seems that, while keeping his critical view of the 'Hindu leaders', he was also in search of the way to his dialogue with 'all Bengal'. The serious communal situation forced him to consider the future of Bengal again in the context of his original idea.

In this respect his article, which appeared in the *Millat* of November 1, 1946, is noteworthy. His statement was published after hearing the news that the riots started again in Calcutta. It is a warning to the Bengali Muslims but also an appeal to the people of Bengal in general (*Banglar Jangan*).[50]

First, Hashim stressed that, in the present condition, it was the responsibility of the Bengali Muslims to maintain peace and order in Bengal, and above all, when their representatives decided to form the ministry, they sincerely took responsibility to keep peace and order in Bangladesh. Therefore they were now responsible for the defence of the dignity, life and property of everyone in Bangladesh irrespective of *jati*, religion and caste. As he said before, here also Hashim criticized the attitudes of the political parties, groups and newspapers which instigated the Muslims to be involved with the riots and tried to create a poor image of the Bengali Muslims and the Bengal ministry in the eyes of the people. His cherished view was that the riots would be of benefit only to British imperialism.

What is to be noted here was that Hashim appealed under the name of the innocent and poor people in Bengal (*Desher nirdosh o nishva Jangan*) to the sense of responsibility for the Muslims and the love of the country for the Hindus. They were asked to desist immediately from the devilish act. If there is a real complaint against any group or *jati* on the side of another group or *jati*, that should be solved peacefully and non-violently. Frenzy, which continued for the past few months, is tantamount to the act of suicide, from which only British imperialism, enemy of both will enjoy its results. Hashim said, "People of Bengal (*Banglar Jangan*) have to decide now whether they want to live, or choose the way to death. I wish people of Bengal (*Bangavasi*) will shun trifling self-respect, violence and hostility, restore peace by unity and integrity, and set Bangla at the peak of greatness".

Under the prevailing communal riots in Bengal, Bihar and other places of India, the editorial of the same issue of the *Millat*, criticized the Indian National Congress, 'the national organization of the Caste Hindus' from the standpoint of the Bengali Muslims.[51]

So far as this statement of Hashim was concerned, he tried to express his view in the name of the people of Bengal. Though he did not refer to the idea of the Bengal State, he appealed for the unity of the people of Bengal. At this critical point of history, he was cautious enough to see that the consciousness of the people as Bangla might not be washed away by the Two Nation Theory. The communal crisis led Hashim nearer to his original idea. His action for an independent Bengal after April 1947 did not come out abruptly, but there was already a sign of it at this stage.

In December 1946, the Bengal Provincial Muslim League Economic Planning Committee was formed. Abul Hashim was elected as its member together with Fazlul Rahman, Khwaja Shahabuddin and others including three members from the Bengal Muslim Chamber of Commerce.[52]

Now, Hashim came to express his idea of East Pakistan with conviction again.[53] In a special interview, he said that British imperialism was exclusively responsible for the fratricidal riots and Hindu-Muslim confrontation. "If the Muslim raj, that is, Pakistan is established in the Muslim majority provinces, the safety of the minorities is completely protected. In the independent East Pakistan the people's raj will be realized with the suffrage for all adults. If we expel foreign interests, Hindu-Muslim confrontation will be weakened. The Cabinet Mission Plan of May 16, 1946 made our two communities look at each other with suspicion." The action and pronouncements of the followers of British imperialism had become lamentable. The comments of the Viceroy, the Minister for State for India and the British Premier divided otherwise united anti-imperialist movement. It may be known from Hashim's pronouncement that he did not expect much of the Cabinet Mission Plan, and wanted to solve the Hindu-Muslim problems to the bitter end by the unity of the anti-imperialist forces in India.

As for the all-India problem, whether the League would cooperate with the Congress in the Constituent Assembly or not, Hashim answered that "we would only do what the Quaid-e-Azam asked us to do." At this stage he did not want to express his view on the central issues, though he was in a position of expressing his idea of East Pakistan freely. Time was on the eve of the election of the Bengal League President. Hashim was considered as a candidate of the ministerial choice. He was also prepared to assume the post of the President.

However, Hashim was soon overtaken by unexpected storms both inside and outside the Bengal League. The storm inside the League forced him to give up his active political life.

Parting with the Communists

The *Millat* dated January 31, 1946 carried the statement of Abul Hashim, who criticized the article of the *Swadhinta*, the organ of the Communist Party in Bengal, as it fabricated a story of his meeting with Sarat Chandra Bose and others.[54] According to this statement the *Swadhinta* carried the exaggerated report that Hashim met Sarat Bose and the provincial workers of the Azad Hind Fauz (Indian National Army) frequently for the increase of the influence of the Muslim League Party in the Bengal Legislative Assembly and the Calcutta Corporation Committee. Hashim approved that he met them and other provincial leaders to discuss the future of India and Bengal in particular. How to organize the front against British imperialism, and how to achieve the independence of all India inclusive of Pakistan and

Hindustan, these were the themes of discussion. There was nothing related to the Bengal Assembly or the Calcutta Corporation.

Hashim said, "I have noticed for some time that the Communists were trying to create estrangement among the League leaders. I did not feel any surprise at such activities of the Communists. Some months before they carried a slogan, wishing for the advance and long-term stability of the Congress and the League. However, against the background of their wish for the Congress and the League unity, there were the Communist activities which tried to dig the tombs for the Congress and the League, and lay the foundation of their organization there." But, the Communists failed in their efforts on the occasion of the last elections, in both Labour constituencies and Rural constituencies. Hashim thought that the Bengal League was far more united than before. Hashim added, "Khwaja Nazimuddin, Suhrawardy and I do not indulge in factionalism. Once there was difference in the general view between Nazimuddin and I. Now we are of the same view in all issues." He ironically 'advised' Communists to leave our organizational problem to Nazimuddin and me, and to find another place for the success of their action.

In his autobiography, Abul Hashim writes that the *Swadhinta* reported that Hashim and Bose talked together about ' A Greater Bengal' with its Muslim minority.[55] Actually there was no talk about it, though they agreed in their view that India was a country of many nations. The man who wrote this story was Shamsuddin Ahmad, a Communist who was close to Hashim, but whose party affiliation was not so far known to him. Nazimuddin made a fuss about the news.

On the eve of the organizational election, Abul Hashim was forced to be defensive again, insisting in the weekly that the Bengal League leadership was united, though the reality was far from it. The fissure between Hashim and the Communists, which had already started before, became decisive, and their 'friendly' relations in the past three years were not recoverable. It affected cooperative relations between the League Left and the Communists seriously.

Election for the Bengal League President

Abul Hashim made one of the most tragic decisions in his political life soon. Immediately after Maulana Akram Khan resigned from the post of the President of the Bengal Provincial Muslim League in early November 1946, Abul Hashim offered himself as a candidate for the President.[56] Later Fazlul Huq, who returned to the League in September 1946, expressed his desire to stand as a candidate for the election to the President on January 31, 1947. Though Huq may have stood with his own will, his candidature was fully utilized for the campaign against Hashim by the Khwaja group to divide the anti-Khwaja forces. The alliance between Huq and the Khwaja group was 'a matter of convenience'.[57] Hashim recollects that, a few days before the day fixed for the Council meeting for the election, Huq requested him to withdraw his candidature, but Hashim did not agree. Hashim adds later, "Now I think my decision was a great blunder".[58] Hashim was not specially interested in his ministerial or organizational post itself during his political life. Suhrawardy had also been criticized by the Khwaja group for his 'appeasing' policy towards the Hindus including the provision of facilities for Gandhi's mission to Noakhali, and the police discrimination in favour of Hindus in Noakhali and Tippera districts.[59] Moreover, the *Millat* wrote in its editorial, "We want to give a special warning that, if the Muslim League government leaves the destiny of the Muslims of Noakhali in the hands of Mr. Gandhi and his co-religionist police and military, they shall only incur their own calamity."[60]

The *Millat* dated February 7, 1947 stated in its editorial that Bengali Muslims wanted a truly competent person as the President.[61] The editorial said that the President Akram Khan submitted his letter of resignation very often due to his old age and bad health. For the same reason he stayed outside Bengal to recuperate for these years. In the last general elections the visit of a man of conviction like Akram Khan was really needed in many constituencies, but he could not come. Not only that, he could not participate in many meetings of not only the Provincial League Working Committee but also the All India Muslim League Working Committee. This editorial did not mention the name of the President to be desired. But, in another article titled "History of the League Movement in Bengal" in the same issue, Alshomim clearly contrasted Fazlul Huq with Abul Hashim, and wrote that, while Huq was neither interested in the League organization, nor wanted the strong organization, Abul Hashim reorganized the Muslim League at both the district and sub-divisional level, and was occupied in the work of the League for 24 hours after 1943.[62]

Before the Council meeting for electing the new President on February 9, 1947, it was propagated inside the League that Shyama Prasad Mukerjee of the Hindu Mahasabha supported Huq as the League President and also the Communists were active behind the scenes to divide the League leadership. They were the 'enemy' of the integration (*sanhoti*) of the Muslims.

The process to the Council meeting was unexpected, as Khwaja Nazimuddin 'betrayed' Fazlul Huq, while Suhrawardy remained 'neutral' and did not support Hashim. According to Hashim's writing, at a meeting with Khwaja Nazimuddin, Fazlul Rahman and Hamidul Huq Chowdhury, Suhrawardy decided to request Akram Khan to withdraw his letter of resignation without the knowledge and consent of Hashim.[63] The way to the President was thus closed for both Huq and Hashim. When this decision was communicated to Hashim is not clear. The *Millat* reported that at the meeting of the League Parliamentary Party on February 8, despite his conviction of victory in the election, Abul Hashim agreed not to stand as a candidate for the President in the name of the Muslim unity. After this, Suhrawardy proposed a resolution in which the Parliamentary Party requested the Council members to ask Akram Khan to withdraw his letter of resignation, and the resolution was passed unanimously. At the Council meeting on the following day, only 21 members voted against the resolution among more than 500 participants.[64] The *'Millat'* did not write about this topic later. Hashim recollects:[65]

> Mr. Suhrawardy did not like that I should be the President of the Bengal Muslim League. Mr. Suhrawardy needed my friendship till he became Chief Minister of Bengal but achieving his objective, he adopted sinister methods to get rid of my vigilance as General

> Secretary of Muslim League over his activities as the Chief Minsiter of Bengal. Like his predecessors in office, he wanted to make the Muslim League subservient to him and his government. Mr. Suhrawardy knew that this was not possible so long as I was Secretary or President of the Muslim League.
>
> In my struggle with the combined forces of Mr. Fazlul Huq and Khwaja Nazimuddin, Mr. Suhrawardy remained neutral. Mr. Suhrawardy did not like Mr. Fazlul Huq either. So he wanted withdrawal of Maulana Akram Khan's resignation and to maintain the status quo.

Abul Hashim opened the way to the Chief Minister of Bengal for Suhrawardy in the Parliamentary Board election, and defended Suhrawardy in the discussion on the motion of non-confidence after the Calcutta Killing. Personally Suhrawardy was a cousin of Mrs. Hashim. Despite their different political stances, both had struggled together, particularly in the provincial elections in 1946.

But, the *Millat* was now critical of the Ministry for its failure to implement any election pledge.[66] For instance, this weekly dated January 10, 1947 warned: "If the Ministry, which has political power in its hands, does not make the life and death efforts for the solution of the problems of vital importance that the people are facing, how will they approve that the Ministry is their representative?"[67] Suhrawardy also started his own paper, *Ittehad* on January 17, whose editor was Abul Mansur Ahmad. The main difference between Suhrawardy and Hashim was their view of the relations between the League government and the League organization. Since the birth of the Suhrawardy ministry and the Kashiara meeting, Hashim wanted the League organization to make the basic guidelines of policies for the ministry, while Suhrawardy wanted, as Hashim wrote, a free hand in the government policy making. This led Suhrawardy to his 'neutrality' and action for the 'status quo' in the presidential problem.

Unlike the description of the *Millat*, Suhrawardy's neutrality and action for the status quo was unexpected and so shocking to Abul Hashim. Hashim submitted his leave from the work of the General Secretary on February 14, and left for Burdwan. At that time, his son, Umar was seriously ill at Burdwan after he played the role of Amal in Rabindranath's drama, *Post Office* at the Burdwan Town School. This leave was received as 'a blessing in disguise' by the Khwaja group. "His retreat from the battlefield in this way was politically a great mistake."[68] Kamruddin Ahmad writes about the historical meaning of this drama as follows:[69]

> It was the conspiracy of the reactionary group, and particularly of Khwaja Shahabuddin. Two tigers became preys with one shot. The left young community was divided by the rivalry between A. K. Fazlul Huq Sahib and Abul Hashim Sahib. Fazlul Huq Sahib faced again his expulsion from politics for seven years, and Abul Hashim Sahib's political life ended.

Kamruddin Ahamd and other leftists workers persuaded Hashim that there was no room for 'sentimentality', and if he left politics, people would forget his contribution to Muslim politics in the past three years. But, Hashim no longer listened to their advice, and left them. He 'lost interest in organizational work.' Later, Hashim's group of workers shifted their centre of activities to Dhaka. "They were disillusioned at what had happened and was happening in the name of religion and decided to draw the attention of the people of East Bengal to the realities of life".[70]

Badruddin Umar also writes that, though Hashim's refusal to agree to Huq's proposal was not 'a political blunder', his request for leave for an unlimited period meant the end of his political life. This action badly affected his role as a leader for an independent Bengal after two months. Umar writes: "In politics there is no room for *Abhiman*."[71] In the dictionary *abhiman* is understood as the 'state of one's feelings being hurt especially owing to undesirable behaviour of a beloved person' (*Samsad Bengali-English Dectionary*, 2nd edition, Calcutta, 1982).

After the start of the Suhrawardy ministry, Hashim's results as the leader of the organization was not satisfactory. No annual party election was held during the period from 1945 to 1947.[72] In 1946 he could not hold the yearly Council meeting, though he tried to call it twice. The *Millat* dated January 24, 1947 stated in its editorial that every Bangladeshi knew the reason for its postponement, but no Council meeting, despite so many problems people were facing, was reproachable and unpardonable guilt.[73] But, the Council meeting held after so many hurdles prepared the way to the end of Abul Hashim's political life. It was a hard fact that Hashim could not secure the support of the majority on his own in the Council meeting, which he once called the *Jatiya Parishad* (National Assembly) of East Pakistan. The leader who appeared at the Council meeting as the man of the organization receded to the background after the unexpected decision of the Council meeting.

How he could take such an important decision promptly is not clear, but, in spite of the popularity of the weekly *Millat*, the lack of active daily communication among the Left workers, which was once consolidated by Hashim's tour to the districts outside Calcutta, and the erosion of the unity of the League Left after the start of the League ministry and the Calcutta Killing, made room for Hashim's isolated decision easier.

Tebhaga Movement

In September 1946, soon after the Calcutta Killing, the Bengal Provincial Kisan Sabha gave the call for the Tebhaga struggle. It was a demand for a two-third share of the crop for *bargadars* (share-croppers), the ratio recommended by the Land Revenue Commission, 1940.[74] The bargadars took the crop to their *khamar* (threshing floor).[75] It was the movement of the Hindu, Muslim and tribal peasants against the Hindu and Muslim jotedars, zamindars and talukdars. The struggle was not confined to north Bengal districts like Dinajpur, Rangpur and Jalpaiguri. It was also intense in Mymensingh district, particularly in Kishorganj subdivision, and in Midnapur district.[76] In Dhaka district too there were many scenes of the united movement of Hindu and Muslim peasants against the jotedars.[77] Under the leadership of the Kisan Sabha, both Hindu and Muslim peasants of Hasnabad in Tippera District provided shelter and relief to the people who suffered in the Noakhali riots which occurred just one mile from their area, and struggled against the spread of the riots.[78] Bhaumik, Eradatullah and others took a leading role in these activities.

The *Millat* also took an interest in the Tebhaga issue.

Mohammad Ali wrote that the Tebhaga movement spread to all parts of Bengal, peasants were awakened and the unjust exploitation of peasants would no longer be workable.[79] Abul Hashim was also conscious of these facts, and said in January 1947: "It is not true that there is lack of our sympathy with the landless peasants. The Bengal government made a promise that they would take steps for them as early as possible. The Provincial Muslim League is the founder of the government. Therefore the provincial League expressed their view to make the government keep their promise."[80] The Bengal Bargadars Temporary Regulation Bill was published in the *Calcutta Gazette* on January 22, 1947. Sunil Sen, who himself participated in the Tebhaga movement in Dinajpur, writes that the immediate effect of the Bill in Dinajpur appeared as the swing of Muslim peasants to the movement, but the jotedars, who constituted a formidable pressure group, exerted considerable influence on the Congress and the Muslim League.[81] He surmises that as the result of this pressure, the government sent an armed police force to the villages to arrest peasants and their leaders.

Sen lists the achievements and problems of the Tebhaga movement as follows:[82]

> Perhaps the single biggest achievement of the Kisan Sabha lay in the fact that it built a secular movement, and achieved considerable success in uniting peasants belonging to different communities on the basis of their class demands. In Dinajpur, Rangpur, Jalpaiguri, Mymensingh and Jessore the Muslim peasants joined the agrarian struggle in large numbers; some of the prominent cadres of the Kisan Sabha were Muslims. In Narail subdivision under Jessore district a sizable number of Muslim kisan cadres under the leadership of Nurul Jalal participated in the Tebhaga movement. In East Bengal the effect of Noakhali riots was felt, and some major districts, notably Chittagong, Dhaka, Comilla (Tippera), Noakhali, Barisal, could not be drawn in the agrarian movement.

Kamruddin Ahmad, who worked as a leader of the young League activists, writes that the wave of the Tebhaga movement did not reach East Bengal.[83]

Sunil Sen, who described the Tebhaga movement in

Dinajpur, writes about the Kisan Sabha organization as follows:[84]

> As the constitution of the Bengal Provincial Kisan Sabha indicates, the organization was based on village level committees ("primary committees"); the Provincial Council was elected by delegates who were elected by primary members. Between the Provincial Council and village level committees there could be district, subdivisional and thana level committees. ... It is not known how many kisans were elected delegates to the provincial conferences which invariably elected bhadralok to the provincial leadership. ...
>
> It is also not clear what business was actually transacted by the district, subdivisional and thana committees. It seems that the district unit of the Communist Party virtually replaced the District Kisan Sabha that maintained a formal existence and came to life when the time for holding the annual conference came. In Dinajpur the District Kisan Sabha did not meet once during the entire phase of the Tebhaga struggle; but communists working in Kisan Sabha managed to meet in Thakurgaon town in December, in Bochaganj in January, in East Thakurgaon in February, in the railway workers' colony in Parbatipur in March. The meetings and demonstrations were however held in the name of the Kisan Sabha.
>
> The real strength of the Kisan Sabha lay in the village level committees that were manned by peasants, the sons of the soil. ... Perhaps these committees did not meet regularly, nor did they maintain an office with a signboard. But in many districts they remained linked with the peasant masses for years, and wherever they existed they brought a new wind to rural life. Over the years communists trained kisan cadres who constituted the core of these committees.

The founding leader of the All India Kisan Sabha, Swami Sahajanand Saraswati already left the Sabha in March 1945. The Kisan Sabha had become actually the class organization under the leadership of the Communist Party of India. The relations between the Bengal League and the Communist Party were no longer 'friendly' as Hashim's pronouncement cited before showed. There was strong sympathy with the Tebhaga movement among the Left activists of the League, but the shadow of the Calcutta Killing and the impact of the Noakhali riots circumscribed their action.

D.N. Dhanagare, who examined the Tebhaga movement,

admitted that the communal politics vastly diminished the scope of the class struggle and, though the situation had potential for a massive peasant rebellion, it did not develop into one.[85] Not only that, while he depended on Sen's work, Dhangare found that the Kisan Sabha committees at the village level were dominated by the middle peasants (mainly petty jotedars or under-raiyats), though the main strength of the Tebhaga movement lay in the poor peasants. Some petty jotedars and under-raiyats active in the Kisan Sabha, employed bargadars for cultivating their lands, and the Tebhaga demand had affected many of them as much as it had affected the rich peasants and big jotedars. This led the middle peasants to turn indifferent to the movement or side with the big jotedars gradually.[86]

Also, the League leadership was almost unanimous in abolishing the zamindari system in the election campaigns as most of the zamindars were Hindus and the majority of the peasants were Muslims, but, after the formation of the Suhrawardy ministry, the government was inclined to abolish the zamindari system with compensation. The *Millat* continued to insist on the abolition without compensation.[87] As for the Bargadars Bill, the League members of the Bengal Legislative Asssemby, many of whom were jotedars, thought that this bill should be withdrawn. Even a rumour spread that, if the bill was brought for discussion, they would submit a motion of non-confidence against Suhrawardy.[88] The bill was finally shelved, and did not come into law before independence.

At the Council meeting of February 9, 1947, the League leaders stressed the need of the unity and integration (*Sanhoti)* of the Bengali Muslims.

On March 11, the Working Committee of the Bengal Provincial Muslim League approved Hashim's leave till June 15, 1947, and instructed Habibullah Bahar to do the work of the General Secretary in the meantime. Thus was completed the system which removed Hashim from the Bengal League leadership.[89] Habibullah Bahar was one of the members of the Khwaja group.[90] The *Millat* also could not resist this trend of thought. Abul Hashim receded to the background without any public notice as if nothing had happened.

Asian Relations Conference

The Inter-Asian Relations Conference was held under the auspices of the Indian Council of World Affairs at the Purana Quila (Old Fort) of Delhi from March 23 to April 2, 1947. Two hundred and fifty delegates from various parts of Asia attended the conference. One of the conspicuous characteristics was the absence of the Muslim League members including the League members of the Interim Government.

The Muslim League party in the Central Legislature decided to boycott the Asian Relations Conference at a meeting held in New Delhi on March 19, 1947. The party explained its reasons as follows.[91]

> The so-called Asian Relations Conference which has been sponsored by the Indian Council of World Affairs, ostensibly for the purpose of fostering cultural relations between Asian countries, is a thinly disguised attempt on the part of the Hindu Congress to boost itself politically as the prospective leader of Asiatic peoples. In convening this Conference through the Indian Council of World Affairs, which has been used for Hindu political propaganda abroad, the Congress did not seek the cooperation of the Muslim League which alone represents the hundred million Muslims of India. It is absurd and ridiculous for a Hindu political party to pose as the sole cultural representative of this vast subcontinent, and its attempt to mislead Asiatic countries into accepting it as such is nothing short of a fraud.
>
> Nor is the present time, when internal conflicts of unprecedented magnitude are inflicting such tremendous wounds on the Indian body-politic and when the future shape of independent India is still to emerge from the welter of the present, opportune for getting together with other peoples of Asia either on the social, cultural or political plane.
>
> The Muslims do not yield to any other section of the peoples of India in their goodwill towards their Asian neighbours, nor are they less anxious to forge cultural and other ties with them. But, they cannot countenance the manner in which this particular Conference has been called, nor the motives of the sponsors.

The Working Committee of the Conference refuted this statement, saying, "The Indian Council of World Affairs is a non-political body, established in 1943 for the objective study of world problems. Its sponsors and founder-members belong to all parties and invitations were sent to over two hundred representative men and women throughout the country, including members of the Muslim League".[92] The Committee added, "The primary object of the Conference is to focus attention on social, economic and cultural problems of the different countries of Asia, and to foster mutual contacts and understanding. Political problems, particularly of a controversial character or relating to the internal affairs of any participating countries are deliberately excluded from the agenda of the Conference." According to the explanation of the Working Committee, Jawaharlal Nehru sought Mr. Jinnah's support for the Conference in August 1946, and at the request of the latter, papers relating to the Conference were sent to him in Bombay. "Mr. Jinnah took no further notice of the scheme."

The *Millat* criticized this explanation with incisive words in its article written by Moyazzem, stating that this was not an 'Inter-Asia Conference' and the Indian National Congress was planning the expansion of their rule under the name of the independence of Asia just as Japan planned the expansion of their empire under the name of Asian independence.[93] He said there were no problems with which politics was not connected. "What was the intention of the Congress which tried to exclude the internal affairs of any participating country while discussing the independence of Asia? If they discuss internal politics, they have to talk about the destruction of the independence movement by one hundred million Indian Muslims. If they take up *varna* discrimination, they have to take up the liberation movement by sixty million Scheduled Caste people. If they take up immigration, they have to discuss the inhuman attitudes of the Congress towards the movement of the people from one province to another. If they discuss colonial economy, they have to take up the monopoly by one class. If they discuss labour problems, they have to take up the destruction of the labour movement by the Congress. In India culture is different between Hindus and Muslims. As the Congress knows these facts, they don't talk about them. The delegates from Asian countries will make a hole in the wall which the Congress built, and see the reality."

It is not clear whether this view was that of the League Left in Bengal, and of Hashim in partucular who already took leave from his work in the Bengal League. Hashim did not support the view that culture was different between Muslims and Hindus, which was the basis of the 'two nation theory'. Otherwise it may be difficult to understand why Abul Hashim again came to Calcutta to work for an independent United Bengal.

ENDNOTES

1. As for Akram Khan as 'a person of modern outlook' in his earlier days, see Dhurjati Prasad De, 1998. *Bengal Muslims in Search of Social Identity 1905-47*, Dhaka, 1998, pp. 18-23. Also see Amalendu De, 1996. *Religious Fundamentalism and Secularism in India*, Baharampur (West Bengal): Suryasena Prakashani, p. 85.
2. "League Councillor Adhiveshan President Keno bandh kariya dilen", *Millat*, May 17, 1946.
3. Syed Abul Maksud, 1994. *Maulana Abdul Hamid Khan Bhasani*, Dhaka: Bangla Academy, pp. 47-8. Also see, Kuwajima, *Muslims, Nationalism*, pp. 187-8.
4. "Kalnar Danga samparke Pradeshik Secretarir Vivriti", *Millat*, June 7, 1946. As for the first serious communal friction in Kalna subdivision in 1935, see Chatterji, op. cit., pp. 214-5.
5. Harun-or-Rashid, 2003. *Inside Bengal Politics 1936-1947 – Unpublished Correspondence of Partition Leaders*, Dhaka: The University Press Limited, p. 143.
6. Anil Chandra Banerjee and Dakshina Ranjan Bose, 1946. *The Cabinet Mission in India*, Calcutta: A. Mukherjee & Co., p. 315.
7. Ibid., pp. 353-60.
8. Harun-or-Rashid, *Inside Bengal Politics*, p. 157.
9. Ibid., p. 158.
10. Hashim, *In Retrospection*, pp. 113-5.
11. Ibid., p. 113.
12. Toaha, op. cit., p. 146-7. Hashim writes in his autobiography; "If the Cabinet Mission Plan could be implemented the partition of the subcontinent could have been avoided without much prejudice to the ideological contents of the Lahore Rsolution." Hashim *In Retrospection*, p. 121.
13. Hoque, op. cit., p. 70.
14. Ibid., p. 60.

15. "Banglar Leager Bhumika". *Millat,* June 21, 1946.
16. Harun-or-Rashid, *Foreshadowing,* p. 243.
17. Hashim, *In Retrospection,* pp. 115-6.
18. Ibid., p. 116 and Umar, *Amar Jiban 1,* pp. 160-1.
19. Hashim, *In Retrospection,* p. 117, and Umar, *Amar Jiban 1,* pp. 155-6.
20. Hashim, *In Retrospection,* pp. 118-9.
21. Wavell, op. cit., p. 335.
22. Ibid., pp. 338-40.
23. Hashim, *In Retrospection,* pp. 117.
24. Ibid, p. 186.
25. Ibid., pp. 185-6. As for the details and the historical meaning of the Calcutta Killing, see Suranjan Das, 1991. *Communal Riots in Bengal 1905-1947,* Delhi: Oxford University Press, pp. 161-192.
26. Hashim, *In Retrospection,* p. 115. Umar mentions the date of the meeting with the revolutionaries as August 20 or 21, 1946 (Umar, "Amar Pita", p. 269).
27. Kalpana Joshi (Dutt), "Chittagong Uprising and the Role of Muslims", in Nitish Ranjan Ray et al. 1984. *Challenge: A Saga of India's Struggle for Freedom,* New Delhi: People's Publishing House, p. 76 and p. 81. Also see Kalpana Dutt, 1979. *Chittagong Armoury Raiders; Reminiscences,* New Delhi: People's Publishing House, 2nd revised edition.
28. Hashim, *In Retrospection,* p. 182.
29. Abul Hashim, "Samrajyavadir jahara Mitra tahara amader Dushman", *Millat,* August 9, 1946.
30. Abul Hashim, "Sankat ki vyarth hoive?", *Millat,* September 13, 1946.
31. Kamruddin Ahmad, *Social History,* pp. 81-2.
32. Toaha, op. cit., p. 138.
33. "Sampadkiya-Dangar Pore", September 13, 1946.
34. "Sampadkiya-Dangar Shiksha", September 20, 1946.
35. Abul Hashim, "Vishwa Manva ki Mukti paive?", October 18, 1946.
36. Das, op. cit., pp. 192-3.
37. Sugata Bose. 1987. *Agrarian Bengal; Economy, Social Structure and Politics, 1919-1947,* Bombay: Orient Longman, p. 183.
38. Ibid. p. 190.
39. Ibid., pp. 194-5.
40. Ibid., pp. 198-9.
41. M.A. Rasul. 1974. *A History of the All India Kisan Sabha,* Kolkata: National Book Agency, p. 37.
42. Swami Sahajanand Saraswati. 1952. *Mera Jivan Sangharsh,* Bihta: Shri Sitaramashram, pp. 527-9.

43. Bose, op. cit., pp. 208-12.
44. Ibid., pp. 231-2.
45. Ghulam Sarwar was defeated by the League candidate in 1946 provincial elections, Ibid., p. 225, and Das, op. cit., p. 196.
46. Ibid., pp. 197-8.
47. K.K. Datta, 1958. *History of the Freedom Movement in Bihar, Vol. 3, 1942-1947*, Patna: Government of Bihar, p. 358.
48. "Sampadakiya-Noakhali ki shikhail?", *Millat*, October 25, 1946.
49. "Noakhali O Tripurar upadrut anchale League Tadant Komiti jaha dekhiyachen". Ibid.
50. "Deshvasir Man-Ijjat O Dhanpran rakshar Jimmedari laite hoive Musalmanke", Ibid., November 1, 1946.
51. "Sampadakiya-Sampradayik Danga", Ibid.
52. Ibid., December 20, 1946.
53. Abul Hashim, "Swadhin Purva Pakistan Jati-dharma nirvishesh Janganer Shasan pratishtit hoive", *Millat*, January 17, 1947.
54. "Muslim League Netrivridder madhya vibhed shrishtir kaje Communist Partir Apcheshta", *Millat*, January 31, 1947.
55. Hashim, *In Retrospection*, pp. 134-5.
56. Harun-or-Rashid, *Foreshadowing*, p. 249.
57. Ibid.
58. Hashim, *In Retrospection*, p. 130.
59. Harun-or-Rashid, *Foreshadowing*, pp. 250-1.
60. "Sampadakiya-matlab ki?" *Millat*, January 3, 1947.
61. "Sampadakiya-League Sabhapati Nirvachan", Ibid., February 7, 1947.
62. Ashomim, "Banglar League Andolaner Itihas," Ibid.
63. Hashim, *In Retrospection*, p. 131.
64. "Banglar League Sabhapati nirvachane Muslim shonhotir Dhushmaner Shadyantra vyarth hoiyachen", *Millat*, February 14, 1947.
65. Hashim, *In Retrospection*, p. 131.
66. Harun-or-Rashid, *Foreshadowing*, p. 253.
67. "Sampadakiya-Janaganer Davi", *Millat*, January 10, 1947.
68. Hoque, op. cit., p. 76.
69. Kamruddin Ahmad, *Atmavikash, 2*, p. 81.
70. Kamruddin Ahmad, *Social History*, p. 84.
71. Umar, *Amar Jiban 1*, p. 173.
72. Harun-or-Rashid, *Foreshadowing*, p. 254.
73. "Sampadakiya-League Counciler Adhiveshan", *Millat*, January 24, 1947.
74. Sunil Sen, 1972. *Agrarian Struggle in Bengal 1946-47*, New Delhi:

People's Publishing House, p. 36.
75. Ibid., p. 37.
76. Ibid., pp. 36-46. Also see, Moni Sinha, op. cit., pp. 90-100.
77. Umar, *Chirsthayee Bandobaste,* pp. 90-91.
78. Hiroshi Sato, "A.K. Fazlul Huq and Muslim Peasants in Bengal" (in Japanese), *Rekishi Hyoron* (Historical Review), April 1972, p. 119. Also see Muhammad Abdullah Rasul, 1980. *Krishak Sabhar Itihas,* 2nd edition, Kolkata: Navajatak Prakashan, pp. 165-6.
79. Mohammad Ali, "Chashider 'Te-bhaga' davi rodh kora jaive na", *Millat,* December 27, 1946.
80. Abul Hashim, "Swadhin Purva Pakistaner Jati-dhram nirvisheshe Janaganer Shasan pratishtit hoive", *Millat,* January 17, 1947.
81. Sunil Sen, op. cit., pp. 47-50.
82. Ibid., p. 84.
83. Kamruddin Ahmad, *Atmavikash, 2,* p. 22.
84. Sen, op. cit., pp. 86-8.
85. D.N. Dhanagare, 1983. *Peasant Movements in India 1920-1950,* Delhi: Oxford University Press, p. 172.
86. Ibid., p. 173.
87. Umar, *Chirasthayee Bandobaste,* pp. 104-8.
88. Moni Sinha, op. cit., p. 100.
89. Hoque, op. cit., pp. 76-7.
90. Umar, "Amar Pita", p. 171.
91. *Indian Annual Register,* 1947, Vol. 1, p. 298.
92. Ibid., p. 299.
93. Moyazzem, "Iha Inter-Asia Sammelan Nahe-Japaner Parikalpna pune Pravarthner Pracheshta matra", *Millat,* April 11, 1947.

7

United Bengal, Partition and Move to East Bengal

For the United Bengal

After his leave from the work of the Secretary of the Bengal Provincial Muslim League, he spent his days in Burdwan as if he was a retired person, though he was 42 years of age. He no longer felt it necessary to know how critical situation was proceeding on in Bengal and India.[1]

Meanwhile, as the partition of the subcontinent had become inevitable, the Working Committee of the Indian National Congress proposed the division of the Punjab into a predominantly Muslim province and a predominantly non-Muslim province on March 8, 1947. Later, Acharya Kripalani, the Congress President, stated this principle of division would apply to Bengal.[2] The Bengal Provincial Congress Committee and the Bengal branch of the Hindu Mahasabha supported the partition of Bengal respectively on April 4 and 6. The business leaders and historians also supported this move, and the Congress and the Mahasabha started the joint work for this campaign.[3]

On April 8, 1947, H.S. Suhrawardy, Chief Minister of Bengal, said in an interview, "I have always held the view Bengal cannot be partitioned. I am in favour of a united and greater Bengal". Again he said at a press conference on April 27, "I speak for myself. I speak for Bengal. I visualize an independent, undivided, sovereign Bengal in a divided India."[4] Hashim writes about his return to Calcutta in his autobiography as follows:[5]

> On April 27, under the leadership of Mr. Deben Dey some young Congress leaders belonging to Mr. Sarat Chandra Bose's group came in a jeep to see me at Burdwan. They requested me to come to Calcutta immediately with them. They said that Bengal was going to be divided. I did not believe them. I asked, "Who is going to divide Bengal? Between 1905 and 1911 the Hindus of Bengal made the greatest sacrifice for annulment of partition of Bengal and the Muslim League of today is against partition of Bengal." I was a fool in thinking like that. I did not take into consideration the latest developments in Indian politics and British diplomacy. Lord Mountbatten pushed his plan in indecent haste as a result of which Indian leaders completely lost their head and fell helplessly into the trap laid by Mountbatten. On the 28th of April I came to Calcutta and issued a statement to the press which was widely published on the 29th of April.

It seems that the incorrect analysis of the developing situation in Bengal was caused by the lack of vivid and free discussion among the League activists who came around Abul Hashim, besides his cherished idea of the Bengal culture shared by both Hindus and Muslims. Hashim's statement issued on the 29th was made as the result of his long attachment to Bengal culture and his persistent efforts which tried to keep the Bengal entity despite the communal disturbances in the later half of 1946, and did not accept the Two Nation Theory. It was not surprising that Hashim could publish his long statement after his two-month 'retired' life. The main points of the statement in his own words were as follows:[6]

> Partition of Bengal bears no analogy to the partition of India. The lamentable perversion in thinking which suggests that the movement for the partition of Bengal is convenient counterblast to Pakistan arises out of a colossal ignorance of the content and implications of the Lahore Resolution to which and which alone and not to this interpretation or that interpretation thereof, Muslims of India owe allegiance. ...
>
> It (the Resolution) merely demands complete sovereignty for those countries which are known to the world as Muslim majority countries, and by implication demands complete sovereignty and self-determination of all the nations and countries of India. It gives Bengal and other cultural units of India complete sovereignty....
>
> Hindus and Muslims of Bengal, preserving their respective

> entities had by their joint efforts, in perfect harmony with the nature and climatic influence of their soil, developed a wonderful common culture and tradition which compare favourably with the contribution of any nation of the world in the evolution of man.
>
> In the free state of Bengal, Hindus and Muslims as such shall have no right exclusively reserved for them except the right of Muslims to govern their society according to their own Shariat and the right of Hindus to govern their own society according to their 'Shastra'. These rights give the Muslims their spiritual need for Pakistan and the Hindus a real homeland for the free development of their own ideology and material realisation of their particular outlook on life.
>
> It is unthinkable that in a free Bengal, the Hindus of Bengal who constitute nearly half of its population will be denied their legitimate share in administration and in the enjoyment of other material resources. Hindu-Muslim population of Bengal is almost balanced. Neither community is in a position to dominate the other. If Bengal is permitted to harness all her resources for the exclusive service of the children of her soil, both Hindus and Muslims shall be happy and prosperous for many a century to come. ...
>
> Mr. C.R. Das is dead. Let his spirit help us in moulding our glorious future. Let the Hindus and Muslims of Bengal agree to his formula of 50-50 enjoyment of political power and economic privileges. I again appeal to the youths of Bengal in the name of her past traditions and glorious future to unite, make a determined effort to dismiss all reactionary thinking and save Bengal from the impending calamity.

Tilt to the religious thought was subdued, except the rights of the Muslims and Hindus to govern their respective society according to the 'Shariat' and 'Shastra'. The expression like 'the resuscitation of the Islamic moral values' in the draft Manifesto of 1945 does not appear here. Hashim appreciated Suhrawardy's posture towards the coalition with the Indian National Congress and other parties in the past despite his most recent feeling of *abhiman*, while he was critical of the Muslim legislators who were busy with the shuffle and reshuffle of the ministry, instead of concentrating on policies and programmes. He appealed to the people of Bengal to return to the glorious tradition of unity. Abul Hashim was still on leave, but he must have thought that the time had come to express his idea of the Bengal nation squarely without any reserved mind. In a sense he freely expressed his idea without worrying about his position as a man of the organization, though this was fatal in mobilizing the mass under his leadership. The *Millat* dated May 2, 1947 carried the full text of Hashim's statement as that of the Secretary of the Bengal Provincial Muslim League.[7]

On April 30 a meeting of the Working Committee of the Bengal Provincial Muslim League under the presidentship of Akram Khan appointed a sub-committee with Nurul Amin, the speaker of the Bengal Assembly, as convenor and Suhrawardy, Habibullah Bahar, Fazlul Rahman, Hamidul Huq Chowdhury and Yusuf Ali Chowdhury as members to negotiate with the leading members of the Hindus about the future constitution of Bengal.[8]

According to Hashim's recollection, in the last week of April a meeting of Muslim League and Congress leaders was convened at Suhrawardy's residence, and a joint committee was formed for drafting the salient features of the constitution of sovereign Bengal. In the Committee the Muslim League was represented by H.S. Suhrawardy, Khwaja Nazimuddin, Mohammad Ali of Bogra, Dr. A.M. Malek, Fazlul Rahman of Dacca and Hashim. Hindus were represented by Sarat Chandra Bose, Kiran Shankar Roy, Nalini Ranjan Sarkar, and Sayyaya Ranjan Bakshi.

How Abul Hashim, who was called to come to Calcutta by Sarat Chandra Bose, but was not a member of the sub-committee of the provincial Muslim League, could participate in the activities of the joint committee as one of the representatives of the Bengal League, is not clear. The *Millat* is silent about this process. However, Hashim, who was brought to Sodepur Ashram, Calcutta by Sarat Chandra Bose, met Gandhi on May 10, and discussed United Bengal. Again, on May 11, Hashim, who accompanied Suhrawardy, met Gandhi.[9] The same members met Gandhi on the 12th too. Hashim and Bose had chances to share their view of a Bengal State before, and Hashim and Suhrawardy also had a common view of a Bengal state composed of Hindus and Muslims for some years. The personal influence of Sarat Bose must have led Suhrawardy to include Hashim into his group of the League representatives.

But, soon Akram Khan, President of the Bengal League, launched a counterattack against the Suhrawardy-Hashim group in his statement on May 4.[10]

> The question of a separate independent state in Bengal isolated from other Pakistan areas does not arise. The Muslims of India constitute a single united nation and we aim at setting up a single united nation and we aim at setting up a single united state which include all the Muslim majority provinces. ...
>
> Those who talk of a Bengalee nation consisting of Muslims and Hindus and of a separate Sovereign Bengal upon that basis are clearly playing into the hands of our enemies ...
>
> I have noticed that the proposals which include joint electorates and the discarded and undemocratic 50:50 formula have been put forward from certain quarters. Let me declare as clearly and unequivocally as possible that these proposals are completely repudiated by the Muslim Bengal. Besides, on such All India issues, the All-India Muslim League and the Qaid-e-Azam are alone competent to express an opinion. I warn the people from whom such proposals have come that the consequences of the game they are playing will be dangerous.

The leadership of the Bengal Provincial Muslim League was far from united in their posture towards a United Independent Bengal. The critical view of Akram Khan and four members of the sub-committee including the Convenor Nurul Amin and Habibullah Bahar,[11] rather strengthened Hashim's conviction that he was on the right road to a United Sovereign Bengal. He replied to his critics, saying: "My statement on the partition of Bengal was merely a suggestion for a possible basis of discussion between the Hindus and Muslims of Bengal. My critics have questioned my authority to do so. No authority is necessary for doing a good thing. In my statement I addressed both Hindus and Muslims and did not speak on behalf of either." And he further clarified his view of the 50:50 suggestion, and concluded as follows:[12]

> My critics conveniently forget that the 50:50 ration is the existing rule which was brought about by an agreement between the

> Hindus and Muslims during the first Muslim League Ministry under the leadership of Mr. Fazlul Huq. In a system of an unadulterated joint electorate, which I have suggested no question of 50:50 or 60:40 arises in the matter of seats in the Legislature or Ministry. My 50:50 suggestion refers merely to the political privileges enjoyed by having a share in the services, and nothing more. ...
>
> I shall appeal most earnestly to the gentlemen of the Negotiating Committee of the Muslim League to go ahead with their job of negotiation with the Hindus and to give a concrete suggestion regarding Bengal's future instead of beating about the bush and vilifying us.

The move for an independent Bengal was crystallized in the form of the Agreement for the Free State of Bengal reached at the meeting attended by Suhrawardy, Hashim, Kiran Shankar Roy, Sarat Chandra Bose, and other leaders at Bose's residence on May 20. The four members out of the six sub-committee members of the Bengal Provincial Muslim League, who belonged to the Khwaja group, were absent at this meeting.[13] After stipulating, "Bengal will be a free state. The Free State of Bengal will decide its relations with the rest of India", the Agreement mentioned, as one of its terms, the election to the Bengal Legislature on the basis of a joint electorate and adult franchise, with reservation of seats proportionate to the population amongst Hindus and Muslims.[14]

Though Gandhi listened to Sarat Bose's appeal carefully, he was not powerful enough to reverse the course taken by Sardar Vallabhbhai Patel, who was the main architect of the partition of Bengal.[15] Gandhi wrote back to Sarat Bose on June 8, 1947, writing: "I have gone through your draft. I have now discussed the scheme roughly with Pandit Nehru and Sardar. Both of them are dead set against the proposal."[16]

Harun-or-Rashid analyses that at a certain stage Jinnah thought it 'much better' to allow Bengal to remain united and independent than to have a divided Bengal with its most prosperous part including the much-coveted Calcutta city joining the Indian Union, but he was also opposed to joint electorates provided under the terms of agreement, and feared that Bengal would take the course of a secular state, and not remain a potential ally of Pakistan 'with the preponderance of the Hindus and the total unreliability of Suhrawardy and Hashim'.[17] Finally, the Working Committee of the Bengal Provincial Muslim League adopted a resolution on May 28 that Jinnah 'alone had the authority to negotiate and settle the future constitution on behalf of the Muslims of India as a whole and the Muslims of Bengal shall stand by his decision', and the sub-committee appointed for negotiations with Bengali Hindu leaders was dissolved.[18]

The meeting of the Council of the All India Muslim League was opened in Delhi on June 3, 1947, and they accepted the Mountbatten Award for the partition of India, Bengal and the Punjab. According to Hashim's recollection, before they left for the meeting, the Council members from Bengal met at Suhrawardy's house, and decided unanimously to oppose the official resolution if the League accepted the Mountbatten Award.[19] But, in Delhi Suhrawardy supported the resolution, and Hashim and Hasrat Mohani were not allowed to speak. On the occasion of voting by the raising of hands, Suhrawardy counted the votes, and said, "Quaid-e-Azam, only eleven votes against us."[20] Those who voted against the official resolution were Hasrat Mohani, Mian Iftikhar-ud-din and 9 delegates from Bengal.

In the evening of June 3, Hashim issued a press statement, saying that the decision of the Council of the All India Muslim League was the results of three fears: firstly, habitual fear of Mr. Jinnah; secondly, fear of an uncertain future; and thirdly, fear of their uncertain status in Pakistan if they incurred the displeasure of Mr. Jinnah.[21] The *Dawn* soon carried the editorial titled 'A Snake in the Grass', and blamed Hashim, writing that he 'has not only fallen foul of the Quaid-e-Azam but also given expression to certain views which are diametrically opposed to the fundamental principles which have always guided the policy of the Muslim League'. This editorial concluded, "In our view Mr. Abul Hashim should be forthwith expelled from the League organization. It would be good riddance."[22]

Suhrawardy did not defy Jinnah, sensing that there would be no chance of United Independent Bengal against the 'adamant' attitudes of Nehru and Patel, whatever postures Bengal Hindu leaders took.[23]

Harun-or-Rashid concludes that the most formidable reason for the failure of the move was the Congress veto.[24] Simultaneously, it cannot be denied that the move for United Independent Bengal was developed through the 'parlour' discussion among the limited members. On April 28, 1947 Abul Hashim appealed to the youths of Bengal to save Bengal from the impending calamity. The Muslim student community tried to mobilize the people behind the demand for United Bengal. On May 25 professors, lawyers, men of letters, thinkers and Muslim League workers participated in the meeting called by the students in Calcutta.[25] Hashim himself gave a talk at the symposium prepared by the Communist Party in May.[26] Despite these efforts the movement was not strong enough to sustain an adverse wind with its mass base. Both Hashim and Sarat Bose never directly appealed to the people for the struggle for a United Bengal beyond the limit of press statements. Hashim was 'on leave', and did not try to return to the post of the Secretary of the Bengal League to lead the movement, while Nazimuddin encouraged the move for the partition of Bengal inside the Working Committee through his man, Habibullah Bahar.[27]

The position was the same with Sarat Chandra Bose. After his work as a minister in the Interim Government for six weeks, he vacated his post to the Muslim Leaguer who joined the government in October 1946, though he remained as a member of the Congress Working Committee. On January 30, 1947 Bose announced the formation of the Azad Hind Party at a meeting of the Indian National Army personnel and others, and began to work separately from the main Congress organization.[28]

The position of both Sarat Chandra Bose and Abul Hashim was situated at the periphery of the Indian National Congress and the Muslim League, while the forces against a United Bengal were developing their 'massive' campaign.[29] Despite his last efforts for the realization of the idea of the Draft Manifesto, Abul Hashim had already lost his group of workers whom he trained with his mission since November 1943. But, it was not only the problem of Abul Hashim's political approach, but here was the shadow of the political situation after the Calcutta Killing on August 16, 1946 on the people's movement in Bengal. The Bengal Provincial Muslim League was seriously divided between the *Akhand* (undivided) Pakistanis and the supporters for a United Bengal.

Kazi Mohammad Idris wrote in his editorial: "Today Bangla was partitioned against the law of nature. We hope that the partitioned Bangla will recover its complete figure again according to the law of nature."[30]

Partition of Bengal

Abul Hashim writes about the process towards the partition of Bengal, and the related move of the Bengal League leaders as follows:[31]

> On the 20th of June, a joint meeting of the Legislatures of Bengal was held at the Assembly Chamber. The joint meeting voted for joining Pakistan. Fifteen minutes after this two meetings were held. One of the Legislators of Hindu majority area of Bengal and the other of the Legislators of Muslim majority area of Bengal. The Muslim majority area voted against partition of Bengal and the Hindu majority area voted for partition of Bengal. Bengal was partitioned. Communist Party members voted for partition. ...
>
> On the 5th of August two meetings were held under the presidency of Mr. Chundrigarh. In the meeting of the Legislators of East Pakistan Mr. Suhrawardy contested Khwaja Nazimuddin for the leadership of the Parliamentary Party of East Pakistan. Mr. Suhrawardy secured 39 votes only. Mr. Suhrawardy immediately after his defeat rushed into the room, with Mr. Abdur Rahman of Bashirhat, where West Bengal members of the Muslim League Parliamentary Party sat to elect their leader. Mr. Abdur Rahman proposed Mr. Suhrawardy's name. Mr. Suhrawardy was elected leader of West Bengal Muslim League Parliamentary Party. This was a sight for the gods to see. A man who a moment ago decided to migrate to Pakistan and aspired to be the Chief Minister of East Pakistan got his name proposed for the leadership of Muslim League Parliamentary Party of West Bengal.

In the election for the leader of the Parliamentary Party of East Pakistan Hashim remained neutral, and did not support

Suhrawardy. Suhrawardy's neutrality in the Bengal League Presidential election in February 1947, and the change of his posture in the move for a United Bengal in the final stage may have influenced Hashim's action or no action. However, Hashim had no idea to move to East Pakistan or Pakistan after the partition. Therefore, there was no reason for Hashim to intervene in the election for the premier of East Pakstan.[32]

In 1947 Abul Hashim lost not only his eyesight, but also his dream, which he described in the Draft Manifesto and had tried to realize through his cooperation with the move for an independent Bengal. On the morning of August 15, 1947 Hashim attended the independence ceremony in Calcutta when the Indian National Flag was hoisted on the Government House and C. Rajagopalachari was installed as Governor of Bengal.[33] In the afternoon he visited Sodepur Ashram to meet Gandhi. Gandhi said to Hashim: "You could not resist partition of Bengal. This is your defeat, but I assure you that you could succeed if you had not lost your vision." Hashim commented in his autobiography: "By 1947 I became almost completely blind. Here he referred to the loss of my eyesight."[34] From his own experience, Gandhi showed sympathy and concern for Abul Hashim who was forced to allow other political leaders to act in their own way.

He was consistent in his critical view of British imperialism, which, he thought, was against the interests of the people of Bengal. He appreciated the movement for the annulment of partition of Bengal at the beginning of the 20th century, did not deny the revolutionary aspect of the Quit India movement of 1942, insisted that the British war and colonial policy was responsible for the suffering of the people in the Bengal famine of 1943, defended Suhrawardy's action in opposition to the top members of the bureaucracy and police after the Calcutta Killing in August 1946, and finally surmised that the divided and weak Bengal would only benefit British imperialism. His criticism sometimes seemed so naïve, but at the base of this thought was his conviction that Hindu-Muslim unity in Bengal could be strengthened on its own historical tradition without the intervention from British imperialism, Indian nationalism or the central 'Muslim nation' leadership. It is in this connection that Ashok Mitra, who critically traced the thought and action of Abul Hashim in the 1940s, writes that the aim in his heart was the rebuilding of a bridge of friendship with the Hindus.[35] However, the reality was that in addition to the intervention of the British and central Congress and League leadership, Bengali leadership was also seriously divided. His conviction was belied by the bankruptcy of a plan for a united independent Bengal.

Gandhi also expressed his deep frustration and observed:[36]

> The world knows Sardar Patel is my 'yes-man', but these days he says 'no' to everything. I say Babu Rajendra Prasad goes out with me in my morning walk but when I come back to my Ashram I feel as though, we shall never meet again; Pandit Jawaharlal Nehru is really a jawahar (jewel) but at times, in sentiment and emotion he makes utterances which he should not do. But he has the courage to admit his mistakes, if he is convinced otherwise. How long shall I live to see these things.

Abul Hashim also noticed that Gandhi deeply realized the defeat of his lifelong struggle. On the day of India's independence, there was something which aroused a response in each other's heart, though the context was different for the two. However, though he resided in India for some years after the partition, Abul Hashim's belief in the theory of multi-nationalism remained, while keeping his critical view of the one or two nation theory.[36]

Riot in Burdwan and Move to Dhaka

In his statement on 'three fears' earlier cited, Abul Hashim said that the partition of Bengal was the result of the British conspiracy and now Bengalis were asked to select one of the two states, Hindustan or Pakistan. Under these conditions the idea of a United Bengal was obstructed. "If Hindus of West Bengal move to Pakistan, or Muslims of East Bengal wish to stay in India, the ideal of a United Bengal may be successful. But there is no probability of both."[37] A divided Bengal and the birth of East Bengal was not what he wanted. After the partition of India and Bengal, he remained in Burdwan, his father's land. Partition, the move of Hindus to West Bengal and Muslims to

East Bengal, communal riots, and the political action of his League leaders who once worked with him were far from encouraging. He lost his eyesight completely, and without help he could not read. Except coming to Calcutta for his work as a member of the West Bengal Legislative Assembly, he was in Burdwan, and friends came to see him there. His main concern was now occupied with the development of his idea of Rabbaniyat.

After Suhrawardy left for Pakistan in 1949, Abul Hashim became an opposition leader, and one of his works in the legislature was the dissolution of the Muslim League Parliamentary Party. Hashim also demanded the Congress Government to stop the oppressive policy towards the Communist Party of India, and prevent atrocities against the detained Communists, though the CPI carried the slogan of the overthrow of the Congress government since its second Congress in Caluctta in February 1948. The Communists also approached Hashim, providing information in this connection.[38] Hashim spoke in the Bengal legislature on February 7, 1950:

> I would ask the Hon'ble Chief Minister of West Bengal if His Excellency was informed that on the 5th of January a member of this Assembly Mr. Ratan Lal Brahmin who was in the Alipur Central Jail was assaulted by lathis and iron bars and he was taken to hospital and that due to high pressure from jail authorities his treatment was abandoned because that would expose the truth. Has His Excellency been informed that on the 15th of December 1949, of the Christian era, within the prison walls of the Alipore Presidency Jail nearly 150 hooligan warders under the leadership of the Superintendent of the Jail himself, who has now been transferred to the Burdwan Jail, being completely drunk scaled the wall of the Female Ward and ruthlessly assaulted unprotected women there and beat them mercilessly with lathis in their attempt to commit violent outrage on the modesty of these unprotected women. ...

Though during this period he was very critical of Communist ideology and was inclined to the philosophy of Rabbaniyat, Hashim was against the use of the extraordinary measures to control the Communists, because "violence breeds violence".[39]

Hashim maintained his multi-nation theory after the

partition of 1947 too. In the general discussion of the budget, Hashim said on February 23, 1948: "India is the home of many nations and unless we are prepared to accept a multi-nation theory, rejecting both one and two, we shall not be able to make India a real temple of peace."[40]

In Burdwan his main daily work was reading. As he lost his eyesight, his son Badruddin Umar read books to him. Among the books he read were Bertrand Russell, *History of Western Philosophy* and Max Mueller, *Six Schools of Hindu Philosophy.* Besides these, Umar read a book written by S. Radhakrishnan and other books on Islamic thought and Indian philosophy.[41]

At the end of 1948 Shamsul Huq of Tangail came to Hashim's house, and stayed for about two months. He was a young activist of the League Left when Hashim was the Secretary of the Bengal League. Shamsul Huq also read books to Hashim, and told him about the political situation in East Pakistan. Already Hashim had his plan to publish a book on Islam, and Shamsul Huq helped him, and prepared two copies of its handwritten draft. Thus the draft of Hashim's first book, *The Creed of Islam* was made. Shamsul Huq took one draft copy to Dhaka. After some time, Kamruddin Ahmad wrote to Hashim that, using this draft, Shamsul Huq published a book titled *Islam from the Revolutionary Point of View* under his own name. Hashim felt surprised and felt sad to hear of it. Hashim prepared the second draft on the basis of the first one. Umar made most of the second draft. Mabinul Huq who later joined, prepared the rest of the second draft, and the last draft for printing. Umar was soon free from reading books for his father, as Mabinul Huq undertook this task.[42] *The Creed of Islam* was published in Dhaka in 1950.

When Shamsul Huq left for Dhaka, Hashim handed another manuscript to him. It was a draft of the Manifesto of a new party in East Pakistan. When the Awami Muslim League was formed in 1949, he submitted this draft. After it was revised, it was adopted as the Manifesto of the League. Shamsul Huq was the General Secretary of the Awami Muslim League.[43]

On January 26, 1950 the Constitution of India came into force. In the Bengal Provincial Assembly Abul Hashim expressed his view of the Constitution on February 7:[44]

> The New Constitution of India has been ushered in an atmosphere of grim disappointment. The new Republic of India came into being equally in an atmosphere of grim disappointment created by inefficient, dishonest and corrupt administration of the Congress Party. The krishak (peasants) and mazdoors (labourers) of India associated themselves actively in India's struggle for independence in the hope of, and I should add relying upon the well-pronounced policy of the then Congress, of having a Krishak Mazdoor Raj. They have been thoroughly disillusioned. There is nowhere in the Constitution any trace of any kind of Krishak Mazdoor Raj.

This view is very close to that of Sarat Chandra Bose, who formed the United Socialist Organization of India (Bharatiya Samyukta Samajvadi Sabha) with Swami Sahajanand Saraswati on October 28-30, 1949. Sarat Bose was elected as its President. This organization stipulated in its statement that the central Congress government was the government of the vested interests.[45] It is not clear whether Abul Hashim sent any message to Sarat Chandra Bose.

There is enough reason for Hashim not celebrating the enforcement of the Constitution of India. The communal situation on both sides of Bengal became very serious around this period. As for the origin of the riot there is a coincidence among political leaders and observers. On December 20, 1949, an assistant sub-inspector of police accompanied by three constables went to the village of Kalshira in Bagerhat sub-division, Khulna district of East Bengal, to search the house where a fugitive communist worker Joydeb Brahma stayed, and the police molested the women at his house. As the local people rushed in to resist it, a constable died while two others sustained injuries. The village was predominantly inhabited by the Nama-Shudras (Scheduled Castes). The policemen were able to escape with the help of Ansars and some local people. The members of the Ansar brigade spread communal sentiment in the neighbouring Muslim dominant areas.[46] Refugees from Khulna districts and others reached Calcutta and other places.[47]

In Calcutta the memory of Sardar Vallabhbhai Patel's speech

at the maidan on January 3, 1948 was still fresh among the Muslims in Bengal. There he said: "As regards the controversy of a secular *versus* a Hindu State, there can be no serious talk of a Hindu State. But one fact is indisputable. There are 4.5 crore Muslims in India many of whom helped the creation of Pakistan. How can one believe that they will change overnight? The Muslims say that they are loyal citizens and therefore why should anybody doubt their bona fides? To them I would say: 'Why do you ask us. Search your own conscience?'"[48] Again, Patel made his speech in the same place on January 15, 1950. He started, "Bengal or India can never forget what was called the 'direct action' by those people. How can the plight of Calcutta in those days be forgotten? Nor can the subsequent events in Noakhali be forgotten by you or India." He also confirmed that, as for the people in East Bengal, the bonds of kinship and economic and social links could not be broken.[49] There was no change in Patel's basic approach to the problem of Bengal as his reference to the 'anger that our Bihari brethren showed' in October 1946 indicated, though he then added, "we must act with discretion, not in anger."[50] His criticism this time was on the action of the Communists and their supporters in West Bengal too. He said, "We have first to set our own house in order. ... I can understand a Communist ideology but how can such vandalism help? But what pains me more is the attitude of the lakhs of other residents of Calcutta. Why don't we understand our duty?" This was about forty days before the Preventive Detention Act came into operation in India on February 25, 1950.[51] Patel's speech warned Muslims, refugees from East Pakistan, Communists and the 'residents of Calcutta' not to hamper his task assigned after India's independence.

On January 24, Muslims were assaulted in Murshidabad and 24 Parganas. On the 30th four Muslims were killed in Calcutta. In February riots spread to Maniktala and Beliaghata of Calcutta. The incident at Kalshira was taken up in a big way by the Indian media and political leaders in India after one month, which raised doubts about India's intention on the side of East Bengal.[52]

Nurul Amin, Chief Minister of East Bengal, made an inflammatory communal speech on February 9, and the riot occurred in Dhaka the next day. After that communal riots spread to other parts of East Bengal.[53]

In his Assembly speech of February 7, cited before, Abul Hashim called 'the spirit of relation' for the solution of minority problems in East and West Bengal.[54]

> Being myself a member of the minority community here I fully appreciate the sufferings and the difficulties that the refugees from East Bengal have to undergo. But what surprised me most is that instead of looking at the Muslims here as their fellow sufferers, they are developing antipathy for them and animus for them. In the like manner the Muslim refugees from here to East Pakistan are developing the same attitude. I would ask them in all seriousness to ponder if the spirit of relation would in any way help the minorities here or there. ... Therefore sir, there is hardly anything to rejoice in the inauguration of the so-called Sovereign Democratic Republic of India.

When Abul Hashim spoke on February 7, he did not imagine that a calamity would befall him soon. Actually Hashim who had been living at his aunt's house located at No. 2, Parkers Road, Burdwan, decided to build his own house at the end of 1947 and moved to his new residence on the outskirts of the city at the end of 1948. So far Burdwan city had been almost free from communal riots. The situation in West Bengal became serious since January 1950, and Shyama Prasad Mukherjee of the Hindu Mahasabha made a fervent speech in Burdwan. In February 1950 a few were killed, and many cases of arson occurred in Burdwan.[55]

On the day when Abul Hashim and family fled to Parkers Road for safety, his house was set fire by the *badmash* (rogue) after sprinkling oil, and a drawing room was burned down. Hashim was deeply shocked. Till then no one in his family, who were free from 'communal thinking', had anticipated that calamity would befall them. Most of Hashim's friends were Hindus, and he helped some of them politically. The second serious shock that Hashim experienced was that some of those friends showed heartless response, instead of giving him a helping hand with sympathy. First Hashim and his family retreated to his village Kashiara, and even there they were not free from insecurity. Hashim went to Delhi and met Jawaharlal Nehru and other leaders. However, Gandhi, with whom Hashim could talk freely was no more. What was most unfortunate was that Sarat Chandra Bose with whom Hashim struggled for a United Independent Bengal, died on February 20. Badruddin Umar recollects that, if Sarat Bose was alive, Hashim might have chosen to remain in India.[56] There was no one with whom he could consult frankly. Umar himself recollects that lack of safety and feeling of disgrace robbed Hashim of his normal thinking.[57]

Once Hashim decided the move of his family to Dhaka, his action followed quickly. He did not hesitate to sell most of his property for a small fraction of its value, and gave the rest free of charge. Some people took unfair advantage of his helpless situation. For his stay in Dhaka, Hashim trusted Abdul Jalil with the arrangement of a rented house. Jalil was once a personal secretary to Hashim when he lived in Calcutta.[58] Badruddin Umar reached Dhaka on April 12, 1950, and Hashim and other family members arrived on April 22. When Abul Hashim reached Dhaka, he had no idea at all about the situation in the city and what he could do there. He had only vague expectations that the erstwhile colleagues of the Muslim League might help him, as Dhaka was the place where once he built the citadel of the League Left.

Not only the riot but the lack of the 'spirit of relations' among the people in 1950 which Hashim proposed only a few days before, forced Hashim and his family to leave India.

Communal riots continued in West Bengal till the end of March 1950, and also spread to Assam. In addition to the line of the armed struggle by the Communists since the second Congress of the Communist Party of India, the communal riots and the movement of a large number of refugees crossing border from both sides of Bengal seriously weakend the peasant and left movement in East Bengal.[59] Innumerable sympathizers and members of the Communist Party left East Pakistan.[60]

ENDNOTES

1. Umar, *Amar Jiban*, p. 174.
2. Harun-or-Rashid, *Foreshadowing*, p. 258.
3. Amalendu De, 2003. *Swadhin Bangabhumi Gathaner Parikalpana-Prayas o Parinati*, 2nd edition, Agarthala: Parul Prakashani, pp. 39-43.
4. Ibid., pp. 6-7.
5. Hashim, *In Retrospection*, pp. 138-9.
6. Ibid., pp. 139-43.
7. Also see, Badruddin Umar, *Bangabhanga O Sampradaik Rajniti*, Dhaka: Shrabon, 2nd ed., pp. 48-53.
8. Harun-or-Rashid, *Foreshadowing*, p. 278.
9. Hashim, *In Retrospection*, pp. 147-9.
10. Amalendu De, *Swadhin Bangabhumi*, p. 81. This part is reproduced from *Star of India*, May 5, 1947.
11. Harun-or-Rashid, *Foreshadowing*, p. 285.
12. Amalendu De, *Swadhin Bangabhumi*, pp. 98-9. For the full text see, *Millat*, May 23, 1947, p. 5. Also see, Umar, *Bangabhanga*, pp. 67-71.
13. Harun-or-Rashid, *Foreshadowing*, p. 294.
14. Ibid., pp. 294-5. Also see, Hashim, *In Retrospection*, pp. 153-4.
15. Amalendu De, *Swadhin Bangabhumi*, pp. 45-55.
16. Hashim, *In Retrospection*, p. 158.
17. Harun-or-Rashid, *Foreshadowing*, p. 277 and p. 313.
18. Ibid., p. 316.
19. Hashim, *In Retrospection*, p. 159.
20. Ibid., p. 160.
21. Ibid. As for other parts of his statement, see "British-Parikalpana keno grihit hoilo", *Millat*, June 13, 1947.
22. *Dawn*, June 14, 1947.
23. Harun-or-Rashid, *Foreshadowing*, p. 316.
24. Ibid., p. 320.
25. *Millat*, May 16, 23 and 30, 1947. For instance, see "Chatra-Samajer Davi-Swadhin Sarvobhaum Bangla", May 23, 1947.
26. Umar, *Bangabhanga*, pp. 78-9.
27. Umar, *"Amar Pita"*, p. 273.
28. Leonard A. Gordon, 1990. *Brothers Against the Raj: A Biography of Sarat and Subhas Chandra Bose*, New Delhi: Viking, pp. 569-73.
29. Umar, "Amar Pita", p. 273.
30. "Sampadakiya-British Prastao", *Millat*, June 13, 1947.
31. Hashim, *In Retrospection*, pp. 162-3. The Central Committee of the CPI thought that, after the Mountbatten Award and its acceptance

by the Congress and the League, 'fight for unity is no longer a fight against the possibility of partition but a fight for reunification of partitioned Bengal in partitioned India'. Therefore, by voting for partition, 'each part of Bengal joins that Constituent Assembly which is the choice, in the present circumstances, of the majority of the people living in that part and thus carry forward the fight for re-unification', defeating 'the reactionaries within.' (*People's Age,* June 22, 1947).

32. Umar, "Amar Pita", p. 274.
33. Hashim, *In Retrospection,* p. 163.
34. Ibid.
35. Ashok Mitra, "Tanr samay aar elo na", Syed Mansur Ahmed, op. cit., pp. 166.
36. Hashim, *In Retrospection,* pp. 163-4.
36. Syed Mansur Ahmed, op. cit., pp. 462-4.
37. *Millat,* June 13, 1947.
38. Umar, "Amar Pita", p. 275.
39. 'On Governor's Speech', February 7, 1950. Syed Mansur Ahmed, op. cit., p. 460-1.
40. 'General Discussion of the Budget', February 23, 1948, Ibid., p. 443.
41. Umar, *Amar Jiban 1,* p. 193.
42. Ibid., pp. 193-5.
43. Ibid., pp. 193-4. Shamsul Huq is known in the history of East Bengal as an independent candidate who fought the by-election for the Tangail constituency against Khurram Khan Panni, the candidate nominated by the Muslim League in March 1949, and won it by a large majority. After the defeat the Muslim League not only tried to prevent his seat in the East Bengal Assembly by all means, but also did not hold any by-election till the general election of 1954 (Badruddin Umar. 2004. *The Emmergence of Bangladesh: Class Struggles in East Pakistan (1947-1958),* Karachi: Oxford University Press, pp. 93-8).
44. 'On Governor's Speech', February 7, 1950. Syed Mansur Ahmed, op. cit., p. 458.
45. Sabhapati, Bihar Prantiya Samyukta Kisan Sabha, 1949, *Bharatiya Samyukta Samajvadi Sabha-Lakshya tatha Karyakram,* Patna: Orient Press, p. 2 and p. 4.
46. Umar, *The Emergence of Bangladesh (1947-1958),* p. 145. Also see Musa Ansari, "Left Politics" in Sirajul Islam, op. cit., p. 509 and Moni Sinha, op. cit., pp. 157-8. Ansars originally mean those who attended Prophet Mohammad when he was forced to leave Mecca. Here Ansars are the paramilitary force in East Pakistan, which

absorbed many members of the Muslim National Guards formed by the Muslim League.

47. As for the process of the spread of communal riots on both sides of Bengal, see Hiroshi Sato, "Communal Riots and Refugee Displacement in South Asia: 1950 Bengal Riot and Nehru-Liyaqat Pact"(in Japanese), *Azia Keizai,* July 2005.
48. G.P. Singh (ed.), 1949, *Sardar Patel: The Working of his Mind,* Delhi, Rajhans Publications, p. 82.
49. Sardar Patel. 1967. *For a United India: Speeches of Sardar Patel 1947-1950,* revised and enlarged edition, Delhi: Publications Division, pp. 156-7.
50. Ibid., p. 158.
51. Ibid., p. 157.
    Bayley writes, "The Preventive Detention Act was first passed on February 25, 1950, thirty days after the commencement of the new Constitution. The bill was introduced, debated, passed, and signed into law all in a precedent-shattering one day. Even more unusual, February 25, 1950 was a Sunday. The bill was piloted through Parliament by the steady and respected Sardar Vallabhbhai Patel, Minister of Home Affairs". (David H. Bayley. 1962. *Preventive Detention in India: A Case Study in Democratic Social Control,* Kolkata: Firma K.L. Mukhopadhyay, p. 11)
52. Sato, "Communal Riots...".
53. Umar, *Amar Jiban 1,* pp. 212-3.
54. Syed Mansur Ahmed, op. cit., p. 459.
55. Umar, *Amar Jiban 1,* pp. 212-3.
56. Ibid., pp. 213-9 and Umar, "Amar Pita", pp. 278-9.
57. Umar, *Amar Jiban 1,* p. 218.
58. Ibid., pp. 219-20.
59. Umar, *The Emergence of Bangladesh (1947-1958),* pp. 148-9.
60. Musa, op. cit., p. 509.

8

From Philosophy of Rabbaniyat to Khilafat-e-Rabbani Party

The Creed of Islam

Azad Subhani published a small booklet on the philosophy of Rabbaniyat, *The Teaching of Islam in Light of the Philosophy of Rabbaniyat* in New York in 1947. According to the introduction written by Abdullah Uthman Al-Sindi, then a Ph.D. student of Columbia University, Subhani arrived in America by the end of October 1946. Subbani never studied English in any school before. He says that it is only in America that he learnt to write and speak English. This leaflet of 33 pages was made within two months after his arrival in America. Subbani is introduced as a thinker who recently retired from politics to his original purpose.[1] Though this introduction says that "his philosophy of Rabbaniyat or Preservation is not merely an abstract or theoretical philosophy, but it is the most constructive and practical philosophy of life", his writing is not so easy for 'beginners' to read through.

By the way, in the midst of the Calcutta Killing Abul Hashim was informed by a friend that he saw Azad Subhani along Bowbaazar Street. Hashim immediately sent volunteers with armed police to Bowbazaar. Fortunately they found Subhani in Bowbaazar Street, and brought him to Hashim's place.[2] At this critical moment how Hashim could get the help of the armed police is a matter to be noted. Besides, how Subhani, who supported the Pakistan movement and was in Calcutta during the Direct Action days, could reach America after only two months 'to collect further data for the development of his Philosophy of Rabbaniyat' is worth considering.

When Abul Hashim first published his book, *The Creed of Islam or The Revolutionary Character of Kalima* in 1950, his idea had departed from his earlier thought which attracted young educated Muslims in 1943-46. In this book Hashim declared: "Time has now come for the re-appearance of the spirit of religion in the full-flood of its pristine glory."[3] While recognizing that organized Nihilism or Marxism played its historic role in liberating the people from the rule of the priests, pundits and mullahs, Hashim observed that Nihilism ignored 'man's potentiality to rise above the influence of his immediate material environments'.[4] The Rabbaniyat is submitted as the philosophy of sublating both capitalism and nihilistic materialism which was the results of capitalist development. Then, what is meant by the Rabbaniyat? It is defined as the 'divinely ordained natural philosophy of creation, sustenance and evolution of the Universe', but if we use Hashim's own words, it is 'a human approach to Islam', and tries to restore the human aspect of Islam which had been deliberately ignored and ultimately forgotten.[5] Hashim explains, "the pragmatic and the operative aspect of the Holy Quran is divided into two parts—duty to God and duty to man. Duty to God is private and personal and duty to man is the public and social part of the teachings of the Holy Quran. The novelty of the Holy Quran is that it makes the performance of duty to God void and invalid when the duty to man is ignored or is not duly performed."[6]

In this book there still remains the thought which encouraged young educated Bengali Muslims in the middle of the 1940s. Besides the human approach to Islam, it is his view of Islam as science and, despite that, flexibility in his idea. Hashim says: "Islam is not a religion as religion is understood today, a mere theology or a set of dogmas and rituals, but is the science which governs man in his individual as well as his collective existence,"[7] but in another place he clarified, saying that, "Islam is the science of Islam in his (man's) being and becoming. In order that Islam may re-assume its grandeur and its progressive role, human contents and values of Islam must be rediscovered and set in a modern setting by the talents of the world—philosophers, scientists, sociologists and historians."[8] Hashim's thought is reflected in his following explanation on the 'stage of development of man'. He writes: "...the contents of the Holy Quran may be likewise classified into two categories namely, the necessary minimum or the immediate and the ideal or the ultimate. At the stage of man's development when the Holy Quran was revealed, the necessary minimum or the immediate was made mandatory for all while the ideal was mandatory for the Holy Prophet. The Muslim social law must now be interpreted in the light of the ideal since humanity has now attained that stage of evolution when some of these ideals can be made mandatory for all. It is, therefore, a gross misrepresentation of facts, wilful or otherwise, to say that Islam is not flexible and dynamic but is rigid and static. The gap between the immediate and the ultimate programme of Islam is so wide and so vast that it can accommodate the ever-expanding progress of man till eternity, that is, till the cycle of creation and evolution of man is complete. To put it in one word the human aspect of Islam is monotheistic materialism and not theology, dogmas, customs and rituals".[9] His basic stance expressed in his following call has not changed in his life: "Let the talents of the world liberate Islam and religion from mullahs, priests and pundits whose only stock-in-trade is ignorance and habitual irrational thinking. Let the talents of the world co-ordinate intellect with intuition, reason with wisdom and faith with action and once again make religion a blessing to humanity."[10] But, he was not an unconditional admirer of modern science. He warned against the anti-humanitarian use of science.[11]

> That religion has been utilized as a means of exploitation is true but that is no reason why it should be put out of court and negated, for there is no invention of science which has not been used as a means of exploitation; the destructive use of atomic energy is the latest example of the anti-humanitarian use of science.

However, in his theory of the nation a delicate change came to be observed. As cited before, in February 1948, Hashim thought India was a home of many nations. Both Hindus and Muslims composed integral parts of the Bangla nation. Hashim was against the Two Nation Theory. In this book Hashim developed the idea of the nation in his own way. At the dawn of civilized existence each family was a nation and a state. In the course of years and centuries the family expanded into tribes, and a tribe became a nation and a state. Then, from common blood, common language and common habits, race consciousness grew. The race was then the nation and their homeland (was) their territory and thus racial and territorial nationality and nationalism developed. Hashim writes that, "mankind must have a common ideology before it can think of establishing the kingdom of God on earth. The Holy Quran gives man that common ideology. So in a secondary sense the Holy Quran defines nationality as a brotherhood based on common ideology when it says, 'The believers are but a single brotherhood'. It is in this specific sense that the Muslims all over the world constitute one nationality but Muslims are never one nation in the racial or ethnological sense of the term".[12] Here a clear distinction is made between brotherhood based on common ideology and nation in the racial or ethnological sense of the term, but as we shall see later, at the end of the 1960s, Hashim removed this distinction, and defined them as two types of 'nation'. Though Hashim refers to Vivekananda in this work, Bengal culture in the late 19th century and early 20th century, which contributed to the formation of his idea of 'nation', is not discussed. His political experience in Bengal of 1946-50 promoted a delicate departure from his earlier idea.

Hashim's idea of democracy also underwent a change. Hashim explains: "A Muslim state is called a Caliphate and the Head of the state is called a Caliph. Caliphate means vicegerency or vicegerency of God on earth and Caliph means vicegerent or vicegerent of God on earth."[13] He mentions the Will of God made manifest in His creation, the Holy Quran, the Holy Prophet, and life and work of the four Caliphs of Islam and life and work of the faithful companions of the Holy Prophet as four sources of Islam. In his analysis of the procedure of the selections of Caliphs, Hashim, who once fought for 'the democratization of the Muslim League', showed his critical view of 'Western

Parliamentary Democracy'.[14]

> Democracy of Islam is the just and equitable distribution of rights and privileges of the state but not equal participation of all in the affairs of the state; it gives absolute freedom of discussion but demands obedience to the decision of the good and the efficient so far as it is consistent with the Will of God or the completely unified knowledge of creation, sustenance and evolution of man.
>
> Here, as also in other matters, the admirers of Western Parliamentary Democracy try to adjust Islam with the wisdom of the West and lay great emphasis on the decision of the majority and advocate the omnipotence and omniscience of the judgment and the will of such a majority. According to this conception of democracy a state is a machinery through which the will of the majority is expressed. A glance at the procedure of the selection of the Caliphs will clarify this issue....
>
> In all these diverse methods and procedures of selection of a leader there is noticed a uniformity of purposes, namely, to select the best man.... Nomination, resignation and subsequent election of Umar (RT.) II clearly show that Islam cares more for the motive than for the procedure of selection of leaders. Whatever procedure may be suitable to the selection of the best man as leaders is valid in Islam. The motives for the selection of the best man must be uniformly present in every case but the method and procedure of selection may vary according to varying circumstances.

In 1947-50 Hashim deepened his understanding of the philosophy of Rabbaniyat, but, as the long introduction of 44 pages showed, he could also discuss the thought of many Western thinkers and others such as Rousseau, Newton, Shakespeare, Darwin, Marx, Spencer, Bacon, Voltaire, Plato, Hume, Nietzsche, etc. He also mentioned the Indian thinkers and a poet like Shankar, Ramanuja and Kalidasa. We can confirm how wide his concern was with the world history of thought even when he was inclined to the philosophy of Rabbaniyat. This is a remarkable characteristic of Hashim's thought compared with that of Subhani expressed in his small leaflet, though we must be cautious enough to make a comparison of two works and come to a hasty conclusion.

Simultaneously it must be admitted that in the first book written by Hashim there was a lack of his analysis of what was proceeding in Bengal in 1943-7 when he worked actively as the Secretary of the Bengal Provincial Muslim League, and how the political situation in Bengal had an impact on his thought. Auschwitz in Europe and the Bengal Famine of 1943 should be considered within the same framework as the problem of war and peace in the contemporary age. But, while discussing war and peace, Hashim interpreted war in Germany and famine in Bengal from his simplistic theory of space and population.[15]

> Nevertheless, at every point of time there is fixed space ratio for man's existence and survival. When the ratio between available space and its population falls below this fixed space ratio of existence, the soil throws off its surplus population. If the surplus population thus thrown off finds space elsewhere, it survives but on the contrary if the thrown off surplus is thrown back into the land of its origin then comes war in case of free and powerful nations, and disease, pestilence and starvation in case of backward peoples to destroy the unbearable surplus. War in Germany and famine in Bengal are recent illustrations of this law of space and population. Therefore, it is clear that all talks of world peace must end in a fiasco, and war, disease and pestilence will not cease until the world's available space be made open for the use of all the needy peoples of the world.

After June 1947 Hashim's thought on Islam went alone on his own axis without making constant contact with the reality of Bengal to which he had been so attached till then, though even in 1947-50 he was not cut completely from it. However, his view of Muslim political leaders, activists and people in general underwent a change.

Abul Mansur Ahmad records in his autobiography an interesting discussion with Abul Hashim. When this talk took place is not clear, but this communication tells something of the direction of the thought of Abul Hashim who did not place a high value on the thought and action of the League leaders and workers.[16] Mansur Ahmad 'provoked' Hashim in their discussion by saying, "You like Islam. I like Muslims." After a few days, Hashim answered, "I not only don't like Muslims, but hate Muslims." Ahmad said, "That means you like medicines, and hate patients." Hashim, a man of wit, answered, "Why don't you hate patients who spoil efficacious medicines?"

Maulana Azad Subhani wrote in the Foreword of *The Creed of Islam:* "The philosophy of 'Rabbaniyat' runs throughout the book from cover to cover although there is a direct mention of it only in one place, viz. the article on the conception of religion".[17] He also added that philosophy of Rabbaniyat was a revolutionary philosophy, but the task of showing, in concrete terms, how to mould the minute details of the everyday business of life of modern civilized society in the light of Rabbaniyat was not the job of ordinary mortals.[18] Even as *The Creed of Islam* was a book of 'revolutionary philosophy', here was no place for the activities of young educated Muslim leaders who once earnestly supported Hashim's idea and movement, and the 'ordinary mortals' of Bengal as the nucleus that carries out 'revolution'.

Despite his tilt to the philosophy of Rabbaniyat, in this book there was something relevant for the contemporary age, which contributed to the formation of the idea of the later generation.[19] That is Hashim's thought on nature and environment. Hashim writes: "Nature is knowable but is not conquerable. Man does not control nature but nature controls man and 'Qudrat' controls nature. An infinite cham (chain?) of cause and effect leads earnest seekers after truth to 'Qudrat', the Cause of all causes.[20] He suggests: "His (Man's) salvation lies ... in seeking a synthesis of two extremes—the state of nature and the state of mechanized life. The end of all religion and philosophy is to make the best out of a bad job, namely, to give man true knowledge of his self and to teach him how to adjust it with what he has made of him without detriment to and risk of his march towards his assigned goal. This balanced existence can be achieved not by establishing sovereignty of the artificially created immediate material environment but by man's knowledge and correct interpretation of his self and its careful and cautious adjustment with the environment."[21]

Language Movement of 1952

When Abul Hashim and his family reached Dhaka, Abdul Jalil helped to find a rented house, but after some time he lost contact with the family. While in Burdwan, Hashim handed him ten thousand Taka for his brickfield, and Jalil responded that, when his work had become profitable, he would return a part of his profit to Hashim.

Among those political leaders and activists who visited Hashim's house occasionally soon after he moved to Dhaka, were Shamsul Huq, Kamruddin Ahmad (then President, East Pakistan Federation of Labour, and Convener, Central Democratic Federation Council), Oli Ahad (General Secretary, East Pakistan Youth League), Tajuddin Ahmed, Ataul Rahman Khan (later Chief Minister of East Pakistan) and Kafiluddin Chowdhuri.[22] Kamruddin Ahmad recollects that, when Hashim moved to East Pakistan after his house was set on fire, he no longer placed his trust in progressive Hindus and socialists.[23] Here it must be added that Hashim had not responded to his adversity in a 'communal' way like instigating one community against the other.[24] But it was also true that Hashim himself lost his earlier passion for political movement. Suhrawardy was cautious so that his political power might not be affected by the appearance of Abul Hashim in East Pakistan. The situation in Dhaka was far from enthusiastically welcoming Hashim who once established a strong League organization there. The 'old and experienced workers' in the Muslim League had all been practically driven out by Akram Khan and other leaders on the pretext that they belonged to the Hashim-Suhrawardy group of the Bengal Provincial Muslim League.[25] The Awami Muslim League, which was formed in June 1949 under the leadership of the President Maulana Bhashani, still remained a very small party without active organizational activities.[26] The East Pakistan Youth League, which started in March 1951, was the only organization which developed meaningful activities of the anti-government forces in East Pakistan before 1952.[27]

Under the circumstances it was quite natural that Abul Hashim joined the Tamaddun Majlis (Cultural Organization) by way of the introduction of Kamruddin Ahmad and, as he was an earnest member, he became one of the leaders of the language movement in 1952.[28] The Tamaddun Majlis was started by some young intellectuals and students of the Dhaka University on September 2, 1947, and it campaigned for making

Bangla the medium of education and legal proceedings during the first phase of the language movement.[29] However, Gafur writes in another essay that it is a mistake to understand that the Majlis was founded for the purpose of the language movement, though it first appeared before the public in this movement. He says that the Majlis was basically the cultural organization, which believed in the Islamic brotherhood. All kinds of activists, both right and left, and particularly the activists of the Hashim-Suhrawardy group joined the Majlis. Kamruddin Ahmad was familiar with the organization and its weekly organ *Sainik.*

Except for Professor Abul Kasem, all were young university or college students. Among the activists who were connected with the activities of the Majlis for a longer period were Shahed Ali and Mohammad Abdul Gafur.[30]

In 1948, when the first session of the Pakistan Constituent Assembly was opened, a Congress member from East Bengal, Dhirendranath Datta tabled a resolution to make Bangla a language of the Assembly along with Urdu and English. Khwaja Nazimuddin, Chief Minister of East Bengal, said: "Most of the inhabitants of East Bengal think that Urdu should be accepted as the only state language".[31] Against this pronouncement of Nazimuddin and the language policy of the central government, the State Language Committee of Action was formed, and the Tamaddun Majlis sent its two members to the Committee along with other organizations. When Mohammad Ali Jinnah, Governor General of Pakistan, visited East Pakistan in March 1948, he warned in his speech in Dhaka against the activities of the subversive elements and conspirators who were out to destroy Pakistan, and kept the same view on the language policy despite his meeting with the leaders of the Committee of Action.[32]

As in 1948, the language movement in 1952 was touched off by the speech of Nazimuddin, then Prime Minister of Pakistan. He said in Dhaka on January 27 that the demand of Bangla as one of the state languages of Pakistan was the expression of 'provincialism', and cited Jinnah's declaration of Urdu as the only state language of Pakistan.[33] On January 31, the All Party State Language Committee of Action was formed.[34] At this founding meeting Abdul Gafur of the Tamaddun Majlis spoke along with other representatives. Abul Hashim who attended the meeting said that, as before partition the Indian National Congress characterized every demand of the Muslim League as communal, now Nazimuddin characterized every progressive movement in Pakistan as the conspiracy by the divisive elements.[35] On February 4, the Dhaka University students resolved to observe a general strike throughout East Bengal on February 21, and the same evening the All Party Committee of Action endorsed the call for a general strike. Abul Hashim and Maulana Bhashani were present at this meeting of the Committee of Action.[36]

On February 20, Abul Hashim presided over the meeting of the All Party State Language Committee of Action. At this meeting Shamsul Huq (Awami Muslim League), Mohammad Toaha (Youth League), Oli Ahad (Youth League), Abdul Matin (Convener, Dhaka University State Language Committee of Action), Abul Kasem (Tamaddun Majlis), Abdul Gafur (editor, *Sainik,* Tamaddun Majlis), Kamruddin Ahmad (Civil Liberty League) and others attended. On this day the District Magistrate of Dhaka promulgated an order prohibiting all public meetings, processions and demonstrations without any permission according to 144 CrPC for 30 days from February 20 in the whole city area of Dhaka.[37]

The majority of the members were against the violation of Section 144. They argued that the language movement had reached a stage when it could not be limited only to the student community. It had become a concern for all sections of the people. They said that the government would try to use the situation to postpone the date of the general election announced for 1953. If that happened, the country's democratic movement would be greatly harmed.[38] It is interesting to note that Abul Hashim, who had earlier criticized Parliamentary Democracy, supported the struggle for democracy this time. The fear of government repression and the adventurism of the movement forced Hashim to return to the mainstream of the language movement and take up the posture as a defender of

Parliamentary Democracy for sometime. Among the supporters of the violation of Section 144, Oli Ahad noted that, if there was no resistance and Section 144 was not violated it would encourage the government to heap further repression and there would be no end to it. Abdul Matin added that the University State Language Committee was the 'parent' body, and since it had decided to violate, the All Party State Language Committee of Action had no authority to decide otherwise. Finally the resolution for not violating Section 144 and cancellation of the programme set for February 21 was put to vote, and was supported by 11 vs. 4. Oli Ahad said that, whatever the decision of the All Party Committee, Section 144 would be violated the next morning. Hashim reacted that in that case there would be no further need for an All Party Committee and the Committee would stand dissolved. Hashim's view was adopted as a resolution by the Committee.[39]

On February 21 students who assembled in the University areas held a meeting, and decided that they would violate Section 144. Clashes between students and the police started. The programme of the students was to surround the East Bengal Assembly which started the budget session on the 20th. Students threw brickbats at the police, who retaliated with tear gas shells as well as brickbats. Then the police suddenly opened fire on the students inside the hostel and on the crowd on the other side of the road. One student and a boy on the roadside were killed, and some were seriously injured. On that evening a meeting of the language movement workers who were available at that time was held, in which it was decided to form a new committee as both the All Party State Language Committee of Action and the Dhaka University State Language Committee of Action had become unworkable. A new student action committee was started, and decided to hold a *gayabi janaza* (funeral prayer without dead bodies). Fazlul Huq and Abul Hashim were present at the *janaza.* At the meeting after the *janaza,* Oli Ahad said they would give a fitting reply to the killings by the Nurul Amin government by the establishment of the full status of Bengali as a state language. But this new committee also could not control the situation, and Kazi Golam

Mehbub (East Pakistan Muslim Students League) and others decided to revive the All Party State Language Committee of Action, by which the message of the movement was delivered by the students to the other parts of East Bengal.[40] Abul Hashim, Kamruddin Ahmad and Mohammad Toaha were present at this critical meeting.

On February 23, 1952 Hashim issued a press statement, in which he criticized the government response. He said it was beyond his imagination how the government officers in a civilized country could open fire on the unarmed students and youth, and kill them inside the university and college campus despite the repeated refusal of the university authorities. Hashim concluded that we lost some of the most excellent students and youth, and the pious memory of their sacrifice would continue to encourage the people of East Bengal for long.[41] Though he was critical of the direction of the movement in violation of Section 144, nevertheless he continued to observe the movement closely on February 21 and 22 and tried to develop the movement as the movement of the people. Abul Hashim was arrested on February 25, and came out of jail on June 5, 1953.

On the basis of the observation of the process of the language movement against the background of the history of Bangladesh 1947-52, Badruddin Umar pointed out a clear difference between the movement in 1948 and the movement in 1952.[42]

> In 1948, when the first Language Movement took place, the working people, with the exception of some Dhaka-based railway workers, had nothing to do with it. It was almost entirely a movement of the middle class intelligentsia, particularly students, teachers and cultural workers. At that time the local people of Dhaka, who lived in the old parts of the town, were quite hostile towards the workers of the language movement, and did not hesitate to beat up the student activists who were engaged in propaganda work. Moreover, it was a completely urban movement.
>
> The situation was quite different (in 1952). This time it ran through the whole of East Bengal, in urban and rural areas, and the people of Dhaka united in support of the movement, in demanding Bengali as one of the state languages of Pakistan....

> The food crisis and the famine situation actually played the most important role in destroying the social basis of the Muslim League.... The famine and food crisis preceding the Language Movement transformed the attitude of the entire peasant population towards the Muslim League.
>
> The Muslim League government closed all doors for constitutional protests and blocked all means for expressing the grievances of the people...
>
> The Language Movement took place at a point when the people of East Bengal had already discarded the Muslim League as their representative organization and were poised for a countrywide revolt against the government. ...
>
> In 1952, it was different. The police firing on February 21 transformed, almost overnight, the Language Movement into a movement of the broad masses of the people for the overthrow of the existing government. The people realized much more clearly the regional character of the Pakistan Government and the need to struggle for establishing not only certain basic rights but for consolidating themselves as a linguistic nation. ...

In a sense, it can be said that, though Bengal was divided in 1947, the idea of the Bengal Nation which Hashim conceived in 1943-7 was in the process of making in the language movement in 1952. Hashim was in the midst of the movement.

Khilafat-e-Rabbani Party and the United Front

Abul Hashim was sent first to Sylhet, but at the end of June of 1952 returned to the Dhaka Central Jail. Hashim's jail life became 'bearable'. Family members visited the jail regularly, and could hand books over to him too. Khairat Hossain, who was in the same jail, read books for Hashim.[43] He was a Muslim League member of the Bengal Provincial Assembly, and left the League in the midst of the language movement.

In the meantime there was a move among the Tamaddun Majlis leaders to form a political party.

Though the Majlis was a cultural organization, they had an idea to form an all Bengal political party and realize the ideal of Islamic Brotherhood, and talked to Abul Hashim in this connection. The language movement of 1952 and police firing encouraged this move, and, while Hashim was in jail, the Khilafat-e-Rabbani Party (Divine Sovereign Party) Standing

Committee was formed with Solayman Khan, one of the Majlis leaders, as Convener.[44] Though this party was started on April 21, 1952, it was formally established in September 1953 with Hashim as its first President, and called for the formation of the anti-Muslim League United Front.[45] Kamruddin Ahmad, who was one of the leaders of the language movement recollects that the importance of the 1952 Movement was that "the younger generation became more secular minded".[46] Under the impact of the most broad based people's movement in 1952, and despite the fact that he was closely connected with the movement, Abul Hashim chose the narrowest path in his later political life.

It was in 1952 before his arrest that Hashim proposed a united front against the Muslim League in a meeting under the chairmanship of Maulana Bhashani. However, Hashim did not support a 'loose and amorphous united platform', but insisted: "They should evolve some principles which could be accepted by all as the basis for organizing a strong and homogeneous party". For preparing its manifesto and organization a committee composed of seven members including Hashim was formed. In a meeting held at the residence of Hamidul Huq Chowdhury (later Foreign Minister, Pakistan Government) it was decided that the future state and society of Pakistan should be secular in spirit and structure. Hashim objected to this principle and left the committee. Later he clarified his idea in his letter to Suhrawardy dated February 7, 1952: "As regards the name of the party, I am of the opinion that a colourless name like Awami League or Awami Jamaat will not inspire the people. The party must bear a name which may contain in it the spirit of Islam and at the same time may give an idea of the future we propose to build. I suggest the name, the Rabbani Party of Pakistan".[47] This is the origin of the Khilafat-e-Rabbani Party.

On the other side there was a strong move for the united front against the ruling party, the Muslim League among the left forces including the Youth League, Ganatantri Dal, and leftist students.[48] Fazlul Huq, who had been Advocate General of the East Pakistan High Court till September 1953, resigned his position and rejoined the Muslim League. After he lost the election for the president of the East Pakistan Muslim League, he started his party called the Krishak Sramik Party (Peasants and Workers Party) and began to draw large crowds to his meetings.[49] Huq's entry into politics was 'God-sent' to the left forces who knew that, as he had no organizing ability, he would have to depend on them 'as a counter-force against Suhrawardy' who, though he resided in Karachi, felt his need to have a solid base in East Bengal again through the Awami Muslim League.[50] On November 14, 1953 the Awami Muslim League decided to endorse the decision to form a United Front in the Council meeting.[51]

Finally the United Front was formed on December 4, 1953, with the Awami Mulsim League and the Krishak Sramik Party as main partners. The United Front was the expression of the strong will of the people in East Bengal against the Muslim League government which was far from responsive to their expectation for a happier life after the birth of Pakistan, but the Front was also not so united. Kamruddin Ahmad wrote:[52]

> The fear of the common enemy, the Muslim League, however kept them together. It was clear to any observer the 'Front' would fail to work together unitedly if the Muslim League collapsed completely. The Front would only remain united if the Muslim League could obtain at least forty-five per cent of the seats.

On the day of the birth of the United Front, Fazlul Huq announced that he had asked Maulana Atahar Ali to join the United Front. The Nizam-e-Islam, which Atahar Ali led, was the organization of the orthodox ulamas of East Pakistan formed in 1953.[53] The reaction was immediate. Atahar Ali made it clear that he would not have anything to do with either the Communist Party or its ally the Ganatantri Dal as a component of the United Front, and he would walk out of the Front if they were included.[54]

Abul Hashim was now critical of the Communist ideology, but Umar writes that personally Hashim was not opposed to the inclusion of the Communist Party. As he knew well the strategy of Fazlul Huq, Hashim advised a Communist leader, who expected his personal influence on Huq, to remain as an outside ally of the United Front. The Communist Party became very bitter against Hashim at one time, but finally accepted that position.[55] It was Suhrawardy who insisted on and succeeded in nominating young men belonging to the Ganatantri Dal and kept a few seats open where there were known Communist candidates.[56] This episode reflected the fragile relations between Fazlul Huq and H.S. Suhrawardy, two main leaders of the United Front. Hashim was on good terms with Fazlul Huq, and was also communicating with the Nizam-e-Islam as well as the Awami Muslim League.

Abdul Gafur describes one scene where Abul Hashim was surrounded by the Communist workers when he entered the residence of Fazlul Huq. They tried to force Hashim to change his idea and allow the Communists to be included in the United Front. Hashim did not flinch, and said: "I am a blind old man. If you like you can take my head off from my shoulders, but you can't take my consent by force."[57] Hashim thought that no group, which stood against the Islamic thought, should not be included in the United Front. As we noted before, he proposed the United Front against the Muslim League at the earliest stage. But, Mafidul Hoque writes that, while Hashim joined the talks on the United Front, he stuck to his anti-Communist stand.[58] It can't be denied that his Islamic political thought based on the philosophy of Rabbaniyat affected his judgment at this critical moment of history. There was no longer room for his dynamic approach to politics which he showed in 1943-45 and in the central and provincial elections in India of 1945-46. The United Front finally comprised the Awami Muslim League led by H.S. Suhrawardy, the Krishak Sramik Party led by Fazlul Huq, the Nizam-e-Islam led by Maulana Atahar Ali and the Ganatantri Dal led by Haji Mohammad Danesh.[59] But it must be noted that formally the Dal had nothing or very little to do with the decision-making process of the United Front, though it was given nominations in 13 constituencies and some other nominated candidates had strong links with the Dal.[60]

The Khilafat-e-Rabbani Party was given only one nomination by the United Front, though the party wanted 10 nominations. Abul Kasem, founder of the Tamaddun Majlis, could stand in Chittagong as a candidate of the United Front. Abul Hashim applied for the nomination by the Front in the

Dhaka East constituency. Fazlul Huq was prepared to provide it, but Suhrawardy was negative. Later Suhrawardy said in his letter to Hashim that they had to give the nomination to an important political worker, Golam Quader Chowdhury of Ganatantri Dal.[61] Earlier Hashim had also felt very sad to hear the blunt response which his family member received when he was sent to meet Suhrawardy to promote the talks on the United Front.[62] Hashim had no financial resources and no organization to carry his election campaign. He fought the election with hand-written posters and actually did not work for any meaningful campaign.

The preparation of the election manifesto of the United Front was left in the hands of Abul Mansur Ahmad, Awami Muslim League. After some adjustments the 21 Point Manifesto was adopted. The number 21 was selected to remember February 21, 1952.[63] In the Manifesto full autonomy to East Pakistan was demanded stating: "In accordance with the historic Lahore Resolution, to secure full autonomy and bring all subjects under the jurisdiction of Unit Governments leaving Defence, Foreign Affairs and Currency under the Central Government."[64]

The election was held on the basis of universal adult franchise, but under the separate electorate system on March 8, 1954. The total seats of the East Bengal Legislative Assembly were 309, and 228 seats of these were reserved for Muslims.[65]

The election results showed a sweeping victory for the United Front. The United Front won 223 seats, and out of these seats 130 belonged to the Awami League, but the ruling Muslim League captured only 9 seats. All five ministers including the Chief Minister Nurul Amin were defeated.[66] The Muslim League was completely routed in the political scene of East Pakistan.

The Communists, who were forced to take an ambivalent position in their relations with the United Front, set up 8 candidates on their own tickets, and won in 4 Hindu seats. Abdul Huq, who were in jail and one of 3 Muslim candidates, was defeated by a margin of a few hundred votes.[67]

The Khilafat-e-Rabbani Party won two seats. Prof. Abul Kasem won the election as a candidate of the United Front. Shahed Ali, who stood at Sunamganj in Sylhet district, won the seat against two candidates, one from the Muslim League and another from the United Front. Hashim widely covered Sunamganj area in the election campaign for Shahed Ali.[68] But, Abul Hashim himself only got 354 votes and lost even his security deposit. The only solace was that the Awami Muslim League and other parties did not feel happy and newspapers reported this miserable result in a small way. Badruddin Umar concluded that the United Front was exalted with its victory, but Hashim's movement was a comedy.[69] Abul Hashim, who stuck to the philosophy of Rabbaniyat, fell a victim to his own ideology and the election tactics of Suhrawardy who knew well the constitutional pathway to power with his cool headed analysis and correctly predicted that the Muslim League would not get even a dozen seats.[70]

After the Election

Abdul Gafur remembers that after the loss of the contest, Abul Hashim thought of making the Khilafat-e-Rabbani Party as the broad based mass organization. The Bengal Provincial Muslim League after 1943 was his model. But it was no longer possible. Soon the discord between Hashim and Prof. Abul Kasem, an undisputed leader of the Tamaddun Majlis for a long time, started. Both stood their own ground. The generation gap was also responsible for the increasing distance between Hashim and the Majlis workers. Young workers had no knowledge of Hashim's political approach in the past and his personal character. Majlis members called each other 'Bhai' (brother or friend). At their meetings even leaders and activists were openly criticized. There was no rule of loyalty to leaders. Gafur found this was unbearable to Hashim. Simultaneously the Majlis at this moment gives us an impression of a 'closed' society, though they were 'free' inside their society. It seems that Abul Hashim felt in fetters under this 'freedom'. He left the Khilafat-e-Rabbani Party in 1956. The philosophy of Rabbaniyat was central to the thought of Hashim, and therefore his secession from the party gave him no place to return. He was forced to live in 1954-58, completely aloof from the critical political situation both in Pakistan and East Bengal. Hashim writes in his autobiography that he joined the Muslim League in 1956, though, in fact, he was politically inactive.[71]

Dhaka was no longer the city of 1943-45 when Hashim organized a strong Muslim League branch. But, the way back to Burdwan was also closed by himself. He had already disposed his properties in Burdwan. Under this situation the only way left to Hashim was to immerse himself in making his own world of thought armed with the philosophy of Rabbaniyat.

Anwar Dil and Afia Dil write about Hashim's activities after his migration to Dhaka as follows:[72]

> Abul Hashim did not have deep ties in East Bengal and in the new political climate with his erstwhile political opponents all at the helm of affairs he found himself totally isolated. He was only approached when his name could add dignity to an undertaking, for example, to the cause of the Bengal Language Movement which was gaining momentum at the time.

However, his isolation from the mass and absorption in his Islamic studies had already started before the Partition. Despite his participation in the people's movement expressed in the Language Movement of 1952, this precious experience was not used for strengthening his political thought. This became fatal in the elections of 1954 in East Bengal and after, though Hashim's attachment to Bengal's language and culture was always there in his life.

As for the behaviour of Hashim in the mid 1950s, Badruddin Umar writes that Hashim said frankly what he thought without considering with whom he was talking. When the content of his talks reached the other side, made-up details were added to the original.[73] In this connection it also needs to examine how political opponents tried to understand the message of Abul Hashim behind his lost eyesight. It was during this period that Hashim finally gave up his plan to go overseas for the remedy of his eye disease as he found no chance of recovery.[74]

H.S. Suhrawardy was the Prime Minister of Pakistan from September 1956 to October 1957. During the Council meeting of the Awami League (since October 1955 the word 'Muslim' was dropped) at Kagmari in February 1957, Maulana Bhashani noted that the rights of East Pakistan were not recognized in the 1956 Constitution of Pakistan, while Suhrawardy claimed that 98 per cent autonomy had been provided for East Pakistan, and the Awami League was in power.[75] On his way back, Suhrawardy came to Dhaka and addressed the students of Dhaka University.[76]

Abul Hashim attended the meeting, and was surrounded by the students after the meeting. Hashim told them an allegory.[77] The gist of the story was like this; one delegation met Khwaja Nazimuddin, carrying their demands. He said: "As I am an old man, there is little that I can do". Then the delegation met Fazlul Huq, who said, "All right, I will do it all", but did not act. Finally they met Suhrawardy. He said, " What I can do is this. What I can't do is this". Despite his agonising days, Hashim was a cool observer of the political scene and political leaders with a sense of humour, but without any prejudice against Suhrawardy. This was the characteristic posture of Abul Hashim who liked to discuss issues with young people.

Kamruddin Ahmad writes that Suhrawardy was a lifelong liberal democrat, but also adds, "It is said that Suhrawardy was a great fighter for people's political rights but when in power he behaved as an autocrat."[78] That may be the reason one writer with a diplomatic career wrote: "Suhrawardy was essentially an autocrat in a democratic mould. He rode too high above the Awami League Party. Often on vital issues they clashed discordantly. In any matter never did Suhrawardy bow before the Awami League working committee. When they differed, he applied his persuasive logic and if it failed he used friendly coercion and threats. But finally he always had the approval of the party".[79] There must have been calculation behind his '98 per cent' speech as a shrewd political leader. But the downfall of his ministry and Ayub's military coup in 1958 was beyond his well-considered calculation.

It is also an irony of history that Ayub Khan's regime, which started 'the political dominance of the civil-military bureaucracies under the total West Pakistani control'[80] after the coup of 1958, tried to use Hashim's idea of Islam, on which people made their judgment in the election of 1954.

ENDNOTES

1. Subbani, op. cit., p. 2.
2. Hashim, *In Retrospection*, p. 118.
3. Abul Hashim. 1985.*The Creed of Islam or the Revolutionary Character of Kalima,* Dhaka: Islamic Foundation Bangladesh p. xiii. Here I am using the 1985 edition of the book.
4. Ibid., p. 10.
5. Ibid., p. 3.
6. Ibid., p. 34.
7. Ibid., p. 14.
8. Ibid., p. 23.
9. Ibid., p. 35.
10. Ibid., p. 16.
11. Ibid., p. 14.
12. Ibid., p. 93.
13. Ibid., pp. 102-3.
14. Ibid., pp. 99-101.
15. Ibid., pp. 122-3.
16. Abul Mansur Ahmad. 1978, *Atmakatha,* Dhaka: Mohiuddin Ahmad, pp. 222-3.
17. Hashim, *Creed of Islam,* p. vii.
18. Ibid., p. vii-viii.
19. Umar, *Amar Jiban 2,* p. 43.
20. Hashim, *Creed of Islam,* p. 21.
21. Ibid., pp. 52-3.
22. Umar, *Amar Jiban 2,* p. 13.
23. Kamruddin Ahmad, *Atmavikash 2,* p. 158.
24. Umar, "Amar Pita", p. 278.
25. Badruddin Umar, 2004. *The Emergence of Bangladesh: Class Struggles in East Pakistan (1947-1958),* Karachi: Oxford University Press, p. 99.
26. Ibid., pp. 187-8.
27. Ibid., pp. 181-3.
28. Hoque, op. cit., p. 92. Also see Mohammad Abdul Gafur, "Nishabde Atikrant hoe gal Darshanik-Rajnitivid Allama Abul Hashimer Janma Shatavarshiki", *Dainik Inkilab,* January 26, 2005.
29. Badruddin Umar, "Language Movement", in Sirajul Islam (ed.), op. cit., p. 424.
30. Mohammad Abdul Gafur, "Amar dekha Darshanik Rajnitivid Abul Hashim", Syed Mansur Ahmed, op. cit., p. 365.
31. Umar, *The Emergence of Bangladesh (1947-1958),* p. 32.

32. Ibid., p. 34.
33. Ibid., p. 190.
34. Ibid., pp. 192-3.
35. Badruddin Umar, 1985. *Purba Banglar Bhasha Andolan O Tatkalin Rajniti, Khand 3,* Chittagong: Bohi Ghar, pp. 222-3.
36. Umar, *The Emergence of Bangladesh (1947-1958),* p. 194.
37. Ibid., pp. 197-8.
38. Ibid., p. 199.
39. Ibid., pp. 199-201.
40. As for the situation in Dhaka on February 21-22, 1952, see Ibid., pp. 202-13 and 215-6.
41. Umar, *Purba Banglar Bhasha Andolan 3,* pp. 361-2.
42. Umar, *The Emergence of Bangladesh (1947-1958),* pp. 222-3.
43. Badruddin Umar, 2008. *Amar Jiban 2 (1950-68),* Dhaka: Sahitya Prokash, p. 68.
44. Gafur, "Amar dekha ... ", p. 366.
45. M.B. Nair, 1999. *Politics in Bangladesh: A Study of Awami League 1949-58,* New Delhi: Northern Book Centre, and Hoque, op. cit., p. 94.
46. Kamruddin Ahmad, *A Socio-Political History,* p. 111.
47. Shahed Ali, "Allama Abul Hashim-Divya Drishthir Adhikari ek annya Manishi", Syed Mansur Ahmed, op. cit., pp. 152-3.
48. Ganatantri Dal (Democratic Party) was formed in January 1953, and its leaders were Haji Muhammad Danesh and Mahmud Ali (Umar, *The Emergence of Bangladesh (1947-1958),* p. 254) and four groups of people—Youth Leaguers who crossed 30 years, some leftist trade unionists, some Muslim Leaguers mainly from Sylhet and Barisal and some old Royists (followers of M.N. Roy) joined it. (Kamruddin Ahmad, *A Socio Political History,* p. 113, fn. 2).
49. Umar, *The Emergence of Bangladesh (1947-1958),* p. 252.
50. Kamruddin Ahmad, *A Socio-Political History,* p. 113.
51. Kamal Uddin Ahmed, "1954 Elections: Issues of Autonomy", Sirajul Islam, op. cit., p. 464.
52. Kamruddin Ahmad, *A Socio-Political History,* p. 114.
53. Y. V. Gankovsky and L. R. Gordon-Polonskaya. 1964. *A History of Pakistan,* Moscow: "Nauka" Publishing House, p. 198.
54. Umar, *The Emergence of Bangladesh (1947-1958),* pp. 257-8.
55. Ibid., p. 258 and Umar, *Amar Jiban 2,* p. 79.
56. Kamruddin Ahmad, *A Socio-Political History,* p. 113.
57. Mohammad Abdul Gafur, "Amar dekha ...", p. 368.
58. Hoque, op. cit., pp. 94-5.
59. Kamal Uddin Ahmed, op. cit., p. 464.

60. Umar, *The Emergence of Bangladesh (1947-1958)*, p. 264.
61. Ibid., pp. 264-5.
62. Umar, *Amar Jiban 2*, p. 78.
63. Abul Mansur Ahmad, *Amar dekha....*, pp. 322-7.
64. Kamal Uddin Ahmad, op. cit., p. 480.
65. Ibid., p. 471.
66. Ibid., p. 470 and p. 473.
67. Umar, *The Emergence of Bangladesh (1947-1958)*, p. 264.
68. Gafur, op. cit., p. 368.
69. Umar, *Amar Jiban 2*, pp. 80-1.
70. Kamruddin Ahmad, *A Socio-Political History*, p. 114.
71. Hopue, op. cit., p. 95.
72. Anwar Dil and Afia Dil, op. cit., p. 292.
73. Umar, *Amar Jiban 2*, p. 78.
74. Ibid., p. 86.
75. Umar, *The Emergence of Bangladesh (1947-1958)*, pp. 334-5.
76. Ibid., pp. 335-6.
77. This episode was provided by an old friend of mine who had attended the meeting as a student of Dhaka University. I am thankful to him.
78. Kamruddin Ahmad, *A Socio-Political History*, p. 105 and p. 132.
79. Kamal Kazi Ahmed. *Politicians and Inside Stories*, Dhaka: A.H. Development Publishing House, p. 83. First published in Dhaka, 1970.
80. Harun-or-Rashid, *Foreshadowing*, p. 339.

9

Under the Ayub Regime and After

Under the Ayub Regime

On April 17, 1959 the Pakistan Government under Ayub Khan took over the Progressive Limited which was publishing the *Pakistan Times* and *Imroze.*[1] Its owner was Mian Iftikhar-ud-din who had been critical of the political process in Pakistan after independence. He was also a leading figure of the 'Progressives' or the Left in the Punjab in the Pakistan movement. He died on June 6, 1962, but till his death he fought against the Martial Law regime.

On the next day after takeover, Mazhar Ali Khan, the Editor, left the *Pakistan Times.* For ten years his pen remained motionless, and he broke his silence on February 7, 1970 by contributing to the *Forum,* published from Dhaka. This article started from the following sentence:[2]

> When the people of our land attain full freedom and genuine democracy, and Pakistan's history is written by honest scholars searching for the truth, and not as a panegyric on, or apologia for, the Ruler of the Day, the Ayub regime will be found guilty of a long and varied list of heinous acts, of defying the most elementary principles of law and justice, of destroying institutions wedded to the public weal, and of victimizing individuals who could not easily be browbeaten or purchased.

On October 7, 1958, the President Iskandar Mirza declared Martial Law in Pakistan and appointed General Mohammad Ayub Khan as the Chief Martial Law Administrator and Supreme Commander of all the Armed Forces. On October 27, Ayub Khan became the President of Pakistan, and Mirza was forced to quit its office. Kamruddin Ahmad got the news as the Ambassador of Pakistan in Burma. In East Pakistan a number of leaders were arrested on charges of corruption. Abul Mansur Ahmad, Sheikh Mujibur Rahman, and Hamidul Huq Chowdhury were among them. Maulana Bhashani and Tajuddin Ahmed were also taken into custody.[3] However, Umar writes there was no discernible resistance to Martial Law in East Pakistan: "The political parties which unitedly destroyed the Muslim League through the 1954 general election had failed to put up any resistance against the dismissal of the United Front Government of the Krishak Sramik Party, the Awami League and others in 1958. ... Their vitality as political forces was sapped and their strength declined owing to internecine conflicts and open feuds."[4] It was in 1962 that the organized movement against the military rule appeared openly in East Pakistan.

After Ayub's coup Shahed Ali, who was one of the founders of the Tamaddun Majlis, had a long talk with Abul Hashim. Shahed Ali told Hashim: " We are not interested in power politics. What we want is the happiness of our people. When Ayub Khan is in office as a dictator, it is not advisable to remain inactive like a tortoise. What we should do is to meet Ayub, let him know our object and advise him. If you can lead him to our idea, you may win an ideal victory. Even as you have got no results, you will lose nothing. You can explain to Allah that you have fulfilled your duty".[5] In March 1959, Hashim met Ayub Khan in Karachi. Who and which side made the first approach is not so clear, but the length of the meeting originally expected showed that Hashim and some people around him were more positive. The meeting was set for only 15 minutes, but it was extended for more than three hours.[6]

Ayub was so attracted by the personality and the Islamic thought of Hashim, and did not take a seat till the latter requested him to sit. After the meeting, Ayub sent Hashim off to the waiting car. Hashim mentioned later that this was the first experience after he moved to Dhaka in 1950 that people of high rank and office paid respect to him.[7] Political leaders at the helm of power whom Hashim trained or with whom he worked before the Partition of 1947 ignored him. Ayub Khan was trained at Sandhurst in England, and had some cultural background. Badruddin Umar characterizes the role of Ayub in the history of Pakistan as follows:[8]

> Ayub Khan, in spite of being a military dictator, emerged as the first real representative of the West Pakistan rising bourgeoisie and it was he who tried for the first time to lay the foundation of a modern industrial state. But, for him, like his predecessors, this state essentially meant West Pakistan. Compared to earlier periods, larger industrial investments were made in East Pakistan during Ayub's government, but surpluses from the East continued to be transferred to the West as before, and on an even larger scale.

In this connection Ayub wanted to reconstruct the teachings of Islam 'in such a way as to bring out its dynamic character in the context of the intellectual and scientific progress in the modern world' while responding to the demands of the religious leaders who wanted to have a say in the political process.[9] It is true that Hashim, who then kept aloof from politics, went to meet Ayub not from his political consideration but from his intention to establish an institution of Islamic studies.[10] But, Hashim saw in the Ayub regime a peerless chance to realize the Islamic way of life in Pakistan which he had so far dreamed, while Ayub saw in Abul Hashim's thought a most effective ideological base to control the upsurge of Bangla nationalism under the name of Islam. From this meeting the most tragic drama was destined for the last years of Hashim's political life. In fact there was an ideological base which was ready to accept Ayub's dictatorship in his theory of the political leadership which appeared in his book, *The Creed of Islam.*[11]

We can notice the continuity of this theory in his book which was published in 1965 in the midst of Ayub's regime:[12]

> Social democracy in Islam means just and equitable distribution of rights and privileges of society and state. Any social superstructure in a given society suitable for implementing this democracy is Islamic. The spirit is eternal, but the form of social machinery necessary for implementing the spirit of democracy changes with varying material conditions of existence. To hold fast to the outer form in colossal ignorance of the spirit is un-

> Islamic. Fundamentals of Islamic social order were as perfectly implemented by the faithful Caliphs of Islam as they could be in the context of the then prevailing conditions of life.

In this book Abul Hashim clarified: "Pakistan is an ideological state and its ideology is Islam", and added that "At a time, when world opinion has firmly settled on the rock-bed of materialism, we have declared that Pakistan would be an Islamic state".[13] The concept of Pakistan as an ideological state seems to have appeared in his thought in the 1960s.

The relationship of mutual trust between Ayub Khan and Abul Hashim, established in their first meeting, was changeless till Ayub's regime was removed. Hashim says that he is not a scholar, but 'merely a humble thinker who tries to think in concrete terms'.[14] Because of this sincerity the scale of tragedy was immeasurable. The result of the meeting soon appeared in the limelight for the 'humble thinker' who felt isolated from the erstwhile opponents, comrades and sympathizers in his political struggle after his migration to Dhaka in 1950. Even in the language movement of 1952, he joined it as a private person.

In October 1960 the government reorganized the Darul Ulm in Dhaka as the Islamic Academy, and on November 8, Abul Hashim was appointed as its first Director, and remained in this post till the middle of 1970.[15] The translation of the Quran into Bangla was one of the main results in the Academy. Hashim was the Chairman of the Board of Translators.[16] In the symposiums, while severely criticizing the materialism in the West, Abul Hashim tried to keep his rational attitudes in his interpretation of Islam and rejected an emotional approach.[17]

However, the shadow of the Ayub regime on the political life of Abul Hashim was obvious.

In August 1962 Hashim was appointed a member of the Islamic Ideology Council of Pakistan. In his autobiography, while recollecting his Law College days in Calcutta, he mentioned one of his main results in the Ideology Council.[18]

> An Anglo-Indian gentleman, Mr. Chependal who was my father's class fellow in Presidency College, took our class on Mohammedan Law. One evening when he was lecturing on the law of inheritance, I remarked, "Sir, orphaned grand-children, in Mohammedan Law,

> are disinherited. This seems to me unjust". Mr. Chependal said, "My dear young man, this is the present law and my job is to teach you Law as it is. You may try to change the Law in future if you can." As Providence would have it I was appointed a member of the Advisory Council of Islamic Ideology in Pakistan in 1960(*sic*). When this Council discussed President Ayub Khan's Muslim Family Law Ordinance I submitted a proposal on the right of inheritance of orphaned grand-children. My proposal was eventually accepted. An Act was passed in 1969 giving the right of inheritance to orphaned grand-children. After passing my Final Law Examination I had to work as an apprentice attached to Mr. Golam Murtaza, an efficient lawyer of Burdwan. I was admitted to the District Bar of Burdwan.

This episode reflects the characteristic of the Islamic thought of Hashim who 'tries to think in concrete terms'. In September 1962 Hashim became the Chief Organizer, East Pakistan Muslim League, Ayub Khan's so-called Convention Muslim League. Though Hashim never wanted this post, and continued to be politically inactive, he could not decline Ayub's proposal. These were the legal and political machineries in accordance with the new Constitution promulgated on March 1, 1962. Under this system, Ayub Khan did not hesitate to meet Maulana Bhashani, a peasant leader and a leading figure of the National Awami Party in East Pakistan. The meeting was held in Rawalpindi on August 22, 1963 at the invitation of Ayub.[19] Soon a delegation under his leadership was sent to China. There was considerable conjecture as to the meaning of the meeting.

Earlier, Suhrawardy, who was arrested on January 30, 1962 and came out of jail on August 19, 1962, declared the formation of the National Democratic Front. The 'democratization of the Constitution' was its main slogan.[20] Bhashani, who became free on November 3, 1962, joined the Front. The election for the President of Pakistan was scheduled for January 2, 1965. But the election was to be held not on the basis of adult franchise, but indirectly by the Basic Democrats who had been elected on adult franchise. On July 21, 1964 the opposition political parties formed a united front called the Combined Opposition Parties and decided to have Fatima Jinnah, sisiter of Mohammad Ali Jinnah, as a candidate against Ayub Khan at the residence of

Khwaja Nazimuddin, who was a leader of the Pakistan Muslim League (Council).[21] In this connection, Badruddin Umar sarcastically expressed his observation that, in the years 1963-64 not only Shahid Suhrawardy but even Khwaja Nazimuddin had become leftists in the eyes of the common people.[22] 1964 was the year when the Ayub regime mounted a full scale attack on any anti-government press, publishers and publications.[23]

In the meantime, the top leaders who were the main actors in Bengal politics in the 1940s and 1950s died one after another.

Fazlul Huq, who led the United Front in 1954 but whose United Front ministry was dismissed in May 1954, died on April 27, 1962. The dismissal of Huq as the Governor of East Pakistan, his last administrative post, on March 31, 1958, had already terminated his long political career.[24] But, it is said that though he was very weak, he observed, "Oh God! I do not want to live in a country where I have no vote. Please take me away."[25] He was far from satisfied with Ayub's regime. Suhrawardy, initiator of the National Democratic Front, died alone in Beirut on December 5, 1963.[26] Though both men were not on good terms, nevertheless Huq and Suhrawardy lived in the age of parliamentary politics, and shared the experience as leading members of the United Front. The death of Suhrawardy provided Mujibur Rahman, who was close to him for long years, a free hand to revive the Awami League as the organization of Bangla nationalism instead of the broad based National Democratic Front. On October 23, 1964 Khwaja Nazimuddin died. Though in the past his pronouncements on the language policy in Pakistan aroused the people's anger, this time he was 'the most important leader of the opposition in East Pakistan'. One of the demands of the Combined Opposition Parties was the right of the people to vote and the introduction of a parliamentary system through direct election.[27]

What was proceeding in East Pakistan of 1963-64 did not cast its shadow on the thought of Abul Hashim who once criticized the Western parliamentary system in his *Creed of Islam*. After the Indo-Pakistan War of 1965, Abul Hashim met Ayub Khan when he came to Dhaka in February or March 1966.[28]

Kamruddin Ahmad writes about the role of Hashim and

Nazimuddin in the party politics under the Ayub regime as follows:[29]

> Ayub hated party politics but Chowdhury Khaliquzzaman of Karachi and Abul Hashim of East Bengal convinced him that politics, even under his own Constitution, could not be successfully implemented without the party system. As a result, ban on formation of party was withdrawn under certain conditions and he decided to revive the Muslim League of Quaid-e-Azam. A Convention was called in Karachi of the pliable Muslim Leaguers in September 1962 and the Muslim League was revived with Ayub Khan as the President. Many old Muslim Leaguers, however, refused to attend the Convention. On the other hand they called a meeting of those people of the Muslim Leaguers who were the members of the Muslim League Council before it was banned by the Martial Law Order. They held a meeting in Dhaka on October 28, 1962. This meeting was presided over by the Al Haj Khwaja Nazimuddin. The meeting also decided to revive the Muslim League, hence two Muslim Leagues came into existence commonly known as Convention Muslim League and Council Muslim League.

Whether Hashim's advice was real or not is not substantiated by other sources. If this really occurred, we can understand one of the main reasons why Hashim could not refuse the post of the Chief Organizer, East Pakistan Muslim League which Ayub proposed, though the former remained politically inactive. But, from this explanation, at least we may be able to understand the meaning of Umar's sarcastic comment.

However, at the end of the 1960s Abul Hashim became very sensitive to the government repression on the Bengal language and culture and freedom of expression. Ayub Khan appointed Abdul Monem Khan, a lawyer, as Governor of East Pakistan. He was also *ex-officio* Chancellor of the Dhaka University, and continued to keep this post till 1969. He was against any thing associated with the culture of the Bengalis and dubbed such practices as un-Islamic and anti-Pakistan.[30] He urged Khwaja Shahabuddin, the Central Minister of Information, to ban the songs of Rabindranath Tagore in the electronic media. The ban on Rabindra Sangeet created a strong protest in cultural circles of East Pakistan.[31] At the meeting in memory of Tagore on

Rabindra Day, July 5, 1968 Hashim said in his presidential address: "Those who prohibited Rabindra Sangeet were not only stupid but evil minded. They understand neither Rabindranath nor Islam."[32] When Abdul Monem Khan, with his violent view against the Rabindra Sangeet, uttered the word, 'Gonyargovind (Bhagwan (God)-like uneducated) man' in his presence, Abul Hashim immediately reminded him how in the non-communal courtyard of Bengal social life Hindu's Govind or Bhagwaṇ exists in the world of colloquial language used by Bengali Muslims.[33] Finally the government had to withdraw their original plan. In September 1968 Hashim was one of forty-two persons who signed the statements which protested against the recommendations of the language reform committee approved by the Dhaka University Academic Council.[34] Later, at the end of 1969, when the Pakistan Government prohibited the publication of Satyen Sen, *Al Beruni,* Kamruddin Ahmad's *The Social History of East Pakistan,* Badruddin Umar's *Sanskritir Sankat* (Cultural Crisis) and *Sanskritik Sampradayikta* (Cultural Communalism) and other books, Abul Hashim said in a meeting held in the compound of the Bangla Academy, "We are at the same time Bengali, Musalmans and Pakistani. Our spirit of Bengali is eternal and unchangeable. Only by encouraging free thought, integrity and brotherhood will be kept. If the writer's freedom of expression is encroached, it will be crushed to pieces."[35]

Syed Mansur Ahmed concludes that Hashim's limitation caused by the loss of eyesight, his work at a semi-government institution, his belief in the integrity of Pakistan and mutual trust between him and Ayub Khan could not silence him. Unlike in the later half of the 1950s, Hashim's work at the Islamic Academy made him much more confident in his attachment to Bengal culture.

Simultaneously, despite his devoted work in the Academy and attachment to Bengal culture, it is difficult to reject another conclusion expressed by Mafidul Hoque (translated by Kuwajima).[36]

> Side by side it must be admitted that, behind the foundation of the Islamic Academy the selfish intention of the ruling class in

> Pakistan was working, namely the utilization of Islam for the purpose of strengthening the system of their rule and exploitation. The Islamic Academy played this role too.
>
> And while he was engaged in the work of the Islamic Academy, his social isolation became deeper. When the political upheaval in the entire East Bengal gradually advanced towards its final stage, and the people were agitated by the development of the national consciousness, we cannot observe its reflection in Abul Hashim. When fissures appeared in the thought of the so-called integration of Pakistan, he published a booklet, *Integration of Pakistan*. Immediately after the people's revolt of 1969, its Bangla translation *Pakistaner Sanhoti* was published.

After his move to Dhaka in 1950, Hashim's idea of a non-communal Bengal and his thought of 'the integration of Pakistan' lived together, though sometimes in acrimonious mutual relations.[37] In the 1960s, Hashim was more well-informed about the situation in East Pakistan than in the 1950s when he had less first hand knowledge. The work in the Islamic Academy provided Hashim with an opportunity to meet people who were working in various fields of society. In spite of this, and partly because of his work at the Islamic Academy his conviction as a thinker of the philosophy of Rebbaniyat including its political theory came to be more equipped with his rigid 'ideological' concept. To that extent he could not trace the development of the critical political situation in East Pakistan correctly. Though Hashim sharply responded to the government attack on Bengal culture as a 'non-communal' thinker, his understanding of the Ayub regime was circumscribed by Hashim's own philosophy. *The Integration of Pakistan* was the product of this contradiction in Hashim's thought.

Two Books: *Integration of Pakistan* and *Arabic Made Easy*

The concept of an 'ideological state' appeared in his earlier work, but now Abul Hashim added the concept of 'ideological nation' in his work, *Integration of Pakistan*.[38] He says:

> Political thinkers define the term 'nation' in two ways. Biologically, a mass of people integrated on the basis of community of blood and language living in a particular geographical condition constitutes a nation. Geographical conditions, by and large, pattern

> conditions of living of man, his habits, customs, history and traditions. Ideologically, people having a common outlook on life and living constitute a nation transcending the bounds of blood, language and geography. Biologically the Germans, the French, the Iranians, the Marathas and the Punjabees are nations. Ideologically, the Muslims and the Communists are nations. An ideological nation is a brotherhood based on common ideology and the Quaranic term for the nationality is 'Millat'.

In his own words, Hashim digests his idea: "Biologically people of Pakistan are not one nation but ideologically they are one nation and Pakistan is an ideological State. Thus ideology of Pakistan is Islam and ideology of Islam is the only basis of the integration of Pakistan. The slightest deviation from this in thought and action would be fatal".[39] In this connection he stresses that "Any individual or party which negates the proposition of an Islamic state is an enemy of Pakistan however honest and sincere they may be in respect of their own ideology", though he adds that Islam does not permit use of force and violence in suppressing freedom of ideas and conscience.[40] Hashim criticized the attitudes of the 'secularists' who "lose no time in taking advantage of the general sense of frustration and make planned efforts to drive the frustrated intelligentsia into the fold of the secularists."[41]

From this standpoint, he traced the political history of East Pakistan succinctly.[42]

> As in the case of food, shelter, etc., they (leaders of the Pakistan Muslim League who were in power in 1947-54) were equally indifferent in respect of their promises for creating in Pakistan an Islamic society and state. Those who captured power after the fall of the Muslim League in 1954 had little or nothing to do with Islam. The Awami Muslim League when in power, dropped the term 'Muslim' for their party name and is now known as the Awami League.

Whether the All India Muslim League aimed at the establishment of an Islamic state or not may need clarification. But Hashim was also critical of the approach of the Awami League under the leadership of Sheikh Mujibur Rahman who was gathering popular support particularly after its Six Point programme of 1966 on the basis of the people's discontent in East Pakistan with regional inequality between two parts of Pakistan. However, as Hashim himself aptly indicated, the people's movement in the later half of the 1960s expressed their protest against the failure of the Ayub regime to come to grips with their problems of 'food, shelter, etc.', that is, daily life. Hashim's following comment was far distant from the reality that the people in East Pakistan was facing, but he also had to admit that those who shared the same idea with Hashim were not an organized unit. Therefore he had to fill it up with Ayub and his party.[43]

> How the principles of Islam can be actually implemented in the second half of the twentieth century, what form and appearance a modern Islamic society and state must have, how individual and collective behaviour of man can be moulded according to the teachings of Al-Quran and the precepts and examples of the holy prophet of Islam can solve the intricate problems of life of a muddled and confused world are the constant care and concern of the Rabbani Islamists. They have the potentiality of representing true Islam but they are stray individuals and not an organized unit. Their stray and individual thinking has not been knit into a composite whole.
>
> The task of the politically conscious people is to organize an honest and efficient party with a clear and well-defined plan and pattern for the future of Pakistan. The Muslim League (so-called Convention Muslim League) which is an All Pakistan political party has the potentiality to reconstruct itself as such.

After conceding that concrete measures must be adopted for implementation of Islamic values with courage and confidence both by the peoples and the government of the nation, Hashim stressed that Ayub Khan as the Head of the state initiated some instruments to this end. "He set up two statutory institutions, the Advisory Council of Islamic Ideology and the Central Institute of Islamic Research. He also set up the Islamic Academy of Dhaka and gave official recognition to two pre-existing institutions the Lahore Institute of Islamic Culture and the Iqbal Academy of Karachi."[44] As we already noted, the Advisory Council of Islamic Ideology and the Islamic Academy of Dhaka with both of which Hashim was connected, were two parts of the ideological mainstay of the Ayub regime.

Abul Hashim also admitted that Ayub Khan, the President of Pakistan, had officially recognized the grievances of East Pakistan in the 1962 Constitution and that recommendations were made for speedy removal of forces of disintegration like mutual suspicion and jealousy. Hashim eulogized that this was a great step towards national integration. To corroborate his view he cited the resolution adopted at the Workers' Conference of the East Pakistan Muslim League held in Dhaka on April 6-7, 1963.[45]

The Islamic Academy published a Bengali edition of *Integration of Pakistan* in 1970.

Already the student movement against the Ayub regime began in October 1968. The Eleven Point programme prepared by the students in Dhaka in January 1969 included the demands for direct election on the basis of adult franchise, full autonomy for East Pakistan, reduction of rents and taxes on peasants, guarantee of fair wages and bonus for workers, withdrawal of the Security Act, non-aligned and independent foreign policy besides their educational demands. This programme provided for a broad-based democratic mass movement by a political student alliance called the Student Action Committee, though the emergence of the question of regional autonomy as the most popular demand overshadowed all other demands.[46] Kamruddin Ahmad writes, "The middle class struggle for democratic rule under the bourgeois leadership was transformed into a revolutionary upsurge of the mass. The working population, the rickshaw pullers, motor drivers and all other sections of day labourers of the city joined hands with the students and defied the law enforcing authorities. The popular explosion shattered the façade of stability of the Regime and the administration collapsed. ... The movement which (was) initially started by the Maulana Bhashani group of NAP in the form of Gherao (act of besiegement) of corrupt officers and government agencies began to spread in the rural areas."[47] On March 25, 1969, Ayub Khan was forced to resign, and General Yahya Khan promulgated Martial Law in Pakistan.

As we already noted, there was a sign in his first book, *The Creed of Islam*, indicating that his Islamic thought was in making within his own isolated axis and without its examination in the context of the changing political situation around him. His meeting with Ayub Khan and his work in the Islamic Academy made him confident of his idea, though he remained as a 'humble thinker' without seeking any worldly spoils. He had a poor experience in his work in the Khilfat-e-Rabbani Party, but he could not abandon his idea of a political party of the true Rabbani Islamists, while he was critical of the Awami League and other 'secular' parties, which had broad support bases among the people in East Pakistan. In his book, *Integration of Pakistan*, the concept of an ideological nation, that is, Muslim nation, was given highest priority compared with a 'biological' nation. Abul Hashim's nation theory reached a point far distant from the stance he took on the occasion of the Delhi Convention of the League legislators in April 1946.

In the *Creed of Islam*, Abul Hashim stresses the role of 'intuition' which leads to seeking after the truth and belief in the unseen.[48] If we use his own logic, there was disunion between 'tuition' and 'intellect' in his thought. And, even his ideological framework expressed in his *Integration of Pakistan* could not control his 'intuition' though he was aloof from the people's movement against the Ayub regime in 1966-69. However, Abul Hashim attended the meeting of the United Committee of cultural workers, with Badruddin Umar as the Convener, on February 21, 1969. Hashim presided over the meeting at the Bangla Academy after the wreaths were placed in the morning at the graves of the language movement martyrs.[49]

Arabic Made Easy written by Abul Hashim was published in July 1969. The book is "Dedicated to Field Marshal Mohammad Ayub Khan".[50] Ayub already resigned as the President of Pakistan. Mentioning his name was of no benefit to Hashim, but he felt a keen sense of obligation to the courtesy extended by Ayub, irrespective of the fact whether he was in office or not. This was his usual attitude as a man of the organization. But, it is also true that it tragically symbolized his role as a man of the Ayub regime, though he was not politically active, and even protested against its repressive policy towards the Bengal culture.

The book itself did not intend to draw any political attention, but was a work composed of 59 lessons prepared in restrained style. In the Author's Preface, Abul Hashim wrote: "The book is intended to help learn the Arabic language within the shortest possible time without the least interference with normal life and work". Hashim learnt a little Arabic till his college days, but started learning it again after he was appointed as the Director of the Islamic Academy.[51] The person who helped his learning at the Academy was Mahmood Mustafa Shaban, Cultural Delegate of U.A.R. in Dhaka. The loss of his eyesight did not affect his strong will to learn.

When Badruddin Umar resigned from his teaching job at the Rajshahi University for political reasons in December 1968, Abul Hashim, his father, did not say anything. He just said, "I have no property, no saving, and no eyesight. I have been thinking of living with you in my last days. You closed this way of life".[52] In the 1960s he lived as a humble person in both public and private life. He himself determined his remuneration for work at the Academy as 1,000 Taka, which was lower than the salary of other office staff.[53]

On November 28, 1969, Yahya Khan, President and Chief Martial Law Administrator, announced the election to the National Assembly to be held on October 5, 1970. Most of the political parties expressed their will to fight the election. Already Maulana Bhashani spoke in his October 6, 1969 anniversary speech at the Islamic Academy that 'maximum' autonomy did not mean anything unless the precise contents of it were adequately spelled out.[54] Unlike other political leaders, Bhashani's immediate response to Yahya's proposal was 'We want rice before election' (*Bhoter aage Bhat chai*) and later, 'full regional autonomy before election'. His final decision to boycott the election was announced only on December 4, 1970. But, by that time his National Awami Party (NAP) had become organizationally very weak with the large scale desertion of the Communist members, though his personal appeal was still there.[55]

In 1970 Abul Hashim left the Islamic Academy. According to Hoque's view, Hashim had already become the person of displeasure in the eyes of the government. They were ready to appoint Ahmed Hossain as the next Director of the Academy while Hashim's tenure of office remained. He was hurt by this process, and left the job on his own. From the news in the journal of the Academy it is known that Ahmed Hossain, Director of the Islamic Academy, made a speech in the symposium held in Chittagong on May 29, 1970. There was no official announcement on the resignation of Abul Hashim.[56] As in the case of the resignation of Hashim as the Secretary of the Bengal Provincial Muslim League in February 1947, he did not stick to his position and chose to resign quietly.

The War of 1971 and After

The first General Election in Pakistan on December 7, 1970, the situation in East Pakistan in March 1971, and the army crackdown on March 25, 1971, which led to the war of independence for Bangladesh, need a separate analysis. Abul Hashim neither extended any support to the action of the Pakistan army despite the repeated request from its highest leaders in Dhaka, nor made any radio and TV talks on Islam as he did in earlier days.[57] Mafidul Hoque writes that Hashim did not participate in the Bangladeshi war for independence positively, but made no contact with the ruling class in Pakistan. He observed that under the circumstances no action indirectly had a positive meaning to a man of great personality like Hashim.[58]

In his last days Abul Hashim prepared his autobiography with the advice of Badruddin Umar. Hashim dictated his talk to Abdus Shaheed, an old Communist. He breathed his last on October 5, 1974 without seeing his book.[59] In his family Abul Hashim belonged to the first generation which learnt the Bengali language, and Bengal literature contributed a lot to his intellectual formation, though his interest was widely open to Indian and Western literature too.[60] In his last book his idea of the 'nation' returned to that of his earliest days. Broad based people's movement and the independence of Bangladesh had a strong impact on the process.

However, when Hashim died, nobody who so often visited his houses in Burdwan, Kashiara or Calcutta in the 1940s, and discussed with him what should be done, came to attend his *janaza* (funeral) and show their sympathy with his wife.[61] One of the few who visited was Kamruddin Ahmad, who was once an active worker of the Bengal Provincial Muslim League, but no longer any party member. He was in jail from August to December 1971, and lost his son, Azad in the war of 1971.[62]

ENDNOTES

1. Tariq Ali, 1970. *Pakistan-Military Rule or People's Power,* New York: William Morrow and Company, pp. 101-4.
2. Mazhar Ali Khan, 1996. *Pakistan; The First Twelve Years: The Pakistan Times Editorials of Mazhar Ali Khan,* Karachi: Oxford University Press, p. 740.
3. Kamruddin Ahmad, *A Socio-Political History,* pp. 146-9.
4. Badruddin Umar, 2006. *The Emergence of Bangladesh Vol. 2: Rise of Bengali Nationalism (1958-1971),* Karachi: Oxford University Press, p. 9.
5. Shahed Ali, op. cit., pp. 153-4.
6. Hoque, op. cit., p. 96.
7. Umar, *Amar Jiban 2,* p. 253.
8. Umar, *The Emergence of Bangladesh* (*1958-1971*), p. xi.
9. Kamruddin Ahmad, *A Socio-Political History,* p. 151.
10. Syed Mansur Ahmed, "Abul Hashim: Bangali O Musalman", Syed Mansur Ahmed, op. cit., p. 333.
11. Hoque, op. cit., p. 98.
12. Abul Hashim. 1980. *As I See It,* 2nd edition, Dhaka: Islamic Foundation Bangladesh, p. 22.
13. Abul Hashim, 1965. *As I See It,* Dhaka: Dhaka Islamic Academy, p. 77.
14. Ibid., Author's Preface.
15. Hoque, op. cit., p. 100 and p. 106.
16. Ibid., p. 104.
17. Ibid., pp. 101-4.
18. Hashim, *In Retrospection,* pp. 11-12.
19. Syed Abul Maksud. 1994. *Maulana Abdul Hamid Khan Bhashani,* Dhaka: Bangla Academy Dhaka, p. 244.
20. Ibid., p. 241.

21. Umar, *The Emergence of Bangladesh (1958-1971)*, p. 92.
22. Hoque, op. cit., p. 113.
23. Umar, *The Emergence of Bangladesh (1958-1971)*, p. 85.
24. Umar, *The Emergence of Bangladesh (1947-1958)*, p. 364.
25. Kamal Kazi Ahmed, op. cit., p. 39.
26. Umar, *The Emergence of Bangladesh (1958-1971)*, p. 90.
27. Ibid., p. 92 and p. 94.
28. Umar, *Amar Jiban 2*, p. 251.
29. Kamruddin Ahmad, *A Socio-Political Histroy*, p. 155.
30. Umar, *The Emergence of Bangladesh (1958-1971)*, p. 123.
31. Ibid.
32. Syed Mansur Ahmed, "Abul Hashim: Bangali O Musalman", p. 335.
33. Ibid.
34. Umar, *The Emergence of Bangladesh (1958-1971)*, p. 141.
35. Syed Mansur Ahmed, op. cit., p. 335.
36. Hoque, op. cit., p. 105.
37. Umar, "Amar Pita", p. 281.
38. Abul Hashim. 1967. *Integration of Pakistan*, Dhaka: Syed Mujbullah, p. 6.
39. Ibid., p. 33.
40. Ibid., pp. 35-6.
41. Ibid., p. 38.
42. Ibid., p. 35.
43. Ibid., pp. 40-41.
44. Ibid., p. 34.
45. Ibid., p. 46.
46. Umar, *The Emergence of Bangladesh (1958-1971)*, pp. 147-50.
47. Kamruddin Ahmad, *A Socio-Political History*, pp. 214-5.
48. Hashim, *The Creed of Islam*, pp. 5-7.
49. Umar, *The Emergence of Bangladesh (1958-1971)*, p. 170.
50. Abul Hashim, 1999. *Arabic Made Easy*, 2nd edition, Dhaka: Bangladesh Cooperative Book Society Ltd., p. v.
51. Umar, "Amar Pita", p. 262.
52. Umar, *The Emergence of Bangladesh (1958-1971)*, p. 170, and Umar, *Amar Jiban 2*, p. 285.
53. Hoque, op. cit., p. 110.
54. Umar, *The Emergence of Bangladesh (1958-1971)*, p. 219.
55. Maksud, op. cit., p. 334 and Umar, *The Emergence of Bangladesh (1958-1971)*, p. 233, pp. 245-6 and p. 269.
56. Hoque, op. cit., p. 106.
57. Umar, "Amar Pita", p. 281.

58. Hoque, op. cit., pp. 111.
59. Ibid., p. 112.
60. Umar, "Amar Pita", pp. 261-2.
61. Ibid., p. 282.
62. Kamruddin Ahmad, *A Socio-Political Histroy,* pp. 381-3, pp. 352-4 and p. 386.

Conclusion
Abul Hashim and His Thought

Mohammad Abdul Gafur, who worked with Hashim in East Pakistan of the 1950s, lamented that Abul Hashim's birth centenary (January 27, 2005) was passing off with no special respect paid to him, despite the fact that he laid the basis of Bangladesh in his idea expressed in his approach to the Lahore Resolution of 1940, and that his followers secured positions of power after her independence. Gafur emphasizes that, unlike other leaders in the Pakistan movement, Abul Hashim's view was not communal, but that Hashim thought that India consisted of not one nation or two nations, but multi-nations.[1]

Hasan Zaheer, who first served in East Pakistan till 1962, and finally as the deputy commissioner to Jessore before his return to West Pakistan, was later posted in Dhaka in May 1971, and found that he 'was not regarded as one of them, or for them'.[2] Though he did not mention the latest activities of Abul Hashim, he remarked that Hashim, in his earlier days, was 'a secular Bengali nationalist, who enjoyed the support of students and was greatly influenced by communist ideology and organizational techniques'.[3]

So far in the historical writings in English, the thought and activities of Abul Hashim were mainly discussed around his remarkable role as the Secretary of the Bengal Provincial Muslim League 1943-47. Wilfred Cantwell Smith, who took notice of the appearance of Abul Hashim and the Progressives in the Bengal Muslim League in the 1940s, later shifted his interest more to the 'crucial role played by ideological and moral factors' in history rather than 'sociological factors', and failed to follow Hashim's work as an Islamic thinker and political leader. G. Adhikari, a Communist who provided the theoretical basis for the CPI's support to the Pakistan movement during the Second World War, admitted in the 1960s that their support to the movement was wrong.

Gafur tried to examine the role of Hashim both as a thinker and a political leader within the same field of vision in his memoir written in Bangla.[4] He concluded that, except for his role in the Pakistan movement, his work as an ideologically based political leader was futile, but his success as a thinker was conspicuous. When Marxism was predominant as the progressive thought, Hashim carried the message of Islam aloft. There was no room for communalism in his idea, and he stressed the need of harmony of mankind with nature. Gafur thinks that, if Hashim was not involved with politics, his thought could have been well accepted.

What is to be examined is whether or not there was a bud in his dynamic thought and action in 1943-46 which led to his later tragic role in the 1960s. Inversely, it also needs to examine whether even in his tragic days there were positive aspects in his thought and action which could be traced to his earlier days.When Hashim was 'a secular Bengali nationalist', it was in the days when he was attracted to the idea of Rabbaniyat. His activities in the Tamaddun Majlis, an Islamic organization, led him to join the 'secular' language movement in 1952. And, when he shared Ayub's idea of 'Islamic' policy, he demonstrated his attachment to the language and culture of Bengal. His philosophy of Rabbaniyat and his theory of multi-nationalism and non-communalism may explain his political action in certain stages of his life. However, there was some ambiguity in his idea, which sometimes played a positive and at other times a negative role in the movement which he led.

Wilfred Cantwell Smith wrote that it was the following, more than the leadership, that emphasized the Islamic aspects of the Lahore Resolution.[5] But, Abul Hashim was a leader who grasped Islam as the system for social change. In spite of that, he did not support the Two Nation theory. There was no room in his idea for a 'Muslim nation', though he once came closer in the 1960s.

Again, Smith interpreted that, ideologically it was not a territorial or an economic or a linguistic or even, strictly, a national community that was seeking a state, but a religious community.[6] However, Umar finds that, though the Muslim League Left activists whom Hashim tried to train listened to his talk of Islam and communism, what encouraged them actually was his idea of the nationalism on the basis of language and his thought of economic emancipation of the people.[7]

It is generally admitted among those reviewers who appreciate Hashim's idea positively that he was a dynamic leader during the period 1943-46, and stimulated young educated Bengali Muslims who fought against the vested interests in the Bengal League represented by the Khwajas and Ispahanis. Hashim's thought and action contributed to the growth of the Bengal Muslim League as a mass organization, or correctly speaking, middle class based organization. Unlike Fazlul Huq, he was a man of the organization. While he was engaged in the election campaign for the League with Suhrawardy, Hashim had the ethos of his age which sharply appealed to the Bengali Muslim youth, though he was wanting in the calculated political technique of the latter as a shrewd organizational leader. The team work of Hashim and his Left followers succeeded in spreading the network of the League organizations in Bengal, and in East Bengal in particular.

As we noted earlier, Nikhil Chakravarty mentioned, as one of the reasons of the growth of the Bengal League, the terrible experience of the famine which, along with 'a timid role' of the League Ministry to tackle the problem, convinced the younger generation of Muslims that the only way to make the League strong was to go out among the people. However, there is a dearth of systematic sources to prove how young League workers had a critical view of the food policy of the League Ministry or went out 'among the people', and extended their relief activities. Asok Mitra's reference to the yeoman's service of the young Leaguers in Munshiganj is one of a few writings in this connection. As for the communist relief activities, we can find some important literature besides the Communist organ, *People's War*,[8] and a Communist, who is critical of the official policy of the Communist Party of India in 1942-47, appreciates the 'dedicated relief work for the victims of the famine in and after 1943' extended by the communists.[9] 'To render social service to all, irrespective of religious or political persuasion' was one of the principles Hashim advised the League workers to practice.

The central and provincial elections in 1945-46 provided the Bengal League the best chance to 'prove' that the League was the only organization which represented the Bengali Muslims. Suhrawardy and Hashim were the main architects of the election campaign, while its President Akram Khan could not come to the scene. Hashim, who declared war against the Khwajas, Ispahanis and Akram Khan immediately after he was elected as the Secretary of the Bengal League, now appealed to the Muslims to 'bundle up all their differences and to preserve them if necessary in cold storage during the pendency of our common struggle', and called landlords and peasants, and ulama and laymen to answer the clarion call of the Quaid-e-Azam. Therefore, Hashim did not mention the abolition of landlordism in his election statement, and the foundation conference of the All India Jamiat-e-Ulama-e-Islam was held in Calcutta in October 1945, in which Azad Subhani, who initiated Hashim to the philosophy of Rabbaniyat, said that the ulama of India had become the supporters of the Muslim League.

Alec Johnson, an Englishman who visited rural towns and villages during this period, observed; "How different in the villages is all this politics! There the elections seem unreal while the town is in a fever. The peasant feels his immediate oppressors to be the zamindar and the hoarder-Bengali oppressors. The town students feel that by the British quitting India or by achieving Pakistan all will be solved. How real is this difference between the town and the country?"[10] In the famine of 1943 the agricultural labourers were the biggest victims, and in the general elections only one fourth of the adult population could have voting rights under the condition restricted by property and education. How did the Indian political parties, the Muslim League, the Indian National Congress, the Communist Party and others, perceive the limitation of the electoral system under the colonial rule? It was in September 1946 that the Communist Party called the start of the Tebhaga struggle in rural Bengal.

In April 1946 Hashim faced the new reality of political situation in both the centre and Bengal.

One is the point of order he raised at the National Convention of the League legislators in Delhi. Though Jinnah admitted the correctness of Hashim's interpretation of the Lahore Resolution, he did not concede in his view of 'a sovereign independent state'. Hashim's demand for an Independent State of East Pakistan was a lonely voice. Since then his original idea was subdued, and was revived only in April 1947.

The Suhrawardy ministry was formed in April 1946. Since then cracks started between Suhrawardy who wanted a free hand, and Hashim who tried to make a guideline for the ministry from the side of the League organization. Many of the League Left leaders were now more interested in the ministerial posts and their spoils.

Failure of eyesight also made it difficult for Hashim to make an extensive tour and discuss with local activists constantly as in earlier days, though he maintained contact with the editorial staff of the *Millat*. His inclination to the philosophy of Rabbaniyat was also deepened. The Calcutta Killing in August 1946 and following communal riots forced Hashim and the League Left activists to face unmeasured challenge. The leave of Abul Hashim from the work of the Secretary of the Bengal Provincial Muslim League in February 1947 was not only the result of his 'wrong decision', but was also the result of the failure of the League Left which could not maintain its strength under adverse circumstances. Hashim's last efforts for 'a United Bengal' were done without the massive support from the League Left and its followers.

Abul Hashim was an independent thinker, and simultaneously a man of discipline in the League organization. The latter part of his work so often made his original idea less discernible in the eyes of the people, though he may have talked freely in informal discussion. In the Manifesto of the Bengal Provincial Muslim League, Hashim reiterated 'the declared and unequivocal goal of the All India Muslim League as set forth in the Lahore Resolution, while using the words of a 'free state of Eastern Pakistan'. On the occasion of the National Convention of the League Legislators in April 1946, in the open session after the discussion with Jinnah, he said that the Bengali Muslims were ready to follow the instruction from the Quaid-e-Azam, though he did not fail to mention himself as a 'servant and soldier of East Pakistan'. As for the call for 'Direction Action Day' under the name of the 'Muslim Nation', Hashim agreed to the call on the condition that their action was against the British imperialism only, and not against any party. Most critical moment as an independent thinker and a man of the organization was after the Calcutta Killing and following communal riots when his multi-nation theory was going to be washed away by the Two Nation theory. On this occasion Hashim appealed under the name of the people of Bengal, and in the tone of his statement there was something different even from the official view of the editorial staff of the *Millat.* It was not accidental that he could participate so readily in the move for 'an Independent United Bengal' from April to June 1947. Though he was 'on leave' from the work of the Secretary of the Bengal League, and partly because he was 'free', Hashim could express his view without any restriction.

Then, what was the substance of the thought that urged Hashim to intensive activities among the Bengali Muslims? Hashim's criticism of the British imperialism was closely connected with his view that the struggle for Pakistan was not against any party or any community. His inclination towards the philosophy of Rabbaniyat was developed within this sphere. The thought of the people's sovereignty clearly expressed in the Manifesto of the Bengal League assumed that the people of Bengal should and could explore their future on their own. It was his consistent view that communal riots would only benefit the British imperialism. He did not show any trust in the British political and administrative leaders including Sir Stafford Cripps and Lord Mountbatten. On the other hand, unlike other

League leaders Hashim appreciated the role of the freedom struggle under the leadership of the Congress or the revolutionary movement in India. How to make his interpretation of the Lahore Resolution of the All India Muslim League understood among others including the Indian National Congress, was one of the most difficult tasks that he faced. The situation did not proceed in the direction as Hashim expected after the general election in 1945-46.

However, because of this basic stance, Abul Hashim never showed a 'communal' response to the critical situation. For instance, even after the Calcutta Killing he was so unruffled in his office, and it irritated an energetic young leader like Sheikh Mujibur Rahman.[11] Hashim's last efforts for 'a United Bengal' was made under the name of the people of Bengal though he was 'on leave' from the secretarial work of the Bengal League, and his co-worker, Sarat Chandra Bose was on the periphery of the Indian National Congress. Bengal was partitioned. His ideal and disappointment is expressed clearly in his words with grief; "If Hindus of West Bengal move to Pakistan, or Muslims of East Bengal wish to stay in India, the ideal of a United Bengal may be successful. But there is no probability of both". Hashim remained in India, but his unexpected and painful experience in February 1950 when his residence at Burdwan was set on fire by rioters forced him to move to East Pakistan. Kamruddin Ahmad, who met Hashim soon, found that he lost trust in progressive Hindus and socialists. However, Hashim never instigated Muslims to fight against Hindus. He continued to be 'non-communal' despite his bitter experience.

What was the image of Bengal which Hashim tried to make? Of course there was his strong attachment to an ancestral land, Burdwan and his village Kashiara. Most central to his idea was Bengal which contributed to his intellectual formation, and for which his father Abul Kasem fought against partition. In this respect Hashim was different from Fazlul Huq who was against the annulment of the partition, but also loved Bengal.

Sumit Sarkar, who wrote about the Swadeshi movement in Bengal 1903-08, analysed the stream of the thought of the Bengal political leaders from the late 19th century to the beginning of the 20th century, and said, "The political leadership of the '70s and '80s had achieved a kind of vision of a united India, secular and modernist in content. But the unity had been fragile and superficial, confined as it was to an Anglicized upper-class elite", while "many in the swadeshi age thought for a time that a basis for a more purely indigenous and popular nationalism could be found in Hinduism-and so we had the curious but by no means unique phenomenon of intellectuals utterly westernized in outlook and way of life striving by a tour de force to turn overnight into orthodox Hindus, imparting to age-old rituals and symbols a political content which was in fact quite untraditional". He added; "By 1908 there were some signs of a return to modernistic ideals, but on a higher plane which recognized more fully than ever before the true complexity of India's problems, the paramount need for overcoming the alienation of the intellectual elite and bringing about genuine and stable Hindu-Muslim fraternity". He found this trend in the works of Rabindranath Tagore.[12]However, while admitting that the nationalist imagination at the time of the Swadeshi movement actually 'naturalized a conception of the nation in history that was quite distinctly Hindu', Partha Chatterjee clarified that "it would be wrong to suppose that this Hindu-centred view of the nation was targeted against Muslims or that it even sought to exclude them from the ambit of the nation. It is noteworthy that even though there was little political campaigning in favor of partition, the Swadeshi movement nevertheless produced an explicit rhetoric of 'Hindu-Muslim unity' as a part of its evocation of nationhood".[13]

While sufficiently conscious of the historical limitation of the Swadeshi movement, Abul Hashim tried to inherit the intellectual tradition of Bengal in the late 19th century and the beginning of the 20th century whose political and literary leaders broadened their eyesight to the world and simultaneously polished the language and culture of Bengal. Later, the rural basis of the 'Bengal nation' was strengthened by absorbing the Krishak Praja movement into the Muslim League organization, and the experience of the provincial government under the Muslim Chief Ministers since Fazlul Huq assumed office in 1937 also made it easier to develop Hashim's idea of the 'Bengal nation' without any restraint. Despite that, the impact of the modern history of Bengal till the beginning of the 20th century in forming intellectual life of Hashim was not ruled out. Though his critical view of the British imperialism lacked detailed analysis, his view that the struggle for Pakistan was not against the Hindus was firmly based on his intellectual formation.

There is no doubt that Abul Hashim thought that India consisted of not one or two nations, but many nations like Europe. The basis of his judgment is language. His view encouraged many young Muslim League workers in Bengal who were critical of the Two Nation theory. But this aspect of his thought was not adequately developed by Hashim and his colleagues. How 'the realization of complete independence for the whole of India' and 'the achievement of Pakistan for the Muslims in the country' mentioned in the Manifesto of the Bengal Provincial Muslim League, should be connected had not become the agenda to be drawn up. The negotiation of the Congress and the League leaders with the British rulers, and communal riots dragged the provincial leaders into endless controversy. The 'unequivocal' trust in the Lahore Resolution was there, but at critical moments Abul Hashim was forced to say that, as for all-India issues he would do what the Quaid-e-Azam told him to do. Even in the case of 'a United Bengal' issue, when Hashim was 'on leave' the Working Committee of the Bengal Provincial Muslim League adopted a resolution that Jinnah 'alone had the authority to negotiate and settle the future constitution on behalf of the Muslims of India as a whole and the Muslims of Bengal shall stand by his decision'.

Hashim writes in his autobiography, "The Muslim League and the Congress accepted the Cabinet Mission Plan. If the Cabinet Mission Plan could be implemented the partition of the Sub-Continent could have been avoided without much prejudice to the ideological contents of the Lahore Resolution".[14] This is his comment in 1974, but it may give a hint to understand what Hashim thought in May 1946. What Abul Hashim really wanted was that the Pakistan issue should have been solved by the anti-imperialist forces in India without any intervention of the British rulers.

As he already noted, in his first book, *The Creed of Islam,* Hashim writes that Muslims all over the world constitute one nationality, but Muslims are never one nation in the racial or ethnological sense of the term. Here Hashim made clear distinction between the brotherhood based on common ideology and nation in the racial or ethnological sense. But, in the book, *Integration of Pakistan* published in 1967, Hashim wrote, "Biologically people of Pakistan are not one nation but ideologically they are one nation and Pakistan is an ideological State". The impact of the fact that Hashim's work had become a part of the Ayub regime can be noticed here. The 'nation' is rather rigidly understood here according to the logic of politics or the fixed idea of ethnology, and is not grasped as the concept to be formed in the movement against the ruling system in history. However, from the end of the 1960s the people's movement in East Pakistan forced the concept of 'ideological nation' to yield to his original idea of the 'Bengal Nation'. Hashim led the struggle for the defence of Rabindra Sangeet as it was crucial to his idea.

The spread of a communal riot to his residence in February 1950 was unexpected and traumatic.[15]Only a few days before Hashim preached in the Bengal assembly the 'spirit of relation' by which the minorities on both sides of the border between two Bengals should sympathize with the minorities on the other sides irrespective of their communities. To Hashim who remained in an ancestral land in India there was no one who extended help readily, and he also lost his usual cool judgment. *The Creed of Islam* published in Dhaka in the same year, but prepared mainly in Burdwan before his move, was the result of his work in the transitional period of his thought. While he appealed to his readers to learn from the talents of the world, his view of political and economic revolution depended on his idea of Islamic political and economic theory without his co-relative analysis of the political and economic situation which he faced in Bengal as the Secretary of the Bengal Provincial Muslim League.

After his move to Dhaka, and after the interlude when he participated in the language movement of 1952, his experiment of the Khilafat-e-Rabbani Party in the middle of the 1950s was a failure without any strong support from those who wanted 'political revolution'. He spent most agonizing days after his miserable results in the 1954 election. After the military coup in 1958 Ayub Khan tried to use the thought of Hashim for the purpose of curving Bengali nationalism under the name of Islam. Ayub was the first person who respected Hashim's profound knowledge of Islam after his move to Dhaka. Though Hashim had to play the tragic role as a part of the Ayub regime, the work of Hashim as an Islamic thinker needs a separate analysis.

His radio talks and public speeches during this period are collected in his book, *As I See It* first published in 1965. In one of his essays, "Philosophy of Islam", he wrote; "Pakistan appeared in the realm of reality as a conditional gift of Allah charged with the responsibility of presenting to the muddled world of today a vigorously living type of Islamic humanity in the second half of the 20th century by moulding the behavior of its individuals, its society and its state according to the ideals of the philosophy of Islam".[16]He had departed from his idea of Pakistan in 1943-46, though the starting point of his thought had not changed, saying that, "In ultimate analysis every system of philosophy is an attitude of the mind towards life and living in the context of the cosmic universe. This attitude of the mind is called *Iman* or faith in the terminology of religion. This 'iman' or the attitude of the mind in the secret chamber of the human mind determines the individual and collective behavior of man and eventually creates history. This is the pragmatic value of philosophy".[17] His basic stance is aptly expressed in the Author's Preface;

> This author does not claim to be a scholar. He is a humble thinker who tries to think in concrete terms. He knows a few words and tries to make proper use of them. The contents of the book are product of his free enquiry, guided more by his intuition than by his intellect.

Even under the military regime, and despite the mutual respect between Ayub and him, Hashim wanted 'free enquiry' in his mind. In his later book, *Integration of Pakistan,* his thought of 'an Islamic state' became stricter; "Any individual or party which negates the proposition of an Islamic state is an enemy of Pakistan however honest and sincere they may be in respect of their own ideology". But, he added; "Islam does not, however, permit use of force and violence in suppressing freedom of ideas and conscience. Force and violence succeed only in sending sedition underground. Parties, having no faith in Islam or inimical to Islam must be liquidated not by force and violence but by pressure of public opinion created by those who believe in Islam".[18] As Hoque remarked, this book was published when 'the integration of Pakistan' was at its critical stage. Hashim also had to struggle for the freedom of expression.

It is difficult to say whether the loss of his eyesight affected Hashim's otherwise cool judgment from 1950 onwards. When people talked to Hashim, they so often did not notice that they were talking to the person who lost his eyesight. It is a suggestive interpretation that Syed Mansur Ahmed, an editor of a collection of essays on Hashim, divided the life of Hashim into five parts, two parts before his loss of eyesight, and three parts after that. The editor explained that in the third stage of life, Hashim got out of his spiritual anguish, and mustered his courage to throw the light of ideal on himself and people around him. In the fourth stage Hashim kept peace in mind and developed his Islamic thought including the completion of the Bangla edition of the Quran. His last stage was four years after 1971.[19]

Abul Hashim wrote in his preface to *As I See It;* "Behavior of man, in everyday business of life, is in conflict with his nature and this conflict perverts his feeling, thinking and action. In order to establish peace and harmony between man's nature and his behavior it is necessary to discover fundamentals of human nature and to evolve an order of human experience based on these fundamentals. This alone can guarantees peace, prosperity and happiness". He also confirmed there; "Islam is the science of man in his being and becoming". This comment is the conclusion learnt from his life's journey in the 1940s and 1950s.

It was unfortunate that Hashim reached mind of peace under the Ayub regime. This was tragic particularly because he, who passed through physical and circumstantial adversity, tried to fulfill his mission sincerely as 'a humble thinker'. However, this mind of peace did not last long. From the latest days of the Ayub regime, Hashim had to protest against the repressive policy of the Pakistan Government, and after the war of 1971 he even refused to talk on Islam on radio or TV. If we use his own words, his 'intuition' was now well corroborated by his 'intellect' under the impact of the growing people's movement.

In 1943-46 Abul Hashim faced the situation in Bengal with his broad outlook which expanded his horizon and learnt from the talents of the world, and expected that the realization of Pakistan might be possible on the basis of the mass based organization, the Muslim League, which he built, and in cooperation with the anti-imperialist political forces, though he was inspired by the philosophy of Rabbaniyat. His rational view, liberated from the traditional interpretation of religion, succeeded in training many young cadres of League workers. This was the most active period of his political life.

In 1947-50, after the partition of Bengal in particular, he was more inclined towards the philosophy of Rabbaniyat, and kept his distance from the real situation, though he sometimes spoke in the West Bengal assembly. The loss of his eyesight may have strengthened this trend. After the partition of Bengal he thought of the 'spirit of relation', mutual sympathy among the minorities of both sides of Bengal with the minorities on the other side.

Unlike Hashim, Umar does not find any difference between the partition of India and that of Bengal and the Punjab.[20]

> The partition of India, Bengal and the Punjab in 1947 instead of solving the religious minority problem, which was the ostensible objective, in fact consolidated much more firmly the rule of religious majorities in what previously constituted British India.
>
> There was nothing surprising in this, because the 1940 Lahore Resolution of the Muslim League proposed to create separate states in the Muslim majority areas of east and west India. Thus, in real terms, there was no question of solving the religious

> minority problems in India either for the Muslims or for the Hindus and other peoples in the declared objectives of either the Congress or the Muslim League.

In 1950, Hashim was forced to realize the fact that his view of minorities did not work at this critical moment.This showed the seriousness of his shock. It took many years for Hashim to free himself from this bondage. In the meantime his action was so often circumscribed by his own 'intuition' and his conviction of political theory based on the philosophy of Rabbaniyat.

But, the young man, who was catholic in his tastes, later in his political life had no interest in ministerial posts, and could accept his modest life after his move to Dhaka. He did not claim to be a scholar of Islam, but tried to be a 'humble thinker' interested in its 'pragmatic value'.

His life was full of conflicts between his 'human approach' and his rigid theory. Hashim's struggle in defence of Rabindra Sangeet expressed not only his firm attachment to the Bengal culture, but also his sympathy with the idea of Rabindranath who worked for the overall development of human faculties, while enough conscious of their limitation under the law of nature.

Abul Hashim will be remembered as a thinker and political leader who embodied in his life the ideal and despair of human activities including politics, and finally in his last few years realized his 'mind of peace' under the impact of the people's movement after so many vicissitudes. He could recollect his political life up to 1947 with his cool observation. The result was his last book, *In Retrospection,* which he could not see in his lifetime.

ENDNOTES

1. Abdul Gafur, "Nishabde Atikrant hoe gel Darshanik-Rajnitivid Allama Abul Hashimer Janma Shatabarshiki", *Dainik Inkilab*, 26 January 2005.
2. Hasan Zaheer, 1994. *The Separation of East Pakistan –The Rise and Realization of Bengali Muslim Nationalism*, Dhaka: The University Press, p. xv.

3. Ibid., p. 8.
4. Abdul Gafur, "Amar dekha—", Syed Mansur Ahmed, op. cit., p. 371.
5. Smith, *Islam in Modern History*, p. 212, fn. 4.
6. Ibid., p. 216.
7. Umar, "Amar Pita", Syed Mansur Ahmed, op. cit., p. 268.
8. Saroj Mukhopadhyay. 1986. *Bharater Communist Party O Amara*, Kolkata: National Book Agency.
9. Arindam Sen, "Indian Communists in Freedom Movement: Yesterday and Today", *Liberation-Central Organ of CPI(ML)*, October 2005.
10. Alec Johnson. 1947. *Another's Harvest*, Kolkata: The Bookman, p. 109.
11. Umar, *Amar Jiban 1*, p. 159.
12. Sumit Sarkar. 1973. *The Swadeshi Movement in Bengal 1903-1908*, New Delhi: People's Publishing House, pp. 494-5.
13. Partha Chatterjee, "The Second Partition of Bengal ", Ranabir Samaddar (ed.). 1997. *Reflection on Partition in the East*, New Delhi: Vikas Publishing House, pp. 37-8.
14. Hashim, *In Retrospection*, p. 121.
15. Umar, "Amar Pita", Syed Mansur Ahmed, op. cit., p. 278.
16. Hashim, *As I See It*, 2nd edition, p. 33.
17. Ibid., p. 11.
18. Hashim, *Integration of Pakistan*, pp. 35-6.
19. Syed Mansur Ahmed, "Pratham Prakashner Bhumika" in Syed Mansur Ahmed, op. cit.
20. Badruddin Umar, "Class Struggles in East Pakistan and the emergence of Bangladesh-Pakistan and the minority question", *Holiday*, 14 August 1998.

Appendix 1

The Districts where the members of the Bengal Provincial Muslim League crossed over 10,000 in 1944

Note: Compiled from Abul Hashim, *In Retrospection*, p. 72

Appendix 2

The Subdivisions Hatched According to Degree of Incidence of Famine Conditions in Bengal of 1943

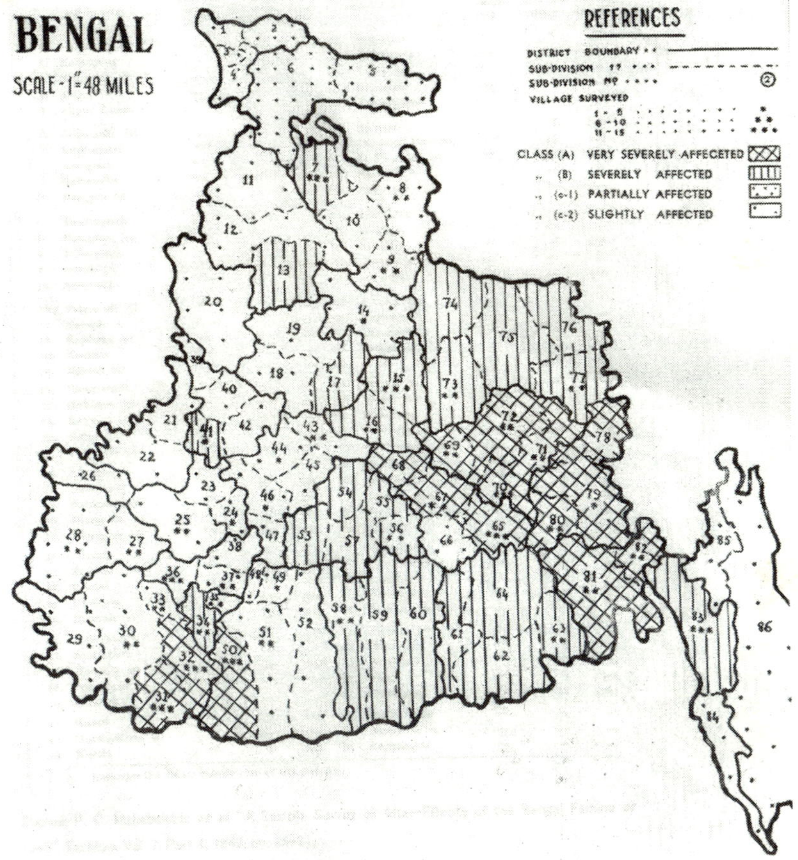

Sketch map of Bengal showing subdivisions hatched according to degree of incidence of famine conditions (Industries Department classification) with intensity of sampling in subdivisions shown by stars.

List of Subdivisions According to Srial Number on the Map with Intensity of Sampling and Number of Villages and Families Included

Subdivision	Intensity of Sampling	Number Surveyed Village	Family
1. Darjeeling (s)	–	–	–
2. Kalimpong	–	–	–
3. Kurseong	–	–	–
4. Siliguri	–	–	–
5. Alipur Duars	–	–	–
6. Jalpaiguri (s)			
7. Nilphamari	***	14	980
8. Kurigram	**	8	281
9. Gaibandha	**	10	450
10. Rangpur (s)	–	–	–
11. Thakurgaon	–	–	–
12. Dinapur (s)	–	–	–
13. Balurghat	–	–	–
14. Bogra (s)	*	4	121
15. Sirajganj	***	12	290
16. Pabna (s)	**	9	238
17. Natore	–	–	–
18. Rajshahi (s)	–	–	–
19. Naogaon	–	–	–
20. Maldah (s)	–	–	–
21. Rampurhat	–	–	–
22 Birbhum (s)	–	–	–
23. Katwa	–	–	–
24. Kalna	*	5	120
25. Burdwan (s)	**	10	350
26. Asansol	–	–	–
27. Bishnupur	**	10	320
28. Bankura (s)	**	10	264
29. Jhargram	–	–	–
30. Midnapur (s)	**	10	254
31. Contaj	***	15	521
32. Tamluk	***	15	599
33. Ghatal	**	10	353
34. Ulubaria	**	10	384
35. Howrah (s)	**	10	405
36. Arambagh	***	15	435
37. Serampore	–	–	–

38. Hoogly (s)	**	10	242
39. Jhangipur	–	–	–
40. Lalbagh	–	–	–
41. Kandi	*	3	149
42. Murshidabad (s)	–	–	–
43. Kustia	**	8	284
44. Meherpur	*	5	165
45. Chuadanga	–	–	–
46. Nadia (s)	*	5	154
47. Ranaghat	–	–	–
48. Barrackpore	–	–	–
49. Barasat	*	5	146
50. Diamond-Harbour	***	15	543
51. 24-Parganas (s)	**	9	322
52. Basirhat	–	–	–
53. Bangram	–	–	–
54. Jhinaidah	–	–	–
55. Magura	–	–	–
56. Narail	**	8	229
57. Jessore (s)	–	–	–
58. Satkhira	**	10	416
59. Khulna (s)	–	–	–
60. Bagherhat	–	–	–
61. Perojpur	–	–	–
62. Patuakhali	–	–	–
63. Bhola	**	10	485
64. Barisal (s)	–	–	–
65. Madaripur	***	14	370
66. Gopalganj	–	–	–
67. Faridpur (s)	**	9	372
68. Goalundo	–	–	–
69. Manikaganj	**	10	187
70. Munshiganj	**	7	633
71. Narayanganj	**	10	369
72. Dacca (s)	**	6	167
73. Tangail	**	10	365
74. Jamalpur	–	–	–
75. Mymensingh (s)	–	–	–
76. Netrokona	–	–	–
77. Kishorgunj	**	8	383
78. Brahmanbaria	–	–	–
79. Tippera (s)	*	5	122

80. Chandpur	**	6	249
81. Noakhali (s)	**	10	773
82. Feni	**	8	348
83. Chittagong (s)	***	14	1931
84. Cox's Bazar	–	–	–
85. Ramgarh	–	–	–
86. Rangamati	–	–	–

(s) indicates the Sadar subdivision of the district.

Source: P.C. Mahalanobis et al, "A Sample Survey of After-Effects of the Bengal Famine of 1943", *Sankhya*, Vol. 7, Part 4, 1946, pp. 16-17.

Appendix 3

Bengal 1946–Areas of Peasant Struggles

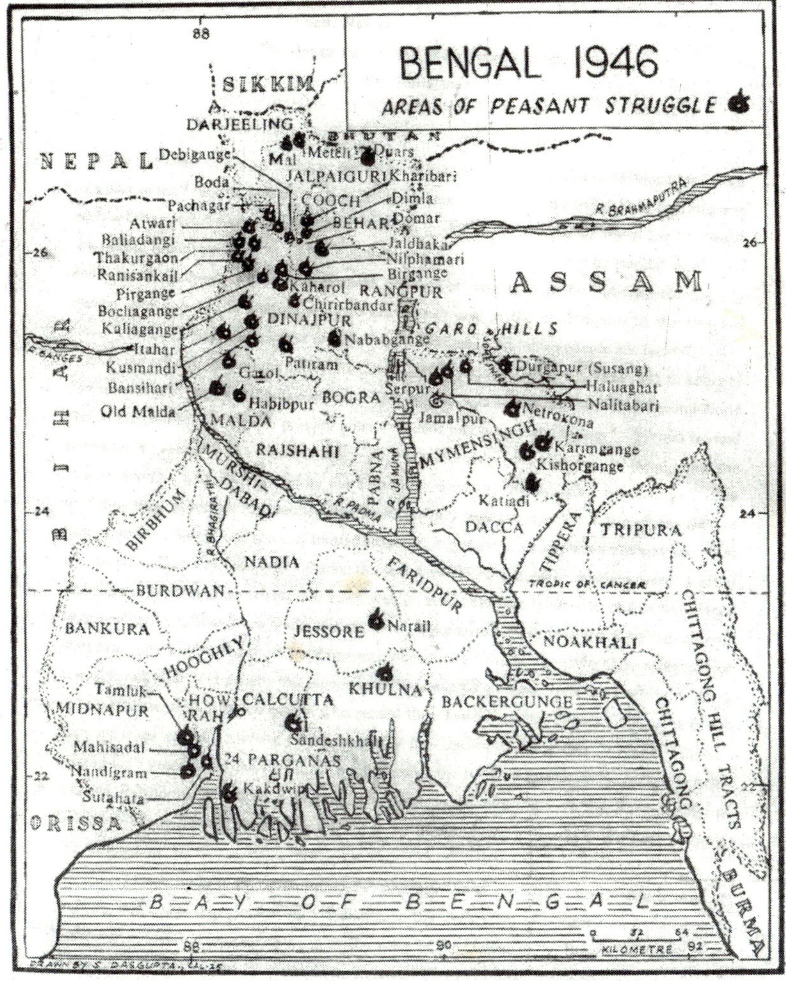

Source: Sunil Sen, *Agrarian Struggle in Bengal 1946-47*, map attached to p. 112.

Appendix 4

Food, War and Anti-Imperialism

The Bengal Famine of 1943 in Asian Context

Sho Kuwajima

In the beginning of the 20th century the National Education movement was developed in Bengal as a part of the Freedom Movement in India, and Calcutta session of the Indian National Congress adopted the resolution on the National Education in 1906. When I started my Indian Studies in the 1950s, I read some works on the National Education in Bengal written by Haridas Mukherjee and Uma Mukherjee. How is the present position of research on the National Education in Bengal, and how has the movement contemporary relevance not only in the contribution to the freedom struggle, but also in the context of the present problems that Indian people are facing?

In Japan primary school was named *Kokumin Gakko* (national school) in April 1941 to educate 'small nationals' as 'small nationalists'. This system was terminated after the Second World War in March 1947. I was a primary school student just during this period. Due to the war, school was short of trained teachers. During the last days of the war, class sessions were so often interrupted by the air raid signals, though we did not face the American air raid. Moreover, one fourth of school buildings was occupied by the army. Why they selected our school is not clear, just as why the American army occupied our small rural town immediately after the war is not clear. Now except those people who record their painful war experiences and want to tell their message to the following generation, very few Japanese know that 'national schools' existed for six years under the rigid state control unlike the National Education movement in India. Besides Rabindranath Tagore's Shantiniketan, the free atmosphere of the Punjab National College in Lahore, which produced a revolutionary Bhagat Singh in the 1920s, is recollected in this connection.

In 2007 I translated Professor Amalendu De's *Amader Bardi*, a small but memorable booklet of requiem, into Japanese. A change in the dietary life of Bengal during the Second World War is depicted in this recollection. Also the voice of the victims in the Bengal Famine of 1943 is recorded, "Ektu fan dau (give me a bit rice soup)". I have been concerned with the Bengal Famine since the 1960s, and wrote a monograph in Japanese under the title, "Anti-Imperialism and Anti-Fascism in India-Bengal Famine (1943)" in the *Rekishigaku Kenkyu (The Historical Jouranl of Japan)*, July 1977. I still remember a strong impression when I saw Zainul Abedin's sketches in the 1960s, and later I saw Satyajit Rai's film, *Ashani Sanket*. My main theme was that the voice of the people for food in Asia was a protest against the war, war mongers and colonial powers including Japan, whatever causes they carried officially.

My view comes from my own experiences as a 'small national' during the war. My native town is located about 40 kilometers north from Tokyo. The profession of my father was to shoe horses. These horses were mainly used for cultivation and transportation, and therefore my house was closely related to rural economy. But, we could not get rice as staple food sufficiently, and as the war proceeded, rice cooked with barley was mixed with beans, potatoes and sweet potatoes. Pumpkin was a daily side dish, but very often became a main dish. Migratory locust, which destroys standing paddy, was my most favorite food during the war.

The problem of food shortage in Japan during the Second World War may give us a hint when we consider the causes of the Bengal Famine of 1943.

1

Till the beginning of the war, food production in Japan could cover only 85% of the need of the people. It needed the import of 3 million tons from outside.[1]In the wartime were added other factors which contributed to the fall of food supply. Many people who were engaged in agriculture were enlisted in the army. Similarly many people in rural areas were recruited and moved to urban areas for work in the military and other related industries. Horses for agriculture were also requisitioned for the military. Chemical goods for fertilizer were transferred for the military purposes. Fish has been always main side-dish in the dietary life of Japan. But, fishery was also affected by the war. Besides the shortage of labor power, boats and fuel, deep-sea fishery was obstructed by the expansion of the war fields.[2]

Food shortage reached a peak in the end of the war and immediately after the war. During the period from November 1944 to October 1945 the load of rice in Korea, Manchuria and Taiwan fell too, and import from other areas was not expected. Yearly import during this period remained at the level of one million eight hundred thousand tons.[3] In 1945, in addition to the administrative confusion accompanying with the end of the war, typhoons and floods damaged harvest. Rice crop in the autumn of 1945 was 5 million 872 thousand tons. With limited quantity of rice, Japan had to support the population which now included civilian repatriates from various parts of Asia and the men discharged from military service too. In the year 1945, she had the military strength of 8 million 263 thousand men.[4]

Under this background it was natural that the post-war struggle for people's right in Japan was closely related to the struggle for food. In 1946, May Day festival was revived after 11 year ban. Later in the same month 'More Food' May Day was held on the 19th, and its leaders staged a sit-in at the Prime Minister's office. General Douglas MacArthur condemned 'the growing tendency towards mass violence and physical processes of intimidation under organized leadership' (*Nippon Times* 21 May 1946). The warning by the head of the occupation army threw the first cold water on the idea conceived by a certain circle of people, who thought that it was the army for liberation from the Japanese military regime.

In September 1947 my town was under dirty water for one week due to the collapse of the bank of the Tone River whose basin is largest in Japan. Paddy field was seriously affected. From that autumn we could eat 'white rice', but that was not white rice which we wanted since the war. Rice washed by the flooded water had unbearably bad smell, but we had to eat it. Though we did not face the American air raid, this flood was the result of the war when the government took the policy, 'Everything for the war', and neglected flood control, which had been one of their main works since olden times.

On 11 October 1947one judge died due to malnutrition. As a keeper of law, he lived only on rationed food, which was far from enough. This episode had strong impact on the people's thinking and my own thinking too. It was the time when we had not recovered from the damage caused by the flood. It proved that both during the war and immediately after the war the government could not protect life of the people under the system prepared by the state.

2

Armed forces generally procure their own food from the areas where they occupy or are active. Food shortage occurred more seriously in the areas where Japan occupied during the Second World War. In north Vietnam it is said that 2 million people died of hunger in 1945. Here I want to make a picture of the famine of north Vietnam in 1945 on the basis of the recent Japanese studies on this problem.

As is well known, Indo-China was once one of the main rice exporting countries in Asia along with Thailand and Burma. In the 1930s Japan heavily depended on the rice imported from Korea then under the Japanese rule. However, in 1939 Japan faced serious drought, and moreover, Korea was affected by drought too.[5] In Europe Paris was occupied by the German army in June 1940, which led to the birth of the French Government in Vichy next month. Under this background the Japanese army occupied north Indo-China in September 1940 and the southern part in July 1941. Thus the diarchy was established in Indo-China under the French Government and the Japanese army. While formally recognizing the French sovereignty, actually

Japan behaved as a supreme ruler, and exerted her influence in economic matters through the French Government, and located one of the military headquarters in Saigon. On 9 March 1945 Japan disarmed the French army, and Vietnam (12 March), Cambodia (13 March) and Laos (8 April) declared their 'independence'.

Japanese army wanted to use rice produced in Indo-China not only for export to Japan, but also as the store for its own use in preparation for the expected long drawn-out war. They started compulsory procurement of rice in 1940 through the French Government, and purchased it at lower price than in the market. This policy brought to naught the store which people had usually at local level. Apart from low temperature and floods, this was a decisive factor which caused the famine in north Vietnam in the first half of 1945.[6] The cultivation of jute and other crops related to the military need like castor oil plants was also forced on peasants. This policy contributed to the drop in food production. In the north people faced food shortage even in regular season, but generally it was covered by the rice transported from the south, or Mekong Delta. But this transportation was obstructed by the frequent American bombing from 1944. In transportation both the French Government and the Japanese army gave their priority to the military need.[7]

According to the Statistical Yearbook prepared by the United Nations, rice production in Vietnam in 1943 was 6 million 686 thousand tons, and in 1944 it decreased to 5 million 917 thousand tons. In 1945 it remained 4 million 491 thousand tons.[8]

People began to starve in January 1945. The famine reached its peak in April.[9] The joint research conducted by Japanese and Vietnamese scholars from 1992 to 1995 made a survey of 23 villages, and proved that the famine prevailed in almost all areas of north Vietnam, and the areas where minorities lived were not free from the famine. The starvation was more serious in the areas where only one crop was grown a year, or the concentration of land in the hands of landlords was observed, and in fishing villages. In many villages the proportion of the victims in the famine was much more than that of the victims in the Vietnamese War in the 1960s and 1970s.

The Famine of Vietnam in 1945 was caused by the Japanese wartime policy. Compulsory purchasing policy robbed people of the traditional system and wisdom to survive in the years of food shortage. A comprehensive picture of the famine in Vietnam is yet to be made, but the Japanese requisition policy in Vietnam has something common with the British 'boat denial' and other policies in the Bengal Famine of 1943. Here was no room for the idea of 'food for people'.

Therefore the 'mobilization of the masses for seizing rice stocks and saving people from starvation' in Vietnam triggered off the revolution which aimed at the end of the Japanese and French rule.[10]

3

There are some common factors among the food shortage of Japan in 1945-46, the Famine of Vietnam in 1945 and the Bengal Famine of 1943.

In 1945 Japan was struck by the visit of typhoons and occurrence of floods. In the same year flood covered vast areas of north Vietnam. In Bengal "the flood and cyclone of 1942 caused havoc to a large slice of coastal territories in the districts of Midnapur and 24 Parganas. — Burdwan was also subjected to a flood in 1943."[11] Famine Inquiry Commission mentioned in the Report on Bengal as one of the basic causes of the famine the low yield of the *aman* crop at the close of 1942, and the shortage of the stocks carried over from the previous year 1942.[12] There is no doubt that the weather condition worked unfavorably to food production in Japan and Vietnam of 1945, and Bengal of 1942-43.

In case of Vietnam peasants were forced to cultivate jute and other crops responsive to the Japanese military need at a short time notice after the Japanese army entered Indo-China. This cannot be simply said about jute production in Bengal. While admitting that "The effect of increase in jute acreage in course of the last 70 years over the production of food-grains in Bengal was, no doubt, considerable in a general sense",

Tarakchandra Das said, "It cannot be, however, pushed too far logically as a serious immediate cause of the last famine". He said nothing farther than to comment that, in the four years preceding the famine when there was a decrease of nearly 4% in the area under jute cultivation, building up of a stock of food-grains from the production of land abandoned by jute might have been possible.[13] However, whether long-term or short-term, what is worth examining is whether colonial forces had their plan of 'food for people' when they expanded jute cultivation, not requisition for the army and 'basic industries'. It was only in September 1942 that the Government of India undertook to prepare the Basic Plan for the procurement and movement of food grains. In December 1942 the Department of Food was started.

The war and threat of bombing obstructed the movement, trade and supply of food grains in Japan, Vietnam and India. Das mentions, among the contributory or immediate causes of famine, 'boat-denial' policy, war requirement and general dislocation of transportation.[14] Except 'boat denial' policy his view is limited to the general comment. He only says that preference was given to the movements of men and materials for war purposes over the railways and steamer lines. Famine Inquiry Commission was a little more specific, and wrote that "The Japanese war enormously increased the strain on the railways. The direction of army operations completely changed and railway traffic which had hitherto centered on India's western outlets had to be oriented to meet the new situation. Rigid control of goods traffic led to be introduced. None but essential traffic could move, and even if supply conditions had not deteriorated, the transport situation alone necessitated rigid control over the movement of foodgrains".[15]

Das who thought, "In science, the end justifies the means. In the present case too the writer was actuated by the same motive", conducted a survey of the Destitutes of Calcutta in September 1943 with his co-workers, and later expanded their investigation into the villages of those districts which had suffered most.[16] In his analysis the threat of the Japanese bombing or aggression does not appear as one of the causes of the famine, except mentioning the failure of supply of rice from Burma, Thailand and Indo-China.[17] Famine Inquiry Commission explained the influence of the air raids on Calcutta from the 20th to the 28th December 1942, and said that the most important effect of the raids was the closing down of a considerable number of food grain shops and the consequent interruption to the city's food supplies.[18] But, the Commission says nothing about the impact of the Japanese air raids on Calcutta in the midst of the famine. The paper on "Calcutta during World War II" written by S. Bhattacharya also does not mention the Japanese air raids in December 1943.[19] The *Statesman* of Tuesday 7 December 1943 carried the news that the air raid on Sunday (5 December) had led to 500 civilian casualties, over one-third of these were fatal. Bayly and Harper's recent work describes the disruption of relief work in the midst of the famine.[20]

> Air-raid posts were transferred into temporary shelters and food distribution points, as a limited charitable operation got underway. This was constantly disrupted as a Japanese air-raids continued. Then the shops closed and already weakened people fled in their thousands back towards the villages.

Here the correct dates of continual air raids are not clear, though it is presumed that Japanese bombing obstructed relief measures extended to the people.

4

Here I do not come into the details of the causes and process of the Bengal Famine of 1943. I only want to show the different pictures described from two sides, British and Japanese.

Bayly and Harper's recent work, *Forgotten Armies–The Fall of British Asia, 1941-1945* spares a part of one chapter to the description of the famine of 1943. They used the British primary sources besides Paul Greenough, *Prosperity and Misery in Modern Bengal–The Famine of 1943-1944* (New York, 1982), Bhowani Sen's view as an eye-witness and the *Statesman*. The *Statesman* is the paper which I also read in the newspaper section of the National Library, Calcutta in 1965-66.

These two authors not only write about well-discussed theme, misjudgment and inaction of both the Indian Government and Bengal Government, but also analyze the role of personal characters and prejudices of the wartime British top leaders in the worsening situation. Here they write,[21]

> Quite apart from the demands of war, it is difficult to escape the impression that the War cabinet was simply hostile towards India. The prime minister believed that Indians were the next worst people in the world after the Germans. Their treachery had been plain in the Quit India movement. The Germans he was prepared to bomb into the ground. The Indians would starve to death as a result of their own folly and viciousness.

They also show that Churchill got the implicit support of the government's scientific adviser Frederick Lindemann who had a derogatory idea of the Bengali people. From this basic stance, it was natural that the British Government at the highest level was 'deaf' though "they had been warned constantly from the early months of 1942 that a serious crisis was building up".[22] According to these authors, L.S. Amery, Secretary of State for India, first adopted 'a lofty political economist's perspective'. "He argued that growing hunger was the 'natural' result of the long-term growth of the Indian population and Bengal's climatic problems, as if this somehow justified the government's lethargy."[23] However, by the early summer of 1943 he was becoming more seriously concerned, and tried to rouse the Cabinet colleagues to action. They also added that the Viceroy Linlithgow's belated but growing alarm seems to have woken up people in London, but "Linlithgow was too old and tired to achieve too much."[24] The reason for delay in the British response to the worsening food situation may lie partly in the idea and behavior of these top leaders but more substantial is the fact that the character of colonialism was exposed under the critical condition of the war by way of the pronouncement and action of these leaders.

The most interesting part of this book is on the role of the ordinary soldiers who forced the British Government to action. Bayly and Harper writes:[25]

> He (Amery) predicted that India's future as a base of military operation would be threatened if the population of Bengal continued to starve and die in the ensuing epidemics. Morale in the Indian army was in jeopardy. A soldier wrote in an intercepted letter, "We come home to our own villages to find that food is scarce and high priced. Our wives have been led astray and our land had been misappropriated. Why does the Sarkar (Government) not do something about it *now* rather than talking about post-war reconstruction?" An even more urgent tone was heard after British and Indian press reports began to use the forbidden word 'famine' in July and August 1943.
>
> The sight of this tragedy all around them was beginning to sap the morale of British as well as Indian troops. Some young British newcomers 'feel personally disgraced that such conditions should have been allowed to develop among the helpless and ignorant of a great province for whose welfare Britain still carries a great share of responsibility'. As the stilted words of one intelligence report had it, the troops were 'adversely affected by the visible evidence of the result of famine conditions. Among British troops there has been some open criticism of government'. One British military unit fed a hundred children, while an Indian battalion collected Rs. 100 as food aid. Against orders, some troops began to share their own food with the starving.

Ordinary soldiers, both British and Indian, who had people's eyes, as well as the movement of the people who fought against hunger, finally led the British Government to action, though hunger and epidemics remained in 1944 too.

5

Since the fall of Rangoon on 8 March 1942, the Japanese army thought that Calcutta and its neighboring area were the pivotal base of counter-attack on Burma and the center of the munitions industry for the British and American army.

Already in January 1942 the Japanese Southern Army was planning the air raid on Calcutta in the last stage of the Burma Operation.[26] However, though the air raid was scheduled for around 15 May, the Fifth Flying Division was forced to suspend the Calcutta air raid before rainy season due to the lack of sufficient preparation and the uselessness of the attack by a few planes.[27]

From June the Japanese Southern Army started their preparation for a plan of operations in India including the attack by the Air Force and the advance to the northeastern part of India by the Land Force. The Third Flying Division also thought that the occupation of Assam which had resources like oil and iron ore might obstruct the work of heavy industries in Calcutta and its neighboring area, and the building of the Japanese air bases inside India and on the other side of the Arakan Yoma would paralyze the function of the air bases in the same areas, and block the air route to China. This plan took a concrete shape as No. 21 Operation by the *Daihonei* (Japanese Military Headquarters). It was expected to start after the middle of October 1942, and included the use of the land force for the occupation of Assam and Chittagong.[28] However, even in the stage of its preparation the *Daihonei* feared that the negative response from the Indian people would incur the 'National War', that is, their all-out resistance to the advance of the Japanese army.[29] It was due to the same reason that the *Daihonei* asked the Southern Army to examine the use of the Indian National Army in this operation.[30] It is to be noted that Mutaguchi, who was then one of the leaders in the 15th Army, and was later positive in the Imphal Operation in 1944, did not agree to the plan at this stage.

Later the proposal of the operation submitted by the Southern Army was finally rejected by the *Daihonei* in consideration of the unfavorable war situation in the south Pacific and the shortage of fighters to be used in the operation.[31] For the moment the air raid on Calcutta was postponed. But, irrespective of the suspension of No. 21 Operation, Japanese military operation was set forward for cutting Indo-China air route. The Fifth Flying force attacked Chittagong from 25 October to 16 December 1942, and then extended their operation to the night attack on Calcutta.[32] [0]On 20 December 1942 the Japanese force made the first night air raid on the Dum Dum Airport and the wharf installations. They continued air raids on the 24th and the 28th. But, on the 15th January 1943, when the

Special Attack Corps under the direct control of the Divisional Commander tried to attack Calcutta, they lost all three bombers due to the counter attack by a British fighter.[33] This affected seriously the morale of the members of the Japanese Air Force. When the second Special Attack Corps were sent again on 19 January, they lost one plane and four crew.[34] In this stage the Fifth Flying Division was asked co-operation with the land operation in Akyab (Burma) by the 15th Army, and also in consideration of their loss in comparison with their results, was forced to change their plan.[35] On 20 January 1943 the Divisional Commander decided to give up further night attack by the Special Attack Corps.[36] Thus ended the first stage of the air raids on Calcutta.

Already in October 1942 the news on the looting of rice stores, rice carrying boats and village bazars, selling a little children in a village and deaths from hunger were collected from various parts of Bengal.[37] In December the Communist Party of India called for the formation of People's Food Committees to face worsening food crisis, and said, "The food crisis can be solved if two key measures are taken; scaling down of speculative prices to such levels as to bring food and other necessities of life within the easy reach of the people, generating at the same time a fair price to the peasant. Secondly, this general reduction of price level can be achieved only if all stocks are controlled, and in the case of food grain, a compulsory storing of all grains in public godowns is enforced. It is not a question of confiscating grain or of interfering with the normal trade profit. The point is to ensure that no stock-monopolists and profit-sharks hold the pistol at the head of the people."[38] It can be imagined from this appeal that, in December 1942 when the Japanese army attacked the military targets in Calcutta, many people in Bengal were well conscious of the coming food crisis or actually facing it. How the life and death struggle for food in Calcutta was affected by the air raids, and how many were the casualties in the military installations and other areas, is not examined in the Japanese military documents. Their main concern was clear grasp of the location of military installations, planes and ships, correct bombing on the targets and the safe return of their crew. The solution of food crisis in Bengal was outside the scope of the Japanese military authorities when they planned the air raids on Bengal.

Japanese newspapers followed the Bengal Famine and Japanese air raids on Calcutta in details. For instance, as for the first night time air raid in December 1942, the *Asahi Shimbun* carried a letter of a young pilot to his mother, saying, "Ah Calcutta! How much I have been longing for this flight of bombing," and concluding that "I feel really happy to find that I can serve the country as a man of the Air Force in the war which destroys an old history and builds a new history".[39] Japan was already enough conscious of the critical food situation in Bengal, and even used the word famine. Therefore, while praising the 'forestalling' action of the Air Force, this paper writes in the editorial titled, "Break the Fetters of India", that, though the air raids seemingly make more suffering of the Indian people, we can definitely say that unlimited love and support of the Japanese Imperial Army to the Indian independence movement is included in a shower of bombs.[40] In this stage Japanese concern with the Indian situation was still camouflaged by a kind of romanticism. However, the Japanese media was entrusted to carry an important duty of handling the public opinion in the direction of supporting the Japanese military operation, which even the *Daihonei*'s announcement felt difficult to manipulate. The sympathy with the people in Bengal who suffered from hunger, expressed in the Japanese media, basically originated from the justification of the Japanese bombardment.

In the beginning of October 1943 three main Japanese papers took up the Bengal Famine in their editorials. It was just before the Provisional Government of India was formed by Subhas Chandra Bose (21 October) and the Greater East Asia Assembly was held in Tokyo, Bose attending it as an observer (5 November). In that year the military situation was developing rapidly unfavorable to Japan.

Though all editorials agreed in their view that the famine was 'man-made' due to the British tyranny in India, the *Mainichi Shimbun* mentioned the refusal of the United States to respond to the Mayor of Calcutta's appeal for help due to their 'fear of offending British sensibilities' (Venkararamani's expression).[41] The *Asahi Shimbun* wrote that Japan was not refusing to send Burmese rice to India as she proposed it through Subhas Chandra Bose, and added that the worsening situation in India was paving way for the growth of the independence movement led by Bose.[42] The *Yomiuri Hochi Shimbun* referred to the start of the non-violent struggle of the Indian people against the famine, and in this connection this editorial reminded that Bengal had a strong peasant movement under the name of the *Krishak Samiti*[43] This may indicate that a Left intellectual, who had some knowledge of the peasant movement in Bengal was included as one of the editorial staff, but they had to write that the people of India were constituent members of the Greater East Asia which Japan conceived during the war. From these editorials we know that Japan had considerable knowledge of the Bengal famine, though this was used to justify Japanese slogan of the Greater East Asia and the Japanese air raids in India, while denouncing the British rule in India, and expressing their sympathy with its victims.

In this context we shall examine the meaning of the first daytime air raid on Calcutta on 5 December 1943. The announcement of the *Daihonei* on its 'outstanding' military results in Calcutta appeared as the lead story of the paper, though generally the report of the *Daihonei* was critically recollected for its stilted expression after the war. First the *Daihonei* published that 5 transport ships were crashed, and 12 planes were shot down (one unconfirmed)[44], but later corrected it as the result of photo finish, and declared that 10 ships were crashed and 19 planes were shot down (5 unconfirmed) besides the damages to wharves, warehouses and railway carriages.[45] Later the *Asahi Shimbun* rated highly the significance of the Calcutta air raid, and wrote that it destroyed at one swoop the munitions which the British and the American forces had stored for the recovery of Burma. This paper carried a memorandum written by a pilot who attacked the Kidderpore (Khiderpur) Dock.[46] However, his description was no more 'romantic' but 'realistic'. In the background of this persistent following of the news on the air raid on Calcutta lay Japan's unfavorable military position in the later half of 1943. Universal conscription system was expanded in Japan. Postponement of military draft for students was suspended on 2 October, draft age was raised up to 45 years of age on 1 November, and lowest draft age also became one year younger, now 19 years after 24 December. On 25 November, in the crucial battle of Makin and Tarawa in the Pacific, the Japanese force was annihilated and the lives of 5,400 men were lost. Japanese wartime journalism may have opined that Calcutta was one of a few war fronts where Japan could impress on her people the 'dramatic results' in the last stage of the war when signs of defeat appeared in many fronts. Time was just on the eve of the approval of the Imphal Operation by the *Daihonei* on 7 January 1944.

The Calcutta attack operation was well in advance prepared as the combined operation of the Japanese Army and Navy after the end of rainy season. Its plan was finalized as one daytime attack on 11 November 1943. They made the details of the operations on 18 and 19 November in Penang, and provisionally decided 3 December as a day of bombing. Its targets were ships, operation materials and wharf installations.[47] However, the central Navy leadership annulled the plan of combined operation in consideration of the serious situation in Makin and Tarawa and the transfer of a part of their force.[48] Though the regional Naval leadership revived the Calcutta operation against the will of the center on 1 December, the Naval participation remained partial.[49] The Army deployed 18 bombers and 74 fighters, and the Navy sent 36 planes to Calcutta. An intelligent operative reported that, besides the damages to the wharf installations, due to the panic caused by the air raid, dock workers escaped from the port, and the work of loading and unloading was seriously affected.[50]

In the first report on 7 December 1943, the *Asahi Shimbun* was still conscious of the famine in Bengal, and wrote, "Despite the fact that the Indian people were in the throes of hunger, and hundreds of them are daily dying of starvation, the British refused our proposal of the transport of rice, and are sending the military men instead of rice. The target of our attack on

Calcutta is not the Indian people, but the cruel American and British army."

This paper also carried a small column without any comment in the form of telegraph from Lisbon that 334 persons were killed by the bombing.[51] A comprehensive picture of the life of the people in Calcutta on 5 December 1943, where people died of starvation, where people died due to bombard, and how air raid and famine condition were related, is not yet clear. It is not so simple as this newspaper claims.

For the moment, at least it can be said that the people's struggle against hunger meant far from a sign of an invitation to the Japanese army, but a protest against the war which brought their calamities, under whichever slogans Japan might have carried. The Japanese concern with the Bengal Famine was an expression of the Japanese aggressive posture on the eve of the Imphal Operation. In March 1944 the *Asahi Shimbun* carried its editorial under the title, 'Crisis of Bengal', and confirmed that Bengal "where Subhas Chandra Bose was born", was then the base for the recovery of Burma and the Indian munitions industry, and a central part of the famine in India too.[52] But Japan also sent her army to India instead of rice, and was elated with her war results in the earlier stage of the Imphal Operation which started on 8 March 1944.

In parallel with the changing situation Japanese concern with the Bengal Famine receded quickly in the background. In March this paper just mentioned the figure of the dead in the Bengal Famine as 6,88,846 as a report from the Department of Health, Bengal.[53] more than 5 million from an English weekly,[54] or 18,73,000 from the statement of Amery, Secretary State for India.[55] Japanese sympathy with the Indian people who were facing the famine was expressed when the Japanese army took aggressive posture in the Indian front, and Calcutta and its surrounding area in particular. But when the Japanese eyes were diverted to other war fronts or their own problems, they lost interest in the destiny of the people who were struggling against hunger. After the 'rearrangement' of the war front, or the start of evacuation in the Imphal Operation, August 1944, this paper was no longer ready to spare space for the Bengal Famine and its aftermath.

6

How the ordinary Japanese soldiers faced hunger, epidemics and death in the Imphal Operation and on their journey of withdrawal are told in Japanese by some of them who could survive and return home. Maruyama Shizuo, a war correspondent of the *Asahi Shimbun* in the Imphal Operation, also left his memoir.[56] He also wrote another book, in which he recorded how the soldiers of the Indian National Army, which had not their own logistics and means of transport, faced different difficulties (for instance, how to get ghee and wheat) besides rain, hunger, epidemics and death.[57] There was something common between those people who fought against hunger and those men of the INA who fought for freedom across Indo-Burmese frontier. That was a critical view of the 'cause' carried by the leaders of colonial powers. Maruyama was later transferred to Saigon branch, *Asahi Shimbun* just before the 'independence' of Vietnam was declared.

When the famine prevailed in north Vietnam actually under the Japanese rule in 1945, the *Asahi Shimbun* kept silent most probably except one article titled, "Dokuritsu no Sakigake Vietnam Teikoku" (The Empire of Vietnam-A Harbinger of the Independence in Indo-China) dispatched from its Saigon branch in the issue dated 24 July 1945.

> The most serious problem that Vietnam is facing now is how to save the destitutes in the north. Three hundred thousand people out of the total of six hundred thousand in the Province of Ha Tinh are on the point of dying from hunger, and in Tonkin the dead caused by hunger are estimated four to five thousand per month. Particularly in Nam Dinh and Vinh Ha Tinh the famine situation is beyond description. People eat snakes, mice and weeds, and even give their children for a bowl of leftover rice.

This article refers to the policy of the 'independent' Vietnam Government which started the Ministry of Food Supply, and adopted all available means like the disposal of the military needs and the import from Laos, without exclusive dependence on the rice from Saigon. It also adds that the Government even used cattle carts for the transport of food to avoid the bombing on the railway lines, and also encouraged the movement of the affected people to the southern part of Vietnam. However, this paper concluded that the famine situation in Vietnam was caused by the French colonial policy which had given priority to the interests of the home country rather than to the interests of the Vietnamese people. Here was no critical examination of the Japanese military policy which caused the food crisis. So far there is no evidence to show that the Japanese media and the Japanese Government, which saw the Bengal Famine of 1943 as the results of the British 'imperialist' policy, learnt lesson for Vietnam from the most recent 'man-made' tragedy. Conversely, this paper cited the pronouncement of the Prime Minister of Vietnam, Tran Trong Kim stating that Vietnam cannot exist without the Japanese support.

The grim reality of the Asian people created by the Japanese bombing or their occupation was not known to the Japanese people under the strict press control till the end of the war. Maruyama recollected in the 1980s that procurement of rice for the Japanese military was the main factor which caused the famine. He also wrote that Vietnam was not provided basic contents of her independence like her right of diplomacy, military affairs and finance.[58] Maruyama met the Prime Minister Tran Trong Kim almost every day, who complained that the demands of the Japanese army was too excessive and too hasty. The most embarrassed matter to his government was procurement of rice. Tran Trong Kim confessed to Maruyama that it was not possible to collect rice in the way Japanese military ordered.[59]

A history of the World War is not a history of the war fronts. How the unarmed people fought against hunger and for food is also a part of the war. During the war food crisis covered the people of the world in an unexpected scale. Quit India movement in Bihar, which was joined by the urban and rural poor, had the character of the struggle for food too.[60] Agricultural laborers suffered most severely in the Bengal Famine.[61] Minorities also suffered from the serious shortage of food caused by the war as Harihar Bhattacharyya's work on the Reang rebellion in Tripura shows.[62] The women of Asia were so often forced to put up with the unbearable burdens caused by the food crisis.[63] Japan did not send food grains, but the army to the Asian scene. Though her media expressed sympathy with the victims of the Bengal Famine, Japanese approach to India and Indian people did not mean any special departure from what they had done in other parts of Asia.

The victory of the United Nations certainly contributed to the formation of the post-war order of the world, and the United Nations Organizations in particular. Similarly, the history of the struggle of the people for democracy and their rights in the post-war years was closely connected with the struggle for food during the war. In Japan people's movement for democratic right after the war was not planted by the American occupation army, but was developed while connecting it with the movement for rice. The development of revolution in Vietnam is unconceivable without the people's struggle against the Famine of 1945. In Bengal the struggle for people's right was developed in the midst of the movement against hunger during the Second World War.

Immediately after the Second World War, "Workers of the world, unite!" was also carried as a slogan in Japan. However, we had little knowledge of the most recent famine situation in Bengal, Vietnam and other parts of Asia under which the toiling people suffered, and their struggle for food though they were closely related in the undercurrent of contemporary history.

A history of the Second World War still awaits rewriting on the basis of the history of the people. It demands not only a comparative study of each area of Asia and the world, but also the integrated studies of these areas. The Bengal Famine of 1943 also needs to be considered in this context.

ENDNOTES

1. Rice Crop in Japan (1,000 tons)

Year	Crop	Year	Crop	Year	Crop
1939	10,345	1945	5,872	1950	9,651
1940	9,131	1946	9,208	1955	12,385
1941	8,263	1947	8,798	1960	12,858
1942	10,016	1948	9,966	2000	9,490
1943	9,433	1949	9,383	2005	9,074
1944	8,784				

Yano Tsunetaro Kinenkai (ed.),*Suji de miru Nihon no Hyakunen-20 Seiki ga wakaru Databook* (Statistical Survey of One Hundred Year Japàn), Tokyo, 2006, pp. 199-200.

2. GHQ/SCAP, *GHQ Nihon Senryo Shi* (History of the Non-Military Activities of the Occupation of Japan, 1945-1951), Japanese edition, Vol. 35, Tokyo, 2000, p. 5.
3. Ibid.
4. Strength of the Japanese Forces (1,000 men)

Year	*Total*	*Army*	*Navy*
1937	1076.9	950.0	126.9
1940	1541.5	1350.0	191.5
1941	2420.0	2100.0	320.0
1942	2850.0	2400.0	450.0
1943	3584.0	2900.0	684.0
1944	5396.0	4100.0	1296.0
1945	8263.0	6400.0	1863.0

Yano Tsunetaro Kinenkai, op. cit., p. 561.

5. Tabuchi Yukichika, "200 Man-nin Gashisha no Koe ga Kikoeru-1944 Nen Vietnam" (Listen to the Voice of 2 Million Starved-Vietnam in 1944), *Rekishi Hyoron* (Historical Review), September 1985, pp. 32-33.
6. Furuta Motoo, "Vietnam Gendaishi niokeru Nihon Senryo" (Japanese Occupation in the Contemporary History of Vietnam), in Kurasawa Aiko (ed.), *Tonan Ajiashi nonakano Nihon Senryo* (Japanese Occupation in the History of Southeast Asia), Tokyo, 1997, p. 515.
7. Furuta Motoo, *Vietnam no Sekaishi-Chuka Sekai kara Tonan Ajia Sekai e* (World History in Vietnam-from the Chinese World to the Southeast Asian World), Tokyo, 1995, p. 124.
8. United Nations, *Statistical Yearbook* (Japanese edition compiled under the supervision of Minobe Ryokichi), Tokyo, 1954, p. 61.
9. Furuta, "Vietnam Gendaishi—", p. 506 and pp. 511-14.
10. Tabuchi, op. cit., p. 36. Also see, *An Outline History of the Vietnam Workers' Party (1930-1974),* 2nd Edition, Foreign Languages Publication House, Hanoi, p. 36. As for *An Outline History,* its author's name is not mentioned, but it is explained that it was the translation of a publication of the Commission for the Study of the History of the Vietnam Workers' Party on the occasion of the 45th anniversary of the founding of the Party (3 February 1930-3 February 1975).
11. Tarakchandra Das, *Bengal Famine (1943)-As revealed in a Survey of the Destitutes in Calcutta,* Calcutta, 1949, p. 118.

12. Famine Inquiry Commission, *Report on Bengal,* Delhi, 1945, p. 103.
13. Das, op. cit., p. 115.
14. Ibid., pp. 121-22.
15. Famine Inquiry Commission, op. cit., p. 23.
16. Das, op. cit., p. 1 and pp. 12-13.
17. Ibid., pp. 117-18.
18. Famine Inquiry Commission, op. cit., p. 37.
19. S. Bhattacharya, "Calcutta during World War II" (translated into Japanese), *Journal of Historical Studies,* November, 1990.
20. Christopher Bayly and Tim Harper, *Forgotten Armies-The Fall of British Asia, 1941-1945,* Cambridge, Massachusetts, 2005, p. 287.
21. Ibid., p. 286.
22. Ibid., p. 285.
23. Ibid., p. 286.
24. Ibid., 291.
25. Ibid., p. 286 and p. 290.
26. Military History Department, The National Institute for Defence Studies, *Nanpo Shinko Rikugun Koku Sakusen* (The Japanese Army Aerial Attack Operations in the Southward), Tokyo, 1970, p. 725. This work is the Volume 27 of the document based *Senshi Sosho* (Series: Military History).
27. Ibid., pp. 728-9.
28. Military History Department, The National Institute for Defence Studies, *Biruma Ran-In Homen Daisan Kokugun no Sakusen* (The Third Flying Force Operations in Burma and Dutch East Indies), Tokyo, 1972, pp. 86-92. This is the Volume 45 of the above mentioned series.
29. Ibid., p. 90.
30. Ibid., p. 91.
31. Ibid., pp. 105-6.
32. Ibid., pp. 169-70.
33. Ibid., pp. 193-94 and p. 202.
34. Ibid., pp. 195-98.
35. Ibid., p. 198.
36. Ibid., pp. 200-1.
37. *People's War,* 8 November 1942.
38. Ibid., 20 December 1942.
39. *Asahi Shimbun,* 29 December 1942.
40. Ibid., 24 December 1942.
41. *Mainichi Shimbun,* 2 October 1943. Also see, M. S. Venkataramani, *Undercurrents in American Foreign Relations-Four Studies,* New York, 1965, p. 17.

42. *Asahi Shimbun,* 6 October 1943.
43. *Yomiuri Hochi Shimbun,* 7 October 1943.
44. *Asahi Shimbun,* 7 December 1943.
45. Ibid., 19 December 1943.
46. Ibid., 25 December 1943.
47. *Daisan Kokugun no Sakusen,* pp. 401-7.
48. Ibid., pp. 406-7.
49. Ibid., p. 407.
50. Ibid., pp. 410-11.
51. *Asahi Shimbun,* 16 December 1943.
52. Ibid., 2 March 1944.
53. Ibid., 16 March 1944.
54. Ibid., 24 March 1944.
55. Ibid., 25 March 1944.
56. Maruyama Shizuo, *Imphal Sakusen Jhugun Ki-Ichi Shimbun Kisha no Kaiso* (The Imphal Operation recollected by a War Correspondent), Tokyo, 1984.
57. Maruyam Shizuo, *Indc Kokumin Gun-Mohitotsu no Taiheiyo Senso* (Indian National Army-Another Pacific War), Tokyo, 1985, pp. 121, 124-25, 134, 136, 141 and 206.
58. Maruyama Shizuo, *Indo-Shina Monogatari* (A Story of Indo-China), Tokyo, 1981, p. 178.
59. Ibid.
60. Sho Kuwajima, "The Character of the Second World War in the Context of the Situation in Bihar", *Journal of Historical Studies,* No. 4, December 1998, Department of History, Patna University.
61. P. C. Mahalanobis *et al,* "A Sample Survey of After-Effects of the Bengal Famine of 1943, *Sankya, Indian Journal of Statistics,* Vol. 7, Part 4, 1946, p. 57.
62. Harihar Bhattacharyya, "The Reang rebellion in Tripura, 1943-45 and the birth of an ethnic identity", *The Indian Economic and Social History Review,* 32-3 (1995).
63. Ela Sen, *Darkening Days-Being a Narrative of Famine-Stricken Bengal-with drawings from Life by Zainul Abedin,* Calcutta, 1944.

P.S. This is a slightly revised version of my paper read at the Department of History, University of Burdwan on 14 February 2008. I would like to express my thanks to Professor Somnath Roy who took trouble to arrange this lecture. I am also thankful to Dr. Pradip Chattopadhyay, Dr.Achinta Kumar Dutta and Dr. Harihar Bhattacharyya for their kind help on the occasion of the seminar. This tour to Burdwan was realized by the friendly care taken by Professor Amalendu De.

Bibliography

1. Works of Abul Hashim

Hashim, Abul. 1974. *In Retrospection,* Dhaka: Subharna Publishers.

Hashim, Abul. 1985. *The Creed of Islam or the Revolutionary Character of Kalima,* Dhaka: Islamic Foundation Bangladesh. First published in 1950.

Hashim, Abul. 1980. *As I See It,* Dhaka: Islamic Foundation Bangladesh. First published in 1965.

Hashim, Abul. 1967. *Integration of Pakistan,* Dhaka: Syed Mujbullah.

Hashim, Abul. 1999. *Arabic Made Easy,* Chittagong and Dhaka: Bangladesh Co-operative Book Society. First published in 1969.

2. Biography and Reminiscences of Abul Hashim

Ahmed, Syed Mansur (ed.). 2007. *Abul Hashim-Tanr Jiban o Samaya* (in Bangla: Abul Hashim-His Life and Time), 2nd edition, Dhaka: Jatiya Sahitya Prokash. First published in 2000.

Hoque, Mafidul. 1990. *Abul Hashim 1905-1974* (in Bangla), Dhaka: Bangla Academy.

Kuwajima, Sho. "Abul Hashim-Islam, Nationalism and Democracy", in Kuwajima, Sho (ed.). 2010. *Life, Freedom and War: Twentieth Century South Asia,* Delhi: Aakar Books.

3. Political leaders and observers in Bangladesh

Ahmad, Abul Mansur. 1975. *Amar dekha Rajnitir Panchash Vochor* (in Bangla: Fifty Years of Politics as I saw it), 3rd enlarged edition, Dhaka: Nawroze Kitabistan.

Ahmad, Abul Mansur. 1978. *Atmakatha* (in Bangla: Autobiography), Dhaka: Khoshroz Kitab Mahal.

Ahmad, Kamruddin. 1382 (Bengal Calendar). *Banglar Madhyabitter Atmavikash* (in Bangla: Growth of Bengali Middle Class), 2, Dhaka: Zahiruddin Mahmud Inside Library.

Huq, A.K. Fazlul. 1977. *Bengal Today*, Reprint, Chakhar: Fazlul Huq College. First published in 1944.

Islam, Sirajul (ed.). 1976. *Fazlul Huq Speaks in Council 1913-1916*, Dhaka: Bangladesh Itihas Samiti.

Khaleque, Muhammad Abdul (ed.). 1395 (Bengal Calendar). *Mahapursh Fazlul Huq* (in Bangla: A Great Leader Fazlul Huq), Dhaka: Sher-e-Bangla Jatyo Gabeshana Kendra.

Maksud, Syed Abul. 1994. *Maulana Abdul Hamid Khan Bhashani* (in Bangla), Dhaka: Bangla Academy.

National Archives of Bangladesh. 1986. *Speeches of Sher-e-Bangla A. K. Fazlul Huq at the Legislative Council of Bengal Vol. 1 (1918-1937)*, Dhaka: Bangla Academy.

Sinha, Moni. 1983. *Jiban Sangram* (in Bangla: Life of Struggle), Dhaka: Jatiya Sahitya Prokashani.

Umar, Badruddin. 2004, 08, 09. *Amar Jiban* (in Bangla: My Life), Vol. 1 (1931-1950), Vol. 2 (1950-1968) and Vol. 3 (1968-1971), Dhaka: Dhaka Sahitya Prokash.

4. History of Bengal

Adhikari, G. 1944. *Pakistan and National Unity*, Bombay: People's Publishing House.

Ahmad, Kamruddin. 1975. *A Socio Political History of Bengal and the Birth of Bangladesh*, Dhaka: Zahiruddin Mahmud Inside Library. First published in 1967 under the title of *The Social History of East Pakistan*.

Bose, Sugata. 1986. *Agrarian Bengal-Economy, social structure and politics 1919-1947*, Cambridge: Cambridge University Press.

Broomfield, J.H. 1968. *Elite Conflict in a Plural Society: Twentieth-Century Bengal*, Berkeley and Los Angeles: University of California Press.

Chakrabarti, S.K. 1978. *The Evolution of Politics in Bangladesh 1947-1978*, New Delhi: Associated Publishing House.

Chatterji, Joya. 1995. *Bengal Divided-Hindu Communalism and Partition 1932-1947*, New Delhi: Foundations Books.

Das, Suranjan. 1991. *Communal Riots in Bengal 1905-1947*, Delhi: Oxford University Press.

De, Amalendu. 1972. *Pakistan Prastab O Fazlul Huq*(in Bangla: Pakistan Resolution and Fazlul Huq), Kolkata: Ratna Prakashan.

De, Amalendu. 1974. *Bengali Buddhijibi O Bichchninnatabad*(in Bangla: Bengali Intelligentsia and Separatism), Kolkata: Ratna Prakashan.

De, Amalendu. 1988. *Islam in Modern India*, Kolkata: Maya Prakashan.

De, Amalendu. 1996. *Religious Fundamentalism and Secularism in India*, Baharampur: Suryasena Prakashani.

De, Amalendu. 2003. *Swadhin Bangabhumi Gathaner Parikalpana: Prayash O Parinati* (in Bangla: Independent Bengal: The Design and its Fate), Agartola: Parul Prokashani. First published in 1975.

De, Dhurjati Prasad. 1998. *Bengal Muslims in Search of Social Identity, 1905-47,* Dhaka: The University Press.

Dhanagare, D.N. 1983. *Peasant Movements in India 1920-1950,* Delhi: Oxford University Press.

Dil, Anwar and Dil, Afia. 2000. *Bengali Language Movement in Bangladesh,* San Diego and Islamabad: Intellectual Forum.

Gankovsky, Y.V. and Gordon-Polonskaya, L.R. 1964. *A History of Pakistan,* Moscow: "Nauka" Publishing House.

Harun-or-Rashid. 2003. *The Foreshadowing of Bangladesh-Bengali Muslim League and Muslim Politics 1906-1947,* Revised and enlarged edition, Dhaka: The University Press. First published in 1987.

Harun-or-Rashid. 2003. *Inside Bengal Politics 1936-1947: Unpublished Correspondence of Partition Leaders,* Dhaka: The University Press.

Islam, Sirajul (ed.). 1992. *History of Bangladesh 1704-1971: Vol. 1 Political History,* Dhaka: Asiatic Society of Bangladesh.

Johnson, Alec. 1947. *Another's Harvest,* Kolkata: The Bookman.

Joshi, P.C. 1944. *They Must Meet Again,* Bombay: People's Publishing House.

Kawai, Akinobu. 1986-7. *'Landlords' and Imperial Rule: Change in Bengal Agrarian Society C1885-1940,* Vols. 2, Tokyo: Institute for the Study of Languages and Cultures of Asia and Africa.

Kosambi, D.D. 1957. *Exasperating Essays-exercises in the Dialectical Methods,* Poona: People's Book House.

Kuwajima, Sho. 1998. *Muslims, Nationalism and the Partition: 1946 Provincial Elections in India,* New Delhi: Manohar.

Mitra, Asok. 1991. *Towards Independence 1940-1947-Memoirs of an Indian Civil Servant,* Bombay: Popular Prakashan.

Mukhopadhyay, Saroj. 1986. *Bharater Communist Party O Amara* (in Bangla: Indian Communist Party and We), Kolkata: National Book Agency.

Osmany, Shireen Hasan. 1992. *Bangladeshi Nationalism-History of Dialectics and Dimensions,* Dhaka: The University Press.

Rasul, Muhammad Abdullah. 1982. *Krishak Sabhar Itihas* (In Bangla: History of the Peasant Union), 3rd edition, Kolkata: Nabjatak Prakashan. First published in 1969.

Samaddar, Ranabir (ed.). 1997. *Reflections on Partition in the East,* New Delhi: Vikas Publishing House.

Sarkar, Sumit. 1973. *The Swadeshi Movement in Bengal,* New Delhi: People's Publishing House.

Sato, Hiroshi. "Development of the Tebhaga Movement and its Background" (in Japanese), *Azia Keizai,* October 1970.

Sato, Hiroshi. "A.K. Fazlul Huq and Muslim Peasants in Bengal" (in Japanese), *Rekishi Hyoron* (Historical Review), April 1972.

Sato, Hiroshi. "Communal Riots and Refugee Displacement in South Asia: 1950 Bengal Riot and Nehru-Liaqat Pact" (in Japanese), *Azia Keizai,* July 2005.

Sen, Shila. 1976. *Muslim Politics in Bengal, 1937-1947,* New Delhi: Impex India.

Sen, Sunil. 1972. *Agrarian Struggle in Bengal 1946-47,* New Delhi: People's Publishing House.

Sinha, Soumitra. 1995. *The Quest for Modernity and The Bengali Muslims 1921-47,* Kolkata: Minerva Associates (Publications) PVT. LTD.

Smith, Wilfred Cantwell. 1969. *Modern Islam in India: A Social Analysis,* Lahore: Sh. Muhammad Ashraf. First published in 1943, and revised edition from London in 1946.

Subhani, Rabbani. 1947. *The Teaching of Islam in Light of the Philosophy of Rabbaniyyat for Beginners,* New York: Academy of Islam International.

Umar, Badruddin. 2004. *The Emergence of Bangladesh-Class Struggles in East Pakistan (1947-1958),* Karachi: Oxford University Press.

Umar, Badruddin. 2006. *The Emergence of Bangladesh-Vol. 2: Rise of Bengali Nationalism (1958-1971),* Karachi: Oxford University Press.

Umar, Badruddin. 1978. *Chirastayee Bandobaste Bangladesher Krishak* (in Bangla: Bengal Peasants under the Permanent Settlement), First Indian edition, Kolkata: Chirayat Prakashan.

Umar, Badruddin. 1985. *Purba Banglar Bhasha Andolan O Tatkalin Rajniti 3* (in Bangla: Language Movement of East Bengal and Contemporary Politics), Chittagong: Bohi Ghar.

Umar, Badruddin. 1987. *Bangabhanga O Sampradaik Rajnity* (in Bangla: Partition of Bengal and Communal Politics), Dhaka: Shrabon.

5. Bengal Famine of 1943

Brown, Michael. 1944. *India Need not Starve!* Bombay: Longmans, Green & Co. LTD.

Das, Tarakchandra. 1949. *Bengal Famine (1943)-As revealed in a Survey of the Destitutes in Calcutta,* Kolkata: University of Calcutta.

Famine Inquiry Commission. 1945. *Report on Bengal,* Delhi: Government of India Press.

Ghosh, Tushar Kanti. 1944. *The Bengal Tragedy,* Lahore: Hero Publications.

Greenough, Paul R. 1982. *Prosperity and Misery in Modern Bengal: The*

Famine of 1943-1944, New Delhi and Oxford: Oxford University Press.

Joshi, P.C. 1943. *Who lives if Bengal dies?* Bombay: People's Publishing House.

Kuwajima, Sho. "Bengal Famine (1943)-Anti-Imperialism and Anti-Fascism in India" (in Japanese), *The Rekishigaku Kenkyu* (The Historical Journal of Japan), July 1977.

Maharatna, Arup. 1996. *The Demography of Famines-An Indian Historical Perspective*, Delhi: Oxford University Press.

Mahalanobis, P.C., et al. "A Sample Survey of After-Effects of the Bengal Famine of 1943", *Sankhya*, April 1946.

Mukherji, Karuna. 1952. *Socio-Economic Survey of 49 Villages: A First-hand Field-work by the author in India & Pakistan*, Kolkata: Karuna Mukherji.

Mukherji, Karunamoy. 1957. *The Problems of Land Transfer: a study of the problems of Land Alienation in Bengal*, Santiniketan: Santiniketan Press.

Sen, Amartya. 1982. *Poverty and Famines-An Essay on Entitlement and Deprivation*, Oxford: Clarendon Press.

Sen, Ela. 1944. *Darkening Days being a Narrative of Famine-stricken Bengal-with Drawings from Life by Zainul Abedin*, Kolkata: Sunil Gupta.

Venkataramani, M.S. 1973. *Bengal Famine of 1943: The American Response*, Delhi: Vikas Publishing House.

6. Literature and Paintings on the Bengal Famine of 1943

Banerjee, Tarasankar. 1380 (Bengal Calendar). "Manubantar" (Great Famine) in *Tarasankar Rachnavali*, (in Bangla: Works of Tarasankar) Vol. 5, Kolkata: Mitra & Ghosh Publishers.

Bhattacharya. 1964. *So Many Hungers*, Bombay: Jaico Publishing House. Originally published in 1947.

Sen, Mrinal. 1983. *In Search of Famine (Akaler Sandhaney): A Film by Mrinal Sen*, Kolkata: Seagull Books.

Zainul Abedin's Famine Sketches-1943, Dhaka: Bangladesh Shilpakala Academy.

7. Periodicals

Dawn
Economic and Political Weekly
Holiday
Indian Annual Register
Millat
Statesman

Index